io 18/00   7⁰⁰

D0206112

A SHEARWATER BOOK

BETRAYAL
of
SCIENCE
and
REASON

PAUL R. EHRLICH

BETRAYAL

of

SCIENCE

and

REASON

How Anti-Environmental Rhetoric
Threatens Our Future

ANNE H. EHRLICH

NORTHCOAST ENVIRONMENTAL CENTER
LIBRARY
822-6918

ISLAND PRESS / Shearwater Books
Washington, D.C. / Covelo, California

A Shearwater Book
Published by Island Press

Copyright © 1996 by Paul R. Ehrlich and Anne H. Ehrlich

First paperback edition published in 1998.

All rights reserved under International and Pan-American Copyright Conventions. No part of this book may be reproduced in any form or by any means without permission in writing from the publisher: Island Press, 1718 Connecticut Avenue, N.W., Suite 300, Washington, DC 20009.

Shearwater Books is a trademark of The Center for Resource Economics.

The "World Scientists' Warning to Humanity" that appears in appendix B is reproduced with permission from the Union of Concerned Scientists; copyright © 1992 Union of Concerned Scientists.

Library of Congress Cataloging-in-Publication Data

Ehrlich, Paul R.
    Betrayal of science and reason: how anti-environmental rhetoric threatens our future / Paul R. Ehrlich, Anne H. Ehrlich.
        p.   cm.
    Includes bibliographical references and index.
    ISBN 1-55963-483-9 (cloth).—ISBN 1-55963-484-7 (pbk)
        1. Anti-environmentalism. 2. Environmental degradation.
    I. Ehrlich, Anne H. II. Title.
    GE195.E37   1996
    363.7—dc20   96-34249
                                                                          CIP

Printed on recycled, acid-free paper ✪

Manufactured in the United States of America

10 9 8

To the memory of Senator John Heinz
and to Teresa Heinz, who carries on his work

Contents

□

Acknowledgments

W<small>E ARE EXTREMELY GRATEFUL</small> to the following colleagues who took time from their busy schedules to read the entire manuscript for this book: Marina Alberti and Gretchen C. Daily (Center for Conservation Biology, Stanford University); Leonie Haimson, Michael Oppenheimer, and David Wilcove (Environmental Defense Fund); John Harte (Energy and Resources Group, University of California, Berkeley); John P. Holdren (Teresa and John Heinz Professor, Kennedy School of Government, Harvard University); Cheryl E. Holdren (Woods Hole, Massachusetts), Sam Hurst (Buffalo Gap Productions); David Layton (Division of Environmental Studies, University of California, Davis); Thomas E. Lovejoy (Assistant Secretary for External Affairs, Smithsonian Institution); Jane Lubchenco (Department of Zoology, Oregon State University, and President, American Association for the Advancement of Science); Peter H. Raven (Director, Missouri Botanical Garden, and Home Secretary, National Academy of Sciences); Kirk Smith (Department of Environmental Health Sciences, University of California, Berkeley); and Wren Wirth (Winslow Foundation).

Many others were kind enough to read selected chapters: Joseph Berry (Carnegie Institution of Washington); Thomas Brooks and Stuart

L. Pimm (Department of Ecology and Evolutionary Biology, University of Tennessee); Michael Dalton and Lawrence H. Goulder (Department of Economics, Stanford University); Lisa Daniel and Timothy Daniel (Bureau of Economics, Federal Trade Commission); Thomas Eisner (Section of Neurobiology and Behavior, Cornell University); Walter P. Falcon and Rosamond L. Naylor (Institute for International Studies, Stanford University); John Froines (Center for Occupational and Environmental Health, School of Public Health, University of California, Los Angeles); Ross Gelbspan (Brookline, Massachusetts); Edward Groth III (Consumers Union, Yonkers, New York); James Hansen (NASA Goddard Institute for Space Studies); Donald Kennedy (Institute for International Studies, Stanford University, and former Administrator, Food and Drug Administration); Gene E. Likens (Institute of Ecosystem Studies); Orie L. Loucks (Department of Zoology, Miami University); Thomas F. Malone (Distinguished University Scholar, North Carolina State University at Raleigh); Pamela Matson (Department of Environmental Science, Policy, and Management, University of California, Berkeley); Tom Meersman (*Minneapolis–St. Paul Star Tribune*); Harold Mooney and Peter Vitousek (Department of Biological Sciences, Stanford University); Dennis Murphy (Center for Conservation Biology, Stanford University); Sandra L. Postel (Global Water Policy Project); William K. Reilly (former Administrator, Environmental Protection Agency); F. Sherwood Rowland (Department of Chemistry, University of California, Irvine, and Foreign Secretary, National Academy of Sciences); Susan Solomon (National Oceanic and Atmospheric Administration); Edward O. Wilson (Museum of Comparative Zoology, Harvard University); and George M. Woodwell (Woods Hole Research Center, Massachusetts).

H. Ronald Pulliam (National Biological Service) and Deanna Richards (Senior Program Officer, National Academy of Engineering) were kind enough to supply critical material, as did Edward Groth III (Consumers Union, Yonkers, New York).

Gretchen Daily, Cheri Holdren, John Holdren, Dennis Murphy, Stuart Pimm, Peter Raven, Sherry Rowland, Steve Schneider, Kirk Smith, and Wren Wirth all deserve extra mention for their time-consuming efforts to review and re-review material and otherwise help us maintain a high standard of scientific accuracy while trying to make environmental science understandable to a general audience. Despite all our colleagues' efforts, some errors and obscurities doubtless got through. For those we are entirely responsible.

The staff of the Falconer Biology Library of Stanford University's Department of Biological Sciences, especially Jill Otto, once again were extraordinarily helpful with literature problems, and Pat Browne and Steve Masley handled our copying chores with their usual dispatch. Working with them all is one of the real pleasures of being at Stanford. And our friends Peggy Vas Dias and Scott Daily did a thousand little things to make our task easier.

Alexander Greenfeld, former libel counsel for the *New York Times* and now a Washington, D.C., attorney specializing in libel law, has cast a careful eye in detail over the entire manuscript. Pat Harris did a fine job of copyediting the manuscript. Finally, Laurie Burnham of Island Press gave us continual sound counsel during the writing of the book. She then edited it with extraordinary care and the scientific insight one might expect from one whose doctoral dissertation was partly overseen by Ed Wilson at Harvard. In many places, we have substituted her words for ours, to the great benefit of the manuscript. She has been by far the most dedicated editor we have ever worked with.

This work has been supported in part by a grant from the W. Alton Jones Foundation and by the generosity of Peter and Helen Bing. And, of course, we always feel that the late LuEsther Mertz is at the barricades by our side.

CHAPTER 1

A Personal Odyssey

□

"One of the penalties of an ecological education is that one lives alone in a world of wounds. . . . An ecologist must either harden his shell and make believe that the consequences of science are none of his business, or he must be the doctor who sees the marks of death in a community that believes itself well and does not want to be told otherwise."

—Aldo Leopold, 1953[1]

THE TIME HAS COME to write a book about efforts being made to minimize the seriousness of environmental problems. We call these attempts the "brownlash" because they help to fuel a backlash against "green" policies. The brownlash has been generated by a diverse group of individuals and organizations, doubtless often with differing motives and backgrounds. We classify them as brownlashers by what they say, not by who they are. With strong and appealing messages, they have successfully sowed seeds of doubt among journalists, policy makers, and the public at large about the reality and importance of such phenomena as overpopulation, global climate change, ozone depletion, and losses of biodiversity. In writing this book, we try to set the record straight with respect to environmental science and its proper interpretation. By exposing and refuting the misinformation disseminated by the brownlash, we hope to return to higher ground the crucial dialogue on how to sustain society's essential environmental services.

In addressing the brownlash, we feel we have come about full circle. We started out in the 1960s, joining forces with others to warn about the environmental damage being caused by the overexpanding human enterprise. For a while, the world responded, and substantial gains were made both in slowing some aspects of the damage and in educating the public about its significance. Now we and other environmental scientists find ourselves once again struggling to preserve those gains and to keep global environmental deterioration from escalating beyond repair.

Yet there is a key difference between then and now. In the 1960s, people were largely unaware of environmental issues; indeed, environmental science as a distinct discipline did not even exist. All that has changed. Human beings know enormously more about how their world works now than they did a mere half-century ago. Our own area of interest—ecology and evolutionary biology—has exploded in that period, revealing (among many other things) that interactions between human beings and their physical and biological environments are far more complex than imagined earlier. What has been discovered is both fascinating and disturbing—ranging from ways people have altered the atmosphere to the evolutionary origins of toxic compounds in plants. This new knowledge could help open the doors to a sustainable future in which human satisfaction could become greater and more widespread than at any time since the invention of agriculture.

Yet at the same time that brownlash activities are intensifying, the conclusions and predictions of concerned environmental scientists are being increasingly substantiated as more data are gathered and computer and analytic models are refined.[2] Indeed, scientists from disciplines as diverse as physics, chemistry, geology, and molecular biology, including many Nobel laureates, now support the conclusions of their colleagues in environmental science, as do most scientific academies around the world.[3]

Despite the evidence and deepening consensus among scientists, humanity seems to be engaged in a remarkable episode of folly. Folly—pursuing policies injurious to self-interest while being advised against them—is nothing new; it has plagued governments since their inception.[4] What has changed through the ages is not the lack of wisdom in politics but rather the price to be paid for that lack. Despite a vastly enhanced understanding of our planet's life-support systems, humanity is continually assaulting them—degrading and destroying within a few generations the ecosystems that provide the very basis of civilization. All the world's nations are pursuing this course despite knowledge of its consequences being available and despite the warnings of many of the world's most distinguished scientists. And that folly is being encouraged and promoted by the individuals and organizations whose efforts we refer to collectively as the brownlash. The opinions and doctrines of the brownlash on the state of the environment and related subjects form the focus of chapters 5 through 10 of this book.

Our interest in environmental matters goes back many decades, to even before we met as students at the University of Kansas. As a teenager in New Jersey with a love for nature, Paul had seen butterfly habitat being replaced by housing developments and often found it impossible to raise caterpillars on local plants because of overspraying with pesticides. As an undergraduate at the University of Pennsylvania, he read the now-classic books *Our Plundered Planet* by Fairfield Osborn and *Road to Survival* by William Vogt,[5] which provided a global framework for things he had observed as a young naturalist. Paul's first job as a graduate student at Kansas was studying the evolution of DDT resistance in fruit flies, and the misuse of pesticides was a hot topic among his evolutionist friends. Anne was an art and French major who also was fascinated with nature and science. As a child, she was always more interested in geography, wildflowers, and airplanes than in dolls. She too had read and was influenced by Osborn's book as an undergraduate.

At the time we met, World War II was still the defining event of our lives and a great source of mutual interest. Both of us remember asking our parents whether the newspapers would still be published daily after the war was over; we couldn't imagine there would be enough other news to fill them. We first got together in the student union of the University of Kansas over a bridge game and a discussion of the battle of Dunkirk, which had taken place fourteen years earlier. Dunkirk is a seaport in northern France that in May 1940 was the site of a successful evacuation of the British Expeditionary Force (BEF) after the collapse of the French army. Threatened with annihilation by encroaching German forces, the BEF evacuation was nothing short of a miracle, accomplished at the last minute by a mixed fleet of naval vessels and small boats.

Our conversation could have been an omen, since the Dunkirk evacuation was a classic result of folly. The British had been thoroughly warned by Winston Churchill and others against appeasing Hitler and neglecting military preparedness. Then, among other things, the French commander in chief of land forces had protested to his superior against a key mistake in French planning—a deployment of substantial forces through Belgium to southern Holland that played a major role in the French army's collapse.[6] The warnings went unheeded, the combined French and British forces were badly beaten, and the British lost almost all their equipment and barely managed to retrieve the vital core of their army—almost a quarter-million professional soldiers. So on first acquaintance, we discussed a folly in which "our" side had barely avoided total catastrophe. Now we're dealing with another case in which the stakes are infinitely higher.

For us personally, discussing Dunkirk was just the start. Keen mutual interests in world affairs, science, and art (among other topics) were soon discovered—and the result was a marriage that has now lasted more than forty years. Both of us had a basic qualification for being scientists: strong curiosity.

In 1955 our daughter, now an economist working for a government agency, was born. By the time she started school, Anne was collaborating in Paul's research, dissecting butterflies under a microscope, illustrating and recording the details of their anatomy for computer studies testing theories of biological classification. Despite the eyestrain from teasing apart and drawing dozens of muscles within structures the size of this "o," she became increasingly interested in science. In the course of a decade of collaboration, we developed a team approach to scientific research and, later, to our work in science policy. Even now, with old age on the horizon, we still have a persistent urge to understand how the world works.

We arrived at Stanford University in 1959 and soon discovered that Paul's senior colleague, the late Richard Holm, shared many of our views. As Paul and Dick started expressing unorthodox views in technical areas of ecology, evolution, and taxonomy,[7] we learned that Dick, too, was deeply concerned about the human impact on the planet. He was the first of our Stanford colleagues to engage in long discussions with us about the human predicament.

Paul's research in evolution and ecology meant that much of his time had to be spent doing fieldwork—going to many different locations to collect and do field experiments with butterflies or to make detailed observations of reef fishes or birds. In our first sabbatical year (1965–1966), we took a field trip around the world.

The purpose of the trip was to gain a worldwide perspective on the taxonomy, evolution, and ecology of butterflies, the natural system that has been the focus of Paul's scientific career.[8] His work on how the size of butterfly populations is controlled has provided insights into such seemingly diverse issues as why Peruvian anchovetas were being overfished and how to control insect pest populations with minimal use of pesticides. And butterflies were central to research Paul did with our friend, plant evolutionist Peter Raven, who was then also at Stanford. They investigated the interrelationships of butterflies and the plants they eat when they are caterpillars.[9] That study launched the increasingly active field of coevolution, which examines the evolutionary relationships between ecologically intimate organisms such as predators and prey or hosts and parasites.[10] Coevolution explains a great deal about problems now faced by humanity such as the increasingly troublesome resistance of human pathogens to antibiotics and that of insect pests to insecticides.

Going around the world in search of butterflies also gave us a personal view of then little-recognized signs of environmental deterioration. We well remember, for example, landing on Yandina, in the Russell Islands (in the Solomons, just north of Guadalcanal), a tiny spot on the map that we had assumed would be a tropical paradise of birds and butterflies. Instead, we found one large coconut plantation, each tree with a metal rat guard and all the vegetation between the trees cut close to the ground. At Mount Hagen in the New Guinea highlands, we also discovered the forests cleared over a huge area and replaced by dense stands of kunai grass. In both places, the natural flora and fauna were in rapid retreat. We were fortunate that our trip to New Guinea and the Solomons had been arranged by a local entomologist, Joe Szent-Ivany, who was well known for helping visiting scientists. Otherwise we would have been hard-pressed to find relatively undisturbed habitat at many of our stops in what we had imagined to be an "unspoiled" tropical paradise.

Indeed, during the next summer, everywhere we went in Asia from Malaysia to Kashmir, it was difficult to find places where anything like the original butterfly fauna was present. In Kashmir, the fabled high-altitude meadows of Gulmarg turned out to be biologically barren, grazed to within a fraction of an inch above the ground.

When we returned to Stanford, conversations with Dick, Peter, neurophysiologist Don Kennedy, botanist John Thomas, attorney John Montgomery, and other friends and colleagues focused with increasing intensity on the population-resource-environment situation. These discussions eventually led to Paul's going public in lectures, then in radio and television appearances, and led to the writing of *The Population Bomb*.[11]

But our experiences in field trips around the world ever since have remained much the same. Since the early 1970s, we've watched the forests of Central America disappear, to be largely replaced by degraded pastures. The coral reef in the Grenadines where we did our first research on reef fishes was soon destroyed by ships' anchors. The watershed in Trinidad in which we studied long-lived tropical butterflies was illegally burned to make way for squatters.

Our fieldwork in central Africa was similarly discouraging. When Jane Goodall first arrived at Gombe Stream in Tanzania in 1960, the forest habitat of her treasured chimpanzees stretched continuously for sixty miles east from the shores of Lake Tanganyika. When we went there a decade later to do research on the dynamics of a butterfly mimicry complex, the forest had been cleared to within two miles of the lake.

In the early 1980s, we traveled through Rwanda to the Parc National des Volcans, home of the rare mountain gorilla. The nation presented a classic picture of overpopulation and environmental deterioration: steep hillsides farmed to the tops with little or no erosion control, patches of exotic (non-native) eucalyptus trees being heavily coppiced for firewood, and rivers running red with eroded soil. We were lucky enough to see the gorillas in their shrinking park; a large chunk had already been destroyed for a failed agricultural scheme. Money was not available even to mark the boundary of the remaining park area, and the trees were disappearing one by one along the forest edges to serve for construction and firewood. The loss of the forest had already changed local rainfall patterns and stream flows, further impoverishing the region's villagers.

Today that park is a dwindling source of firewood for hundreds of thousands of refugees. We fear that the gorillas, the prime tourist attraction and source of foreign exchange for Rwanda, are now severely threatened—as are the myriad other mammals, birds, insects, plants, and other organisms that had survived under the "umbrella" of gorilla protection. Without the gorillas, we doubt that any substantial protection could be provided for the remainder of the park's once-rich flora and fauna.

In the United States, we have witnessed similar trends. Much of the East has been converted into a sprawling suburbia during our lifetimes, and in California the process has progressed even faster. In that state our research group has recorded the disappearance of butterfly populations one after another as a result of various "developments." Extensive field research in the desertified intermountain West has produced no better news. Back in the 1980s, Stanford University conservation biologist Dennis Murphy and Paul traveled into an isolated Nevada mountain range to sample a known population of checkerspot butterflies only to find the site devoid of even a single food plant for their caterpillars, grazed bare, trampled, and coated with sheep droppings. Even at the remote Rocky Mountain Biological Laboratory, over 9000 feet high in the Elk Mountains of Colorado, encroaching ski and suburban development is slowly destroying the area's living resources.

In short, around the world, we have watched humanity consuming its natural capital and degrading its own life-support systems. Virtually everywhere—be it the Comoros Islands or California, Delhi or Detroit, Antarctica or Alaska, Fiji or Florence, Tanzania or Tokyo, Australia or the Amazon, Beijing or Bora Bora—we've seen the results of gradually building pressures caused by increasing human numbers, overconsumption, and the use of environmentally damaging technologies and practices. It was and is a classic picture of a species overshooting the carrying capacity of its environment because the ability of that environment to support people in the future is being reduced.

During the 1960s and early 1970s, a growing number of our colleagues also became greatly concerned about the global environmental situation. As a result, Peter Raven, John Holdren, George Woodwell, John Harte, Gene Likens, Sherwood Rowland, Stephen Schneider, and many others began to apply the knowledge of environmental systems being acquired by ecologists, evolutionary biologists, physicists, geologists, and chemists to the rapid changes they were observing in the biosphere. The more environmental scientists learned about the population-resource-environment situation, the more worried we all became about the long-term human future.

Perhaps more important, early on some of us started to take these findings to the public. To do that was perhaps the most traumatic act of Paul's career. In the 1960s, the dominant view in science was expressed in the old saying "Shoemaker, stick to your last." In other words, work in your own specialty, don't transgress disciplinary boundaries, and certainly don't get involved in public policy issues—especially highly controversial ones. Some nuclear physicists had already broken this rule in the 1940s and 1950s as they helped develop atomic weapons, were horrified by the impact of their detonation in Japan, and began speaking out against the nuclear arms race.

Biologists, however, had been pretty quiet until the catastrophic misuse of pesticides began to draw them into the public arena. Paul's first venture in that area occurred in 1958, at the behest of our longtime friend Ed Wilson. The U.S. Department of Agriculture (USDA) had announced a deeply flawed plan to blanket much of the southeastern United States with broad-spectrum pesticides in order to "exterminate" the imported fire ant. Despite the protests of many biologists,[12] the USDA proceeded; and as predicted the plan was an environmental disaster that failed to eliminate the ant (which remains a major pest to this day).

Leading the way, Rachel Carson had made the first major public statement on an environmental issue with *Silent Spring* in 1962, for which she was mercilessly abused by economic entomologists and the pesticide industry for her forthright condemnation of their behavior.[13] It was therefore with some trepidation that Paul began to appear on radio and television to condemn the behavior of human beings in general. The possible public response worried him less than his colleagues' reactions because, as is the case with most scientists, Paul's ego rewards come mostly from the approval of his peers. Condemnation from them could have cut him off from a career he loved. But he felt compelled to take the chance and was encouraged to do so by the support of his closest colleagues at Stanford.

He needn't have worried. We have received more than enough abuse from the far left, the far right, classical economists, the business press, and elsewhere—but we've had nothing but wonderful support from our colleagues in ecology, evolutionary biology, and animal behavior (together known as "population biology"). For example, the dean of evolutionary biology is Ernst Mayr of Harvard, now over ninety years old. In the 1960s, Paul (then a young turk) and Ernst (a scientist of great stature) had friendly debates over details of taxonomic practice and evolutionary theory. But since the publication of *The Population Bomb,* hardly a year has gone by without at least one letter of encouragement from Ernst.

The support of fellow population biologists and the opportunity to work with friends from other scientific disciplines in a growing "band of brothers and sisters" trying to find solutions to the human predicament have helped to smooth the bumps in the long road to this book. We finished this chapter while working with John and Cheri Holdren on technical revisions over the Christmas break in 1995. Visiting them reminded us once again of what deeply social animals we all are and how critically important friends are to maintaining our equilibrium as human beings. We hope our three bright and beautiful granddaughters—and everyone else's grandchildren—will be able to live in a world where friendships like ours will be able to thrive; where, indeed, friendship will be the dominant human interaction.

CHAPTER 2

"Wise Use" and
Environmental Anti-Science

□

HUMANITY IS NOW FACING a sort of slow-motion environmental Dunkirk. It remains to be seen whether civilization can avoid the perilous trap it has set for itself. Unlike the troops crowding the beach at Dunkirk, civilization's fate is in its own hands; no miraculous last-minute rescue is in the cards. Although progress has certainly been made in addressing the human predicament, far more is needed. Even if humanity manages to extricate itself, it is likely that environmental events will be defining ones for our grandchildren's generation—and those events could dwarf World War II in magnitude.

Sadly, much of the progress that has been made in defining, understanding, and seeking solutions to the human predicament over the past thirty years is now being undermined by an environmental backlash, fueled by anti-science ideas and arguments provided by the brownlash. While it assumes a variety of forms, the brownlash appears most clearly as an outpouring of seemingly authoritative opinions in books, articles, and media appearances that greatly distort what is or isn't known by environmental scientists. Taken together, despite the variety of its forms, sources, and issues addressed, the brownlash has produced what amounts to a body of anti-science—a twisting of the findings of empirical science—to bolster a predetermined worldview and to support a political agenda. By virtue of relentless repetition, this flood of anti-environmental sentiment has acquired an unfortunate aura of credibility.

It should be noted that the brownlash is not by any means a coordinated effort. Rather, it seems to be generated by a diversity of individuals and organizations. Some of its promoters have links to right-wing ideology and political groups. And some are well-intentioned individuals, including writers and public figures, who for one reason or another have bought into the notion that environmental regulation has become oppressive and needs to be severely weakened. But the most extreme—and most dangerous—elements are those who, while claiming to represent a scientific viewpoint, misstate scientific findings to support their view that the U.S. government has gone overboard with regulation, especially (but not exclusively) for environmental protection, and that subtle, long-term problems like global warming are nothing to worry about. The words and sentiments of the brownlash are profoundly troubling to us and many of our colleagues. Not only are the underlying agendas seldom revealed, but more important, the confusion and distraction created among the public and policy makers by brownlash pronouncements interfere with and prolong the already difficult search for realistic and equitable solutions to the human predicament.

Anti-science as promoted by the brownlash is not a unique phenomenon in our society; the largely successful efforts of creationists to keep Americans ignorant of evolution is another example, which is perhaps not entirely unrelated.[1] Both feature a denial of facts and circumstances that don't fit religious or other traditional beliefs; policies built on either could lead our society into serious trouble.

Fortunately, in the case of environmental science, most of the public is fairly well informed about environmental problems and remains committed to environmental protection. When polled, 65 percent of Americans today say they are willing to pay good money for environmental quality.[2] But support for environmental quality is sometimes said to be superficial; while almost everyone is in favor of a sound environment—clean air, clean water, toxic site cleanups, national parks, and so on—many don't feel that environmental deterioration, especially on a regional or global level, is a crucial issue in their own lives. In part this is testimony to the success of environmental protection in the United States. But it is also the case that most people lack an appreciation of the deeper but generally less visible, slowly developing global problems. Thus they don't perceive population growth, global warming, the loss of biodiversity, depletion of groundwater, or exposure to chemicals in plastics and pesticides as a personal threat at the same level as crime in their neighborhood, loss of a job, or a substantial rise in taxes.

So anti-science rhetoric has been particularly effective in promoting a series of erroneous notions, which we will analyze in detail in this book:

- Environmental scientists ignore the abundant good news about the environment;
- Population growth does not cause environmental damage and may even be beneficial;
- Humanity is on the verge of abolishing hunger; food scarcity is a local or regional problem and is not indicative of overpopulation;
- Natural resources are superabundant, if not infinite;
- There is no extinction crisis, so most efforts to preserve species are both uneconomic and unnecessary;
- Global warming and acid rain are not serious threats to humanity;
- Stratospheric ozone depletion is a hoax;
- The risks posed by toxic substances are vastly exaggerated; and
- Environmental regulation is wrecking the economy.

How has the brownlash managed to persuade a significant segment of the public that the state of the environment and the directions and rates in which it is changing are not causes for great concern? Even many individuals who are sensitive to local environmental problems have found brownlash distortions of global issues convincing. Part of the answer lies in the overall lack of scientific knowledge among United States citizens. Most Americans readily grasp the issues surrounding something familiar and tangible like a local dump site, but they have considerably more difficulty with issues involving genetic variation or the dynamics of the atmosphere. Thus it is relatively easy to rally support against a proposed landfill and infinitely more difficult to impose a carbon tax that might help offset global warming.

Also, individuals not trained to recognize the hallmarks of change have difficulty perceiving and appreciating the gradual deterioration of civilization's life-support systems.[3] This is why record-breaking temperatures and violent storms receive so much attention, while a gradual in-

crease in annual global temperatures—measured in fractions of a degree over decades—is not considered newsworthy. Threatened pandas
are featured on television, while the constant and critical losses of insect populations, which are key elements of our life-support systems,
pass unnoticed. People who have no meaningful way to grasp regional
and global environmental problems cannot easily tell what information
is distorted, when, and to what degree.

Decision makers, too, have a tendency to focus mostly on the more
obvious and immediate environmental problems—usually described as
"pollution"—rather than on the deterioration of natural ecosystems
upon whose continued functioning global civilization depends.[4] Indeed,
most people still don't realize that humanity has become a truly global
force, interfering in a very real and direct way in many of the planet's
natural cycles.

For example, human activity puts ten times as much oil into the
oceans as comes from natural seeps, has multiplied the natural flow of
cadmium into the atmosphere eightfold, has doubled the rate of nitrogen fixation, and is responsible for about half the concentration of
methane (a potent greenhouse gas) and nearly a third of the carbon
dioxide (also a greenhouse gas) in the atmosphere today—all added
since the industrial revolution, most notably in the past half-century.[5]
Human beings now use or co-opt some 40 percent of the food available
to all land animals[6] and about 45 percent of the available freshwater
flows.[7]

Another factor that plays into brownlash thinking is the not uncom-
mon belief that environmental quality is improving, not declining. In
some ways it is, but the claim of uniform improvement simply does not
stand up to close scientific scrutiny. Nor does the claim that the human
condition in general is improving everywhere.[8] The degradation of
ecosystem services (the conditions and processes through which natural
ecosystems support and fulfill human life) is a crucial issue, which is
largely ignored by the brownlash and to which we will return. Unfortunately, the superficial progress achieved to date has made it easy to
label ecologists doomsayers for continuing to press for change.

At the same time, the public often seems unaware of the success of
actions taken at the instigation of the environmental movement. People
can easily see the disadvantages of environmental regulations but not
the despoliation that would exist without them. Especially resentful are
those whose personal or corporate ox is being gored when they are

forced to sustain financial losses because of a sensible (or occasionally senseless) application of regulations.

Of course, it is natural for many people to feel personally threatened by efforts to preserve a healthy environment. Consider a car salesman who makes a bigger commission selling a large car than a small one, an executive of a petrochemical company that is liable for damage done by toxic chemicals released into the environment, a logger whose job is jeopardized by enforcement of the Endangered Species Act, a rancher whose way of life may be threatened by higher grazing fees on public lands, a farmer about to lose his farm because of environmentalists' attacks on subsidies for irrigation water, or a developer who wants to continue building subdivisions and is sick and tired of dealing with inconsistent building codes or U.S. Fish and Wildlife Service bureaucrats. In such situations, resentment of some of the rules, regulations, and recommendations designed to enhance human well-being and protect life-support systems is understandable.

Unfortunately, many of these dissatisfied individuals and companies have been recruited into the self-styled "wise-use" movement, which has attracted a surprisingly diverse coalition of people, including representatives of extractive and polluting industries who are motivated by corporate interests as well as private property rights activists and right-wing idealogues. Although some of these individuals simply believe that environmental regulations unfairly distribute the costs of environmental protection, some others are doubtless motivated more by a greedy desire for unrestrained economic expansion.

At a minimum, the wise-use movement firmly opposes most government efforts to maintain environmental quality in the belief that environmental regulation creates unnecessary and burdensome bureaucratic hurdles, which stifle economic growth. Wise-use advocates see little or no need for constraints on the exploitation of resources for short-term economic benefits and argue that such exploitation can be accelerated with no adverse long-term consequences. Thus they espouse unrestricted drilling in the Arctic National Wildlife Refuge, logging in national forests, mining in protected areas or next door to national parks, and full compensation for any loss of actual or potential property value resulting from environmental restrictions.

In promoting the view that immediate economic interests are best served by continuing business as usual, the wise-use movement works to stir up discontent among everyday citizens who, rightly or wrongly, feel abused by environmental regulations. This tactic is described in detail in David Helvarg's book *The War Against the Greens:*

> To date the Wise Use/Property Rights backlash has been a bracing if dangerous reminder to environmentalists that power concedes nothing without a demand and that no social movement, be it ethnic, civil, or environmental, can rest on its past laurels. . . . If the anti-enviros' links to the Farm Bureau, Heritage Foundation, NRA, logging companies, resource trade associations, multinational gold-mining companies, [and] ORV manufacturers . . . proves anything, it's that large industrial lobbies and transnational corporations have learned to play the grassroots game.[9]

Wise-use proponents are not always candid about their motivations and intentions. Many of the organizations representing them masquerade as groups seemingly attentive to environmental quality. Adopting a strategy biologists call "aggressive mimicry," they often give themselves names resembling those of genuine environmental or scientific public-interest groups: National Wetland Coalition, Friends of Eagle Mountain, The Sahara Club, the Alliance for Environment and Resources, The Abundant Wildlife Society of North America, The Global Climate Coalition, the National Wilderness Institute,[10] and the American Council on Science and Health.[11] In keeping with aggressive mimicry, these organizations often actively work *against* the interests implied in their names—a practice sometimes called "greenscamming."

One such group, calling itself Northwesterners for More Fish, seeks to limit federal protection of endangered fish species so the activities of utilities, aluminum companies, and timber outfits utilizing the region's rivers are not hindered. Armed with a $2.6 million budget, the group aims to discredit environmentalists who say industry is destroying the fish habitats of the Columbia and other rivers, threatening the Northwest's valuable salmon fishery, among others.[12]

Congressman George Miller, referring to the wise-use movement's support of welfare ranching, overlogging, and government giveaways of mining rights, stated: "What you have . . . is a lot of special interests who are trying to generate some ideological movement to try and disguise what it is individually they want in the name of their own profits, their own greed in terms of the use and abuse of federal lands."[13]

Wise-use sentiments have been adopted by a number of deeply conservative legislators, many of whom have received campaign contributions from these organizations. One member of the House of Representatives recently succeeded in gaining passage of a bill that limited the annual budget for the Mojave National Preserve, the newest addition to the National Park System, to one dollar—thus guaranteeing that the park would have no money for upkeep or for enforcement of park regulations.[14] Fortunately, the bill did not become law.

These same conservative legislators are determined to slash funding for scientific research, especially on such subjects as endangered species, ozone depletion, and global warming, and they have tried to enact severe cutbacks in funds for the National Science Foundation, the U.S. Geological Survey, the National Aeronautics and Space Administration, and the Environmental Protection Agency. Many of them and their supporters see science as self-indulgent, at odds with economic interests, and inextricably linked to regulatory excesses.

The scientific justifications and philosophical underpinnings for the positions of the wise-use movement are largely provided by the brownlash. Prominent promoters of the wise-use viewpoint on a number of issues include such conservative think tanks as the Cato Institute and the Heritage Foundation.[15] Both organizations help generate and disseminate erroneous brownlash ideas and information. Adam Myerson, editor of the Heritage Foundation's journal *Policy Review,* pretty much summed up the brownlash perspective by saying: "Leading scientists have done major work disputing the current henny-pennyism about global warming, acid rain, and other purported environmental catastrophes."[16] In reality, as we will show, most "leading" scientists support what Myerson calls henny-pennyism; the scientists he refers to are a small group largely outside the mainstream of scientific thinking.

In recent years, a flood of books and articles has advanced the notion that all is well with the environment, giving credence to this anti-scientific "What, me worry?" outlook. Brownlash writers often pepper their works with code phrases such as "sound science" and "balance," words that suggest objectivity while in fact having little connection to what is presented. "Sound science" usually means science that is interpreted to support the brownlash view. "Balance" generally means giving undue prominence to the opinions of one or a handful of contrarian scientists who are at odds with the consensus of the scientific community at large.[17]

In this book, we will investigate many examples of what the brown-lash calls "sound science" and "balance"; some of the most dramatic ones are in the area of atmospheric anti-science. We'll take a hard look at the claims of the brownlash, mostly using its own words to represent its positions, and will then set the record straight with respect to the underlying science. In our view, not all but the vast majority of brownlash pronouncements are based in either faulty science or the misinterpretation of good science. Our principal sources of brownlash ideas and erroneous information are a series of books that although convincing to some lay readers, are replete with gross scientific errors and severely twisted interpretation, as we will document in considerable detail.

Of course, while pro-environmental organizations and environmental scientists in general may sometimes be dead wrong (as can anybody confronting environmental complexity), they ordinarily are not acting on behalf of narrow economic interests. Yet one of the remarkable triumphs of the wise-use movement and its allies in the past decade has been their ability to define public interest organizations, in the eyes of many legislators, as "special interests"—not different in kind from the American Tobacco Institute, the Western Fuels Association, or other organizations that represent business groups.[18]

But we believe there is a very real difference in kind. Most environmental organizations are funded mainly by membership donations; corporate funding is at most a minor factor for public interest advocacy groups. There are no monetary profits to be gained other than attracting a bigger membership. Environmental scientists have even less to gain; they usually are dependent on university or research institute salaries and research funds from peer-reviewed government grants or sometimes (especially in new or controversial areas where government funds are largely unavailable) from private foundations.

One reason the brownlash messages hold so much appeal to many people, we think, is the fear of further change. Even though the American frontier closed a century ago, many Americans seem to believe they still live in what the great economist Kenneth Boulding once called a "cowboy economy."[19] They still think they can figuratively throw their garbage over the backyard fence with impunity; they regard the environmentally protected public land as "wasted" and think it should be available for their self-beneficial appropriation; they believe that private property rights are absolute (despite a rich economic amd legal literature showing they never have been).[20] They do not understand, as Pace

University law professor John Humbach wrote in 1993, that "the Constitution does not guarantee that land speculators will win their bets."[21]

The anti-science brownlash provides a rationalization for the short-term economic interests of these groups: old-growth forests are decadent and should be harvested; extinction is natural, so there's no harm in overharvesting economically important animals; there is abundant undisturbed habitat, so human beings have a right to develop land anywhere and in any way they choose; global warming is a hoax or even will benefit agriculture, so there's no need to limit the burning of fossil fuels; and so on. Anti-science basically claims we can perpetuate the good old days by doing business as usual. But the problem is, we can't.[22]

Thus the brownlash helps create public confusion about the character and magnitude of environmental problems, taking advantage of the lack of consensus among individuals and social groups on the urgency of enhancing environmental protection. A widely shared social consensus, such as the United States last saw during World War II, will be essential if we are to maintain environmental quality while meeting the nation's other needs. By emphasizing dissent, the brownlash works against the formation of any such consensus; instead it has helped thwart the development of a spirit of cooperation mixed with concern for society as a whole. In our opinion, the brownlash fuels conflict by claiming that environmental problems are overblown or nonexistent and that unbridled economic development will propel the world to new levels of prosperity with little or no risk to the natural systems that support society. As a result, environmental groups and wise-use proponents are increasingly polarized.

Unfortunately, some of that polarization has led to ugly confrontations and activities that are not condoned by the brownlash or by most environmentalists, including us. As David Helvarg stated, "Along with the growth of Wise Use/Property Rights, the last six years have seen a startling increase in intimidation, vandalism, and violence directed against grassroots environmental activists."[23] And while confrontations and threats have been generated by both sides—most notably (but by no means exclusively) over the northern spotted owl's protection plan—the level of intimidation engaged in by wise-use proponents is disturbing, to say the least.

One of the most egregious cases involves a U.S. Forest Service officer in central Nevada who has had several attempts made on his life.[24] Why?

Because he tried to enforce Forest Service regulations in ways that offended local ranchers. In late 1995, the Forest Service transferred him to another state, literally to save his life. Meanwhile, the rebellious ranchers of Nevada have gone so far as to proclaim that county rights have precedence over the federal management of public lands. In early 1996, however, a federal court rejected their claim and reaffirmed federal jurisdiction over national lands.[25]

For Stanford scientists, of course, it's all too easy to talk about saving old-growth forests, shutting down coal mines, restricting pesticide use, or limiting fish harvests. It's more difficult for us to address the legitimate concerns of those who might pay heavy costs for those actions. Nonetheless, more must be done to address those concerns. After all, the loggers, miners, farmers, and fishers are no more responsible for the human dilemma than those of us who demand and consume their products.

Indeed, most people find it more and more difficult to do what's right environmentally. People are mostly conservative; they don't want to change their ways of life. Furthermore, especially in rich countries, citizens are bombarded by advertising that urges them to consume more and more, while technology, mobility, and an urban lifestyle have largely concealed their dependence on the natural systems and resources that are damaged by overconsumption.

For years, we owned and flew a light aircraft—and loved it. It was extremely convenient for getting to remote field sites or out-of-the-way places for lectures. But we paid a price in some environmental guilt. We worry about driving a car that's too small for safety, and we spend too much time roaring around on airline jets. Like most Americans, we have more gadgets than we need. As Pogo said, "We have met the enemy and he is us."

We have less excuse than most people, since so much of our time is spent trying to figure out how Earth's life-support systems work and how to do what's necessary to keep them working. That's why years ago we decided to have only one child; having a small family was, for us, one very effective way to lessen dramatically our "footprint" on the planet. But like many others, we feel the tension between doing what we think is right for other people, our descendants, and humanity as a whole on one hand and trying to have a pleasant and convenient life for ourselves on the other.

But, of course, timbering, coal mining, and fishing are honorable and useful jobs, and if society suddenly determines that some of those must disappear, society (including Stanford professors) should help bear the costs of easing the transition for those displaced. Sure, nobody helped the employees of horse collar manufacturers when, with the advent of the automobile, the "market" decided they should lose their jobs. But there was no general social decision that horsecollars threatened everyone, and the cooperation of workers who made them was not required for the general good.

Fortunately, despite all the efforts of the brownlash to discourage it, environmental concern in the United States is widespread.[26] Thus a public opinion survey in 1995 indicated that slightly over half of all Americans felt that environmental problems in the United States were "very serious." Indeed, 85 percent were concerned "a fair amount" and 38 percent "a great deal" about the environment. Fifty-eight percent would choose protecting the environment over economic growth, and 65 percent said they would be willing to pay higher prices so that industry could protect the environment better. Responses in other rich nations have been similar, and people in developing nations have shown, if anything, even greater environmental concerns. These responses suggest that the notion that caring about the environment is a luxury of the rich is a myth. Furthermore, our impression is that young people care especially strongly about environmental quality—a good omen if true.

Nor is environmental concern exclusive to Democrats and "liberals." There is a strong Republican and conservative tradition of environmental protection dating back to Teddy Roosevelt and even earlier.[27] Many of our most important environmental laws were passed with bipartisan support during the Nixon and Ford administrations. Recently, some conservative environmentalists have been speaking out against brownlash rhetoric.[28] And public concern is rising about the efforts to cripple environmental laws and regulations posed by right-wing leaders in Congress, thinly disguised as "deregulation" and "necessary budget-cutting." In January 1996, a Republican pollster, Linda Divall, warned that "our party is out of sync with mainstream American opinion when it comes to the environment."[29]

Indeed, some interests that might be expected to sympathize with the wise-use movement have moved beyond such reactionary views. Many leaders in corporations such as paper companies and chemical manufacturers, whose activities are directly harmful to the environment, are concerned about their firms' environmental impacts and are shifting to less damaging practices.[30] Our friends in the ranching community in western Colorado indicate their concern to us every summer. They want to preserve a way of life and a high-quality environment—and are as worried about the progressive suburbanization of the area as are the scientists at the Rocky Mountain Biological Laboratory. Indeed, they have actively participated in discussions with environmentalists and officials of the Department of the Interior to set grazing fees at levels that would not force them out of business but also wouldn't subsidize overgrazing and land abuse.[31]

Loggers, ranchers, miners, petrochemical workers, fishers, and professors all live on the same planet, and all of us must cooperate to preserve a sound environment for our descendants. The environmental problems of the planet can be solved only in a spirit of cooperation, not in one of conflict. Ways must be found to allocate fairly both the benefits and the costs of environmental quality. Environmental scientists have been arguing this for decades,[32] but unhappily, things have not always worked out as those scientists would wish.

In writing this book, we are trying to achieve three goals. The first and most important goal is to counter the erroneous information and misrepresentations put forth by the brownlash, giving a point-by-point rebuttal to the more prominent fables of environmental anti-science. Second, we want to reach out to a broad audience of readers, whether they be interested citizens, journalists, scientists, or policy makers, and provide them with accurate scientific information they can use to evaluate critically and counter the commentary of the brownlash. We hope everyone will learn that environmental conditions and processes are more crucial to human well-being, and more threatened by human activities, than most people realize. To facilitate the process, we have provided important background material and provided references to pertinent scientific literature.

And third, we want to encourage other scientists to speak out and become involved in such issues. To that end, we provide our own insights into how a scientist can become a spokesperson on matters of societal urgency yet retain scientific integrity and the support of the scientific community.

Paul and political scientist Dennis Pirages once wrote: "We are all now caught in a gigantic tragedy of the commons; each person, each family, and each nation is struggling to stay ahead while the whole system is on the verge of collapse. Many people are now coming to realize the predicament, but it remains to be seen if enough people are willing to break the individual patterns of behavior that are leading to social destruction."[33]

Sadly, one consequence of brownlash activities is to stifle any inclination citizens might have to break away from their existing patterns of behavior. Because seeds of doubt and confusion have been sown by the brownlash about the environmental prognosis, Americans hesitate to embark on changes that might entail some sacrifice or inconvenience. Change does not come easily when its necessity and purpose are questioned, when people are told our environment is adequately protected and that reform is promoted only by environmental doomsayers. Americans today are being told that the environmental movement is "the greatest single threat to the American economy"[34] and that environmental reform would make U.S. factories grind to a halt, throwing the nation further down the economic ladder.

If citizens were convinced that some changes in the American way of life were necessary and if attractive options were offered, most would gladly oblige, as they did during World War II. They certainly would be willing to support changes if they understood that those changes could *enhance* their quality of life and that of their children. In our view, the brownlash has achieved some success partly because much of society remains woefully uninformed about environmental science. We hope the ensuing chapters will provide some basic understanding that puts the messages of the brownlash into perspective.

CHAPTER 3

In Defense of Science

◻

IN THE UNITED STATES TODAY, a surprising number of people believe in horoscopes, "out-of-body" experiences, the magical powers of crystals, and visitors from space. Our society is also witnessing a resurgence of creationism. In state after state across the Bible Belt, religious doctrine is creeping back into school science curricula as legislators and local school boards pressure teachers to give equal time to the teaching of creationism and to characterize evolution as an "unproven" theory.

In response to the popular surge of superstition and belief in the supernatural, in 1995 some two hundred concerned scientists, educators, and philosophers were convened by the New York Academy of Sciences for a three-day conference called "The Flight from Science and Reason."[1] Far from being a run-of-the-mill event, this gathering was a clarion call in defense of science, an opportunity to denounce the rising influence of astrology, supernaturalism, religious fundamentalism as science, and other irrational notions. Such beliefs, and the activities they inspire, threaten rational scientific inquiry by rejecting the methods and procedures—such as statistical analysis, controlled experimentation, computer modeling, and peer review—that characterize modern science. In the words of Malcolm Browne, a *New York Times* reporter, the need for such a meeting reflected a growing fear "that the fabric of reason is being ripped asunder, and that if scientists and other thinkers continue to acquiesce in the process, the hobbling of science . . . seems assured."[2]

Of course, science couldn't be hobbled this way in a society that valued it as much as it values, say, mass marketing or organized sports. The sad truth is that most Americans lack any credible education in science and are at best vaguely aware that science and technology comprise a substantial and crucial portion of their culture.[3] They are profoundly ignorant of that culture and, thus, of the most basic forces that shape and influence the nation.[4] To the average person, the scientific process is a sort of black hole, an alien world of arcane experiments, unintelligible or confusing results, and peculiar people.

Reflecting the general lack of scientific knowledge among citizens, only about half of 534 newspaper editors in a survey disagreed strongly with the statement "Dinosaurs and humans lived contemporaneously," and the views on evolution of about half of them were divergent from those of the scientific community.[5] American education thus has failed to provide an adequate science background even to relatively well educated journalists. They are not alone among prominent citizens; Pat Buchanan, a candidate for the presidency of the United States, made his creationist position clear during the primary campaign of 1996.[6]

The rise of creationism has prevented a majority of Americans from understanding the origins of *Homo sapiens* and numerous public issues with biological underpinnings, including many health issues. Indeed, the widespread lack of familiarity with evolutionary processes has helped set the stage for a potentially catastrophic public health crisis from a surge of antibiotic-resistant diseases (such as tuberculosis, now becoming a serious problem in much of the world) and emergent viruses (such as AIDS and Ebola),[7] as has been described in many popular articles and was portrayed fictionally in the novel and movie *Outbreak*. One reason antibiotic-resistant strains of microorganisms and emergent viruses have become so troublesome is the lack of understanding of evolution and coevolution among physicians and the public at large.

Poor as the public's knowledge is of the findings of science, though, understanding of scientists and the processes by which those findings are made is even more sketchy. Scientists generally are doing what they love; they often work very long hours for relatively small financial rewards. Like athletes or musicians, they are always "in training" or performing—trying to keep up with an ever-more-voluminous literature, seeking novel hypotheses and ways of testing them, or carrying out difficult experiments or laborious sets of observations to find out how the world works.

Like professional athletes or musicians, scientists are subject to continuous open testing and scrutiny. In order to get the financial support required for their work, they must convince tough-minded colleagues on review panels that the research they are proposing is soundly designed and deserves funding. To build a reputation, to get promotion and tenure in universities, to earn the approval of colleagues and gain the satisfaction that one has added to human knowledge; indeed, to get any of the non-financial rewards available in science, scientists must publish regularly in peer-reviewed journals. For a first-rank scientist, this may mean 200 or more published papers over the course of a career.

Most scientists are competitive—just as a hitter delights in spoiling a pitcher's day with a home run, a scientist often delights in beating others to an important discovery or showing that earlier ideas were wrong. With trivial exceptions, cheating is not possible; a person can't fake being a world-class scientist any more than one can fake being a world-class pitcher or concert pianist. It's not that scientists are intrinsically more honest or more objective than other human beings, it's that the system is fundamentally adversarial, and nature itself is the ultimate judge of who is correct.

This system works very well, but even so, science can never provide absolute certainty or the "proof" that many who misunderstand science often say society needs. Certainty is a standard commodity for some religious leaders and political columnists, but it is forever denied to scientists. Some things, such as the role of natural selection in evolution, gravity, or the laws of thermodynamics, have never been conclusively "proven." Yet these concepts are supported by such massive evidence that scientists treat them as certain in their daily operations. Thus everyone accepts gravity as a given: if you let go of an ordinary wine glass three feet above a concrete floor, it will drop and shatter. Neither the drop nor the shattering is certain, but the odds of the glass rising rather than falling, or bouncing unbroken off the concrete onto a nearby rug, are sufficiently minuscule that everyone ignores them.

Similarly, scientists try to ignore creationists, flat-earth believers, alchemists, and builders of perpetual-motion machines. If they didn't accept well-founded concepts like those mentioned above as axiomatic, the scientific process would be paralyzed. But that doesn't mean that these concepts can never change or be overthrown; history is littered with ideas that science has discarded—such as the belief that a medium (known as "ether") permeates all of space or that most species were formed in single steps by major mutations. Science is constantly evolving as new ideas and new data become available.

But ideas are not accepted without question; scientists attempt first to disprove a new hypothesis. In many cases, they can evaluate new ideas by doing experiments and then submitting the results to a battery of statistical tests to see whether the results are "significant." A "significant" result is often defined as one for which the probability that it happened by chance alone is less than 5 percent (.05), and a "highly significant" result is defined as one for which the probability of a chance result is less than 1 percent (.01).[8] For example, five consecutive heads in five flips of a coin would be a significant result, suggesting that the coin was loaded or the flipper dishonest, since the odds of getting five consecutive heads by chance is about 0.03. Seven consecutive heads would be highly significant, since the odds of that occurring with an unloaded coin are about 0.008—that is, it would happen on average eight times in every 1000 sets of seven flips.

So when numerous studies indicate that cigarette smoking is strongly associated with development of lung cancer, the hypothesis that smoking is not a cause of lung cancer tends to be falsified.[9] In the rest of environmental science, it is almost never possible to obtain the clarity of understanding now available about the relationship of smoking to health. When it comes to other pollutants that directly injure human health, such clear evidence on cause and effect is rare. A person can tell an investigator how many packs of cigarettes were smoked per day and for how many years. Only other smokers have similar levels of exposure. But no one knows with remotely the same level of precision the quantity of various toxic synthetic organic chemicals or heavy metals such as lead or mercury to which he or she has been exposed. Even so, clarifying the relationship of smoking to health has taken many decades.

With most environmental problems, the analysis is considerably more difficult. Neat experiments and simple statistical tests usually are not adequate or feasible, and attempts to find statistical correlations (as in the case of smoking and health) between possible causes and effects seldom yield clear-cut results. Scientists often say, "Correlation is not causation." But a conclusion drawn on the basis of correlations can often be bolstered if possible mechanisms of causation, or similar correlations in other systems, are found. Thus, when particular components of cigarette smoke were shown in animal tests to be carcinogenic, it strengthened the case against cigarettes.

For large-scale problems such as population growth, climate change, ozone depletion, land degradation, declining biodiversity, and the general loss of ecosystem services, the difficulties are even more severe. Humanity is running a vast experiment on the biosphere and on itself, causing changes in the planet's fundamental life-sustaining processes, and all the changes are interrelated. How can anyone possibly know in advance what ancillary effects might accompany something like warming of the oceans? Unlike the case with cancer research, laboratory analysis is of little use. For the global experiment, the system is unique, there can be no replicates, and the experiment cannot be repeated. To a large degree, scientists must rely on computer simulations, analyses of government statistics, and conclusions based on first principles in lieu of laboratory or field experiments to gain an understanding of the potential consequences of this uncontrolled global experiment. Consequently, many uncertainties about human impacts on planetary processes will persist.

Of course, investigations exposing plants to ultraviolet-B (UV-B) radiation or carbon dioxide (CO_2) enrichment in greenhouses, or looking at the effects of drought stress on experimental plots with different levels of biodiversity, can supply very useful information on some possible effects.[10] For instance, our colleague at the Rocky Mountain Biological Laboratory, John Harte, and his group are doing small-scale warming experiments in a mountain meadow to gain insight into mechanisms of ecosystem response to global warming. Their results have shown a variety of effects on plant growth and changes in abundance among species as well as interesting changes in soil flora and fauna.[11] But drawing broad conclusions from such experiments is subject to severe problems of scale, and the results require conservative interpretation, as the scientists doing the work are well aware. In dealing with systems of such complexity, individual scientists might reasonably evaluate the same evidence differently, and differing or unorthodox conclusions are legitimate. Science does not often progress by consensus.

Fakhri Bazzaz, a plant physiologist at Harvard, has found that CO_2-enriched air accelerates short-term plant growth. But his studies were carried out under controlled greenhouse conditions, and his results are difficult to translate to a larger scale. No one yet knows what will happen when an entire ecosystem is enriched over a longer time period—as is now happening because of the CO_2 humanity is adding to the atmosphere.

In many cases, scientists can predict that plant growth in natural ecosystems will be constrained by a shortage of soil nutrients despite the greater availability of CO_2. Competitive relations among the plant species will shift as plants vie for a limited pool of nutrients, as will the interactions of the plants with the herbivores and diseases that attack them, thus changing the dynamics of the ecosystem. It is also highly likely that changes in climate will exert significant effects, further perturbing the system. Because of such complexities and the problems of scale, scientists can at best make informed guesses about whether any positive effects of CO_2 fertilization will compensate for negative effects of CO_2-induced rapid climate change. Thus a reasonable consensus may not be achieved until the global experiment starts producing dramatic results.

Climate change in general has been an area of both substantial uncertainty and great concern to scientists. Scientists who have studied atmospheric physics and the past history of climate know that quite rapid shifts in climatic patterns can occur. They also know that adding large quantities of greenhouse gases to the atmosphere will alter the climate. This is so well established that scientists treat it as a fact. The uncertainties lie in how fast changes will take place and exactly what sort of changes will occur in specific places.

Nevertheless, the majority of climatologists are now convinced that the human-caused additions of greenhouse gases are already causing climate change, and many of them believe that the changes ahead might be very rapid and could cause great hardships for humanity and nature. This view is clearly expressed in the reports of the very conservative Intergovernmental Panel on Climate Change—reports that represent a consensus of hundreds of atmospheric scientists.[12]

On the other hand, a very few qualified atmospheric scientists, among them Richard Lindzen of the Massachusetts Institute of Technology and

S. Fred Singer of the Science and Environmental Policy Project, apparently see little to be concerned about. They speculate that increased CO_2 will trigger various feedback systems, such as greater cloud cover and higher rates of CO_2 absorption by the oceans, thereby dampening the impact of CO_2-induced climate change. (We discuss feedbacks in more detail in chapter 8.) Thus they argue that little change is likely and they advise no action to curb CO_2 emissions. We hope they are correct. With the information available today, however, most climatologists think feedbacks are just as likely to reinforce as to offset each other, possibly leading to a snowball effect and a greater disaster than most anticipate. But if we listen to the dissenters and take no action to slow the atmospheric buildup of greenhouse gases, we will be betting our children's futures that all the possible climatic feedbacks—against most current evidence—will happily cancel each other out.[13]

The issue is not likely to be settled soon. It could be a long time before scientists begin to treat the consequences of enhancing the greenhouse effect as facts. But, while scientific research is not properly carried out by consensus, as Stanford climatologist Stephen Schneider always says, *science policy should be.* That is, in most cases, society's best bet is to rely on the scientific consensus—even though once in a while, the contrarians will prove to be correct and will eventually change that consensus. Society normally cannot afford to act solely on far-out views on scientific issues—most of which eventually prove to be wrong.

In the case of global climate change, we believe that taking no action, based on an assumption that global warming is inconsequential, is too risky. A society totally unprepared for the disruptions caused by prolonged droughts, severe storms, and coastal flooding, for instance, could undergo a devastating breakdown. But taking action on the basis of worst-case prognoses would also be inappropriate and costly; suddenly imposing fuel rationing and high taxes on industrial activity with no tangible justification would cause economic disruption and most likely would backfire. In the end, society must decide where to place its bets and what (if any) price to pay to insure against possible disaster. In democratic societies, this is done through the political process with input from credible scientists.

This is not a novel exercise; virtually everyone who can afford it carries some kind of insurance. Taking out insurance is not even novel for societies. For instance, from the 1950s until about 1990, Americans paid trillions of dollars to insure against the risk of a Soviet invasion of western Europe, an event many experts now think was never a realistic possibility. Yet, even today, some conservative groups favor investing in enormously expensive insurance against the possibility of an unexpected nuclear attack by deploying an anti-ballistic missile (ABM) system. Although such a move would violate a signed treaty and is probably the most expensive and least effective form of insurance against such a risk, it would have the advantage of enriching the patrons of those institutions with taxpayers' money—an all-too-common outcome of the political process.

In contrast, insuring against the most serious consequences of global warming by investing more federal dollars in research and development of energy-efficient technologies and renewable energy sources (especially solar), thereby eventually lowering CO_2 emissions, makes very good sense to us. Similarly, research into ways of reducing emissions of other important greenhouse gases such as nitrous oxide and methane is needed.[14]

Of course, we too are trying to influence the political process by educating the public and decision makers about what we believe environmental science has to say about the human predicament. We hope that if the public becomes familiar with what we and our colleagues believe to be the best assessment of the environmental situation, it will support adopting a more conservative approach, including initiatives to insure against environmental disasters.

Above all, remember that there *is* a consensus in the scientific community about the human dilemma. To a very large degree, that consensus is based on first principles, such as the following: it is impossible to have exponential growth of the human population at anything like today's rates for very much longer; adding greenhouse gases to the atmosphere will change the climate; agriculture is dependent on reasonably stable climates; habitat destruction causes extinctions, and so forth. Besides these principles, the consensus is also based on the results of innumerable field experiments and observations, detailed examinations of demographic and food production statistics, computer modeling, and the like. We share in that consensus and believe that it supports the overall viewpoint expressed in this book.

That is not to say scientific studies are always error-free, or that scientists' interpretations and projections are always right, or that unexpected results never occur. This goes for our own work as well. We would write a different *The Population Bomb* if we were doing it today (as, in a sense, we did with *The Population Explosion*).[15] The predictions we would make now, after digesting nearly thirty more years' data and interactions with hundreds of colleagues and students working ever more intensively on the human predicament, would be different in many details from those we made in the distant past. But they would not differ greatly in substance. Most of the same trends still concern us: rapid population growth, the widening gap between rich and poor, and increasing environmental impacts of agricultural and industrial activities.

Moreover, we and other environmental scientists don't lack for intelligent, competent critics. As examples, Kenneth Arrow (Professor Emeritus of Economics, Stanford University), Samuel Preston (Professor of Demography, University of Pennsylvania), Vernon Ruttan (Professor of Agriculture and Applied Economics, University of Minnesota), Walter Falcon (Director, Institute for International Studies, Stanford), and William Nordhaus (Professor of Economics, Yale University), all distinguished academicians, have disagreed with us on issues of the proximity of limits to growth, the impact of population growth, the future of agriculture, the consequences of international trade, and what might be a reasonable level of social response in anticipation of climate change, respectively.

Such disagreements sometimes even become intense. But these are serious people with many publications in the refereed literature. They have contributed to the technical analysis of the human predicament, and they cite the primary literature accurately and fairly. The views of such critics merit careful consideration. Their backgrounds and their approaches are different from those of ecologists, and we can invariably learn from them even when our conclusions are somewhat divergent.

Like all scientists, we're accustomed to being criticized and accustomed to changing our views as new data come in. We would rather be wrong for the right reasons than right for the wrong reasons. For example, based on the data in hand and the concerns of agricultural scientists in the mid-1960s, we underestimated the potential of the "green revolution" to boost crop yields and predicted crop shortfalls and famines in the 1970s two or three times as severe as those that actually occurred. The average nutritional status of humanity has significantly improved since *The Population Bomb* was written—possibly in part be-

cause the warnings it conveyed helped stimulate global efforts to support increased food production and improved food distribution.[16] Another factor that no doubt helped was the modest but real slowing of
population growth that began around 1970.

Nevertheless, we were wrong in assuming that per-capita food supplies would deteriorate significantly over that period. A smaller proportion of the population is hungry today than in 1968, and it is possible
that the absolute numbers of malnourished people have declined, even
though the population has grown by some 65 percent. Still, in some of
the world's poorest regions (especially sub-Saharan Africa), things are
considerably worse than they were in 1968. But since people in both industrialized and middle-income nations are almost all better fed and
paying less (in relation to their incomes) for food than they were in
1968, our projections were inaccurate—and we're glad they were.

Naturally, we're not the first scientists to have made faulty predictions,
and we won't be the last. There are plenty of instances in which warnings and predictions have turned out wrong because information was
incomplete, the warnings were heeded and policies changed, or circumstances changed. For example, predictions of future climate trends
by Stephen Schneider and other leading climatologists, based on the
prevailing knowledge of the atmosphere in the early 1970s, gave more
weight to the potential problem of global cooling than it now appears
to merit. But then, although increasing human-caused additions of CO_2
to the atmosphere were known and could be predicted, the role of several other important greenhouse gases—chlorofluorocarbons (CFCs),[17]
methane, and nitrous oxide—hadn't yet been discovered.[18] The addition
of these gases roughly doubles the rate of greenhouse gas buildup and
speeds up the global warming process accordingly.

The point we wish to emphasize here is that we and our colleagues
in environmental science make no claim to perfection, only to doing science as it should be done and to having our work constantly reviewed
by peers so that it represents more than our own idiosyncratic opinions.
If scientists waited for "proof" or perfection, no scientific papers would
ever be published. We firmly believe that increased scientific knowledge, and especially much wider dissemination of the knowledge we already have, will be an essential ingredient of resolving the human
predicament.

One should not make the mistake of assuming that because science
and its conclusions evolve, science will not be essential to solving civi-

lization's most pressing problems. Nothing could be further from the truth. The problem-solving power of science can be seen in the success of everything from the air transport system and the ubiquity of computers to the dazzling variety of products in stores and supermarkets. Technology (the practical application of scientific findings) has shaped the world in which we live to an overwhelming degree.

The power of science rests in the very thing that leads naive critics to attack it: the obligation of scientists to change their views as new data come in and hypotheses are tested. Science cannot provide certainty, but it can provide a continually upgraded assessment of the environmental situation, and it can help design and implement strategies to improve that situation. Science's assessments and advice will be *relatively* objective; it strives to be (but, being itself a social institution, never fully becomes) value-free. In comparison with estimates and advice not subject to the procedures required in science, it usually succeeds.

Civilization's future (and the long-term ability of Earth to support human beings) will depend heavily on an increasingly careful and wise use of science and technology and on the rate and direction of technological innovation. Thus it is crucial that the public gain a realistic view of science and what it can and can't provide.

The basic goal of environmental scientists is to understand the world better; and the values of most of us compel us to use that understanding to strive for a better future for family, friends, and descendants— and for all humanity. Our egos, of course, are involved in our work. Like all scientists, we and other environmental scientists want to be "right" and earn the approval of the scientific community. We also bring our cultural baggage to our work, as does every scientist.

But that's one place where science has an advantage over most other approaches to understanding the world—to be successful, we must convince other scientists, who may have very different cultural and disciplinary backgrounds, that our worldview is credible—and nature is always present as a final arbiter. Thus a scientist who takes a heterodox position must understand the orthodoxy better than most of its adherents if he or she is to have any real chance of success within the scientific community. Convincing the general public of a contrarian view is a different matter, though.

It is clear that most brownlash proponents have an agenda very different from that of most scientists; their conclusions generally support the view that immediate economic interests are best served by continuing business as usual and that long-term interests are not threatened by that policy. Taking the lead from contrarian scientists on many issues, they question conventional views and frequently reject mainstream scientific thinking. With a few exceptions, brownlash writers don't publish their attacks on environmental science in peer-reviewed journals, where their views would be exposed to the rigorous criticism of the scientific community. Nor do they constantly carry out research to test and retest ideas, as most scientists do.

Contrarian scientists with compatible views are often featured in brownlash literature as purveyors of "sound" science: modern equivalents of Copernicus about to shatter the current version of a Ptolemaic paradigm. And there always is a chance they are. After all, in the history of science, contrarians have played critically important roles in pointing out antiquated patterns of thought and generating creative change.[19] But one should always remember that for every Copernicus, Galileo, Darwin, or Einstein, there are thousands of scientific pretenders with perpetual-motion machines, flat-earth theories, and creationist beliefs.

Who are the brownlash contrarians? Some are legitimate scientists with appropriate credentials who adhere to scientific rules and procedures; others are less qualified individuals more clearly aligned with right-wing organizations or private interests. Among the legitimate scientists are atmospheric scientists Richard Lindzen of MIT and S. Fred Singer, Director of the Science and Environment Policy Project, and molecular biologist Bruce Ames of the University of California, Berkeley, who has made important contributions to carcinogenicity testing, but now downplays the health risks of toxic substances produced by industry. A few other scientists cooperate with elements of the brownlash, often just on limited issues. In general, though, respected scientists are not prominent figures in the brownlash. And for the most part, contrarian scientists are notably absent from the ranks of scholars who, besides doing research on the human predicament, are also systematically seeking solutions (since they deny that solutions are needed).

Why would a qualified scientist help disseminate brownlash ideas? We can think of only two reasons. He or she believes that the scientific consensus is in error (a perfectly valid position, provided it is well reasoned and supported by evidence) and/or enjoys financial support from anti-environmental elements (not so valid). In the latter group one finds Patrick Michaels, a University of Virginia climatologist and Cato Institute senior fellow, who downplays the effects of global warming while accepting six-figure consulting fees from coal and other energy interests.[20] Fred Singer has been a paid consultant for ARCO, Exxon Corporation, Shell Oil Company, Sun Oil Company, and Unocal Corporation; he is on record for telling these companies that they had better stand up for their interests or they will be threatened in the same way as CFC manufacturers, who, Singer claimed, were forced to phase out CFC production on the basis of "insubstantial science."[21]

Being paid for consulting is normal practice among professionals, who are—and should be—paid for sharing their expertise with the non-academic world. At issue here are whether their consulting activities blur the line between objective and subjective reporting of the facts and whether the data are presented in a way that supports a predetermined conclusion. The brownlash contrarians claim that their sources of support do not influence their science. But often they are financed by industries with a strong economic interest in rolling back environmental regulations and in preventing the enactment of new ones. One certainly has to wonder about the objectivity of a scientist's findings when she or he supports views friendly to those interests.[22]

Ross Gelbspan, a Pulitzer Prize–winning journalist, referring to the small cadre of atmospheric scientists who deny that global warming is real, wrote: ". . . in this persistent and well-funded campaign of denial they have become interchangeable ornaments on the hood of a high-powered engine of [misinformation]." At the very least, the views of atmospheric contrarians have been magnified far out of proportion compared with those of the vast majority of their climatological colleagues by the multimillion-dollar publicity campaigns of industry groups attempting to quell public worries about climate change.[23] Industry may not have bought the contrarians, but it certainly has bought them a megaphone.

Of course, scientific findings that imply a need for new or changed policies are not immune to political controversy. The consensus of the scientific community that population, consumption, and environmental problems are extremely serious (as represented in the opinion of fifty-eight of the world's scientific academies or in the World Scientists' Warning to Humanity—see appendix B) has come under attack from both ends of the political spectrum. It has been portrayed as doctrinaire and under the control of radicals: leftists, socialists, or communists in the view of the right wing;[24] capitalists, racists, or fascists when viewed by the far left. But there is a big difference between conducting rational and honest discussion of the weight to be given to scientific conclusions and uncertainties in making policy decisions and launching attacks on scientists if their findings are unpalatable.

More subtle is the brownlash approach of downplaying or denying unpalatable scientific findings or presenting contrary views as if they had equal support by scientists. Most scientists have a difficult time dealing with assertions that in their view distort or misstate research findings; they know that nature can be exceedingly complex, but they also are confident that nature does not deliberately try to fool them. Nature is tough but honest. They also expect other scientists to be clear and accurate in describing scientific findings.

But the brownlash apparently doesn't operate under such rules. To our dismay and that of our colleagues, the contrarians, aided allies in the media, have been surprisingly effective in getting brownlash messages across to the public. In some cases, the messages simply confuse the issues; in others, they offer a seemingly credible (though generally unfounded) rationale for relaxing or eliminating environmental regulations or forestalling development of new policies to address serious global problems.

Especially worrisome is the skewing of facts by contrarians and their allies, turning seemingly objective communications into advocacy pieces. Fred Singer, who writes a regular column for the *Washington Times,* wrote one in 1994 titled "Climate Claims Wither Under the Luminous Lights of Science."[25] It attacked the accuracy of climate models, using careful selection of data to imply that the models cannot be trusted when they predict global warming. With it was a graph titled, "Global Warming's Phantom Threat," which compared "temperature change predicted from climate models" with two actual temperature records.

Anyone looking at the graph could see that between 1950 and 1980, the climate model projection deviated significantly from the actual temperature records. A reader might well conclude that this indicated that global warming hasn't occurred. Yet climatologists know that the model-derived data plotted by Singer were inaccurate because they failed to account for the cooling effects of aerosols in the atmosphere. Once the aerosol effect was incorporated into improved models in the early 1990s, predictions were much closer to the recorded trend. Worst of all was Singer's failure to include the actual temperatures of the 1980s; collectively, they were the warmest years in recorded history. If the models had been properly represented and the actual record taken into the 1990s, the predictions would have been shown to be reasonably accurate.

The strenuous efforts of the brownlash to refute a growing mountain of scientific evidence on global warming are especially interesting now that the scientific community is becoming more united in its concern about it.[26] Can we expect brownlash advocates to change their views as new data flow in? Perhaps, but our prediction is that they will simply switch their emphasis from "global warming is a hoax" to "global warming is real, but not to worry, keep doing business as usual; its effects will be minor and may even be good for us."

A major element of the brownlash is the work of a handful of journalists who write authoritatively yet draw erroneous conclusions based on their own interpretations of science. In 1995, Stephen Budiansky, senior writer for *U.S. News and World Report,* published a scathing review of *The Value of Life* by Stephen R. Kellert, a Yale professor well known for his work on biophilia—the innate affinity he believes human beings have for the natural world.[27] Budiansky presumptuously sneered at the need to preserve biodiversity while at the same time revealing a poor grasp of the subject. He wrote: ". . . you wonder what will happen when biotechnology and rational drug design make natural products obsolete, as they surely will in time."[28] The biotechnologists we know would consider that a dubious prediction at best.

Budiansky also has suggested that because disequilibrium and instability have in some ways made life on Earth possible, human-induced damage can hardly upset Earth's not-so-delicate ecosystems, an attitude he happens to share with radio talk-show host Rush Limbaugh. Such thinking is clearly a corollary to the brownlash argument that since extinction is a natural process, human-driven extinctions are nothing to worry about. We explain what is wrong with Budiansky's claim in chapter 7, although Kellert summed it up nicely in a rebuttal he wrote to *New Scientist:* "It seems curious that Mr. Budiansky, a senior writer (I suppose journalist) at *U.S. News & World Report,* knows more about the current scientific data than the eminent scientist, Professor Edward O. Wilson of Harvard, a wide range of other well-known scientists cited in the book, or, for that matter, myself."[29] Curious indeed.

Brownlash writers also cheerfully exploit any dissent that occurs among scientists. If scientists don't agree on rates of species extinction, or on strategies for ecosystem management, or on details of model projections of global warming, brownlash advocates are quick to point out—and exaggerate—those differences. Thus Gregg Easterbrook, Ronald Bailey, and other brownlash writers make much of the news that climatologists don't agree on the details of global warming, although it isn't the warming itself but the probable *rate* of warming and changes in precipitation patterns that are under dispute. In doing this, they help perpetuate the myth that a basic consensus on warming doesn't exist within the scientific community, justifying their view that any action undertaken to reduce greenhouse gas emissions should be delayed until "all the data are in."

The congeniality of brownlash views with short-term economic gain is indicated by their repeated coverage in the American business press—especially in *Forbes* magazine and in the editorial section of the *Wall Street Journal,* which are favored outlets. Indeed, the *Wall Street Journal* frequently lavishes praise on brownlash writers, thus further elevating their work in the eyes of its readers (mostly non-scientists). The difference between the preponderance of views in the editorial pages of the *Wall Street Journal* and those of the scientific community speaks volumes about the *Journal*'s positions on matters of environmental science.

For instance, an editorial in that newspaper referred to Gregg Easterbrook's book *A Moment on the Earth*[30] as "an update on the state of Mother Earth today."[31] Yet the book contains so many serious errors that it has spawned a virtual cottage industry among scientists trying to correct them.[32] Typical were the comments of entomologist Jack Schultz of Pennsylvania State University: *Moment* "contains some of the most egregious cases of misunderstood, misstated, misinterpreted, and plainly incorrect 'science' writing I've ever encountered."[33] Ecologist Thomas Lovejoy, Undersecretary for External Affairs at the Smithsonian Institution, wrote: "I was stunningly disappointed by the book's rambling prose and profusion of inconsistency and error."[34] Physicist-ecologist John Harte of the Energy and Resources Group at the University of California, Berkeley, stated, "On far too many pages of this vexing book, I found examples of . . . misquoted and misinterpreted segments of scientists' writings, and of illogical thinking."[35] But Easterbrook, a journalist and contributing editor to *Newsweek* and the *Atlantic Monthly,* is only one of the more prominent brownlash writers and is far from the most extreme in his views.

In an effort to appear credible, brownlash writers frequently cite one another, often leaning on statements by the Ph.D. contrarians, which imbues their work with an aura of validity. Much of the nonsense promulgated by Rush Limbaugh in his bid to convince the public to ignore the threat of stratospheric ozone depletion[36] can be traced to *21st Century Science and Technology.* Among other things, that magazine has carried out a very effective campaign of misinformation on the issue of ozone depletion—one detailed in *Science,* the premier North American scientific journal.[37] We'll deal later with the science that shows Limbaugh's position to be nonsensical; here we primarily trace the brownlash linkages. Limbaugh credits his views to marine biologist Dixy Lee Ray's *Trashing the Planet.*[38] Ray in turn cited S. Fred Singer and Rogelio Maduro.[39] Maduro is an associate editor of *21st Century Science and Technology* and coauthor (with R. Schauerhammer) of *The Holes in the Ozone Scare: The Scientific Evidence That the Sky Isn't Falling,* published by 21st Century.[40]

Maduro and Schauerhammer argue vehemently that natural sources of ozone-destroying chlorine in the atmosphere are much more important than the synthetic chlorofluorocarbons (CFCs) that the scientific community has identified as the leading culprits.[41] Leaning on the Maduro and Schauerhammer book, Limbaugh and his collaborator John Fund (who writes editorials for the *Wall Street Journal*)[42] state that "Mt. Pinatubo in the Philippines spewed forth more than a thousand times the amount of ozone-depleting chemicals in *one* eruption than all the fluorocarbons manufactured by wicked, diabolical corporations in history. . . . Conclusion: mankind can't possibly equal the output of even one eruption from Pinatubo, much less a billion years' worth, so how can we destroy ozone?"[43]

This is classic anti-science. It sounds authoritative, but it is well known among scientists as a totally incorrect conclusion. The chlorine-containing compounds released by volcanoes do not contribute much to ozone breakdown in the stratosphere because they don't end up there. Nonetheless, Ray continued to publish erroneous information on the impact of volcanoes on ozone in her 1993 book *Environmental Overkill.*[44]

Interestingly, contrarian Fred Singer told *Science* in 1993 that atmospheric scientists had done "a very careful job of tracing the amount of chlorine and fluorine in the stratosphere. . . . I'm now reasonably convinced that CFCs make the major contribution to stratospheric chlorine, and what has convinced me is the published data."[45] *Science* added, "And that leaves the critics with little basis for claiming that the ozone layer has long withstood high levels of chlorine without harm."[46] We wonder how vigorously Rush Limbaugh has retracted his error.

The ozone backlash provides an excellent example of how non-scientific publications can influence public perceptions of scientific issues. Maduro's views "percolated from Ray to Limbaugh" and also served as the basis for an article in the June 1993 issue of *Omni,* which reaches more than 1 million readers, "claiming to expose ozone research as a politically motivated scam."[47] Maduro's book sounds so authoritative that atmospheric researchers have said "they can see how readers who are not experts in the field might find the arguments compelling."[48] Harvard atmospheric chemist James G. Anderson commented, "Part of the strategy in this backlash is to try to entrain apparently responsible scientists who clearly don't understand the problem and have not gone over the data before they've commented."[49]

We can sympathize with the plight of the ordinary reader (or even the ordinary talk-show host) when faced with such a campaign. It does not augur well for the future of an increasingly scientifically illiterate population when even scientists can be taken in. The bottom line is that the battle with the brownlash is not some kind of scholarly discourse. It is actually more like a street fight,[50] and within the bounds of scientific accuracy it must be fought as such.

A major part of the problem, of course, is that all of us have difficulty perceiving large-scale or slowly developing environmental problems.[51] Human beings evolved, both culturally and genetically, in situations in which there was no advantage to perceiving changes occurring slowly, decade by decade. People have been programmed to react quickly and appropriately to a sudden environmental change, as when a leopard appeared in the path ahead. But there was no advantage to registering a change in climate—if it occurred, it was not human caused, and there was precious little a band of hunter-gatherers could do about it except seek greener pastures. Indeed, there is reason to believe that our nervous systems evolved to keep the general environmental backdrop of our lives seemingly constant in order to allow us to concentrate on short-term changes happening against that backdrop.[52]

Now many critical changes are taking place in our backdrop because of human activities, but most of them are happening too slowly for people to notice. Many changes might be detected more easily by organisms with sensory capabilities different from those of human beings. Like birds, people are sight-oriented animals and have relatively poorly developed chemosensory abilities. Toxification of the planet might be much more obvious to dogs, which live in a world shaped to a great extent by their sense of smell. One can barely imagine how we would perceive changes in our environment if, like some fishes, we oriented to it primarily by detecting distortions in electrical fields, or if we responded primarily to sonar returns as bats do.

But people can't detect the buildup of greenhouse gases by sight, hearing, or smell. We know the concentration of CO_2 is increasing because of a climbing zigzag line on a graph attached to a machine that measures the concentration of CO_2 in the air over Hawaii. Even some trained scientists have trouble emotionally grasping the potential for disaster suggested by that zigzag line. Dirty air and dirty water are easy to spot and react to; declining biodiversity, soil erosion, and overpumped aquifers are harder to perceive.

Indeed, people seem incapable of directly perceiving even threats as dramatic as the linkage between cigarettes and poor health. Compared with risks from exposure to most other environmental hazards, the direct risk to health from smoking is astronomical—one out of every three smokers dies prematurely because of the habit. Yet people persisted in smoking for hundreds of years without fully realizing the danger, and it took a large scientific effort over decades to persuade the medical community and most of the general public of the hazards of tobacco. In fact, many people remain unconvinced, often citing the common (but irrelevant) experience of knowing healthy octogenarians who have smoked for sixty years.

It is not surprising that if a one-in-three risk of early death is not directly detectable by many people, the majority cannot detect risks on the order of one in a hundred. Nevertheless, with regard to pollutants, one death among every hundred people exposed would be considered unacceptably high. Only scientific analysis, properly communicated to an educated public, is likely to generate appropriate responses to risks of that magnitude or less.

Thus our evolutionary heritage, both biological and cultural, combined with the public's lack of appreciation of statistical reasoning, works in favor of the brownlash. People are not disposed to embrace news that implies a need to change their ways to begin with. If the need for change is justified by environmental changes they don't understand and can barely perceive, they will be susceptible to a contrary view that assures them all's well with the world.

Moreover, an attitude of many knowledgable environmental scientists also plays into the hands of the brownlash. While the scientists appreciate the progress that has been made in treating the symptoms of environmental deterioration, they remain pessimistic because the underlying disease remains largely untreated and threatens to flare out of control. But people need hope for the future, and they deserve credit for their accomplishments. That's why we and others have been remiss in not emphasizing sufficiently what good news there is. In the next chapter, we take a stab at correcting that failure, while still recognizing a fair amount of unfinished business as well as emerging challenges.

CHAPTER 4

The Good News . . . in Perspective

A MERICAN ENVIRONMENTALISTS are often accused of never being satisfied with the progress that has been made in environmental protection. Instead of applauding hard-won gains, they keep pointing out new or intensifying problems and calling for new policies or stricter laws and enforcement. On the other side, environmental critics have increasingly complained about the burdens of compliance with what they see as proliferating and troublesome environmental regulations—with little appreciation of the positive difference they have made in the quality and safety of American life.

Clearly, the United States has come a long way since the days when toxic chemicals were dumped indiscriminately, rivers burst into flames, and lakes were so polluted that fish couldn't survive. Even the most ardent opponents of environmental regulation would probably concede that our lives today are much safer, healthier, and more pleasant than they would be without America's efforts in environmental protection.[1]

Moreover, in the past decade or two, environmental consciousness has become well integrated into American life and business, in itself a remarkable and important social change. Hardly a day goes by without at least one environmental report in the newspapers or on television, and environmental studies programs proliferate in schools and colleges. Citizens willingly cooperate in curbside recycling programs despite some inconvenience, spend extra money for "organic foods," and buy "green" products such as compact fluorescent lightbulbs and energy-efficient refrigerators. Not only have many businesses and industries risen to meet the demand for greener products and services, many have also been shifting to more environmentally responsible behavior than in the past. And the environmental movement has become a prominent element of the American social and political mainstream. In short, the United States has much to be proud of, with a record of environmental protection that ranks among the world's best.

Yet environmental protection is not just a matter of safeguarding the health of citizens; it includes a very broad range of issues beyond controlling pollution. But rather than deal with all these broad topics here, we focus first in this chapter on pollution abatement, which is both a major component of environmental policy in the United States and an area of good news that often goes unrecognized. We also describe the role of Americans as international environmental leaders. In later chapters, we discuss various other issues that have been successfully addressed, such as protection of biodiversity by the Endangered Species Act, among other measures, and efforts to reverse ozone depletion.

Americans certainly can—and should—be proud of their success in reducing many kinds of pollution, especially pollution of air and water. The average number of days per urban area per year during which air quality was deemed "unhealthy" fell from nearly twenty in the early 1980s to about six in 1993.[2] Even Los Angeles, famous worldwide for its smog, is a salient success story—all the more so given its substantial population (and car population) growth in recent decades.[3]

The improved air quality reflects dramatic reductions over the past twenty-five years in emissions of some important pollutants that are produced when fossil fuels (coal, oil, and natural gas) are burned. Moreover, the efficiency of energy use has risen substantially, and emissions are lower when less fuel is used to produce the same goods and services. Water quality also has greatly improved in many important respects, especially the treatment of urban sewage and industrial effluents. And significant progress is being made in cleaning up thousands of places contaminated in the past with toxic wastes and protecting the public from current and future exposures to toxic substances.

But all this regulatory activity no doubt helped generate the recent backlash. No one seriously objected to curbing air or water pollution, which can readily be seen and smelled and can make people sick. And the public demanded action when pesticides and toxic waste sites were shown to be sources of illness, birth defects, and cancer. But regulation seems to have become increasingly intrusive, so new questions are being raised: How clean is clean? Haven't the costs exceeded the benefits of pollution abatement or cleanup measures? Isn't the Environmental Protection Agency too focused on "command-and-control" bureaucratic solutions, using too much stick and too little carrot? Such questions are clearly legitimate and appropriate, yet they imply that regulation has gone too far, that it is overly burdensome, too expensive, and unnecessary.

So why do environmentalists—to the great consternation of conservatives and wise-use proponents—keep pushing for tighter controls and new laws? There are two reasons for this persistence. First, environmental protection means much more than controlling pollution and disposing safely of wastes. More than anything, it means preserving the stability of natural processes and the ecosystem services that support civilization—concerns that have only recently appeared on the policy agenda. Only in the past few decades have environmental problems transcended national scales and become worldwide in scope; global warming, ozone depletion, acid precipitation, and the loss of biodiversity all were unsuspected or little known before 1970. Concern over these difficult global problems explains why so many scientists haven't been as forthcoming with "good news" as many people, especially brownlash advocates, claim they should be.

Second, just to stay in place, it is necessary to keep moving forward. As more and more people are added to the population, each consuming more and more resources and materials, they generate more and more waste and pollution. If, in the face of this constant escalation of consumption and waste, we don't keep ratcheting up environmental regulations, we'll slide backward as deterioration outpaces abatement. It's rather like trying to run up an escalator that is going down. This is why urban air quality continues to be a serious problem in many cities, with ozone alerts now commonly included in weather reports. In some cities, such as Dallas, it has gotten worse. And that's why water pollution is still troublesome—even more so in some ways because the remaining sources are numerous, diffuse, and not as easily controlled as when water pollution came mostly from sewage or factory discharge pipes.

Sliding Backward, Struggling Forward

Automobile tailpipe emissions illustrate the running-up-the-down-escalator dilemma. Since 1970, when the first strong amendments to the national Clean Air Act were enacted, the U.S. population has grown by 31 percent—from 203 million to 266 million in 1996—while the number of vehicles (cars, trucks, and buses) grew a whopping 62 percent—from 120 million to almost 195 million. Moreover, since 1980, the average number of miles driven annually per vehicle has risen by about 20 percent.[4] In other words, not only are there more Americans buying more cars, they are also driving them longer distances.

With no change in cars and emissions, the result would have been a near doubling of pollution. But the average vehicle's fuel efficiency was improved by more than 60 percent (a figure that would have been even greater if gas-guzzling light trucks and recreational vehicles hadn't become so popular), so the total amount of fuel consumed each year by U.S. motor vehicles rose only about 42 percent.[5]

In addition, tailpipe emissions of particulates and carbon monoxide (CO) were substantially reduced. Perhaps the biggest success story was the 96 percent reduction in lead emissions made possible by removing lead from gasoline in the late 1970s.[6] But there has been little or no reduction in total emissions of some important pollutants such as nitrogen oxides, which in 1990 were some 7 percent higher than in 1970. And hundreds of other air pollutants still are not controlled at all. The bottom line is that progress was made, but not as much as might have been expected.

Meanwhile, hefty increases have occurred in emissions of some uncontrolled substances, particularly carbon dioxide, the leading culprit in global warming. Not surprisingly, since CO_2 emissions rise in tandem with fuel consumption, the U.S. transportation sector alone adds 40 percent more to the atmosphere now than it did in 1970. And, of course, the raising of highway speed limits in 1995 was a step backward for both fuel conservation and emissions control, to say nothing of public health.

Despite all the hurdles, American achievements in pollution control are very real and substantial, all the more so since the number of pollution-generating sources (of which motor vehicles are only a part) is so enormous. Energy use per capita in the United States is 25 to 60 percent higher than that of most other industrialized nations with comparable standards of living and five to 100 times higher than in developing nations. High per-capita energy use multiplied by a very large population (the third largest in the world) makes us the world's biggest consumer of energy.

Yet our urban air quality is as good or better than that of most other industrial nations and a lot better than that of cities in eastern Europe or the developing world.[7] Similar statements can be made for other aspects of environmental protection in the United States, such as reducing water pollution and dealing with hazardous substances. Indeed, our pollution-control and pollution-prevention technologies are among the best in the world and are increasingly in demand as export commodities.

The Benefits and Costs of Controlling Air Pollution

Following the passage of Clean Air Act amendments in 1970, and most recently, in 1990, the United States has significantly stemmed the flow of toxins into the air. Although estimates of the dollar value of controlling air pollution in the United States vary enormously,[8] as do estimates of the costs, Americans clearly have gained enormous benefits, especially in the protection of health. The principal pollutants addressed by the Clean Air Act—carbon monoxide, hydrocarbons, particulates, oxides of nitrogen and sulfur, and the ozone formed by the action of sunlight on hydrocarbons and oxides of nitrogen—are precisely those that are most damaging to human health.[9] Controlling emissions of these substances saves many thousands of people from premature death every year. And billions of dollars are saved by reducing losses of productivity because of asthma, emphysema, bronchitis, and other respiratory diseases.

The benefits of eliminating lead from gasoline have ironically become clearer after the fact, spurring regulators to keep lowering tolerances. Improved technologies allowed detection of mental impairment in children caused by very low concentrations of lead from paint, plumbing, and other sources only after blood levels in the general population had declined far enough to make comparisons feasible.[10]

Important indirect benefits of controlling air pollutants, especially sulfur dioxide (a prime component of acid precipitation), also accrue to natural and agricultural ecosystems and to the built environment. Thus additional billions are saved through reduced losses of crop and forest productivity and reduced damage to buildings and materials.

Many of the easy reductions, accomplished with scrubbers, catalysts, and other pollution-control technologies, have already been achieved. But controls must be continually tightened to compensate for population growth and the accompanying increase in polluting activities. Unfortunately, as control is tightened, costs generally rise; capturing the last 5 percent of emissions of a pollutant from stacks or tailpipes may cost as much or more than removing the first 50 percent. So, although the problem can sometimes be sidestepped through process changes or substitution of materials that generate less pollution, abatement costs by and large have risen faster than pollution could be reduced.

As costs have climbed, resistance to increased pollution controls by some business and industry groups has also risen, contributing to the environmental backlash. Particularly hard hit have been small businesses in California—paint dealers, gas stations, and dry-cleaning establishments—which the state began regulating in 1990. Unlike large corporations, which are better positioned to absorb regulatory expenses, many of these small businesses can ill afford the costs and have been threatened with bankruptcy. Not surprisingly, their angry owners are a growing presence in the backlash.

Many conservative members of Congress are angry too and since early 1995 have made strenuous attempts to dismantle environmental regulations. They denounce what they consider wrongheaded laws that specify not only results but also methods for meeting standards. In some cases, their point is well taken. For instance, the 1977 amendments to the Clean Air Act required power plants to meet standards for sulfur dioxide emissions by technological means (that is, by installing scrubbers) rather than by switching to low-sulfur coal. To save a few thousand jobs for eastern coal miners, power companies had to spend roughly ten times the miners' collective incomes to install and operate scrubbers. Another cost-saving opportunity was lost when Congress refused to allow pollution trade-offs for carbon monoxide and nitrogen oxides between vehicles and stationary sources. During the 1980s, an estimated $2.4 billion per year could have been saved by imposing stiffer controls on stationary sources rather than on vehicles.[11]

Recent Congresses have adopted more cost-effective approaches to controlling air pollution. The 1990 Clean Air amendments initiated various forms of emissions trading, and others have been proposed by the Clinton administration. The 1990 law established a market for tradeable emissions allowances among power plants that will save the utility industry about $1 billion per year while reducing overall sulfur dioxide emissions by more than half by 2000.[12] The strength of the new law lies in its flexibility. Companies are given financial incentives to invest in whatever clean technologies are most cost-effective for themselves, whether that means switching to cleaner fuels, conserving energy, or buying emissions permits from other, more efficient companies. Meanwhile, total allowable emissions will be gradually cut throughout the 1990s, giving companies time to adjust cost-effectively. Shifting away from traditional command-and-control regulation creates a win-win situation: more efficient pollution control and less opposition from polluting industries.[13]

Water Quality

Abatement of water pollution in the United States, like that of air pollution, has been largely a success story. It also is one of the longest running, with legislative origins that go back to the turn of the past century. Until the 1970s, most legislation addressed public health issues and included provisions for helping communities build water and sewage treatment plants.[14] With passage of the Water Pollution Control Act in 1972 (later called the Clean Water Act), the federal government turned its attention to cleaning up the nation's waterways, which had become badly polluted from industrial effluents and inadequately treated sewage.

Although the Clean Water Act was vetoed by Republican president Richard Nixon, members of both parties overwhemingly voted to override his veto, stirred by eloquent pleas from various members of Congress, including Senator Edmund Muskie of Maine:

> Can we afford clean water? Can we afford rivers and lakes and streams which continue to make life possible on this planet? Can we afford life itself? Those questions were never asked as we

destroyed the waters of our Nation, and they deserve no answers as we finally move to restore and renew them. These questions answer themselves.[15]

The 1972 Clean Water Act gave the government power to set and enforce national standards and to regulate effluents of organic materials, suspended solids, bacteria, and some toxic substances.[16] By the 1990s, most "point sources"—that is, readily identifiable, single-outlet sources such as sewage outlets and industrial discharge pipes—had been brought under control. Regulations and treatment of surface waters have considerably reduced eutrophication, a process in which a water body first becomes overenriched from sewage or fertilizer runoff, then falls victim to excessive bacterial growth and oxygen depletion. Massive fish kills linked to pesticide contamination also are largely a problem of the past.[17] Even Lake Erie, declared "dead" from pollution and eutrophication in 1969, has come back to life, although the array of fish species available to fishers is not what it once was.

Overall, the quality of water in lakes and streams in the United States has improved or at least has not significantly deteriorated. This is no small achievement given the escalating growth of pollution-generating activities. Not only has the scale of such activities increased on all fronts—mining, industry, consumer use of polluting products, and chemical-based farming—but also the variety of harmful substances that can find their way into water bodies has proliferated, including thousands of chemical compounds previously unknown to nature. Indeed, some toxic chemical compounds and heavy metals in industrial effluents were not individually regulated until 1986.[18] Moreover, serious problems remain in estuaries such as San Francisco and Chesapeake Bays and Boston Harbor and in the Great Lakes. These water bodies have for decades been receiving accumulations of pollutants such as organic compounds that cause eutrophication, heavy metals, and long-lived toxic chemicals that are difficult to clean up. The latter substances often concentrate in food chains and have disruptive effects on aquatic ecosystems, including commercially valuable fish and shellfish populations, thus posing potential threats to human health.[19]

In the past quarter-century, by using increasingly sophisticated and stringent controls, Americans have managed in most cases to stay ahead of their capacity to generate pollution—but only just. Even as pollution from point sources has fallen, non-point sources (mainly runoff from farms, lawns, and city storm drains) have emerged as the dominant water pollution problem. Lacking identifiable discharge sites, non-point sources are much harder than factory or sewage outlets to regulate.

At the same time, toxic substances are turning up with ever greater frequency in groundwater, the source of drinking water for one of every two Americans. Once contaminated, groundwater is extremely difficult and costly to clean up.[20] The shift to no-till cultivation in the Midwest has done much to reduce soil erosion, but the price has been a widespread influx into aquifers of herbicides (needed to suppress weeds formerly destroyed by plowing). Even more worrisome has been the contamination of groundwater in many parts of the country with radioactive and toxic substances resulting from military activities and especially the nuclear weapons–making enterprise of the cold war.[21]

Even though Americans today take safe drinking water for granted, it is essential to guard against complacency. Even in recent years, frightening outbreaks of waterborne diseases have occurred.[22] The best known was an outbreak in 1993 of waterborne cryptosporidiosis in Milwaukee. Some 400,000 people got sick, and the lives of AIDS victims and other people with impaired immune systems were seriously threatened. Among contributing factors was a new strain of *Cryptosporidium* (a pathogenic protozoon) that was resistant to the chlorination used to treat Milwaukee's water.[23]

When activists opposed to further regulation of water pollution cite figures indicating that the costs of abatement (roughly $15 to $30 billion per year in the mid-1980s)[24] exceed the benefits, their calculations generally underestimate the value of clean water to society. Who can put a price on the social value of clean water? How much would Americans be willing to pay to avoid the loss of swimmable waters, clean beaches, edible catches, and placid blue lakes, to say nothing of potable tap water? How does one quantify the link between clean water and property values or recreational pursuits such as swimming, boating, fishing, and tourism? Such questions must be part of any regulatory discussion.

Abolishing or crippling water pollution–control legislation seems more likely to anger citizens than win their approval. Nevertheless, regulations could be made less onerous and costly without significantly reducing water quality. Permitting pollution trade-offs similar to those for air pollutants is one possibility.[25] Another approach, utilized in Germany, is to charge companies for their discharges, which provides a strong incentive to minimize them.[26]

Managing Toxic Substances

Ever since the Love Canal scandal burst upon the scene in 1978, Americans have been aware of and outraged about toxic waste dumps and other sources of exposure to hazardous substances.[27] Love Canal was a national wake-up call; it soon proved to be just the tip of a very large iceberg. By the late 1980s, some 30,000 old and abandoned toxic waste sites in the United States had been listed by the Environmental Protection Agency (EPA) as needing to be cleaned up; other agencies estimated that as many as a half-million might exist. Thousands more sites were later found at various federal facilities, including military sites.[28] By 1995, the 1300 most dangerous sites had been assigned to the National Priorities List and were undergoing treatment.[29]

These old sites represent a legacy of nearly two hundred years of industrial activity during which wastes of all kinds were discarded in almost any convenient place, often with no record kept of their disposal. Spills and dumpings from factories, refineries, smelters, mines, metal and chemical works, town dumps, and even gas stations were left with no attempt to remove noxious residues. The public was blissfully unaware, and no one cared unless some toxic brew exploded. As in Love Canal, new housing or other facilities such as schools sometimes were built over an old site, thus exposing families and especially children (who generally are more vulnerable) to any lingering toxicity.[30] Indeed, the great majority of waste sites are in residential areas, and nearly all are within a mile of a well providing drinking water.[31]

With passage in 1976 of the Resource Recovery and Recycling Act (RCRA; known in the trade as "Rickra") and the Toxic Substances Control Act (TSCA or TOSCA), the federal government began regulating hazardous wastes. Industrial wastes—amounting to well over 250 million metric tons generated every year in the 1980s—are now managed under license by independent companies, by the waste-producing industries, or by operators of industrial landfills.[32] TOSCA requires corporations to record their acquisition or creation, use, and disposal of potentially toxic materials.[33] This information is filed with the EPA, which can ban or limit production of any substance found to pose an unreasonable risk. Thus currently produced, used, and discarded chemical substances—more than 60,000 chemicals by 1990—are carefully tracked from "cradle to grave."

A separate set of regulations covers pesticides: the Federal Insecticide, Fungicide, and Rodenticide Act (FIFRA).[34] DDT and some other pesticides that posed threats to human health or the environment have been banned under FIFRA. Both TOSCA and FIFRA differ from other environmental laws in assigning the EPA responsibility to balance costs and benefits in its decisions.[35]

Many uncertainties surround the risks from toxic substances, and these uncertainties cannot be entirely resolved by scientific testing before introduction. Such tests are required for new drugs, food additives, and pesticides but not for new chemicals entering the market under TOSCA, unless the EPA challenges their introduction. The toxic effects of many substances (cancers, developmental problems, or long-term environmental impacts), however, may appear only decades later. And, since the regulatory action is largely preventive, the damage a hazardous substance might cause remains unknown if it is never introduced.

The legacy of old waste sites, however, was not addressed by RCRA, TOSCA, or FIFRA. Galvanized by Love Canal and the rediscovery of thousands of other forgotten dump sites, Congress in 1980 passed the Comprehensive Environmental Response, Compensation, and Liability Act (CERCLA). Of all the laws regulating toxic substances, this one— widely, though not affectionately, known as Superfund—has aroused the most passionate opposition, serving as a lightning rod for anti-regulatory fervor. Polluters seemed to be clogging the courts, channeling money into lawyers' pockets instead of into cleanup efforts. Many citizens concluded that the law was a failure; at the least, progress seems dishearteningly slow and incredibly expensive.[36] One estimate for the final bill over a thirty-year period (within a wide range of possibilities) was $750 billion.[37] And, of course, the public's irritation has been both promoted and exploited to considerable effect by the brownlash (see chapter 9).

The purpose of Superfund was to make the original polluters pay for cleaning up their old toxic waste dumps. Unfortunately, many of the original polluters are no longer in business or cannot even be identified; often several parties are involved. This situation and the complexities of liability have led to a plethora of lawsuits among the guilty parties and their insurance companies.[38] The RAND Institute for Civil Justice found that 88 percent of insurance companies' Superfund-related costs in the late 1980s went to legal fees paid in largely successful efforts to avoid cleanup liability.[39]

Responding to the public's concerns, in 1986 Congress passed the Superfund Amendment and Re-authorization Act (SARA), which broadened the fund's tax base and eased the requirements of responsibility, thus (it was hoped) speeding up the process and lowering the angst. The EPA also became more flexible in negotiating with small companies or with larger firms whose involvement in the original site had been minimal. By the 1990s, many more cases were being privately settled and cleaned up without controversy.

Even without seemingly endless legal delays, the cleanup process is lengthy and expensive; assessing and ranking a site, designing remedial action, and carrying out the action can take a dozen years or more, especially when, as often happens, groundwater contamination is involved.[40] In these cases, an ounce of prevention would be worth a ton of cure. Yet by 1989, nearly all of the original 30,000 Superfund sites had been assessed and ranked, and by 1993 some 150 of the nearly 1300 sites on the National Priority List (NPL) had been fully cleaned up.[41] Critics have called this a dismal record, but they neglect to mention other accomplishments. By 1993, long-term remediation was under way at more than half of the NPL sites, and planning for 200 more had begun. And preventive and remedial actions—removing leaking drums of wastes and contaminated debris, draining polluted ponds, and so on—had taken place at some 2600 other sites.

Moreover, the perception that most of Superfund's money has gone into lawyers' pockets is not accurate. The same RAND study that revealed the insurance companies' penchant for legal battles found that only 21 percent of the Superfund expenses paid by large industrial firms went for court costs, and only 11 percent of EPA's did.[42] The great bulk of funds from both sources went into cleanups.

Also passed in 1986 was the Emergency Planning and Community Right to Know Act (also known as SARA Title III), which requires manufacturers to report the types and amounts of chemicals they release to air, water, and land each year. The information is then published by the EPA in an annual report, the Toxics Release Inventory (TRI).[43] Even though no regulation of the toxic compounds on the TRI list (more than 600 by 1996) is involved, the law had startling effects. Not only were people shocked by the huge volume of these materials being discharged into the environment, the disclosures motivated many industries to clean up their acts. No doubt, concern for corporate images was a big factor, but another seems to be a widespread belief among business-people that clean operations are better run, more efficient, and more competitive than dirty ones.[44]

The program's success is evident. Soon after TRI reports began to be required, the EPA saw a significant drop in reported emissions—all without any regulatory pressure or cumbersome rule making. Industries voluntarily made the changes for their own reasons and, evidently, considered them worth the investment.[45] Today, many corporations can boast of substantial reductions in their toxics output. For instance, the Monsanto Company's chemical division in 1995 reported a 90 percent reduction in its TRI emissions,[46] and the Procter & Gamble Company announced reductions of 75 percent in its U.S. operations.[47]

Many companies now adhere to the mantra of "reduce, reuse, and re-cycle," an integrated approach to waste management that minimizes waste at every stage of the industrial cycle rather than simply at the end of the pipe. Waste reduction strategies include materials substitution (finding less hazardous substances to use), packaging redesign (result-ing in lighter weights and less need for raw materials), recycling of by-products (materials once discarded are now reclaimed and either sold for profit or reused in the company), and improved emission controls. People involved in this new approach to industrial management refer to it as "industrial ecology" because of its similarities to the closed loop systems of natural ecosystems in which nutrients and organic matter are continuously recycled through the biosphere.[48]

Even before emissions reporting was required, some companies rec-ognized the link between economic and environmental benefits. Among the pioneers was the Minnesota Mining and Manufacturing Company (3M), which introduced its widely regarded Pollution Prevention Pays program in 1975.[49] The program led to the elimination of more than 1 billion pounds of polluting emissions for 3M factories and saved the company some $500 million.[50] Other companies have since jumped on the bandwagon, including Monsanto, E. I. du Pont de Nemours and Company,[51] the Dow Chemical Company, Xerox Corporation, and Procter & Gamble, earning greener reputations in the process.[52] Even the American Chemical Manufacturers Association, to its credit, has encouraged the trend toward cleaner industrial processes and production through its Responsible Care program.[53] Indeed, a whole new industry has arisen in response to the need for technologies to manage and detoxify toxic substances.

Thus the implementation of RCRA, TOSCA, and other toxics regulations has quietly revolutionized the way hazardous substances of all kinds are handled in the United States. Illegal midnight dumpings and other abuses that regularly made headlines in the 1970s are now essentially a thing of the past. Most major corporations have assumed much more responsible practices than those that led to the passage of RCRA and Superfund. Even so, Superfund and other toxics regulations remain exceedingly sore points for some members of the business community, inspiring many of Congress's recent efforts to extract the EPA's regulatory teeth. At least one congressman has even targeted the TRI reporting requirement for elimination as an unnecessary burden on business—a rule that costs practically nothing (except perhaps some embarrassment to businesses) and has led to substantial reductions in toxic emissions without any enforcement action at all!

Providing Perspective

The difficulty with assessing the real value of environmental regulation in the United States is that Americans haven't experienced the consequences that would have occurred without it. Some of the horrendous problems experienced in the past before environmental laws began protecting us have been forgotten or were never known by a generation of young people. Environmental protection has been swept along with myriad other factors that have made life materially better for most people today compared with several decades ago. Like credit cards, computers, jet airliners, and freeways, environmental protection is taken for granted.

Furthermore, most Americans don't realize how much of the progress made has been swallowed up by increased energy use and economic activity. For instance, without catalytic converters and increased fuel efficiency, the near doubling of miles traveled per year since 1970 would have doubled air pollution emissions from cars and trucks. This is why improvements in air and water quality seem scarcely noticeable, while the hassles and costs of compliance seem to have escalated to intolerable levels.

To see just how different American life would be without environmental laws, suppose one of the states opted out of federal regulation. For a realistic comparison, most industrial infrastructure, vehicles, homes and appliances, and water treatment facilities in the state would have to be state-of-the-art 1970. The inhabitants of the unlucky state no doubt would strenuously object to being made guinea pigs; Americans are not notably fond of smog or polluted water. Since the gains in energy efficiency since 1970 would be lost, there probably would be howls of protest over the higher prices for many goods and services, especially electricity and fuel.

But these complaints might well be drowned out by the clamor over irritating air pollution and a substantial rise in incidence of lung ailments such as asthma, bronchitis, and emphysema—to say nothing of an increase in waterborne diseases and chemical hazards in drinking water. Farmers might also notice a drop in crop yields, while forests, rivers, and lakes would show signs of declining health and productivity.[54] Rising rates of cancer and birth defects might cause alarm, although pinning down the causes would be difficult. All this would, of course, carry economic costs. Meanwhile, polluting companies would be busy trying to convince the public that their activities had nothing to do with the problems and that people were certainly better off without burdensome regulation.

Anyone who still doubted the benefits of environmental regulation might benefit from a field trip to developing regions. Huge cities such as Mexico City, São Paulo, Jakarta, Bangkok, Beijing, Delhi, and Nairobi have horrific smog despite being located in countries with far less industry than the United States. Tens of thousands to millions of cars, trucks, and buses with no smog controls cram the streets; hundreds of uncontrolled factories, smelters, and power stations belch smoke and pollutants; and in some cities millions of open cooking fires foul the air. Third world rivers are often essentially open sewers spiked with pesticide cocktails. Many areas have yet to reach state-of-the-art-1970 U.S. pollution-control standards.

Equally enlightening might be a visit to industrialized regions of eastern Europe and former Soviet Union republics. Even though fairly strong pollution-control laws have long been on the books in those nations, they have seldom if ever been enforced. Nor was any effort made toward energy efficiency. The result, given a high level of industrial activity, has been horrendous pollution and a related severe decline in the population's health.[55]

During the 1970s, mortality rates in the Soviet Union stopped falling and began rising, and the government, presumably embarrassed, stopped publishing mortality statistics. The trend worsened after the Soviet Union's breakup. Even though a faltering health care system and inadequate supplies of equipment and medicines have played a role, most medical authorities blame the public's exposure to various forms of pollution, from common air pollutants to pesticides, heavy metals, and radioactivity. By 1995, infant deaths from severe birth defects were five times as frequent in Russia as in other industrialized nations, presumably resulting from parental exposure to high levels of toxic and radioactive substances.[56]

Serious impacts have also been seen on agriculture, forests, and wildlife throughout the former Eastern Bloc. The tragedy of the Aral Sea region is relatively well known in the West, although not everyone realizes that pollution, especially by pesticides, was a major factor in the area's problems. The devastating effects of acid precipitation and industrial air pollutants on forests in Czechoslovakia, Poland, and parts of Russia are also familiar to environmentally conscious westerners, as is the aftermath of the Chernobyl disaster. But the widespread contamination of rivers and farmland, and its connection to declining health and reduced agricultural production, is not so well known. After the cold war ended, American companies sent representatives to forge partnerships and help former Soviets and eastern Europeans convert to capitalism, but the Americans often found the air, water, and soils too polluted to support the high-technology operations they were planning. Vaclav Havel, president of the Czech Republic, eloquently summarized the situation in his country: "The environmental desolation created by the Communist regimes is a warning for the whole of civilization today."[57]

America's International Role

Over the past few decades, while the United States has developed a strong domestic program of environmental protection it has also played a role as a world leader in this area. But the U.S. government's record on international environmental action has at best been uneven, mainly restricted to participation in conferences, treaties, and agreements. Active leadership has generally depended on the attitude of the administration in power. During the Reagan and Bush administrations, the U.S. government abandoned leadership on population and many environmental matters, sometimes even opposing appropriate policies.[58]

American leadership has often been accomplished by example. American environmental laws are frequently copied and set the standard worldwide; American environmental science and technologies are widely recognized as the best overall.[59] So it is not surprising that U.S. scientists, many of whom first called the world's attention to global problems such as global warming and the loss of biodiversity and their potential consequences,[60] have become prominent voices in international deliberations. Similarly, environmentalists in U.S. non-governmental organizations (generally known as NGOs) have become increasingly influential in global policy making, with the government acting as a sometimes reluctant partner.

Some transnational corporations, with their ever-expanding global presence and foresight capabilities often greater than those of governments, have considerable potential for positive influence, despite the manifold problems they pose.[61] Those corporations hold many of the keys to global environmental impacts, for good or ill, by influencing environmental thinking in countries where they do business. That potential was clearly shown in the negotiations for the Montreal Protocol to phase out production and use of chlorofluorocarbons (CFCs) and protect the stratospheric ozone shield.[62] Without the active cooperation of corporate decision makers and staff scientists, the agreement could never have been made.[63]

Over several decades, urged on by NGOs and the scientific community, governments have established landmark agreements on a variety of environmental matters from protection of whales and forests to the Law of the Sea Treaty, the Montreal Protocol, and the Biodiversity Convention. With no means to enforce international agreements, that governments have not only signed but also to a large extent honored them is remarkable to say the least. Some, of course, have been honored largely in the breach, such as the Framework Convention on Climate Change to restrain greenhouse gas emissions, signed at the International Conference on the Environment in Rio de Janeiro in 1992. But that agreement was presented as a weak first step in any case, and it's too early to judge the outcome. Given the complexity and uncertainties of global warming and the enormous economic and political interests at stake, a strong, universally acceptable agreement was unlikely to appear on the first attempt.

The United States has also served as a leader, with some success, in addressing global population growth. Population growth in the second half of the twentieth century has been the most rapid in history. Yet, thanks to worldwide efforts and rising awareness of the risks of overpopulation,[64] that growth has been significantly slowed in recent years. In the 1960s, the world population was growing by more than 2 percent per year; since then the rate has fallen below 1.6 percent.[65]

Modest though it seems, this change represents a drop in the average family size from about five children to just over three.[66] Without it, the world population would have been almost 6.2 billion in 1996, not 5.7 billion, with an increase of more than 120 million people every year instead of about 85 million. This gap will widen in years ahead; assuming birthrates keep falling, by 2030 it will be almost 4 billion—as many people as existed on Earth in 1972. Obviously, given the compound-interest effects of population growth, even small changes in birthrates can make a huge difference in the future population size—in this case, the difference between a projected population size of about 8.6 billion and 12.4 billion in 2030.

The slowing of population growth has been achieved despite falling death rates, as birthrates have declined even faster virtually everywhere, including in industrialized nations.[67] Unfortunately, some have greeted this news with alarm over imminent population declines in developed countries.[68] Meanwhile, deteriorating conditions in the former Soviet Union have produced a more genuine demographic debacle: rising death rates, precipitously falling birthrates, and shrinking populations.[69]

The population issue, more than most, has suffered from shifting government political positions and allegiances. Until Ronald Reagan beame president in 1981, the United States led the way in establishing and supporting family planning programs in developing nations, both to benefit health and well-being and to reduce the rapid population growth that was seen even then as hindering economic development.[70] President Reagan withdrew American support for family planning assistance, and his policies were continued by President George Bush.[71] Although other nations picked up some of the lost funding, financial support for family planning programs fell significantly. For that and other reasons, the decline in global population growth essentially stalled during the 1980s.[72]

President Bill Clinton quickly reversed the Reagan-Bush policy in 1993 and increased U.S. funding for family planning aid. Since about 1990, birthrates have been declining again in many regions, even in parts of sub-Saharan Africa, where no decline had previously been seen. Particularly important in reasserting American leadership was the Clinton administration's strong participation in the 1994 International Conference on Population and Development in Cairo and the 1995 World Conference on Women in Beijing, which dealt with many related issues.

Unfortunately, Clinton's population policies have clashed with the attitudes of the Republican-dominated Congress elected in 1994, which has shown little interest in global affairs or sympathy toward developing nations. Just as the success of past population policies is beginning to be felt, U.S. efforts to deal with the problem may fall victim to domestic politics.

By a curious irony, some new leaders of the nation that has led the world in identifying the costs and risks of overpopulation and environmental deterioration, and in developing policies to lower them, are now trying to deny the very existence of the problems and reverse the policies. The battles that have been won for environmental protection are substantial and important, but the war will continue to rage as long as the human enterprise keeps on expanding in all dimensions, not only in sheer numbers of people but also in per-capita consumption and the deployment of environmentally damaging technologies. The myths that environmental protection damages the economy and obstructs personal freedom are seductive but dangerous.

While no one denies that progress has been made in environmental protection, a realistic assessment of how much optimism is justified is in order. In the following chapters, we evaluate the principal fables promoted by brownlash anti-science and contrast them with the consensus views of environmental scientists on different aspects of the human predicament. In doing so, we hope to present a realistic assessment of the actual dimensions of that predicament.

CHAPTER 5

Fables about
Population and Food

E VER SINCE REVEREND THOMAS MALTHUS at the end of the eighteenth
century warned about the dangers of overpopulation, analysts
have been concerned about maintaining a balance between human
numbers and the human food supply.[1] That concern remains valid today
in a world where a tenth of the population goes to bed hungry each
night and millions die every year from hunger-related causes. Few subjects have been closer to our hearts and minds for the past three
decades than the race between population growth and increasing food
production. That race was a major focus of Paul's first popular book,
The Population Bomb, published in 1968;[2] it was also the principal focus
of our 1995 book, written with our colleague Gretchen Daily, *The Stork
and the Plow.*[3]

The world food situation has been a favorite arena for brownlash writers and spokespeople who deny, often vehemently, that a growing
population might someday run into absolute food shortages. The
essence of their argument takes two forms: population growth is not a
problem and (for some of them) is even virtually an unmitigated bless-
ing; and food production can be increased more or less forever without
constraint. Some of the more extreme holders of the latter view still oc-

casionally quote an old and long-discredited estimate publicized by Catholic bishops several years ago that theoretically 40 billion people could be fed on Earth.[4] Needless to say, these groups aren't fond of our positions on these matters, and the brownlash attacks our analyses regularly.

Let's take a look at some of the brownlash claims about population and food. Here and throughout the rest of this book, we summarize or directly quote brownlash statements in boldface, then present what we believe to be the consensus or majority view of environmental scientists. We begin with one of the most extreme brownlash claims.

☐ **"We now have in our hands—in our libraries, really—the technology to feed, clothe, and supply energy to an ever-growing population for the next 7 billion years." (Julian Simon, 1994)[5]**

Does Julian Simon really mean to suggest the world's population can continue to grow for billions of years at the rate it was growing when he wrote that statement? The world population was growing in 1994 at the rate of about 1.6 percent per year, which corresponds to a doubling time of about 43 years.[6] A bit of arithmetic reveals that such a population growth rate could not persist even for hundreds of years, let alone millions of years.[7] To suggest that an "ever-growing" population can persist for billions of years is, of course, ridiculous.

Consider how long it would take for the 1994 world population of 5.6 billion to increase to a size where there were *ten human beings for each square meter* of ice-free land on the planet. At the 1994 growth rate, it would take only 18 doublings to bring the population to that point, and the population was then doubling every 43 years. Thus the required doublings would take only 18 × 43 = 774 years—somewhat short of 7 billion. After 1900 years at this growth rate, the mass of the human population would be equal to the mass of the Earth; after 6000 years, the mass of the human population would equal the mass of the universe.[8]

Of course, Professor Simon may have had a somewhat lower population growth rate in mind than that of 1994, the year he made his remarkable statement. But if the growth rate were *one million times* smaller than the actual 1994 value—that is, if it were only an infinitesimal 0.0000016 percent per year—Earth's population would still reach a mass exceeding that of the universe before the end of the 7-billion-year period Simon mentioned.[9] Such is the power of exponential growth. Simon's statement is nonsense, pure and simple. But it is only an extreme version of claims of other technological optimists who, living on a planet rife with human hunger, glibly assert that many multiples of the present population can be fed.

☐ **There is no overpopulation today.**

This is a popular theme with many brownlash writers.[10] To understand how fallacious this statement is requires recognizing that overpopulation can be reached very quickly by exponentially growing populations in situations of seeming abundance. There is overpopulation when organisms (people in this case) become so numerous that they degrade the ability of the environment to support their kind of animal in the future. The number of people Earth can support *in the long term* (without degrading the environment)—given existing socioeconomic systems, consumption patterns, and technological capabilities—is called the *human carrying capacity* of the planet at that time.[11] And carrying capacity can be exceeded without causing immediate effects obvious to the untutored observer. "Overshoots" commonly occur in nature with all kinds of organisms. A population has an "outbreak," grows far beyond its carrying capacity, consumes its resources (for animals, usually food), and "crashes" to a size far below the previous carrying capacity.

The surprise element in overshoots and the finite nature of all habitats (including Mother Earth) to support organisms is recognized in the saying, "A long history of exponential growth does not imply a long future of such growth." This can be illustrated simply. Suppose you have an aquarium that has a carrying capacity of 1000 guppies—more than that will start to exhaust the oxgen supply. Suppose the tank is stocked with a pair of adult guppies, and that their numbers grow exponentially with a doubling time of one month. After eight doublings, taking eight months, the guppies reach half the tank's carrying capacity: $2 \rightarrow 4 \rightarrow 8 \rightarrow 16 \rightarrow 32 \rightarrow 64 \rightarrow 128 \rightarrow 256 \rightarrow 512$ guppies. For this whole period, the population is safely far below the tank's carrying capacity. Then, in the ninth month, a further doubling to 1024 suddenly results in an overshoot of carrying capacity—with the last 100 guppies added in less than five days. After 35 weeks of apparent prosperity, overshoot occurs within a week. At first, there are no obvious symptoms, but gradually more and more of the fishes are gasping at the surface, and then they begin to die.[12]

Overshoots can occur in human populations, too.[13] Humanity has already overshot Earth's carrying capacity by a simple measure: no nation is supporting its present population on *income*—that is, the sustainable flow of renewable resources. Instead, key "renewable" resources, the natural *capital* of humanity, are being used so rapidly that they have become effectively non-renewable.[14] *Homo sapiens* is collectively acting like a person who happily writes ever larger checks without considering what's happening to the balance of the account.[15]

Warning signs that the human enterprise is nearing the end of exponential growth include declines in the amount or availability of good farmland,[16] soil,[17] fresh water,[18] and biodiversity,[19] all of which are crucial elements of natural capital essential for sustaining humanity and especially for sustaining agricultural production.[20] A more fundamental but indirect indicator of how close humanity is to its limits is that it is already consuming, co-opting, or destroying some 40 percent of the terrestrial food supply of all animals (not just human beings).[21]

Deep, rich agricultural soils are being eroded away in many areas at rates of inches per decade; soils are normally formed at rates of inches per millennium.[22] Accumulations of "fossil" fresh water, stored underground over thousands of years during glacial periods, are being mined as if they were metals—and often for low-value uses such as irrigating forage crops. Water from aquifers that are recharged at rates measured in inches per year is being pumped out at rates measured in feet per year—and the freshwater-holding capacity of the aquifers is being compromised in the process. Becoming dependent on such largely irreplaceable sources of water—especially for non-essential purposes such as irrigating feed crops in arid regions—is both shortsighted and risky.[23]

The worst form of capital depletion is biological. Microorganisms, plants, and other animals are being exterminated at a rate unprecedented in 65 million years—on the order of 10,000 times faster than the stock can be replaced.[24] These are the working parts of our global life-support system; if we destroy them, the price will be a catastrophic decline in carrying capacity. Natural ecosystems and the species they contain maintain biodiversity and the production of ecosystem goods[25] such as forest products and food from the sea, the harvesting and trading of which are familiar and important parts of the human economy.

Ecosystems also provide essential life-support functions of cleansing, recycling, and renewal, upon which the economy is utterly dependent. From the perspective of agriculture alone, these ecosystem services are vitally important. Among them are amelioration of climate and weather; generation and maintenance of soils and soil fertility; recycling of nutrients; running of the hydrological cycle, which supplies rainfall and irrigation water; control of more than 95 percent of the potential pests of crops; and maintenance of a vast natural library of biodiversity. That library is the source of the innumerable potential and actual ecosystem goods such as medicines and genetic material essential for development of crop varieties resistant to pests and diseases and able to cope with changing conditions, such as adverse weather or increasing soil salinity.

The depletion of environmental capital by people or other animals is a sure sign of overpopulation. But the carrying capacity of an environment is not fixed. Through evolution, organisms can become more efficient in the ways they exploit their environments and thus expand their carrying capacity. In non-human animals, this evolution is mostly genetic and requires numerous generations. Since the animals' environment is also perpetually changing (for example, plants being devoured by a herbivore are coevolving with the herbivore in response to its attacks),[26] it is usually impossible to track changes in carrying capacity.

But human beings are specialists in cultural evolution, which can proceed much more rapidly than can genetic evolution. Through ingenuity and invention, it is possible to enlarge human carrying capacity—as indeed has happened in the past. Today, widespread behavioral changes—such as becoming vegetarian—potentially could increase Earth's carrying capacity for human beings in a short time as well. Assuming full cooperation in the needed changes, it might be possible to support 6 billion people indefinitely (that is, to end human overpopulation, if there were no further population growth). But we doubt that most people in today's rich nations would willingly embrace the changes in lifestyle necessary to increase global carrying capacity. How many Americans would be willing to adjust their lifestyles radically to live, say, like the Chinese, so that more Dutch or Australians or Mexicans could be supported? How many Chinese would give up their dreams of American-style affluence for the same reason? Such lifestyle changes certainly seem unlikely to us, since most current trends among those who can afford it are toward more affluence and consumption, which tend to *decrease* carrying capacity and intensify the degree of overpopulation.

Consider the rise in consumption of animal products that almost always accompanies rising affluence. That behavioral change, now seen around the world, is contributing to the human overshoot. The feeding base for humanity is the 1.8 billion metric tons of cereal grains produced each year by the world's farmers, which amounts to roughly half of all the food produced. Of the grain harvest, about one-third is fed to livestock to produce meat and dairy foods. Unfortunately, anywhere from 60 to 90 percent of the calories fed to animals are lost in the process of supplying the animals' needs first before passing on the energy to people. At least three times as many people could be sustained by directly eating the grain as by eating products from grain-fed animals.[27]

Unfortunately, when nations industrialize and attain higher incomes, a strong trend usually develops toward consumption of more animal products. This trend is spectacularly under way in China today, where the rapid switch of a billion-plus people from almost entirely vegetarian diets to diets based more on meat could have profound repercussions on the world food supply.[28] Although China has been essentially self-sufficient in food production for decades, the country's increasing consumption of animal foods may mean that massive amounts of grain will need to be imported for livestock feed. This would intensify the pressures on the world's agricultural resources, thereby further increasing global overpopulation.

> One needn't worry about population growth in the United States, because it's still nowhere near as densely populated as the Netherlands. (Malcolm Forbes, 1989)[29]

The idea that the number of people per square mile is a key determinant of population pressure is as widespread and persistent as it is wrong—Paul and physicist John Holdren (now at the Kennedy School of Government at Harvard) long ago named it the "Netherlands fallacy."[30] Nicholas Eberstadt, in his contribution to the Competitive Enterprise Institute's book *The True State of the Planet,* wrote: "What are the criteria by which to judge a country 'overpopulated'? Population density is one possibility that comes to mind." He then proceeded to extend the Netherlands fallacy to Bermuda and Monaco.[31]

The fascination with how many people can be crowded into how much land is common to many brownlash writings. In *Eco-Scam,* Ronald Bailey repeats the tired Netherlands fallacy and quotes Eberstadt to the effect that "There is absolutely no content to the notion of over-population."[32] In *Apocalypse Not,* Ben Bolch and Harold Lyons point out correctly that if the 1990 world population were placed in Texas, less than half of 1 percent of Earth's land surface, "each person would have an area equal to the floor space of a typical U.S. home."[33] They also say: "Anyone who has looked out an airplane window while traveling across the country knows how empty the United States really is."[34]

Our response is perfectly straightforward. First, the key issue in judg-ing overpopulation is not how many people can fit in any given space but whether the population's requirements for food, water, other re-sources, and ecosystem services can be met on a sustainable basis. Most of the "empty" land in the United States either grows the food essential to the well-being of Americans and much of the world (as in Iowa) or supplies us with forestry products (northern Maine), or, lacking water, good soil, and a suitable climate (as in much of Nevada), it is land that cannot directly contribute much to the support of civilization.

The key point here is that the Netherlands, Bermuda, and Monaco (and Singapore, Hong Kong, São Paulo, Mexico City, Tokyo, London, and New York) *can be crowded with people only because the rest of the world is not.* The Netherlands, for example, imports large amounts of food[35] and extracts from other parts of the world much of the energy and virtually all the materials it requires. It uses an estimated seventeen times more land for food and energy than exists within its borders.[36]

□ "Predictions of a 'population explosion' . . . were wrong because they were based on projections of past trends." (Joseph Bast, Peter Hill, and Richard Rue, 1994)[37] "Nor does [Ehrlich] acknowledge that predicted population growth has not exploded, as he had predicted [sic]." (Dixy Lee Ray and Lou Guzzo, 1993)[38]

When Paul wrote *The Population Bomb* in 1968, there were 3.5 billion people on Earth. Two years later we published a book in which we cited a *projection* of the United Nations, which "predicted" there would be 5.65 billion people in 1995.[39] In 1995 the actual population size turned out to be 5.70 billion, just a little higher than our "prediction." Although our critics continually claim otherwise, we have never "pre-dicted" a future population size or rate of growth but instead have depended entirely on (and have always cited) the work of professional demographers, primarily those at the United Nations and the Population Reference Bureau.

We're perpetually (and correctly) cited as population alarmists, and while we deserve partial credit for sounding the alarm, we can't take credit for the accuracy of the projections we cite. Those projections are made by demographers, who build on history and existing population structures and say what will happen if certain trends continue. The projections are based on reasonable assumptions about birth, death, and migration rates but over time those assumptions may well be violated, moving a population's trajectory away from the projection. Yet given all the variables, the demographers do remarkably well. For example, in 1977, we and John Holdren reprinted demographer Tomas Frejka's high and low projections for 2000—6.67 and 5.92 billion, respectively.[40] At the moment, Frejka's projections, made in 1974, seem pretty close to the mark: the world's population in 2000 seems likely to fall somewhere between 6.1 and 6.2 billion.

Whether our "predictions" of a population explosion were wrong is not a matter of projection but a matter of history. In the nearly thirty years since the *Bomb* was written, some 2.3 billion people have been added to Earth's population—more than existed when we were born. That's equivalent to the *addition* each year of roughly the present population of Germany. We've already seen more than a doubling of America's population in our lifetime, and the most recent U.S. population projections indicate continued growth well beyond 2050.[41] If we are lucky enough to live to the turn of the century, we'll have seen a *tripling* of the number of human beings with which we share Earth. If that isn't a population explosion, we don't know what is!

☐ **Enviros hate people.**[42]

In *A Moment on the Earth*, Gregg Easterbrook correctly quotes something we have been saying in speeches for decades—that no one has ever suggested a sane reason for having more than 135 million Americans. We chose that number because one can make the argument (although it's not a very good one) that a population of that size was necessary to put together a military force large enough to win World War II.[43] That was the largest land war ever likely to be fought, one requiring a lot of "cannon fodder." But Easterbrook came up with a counter-argument: a sane reason for wanting more than 135 million Americans is that "people like to be alive."[44]

One can imagine some ripostes to this statement, such as "Do people hate not being born?" or "Would people like to be alive if they had to live like chickens in factory farms?" But ripostes are unnecessary. As we often point out, the best way to maximize the number of Americans (or Chinese, or Nigerians) who live isn't accomplished by cramming into the United States (or China, or Nigeria) as many people as possible in the next few decades until those nations self-destruct. Rather, the way to maximize the number of lives lived is to have permanently sustainable populations in those nations (and on this planet) for tens of thousands, perhaps millions, of years.[45]

As for hating people, virtually everyone we know who is concerned about the population problem is gregarious and likes people—likes them enough to think beyond their brute numbers at any given time and care deeply about the conditions in which they live. Interestingly, many individuals who claim to love people and want the population to keep growing shield themselves from the growing numbers in their own vicinity. For instance, the Vatican relentlessly pushes for unlimited immigration into the United States and other countries while also opposing most forms of birth control. Yet the Vatican City doesn't admit immigrants or refugees, even though it has one-fourth the population density of New York City.[46]

Like the Vatican, many brownlash writers who express a supposed devotion to people are carrying on an old tradition of the upper classes and the Vatican (*not* of Catholics in general): promoting reproduction among the poor. They do this by downplaying the seriousness of the population problem and opposing programs to give people control over their reproductive activities.[47] Not surprisingly, their views are often supported by agribusiness and big corporations, which naturally are still interested in abundant cheap labor, as evidenced by their lobbying efforts against immigration reform.[48] Overall, it seems to us that "enviros" care a lot more about people than do the promoters of the brownlash.

> **Modern medicine has eliminated one big threat connected with overpopulation: the rampant spread of infectious diseases.**

Brownlash writers generally overlook the deterioration of the epidemiological environment, which is quite directly related to population size as well as to poverty and environmental deterioration.[49] In *A Moment on the Earth,* Gregg Easterbrook does not discuss what the epidemiological risk means for people—especially poor people—even though the hazards are widely discussed in the literature he attacks.[50] Indeed, in an earlier piece criticizing us,[51] he ridiculed (and quoted out of context) Paul's 1968 statement in *The Population Bomb* that it was "not inconceivable" that a novel viral disease could kill 500 million people.[52]

Yet scientists who grapple with outbreaks of infectious disease care deeply. It is instructive to note that the World Health Organization estimates that as many as 40 million people could be infected with HIV (the virus that causes AIDS) by the year 2000;[53] virtually all infected people can be expected to die of the disease unless some other cause of death intervenes or a miracle cure is found in time. Consider the words spoken in 1989 by Joshua Lederberg, microbiologist at Rockefeller University and recipient of a Nobel Prize for his work on the sharing of genetic material by bacteria: "Nature is not benign. . . . The survival of the human species is *not* a preordained evolutionary program. Abundant sources of genetic variation exist for viruses to learn new tricks, not necessarily confined to what happens routinely or even frequently."[54]

For a number of population-related reasons, human beings are more vulnerable than ever to epidemics. For one thing, the increase in human numbers alone makes us more susceptible.[55] Some infectious agents can persist only in populations above a certain size (the measles virus, for example, requires 50,000 or more). Thus an ever-increasing population opens the door to a new range of pathogens. Many human groups are coming into more frequent contact with wild animal populations, and other animals are the source of most epidemic diseases. Recently, exposure to infected wild animals has led to transfers of viruses such as those that cause AIDS and various hemorrhagic fevers (among them the Marburg, Ebola, Hanta, and Machupo viruses). Increased contact by larger groups of people, frequently associated with the clearing of forests, raises the chances both of a transfer from a wild animal into the human population and of the new disease causing an epidemic. Larger human populations also lead to urbanization, so infected and susceptible people are jammed together in cities, where sexual promiscuity and drug use are often rampant. Cities have rightly been called "ecosystem[s] that can amplify infectious diseases"[56] or, more bluntly, "graveyards of mankind."[57]

To make matters worse, international air travel creates a mechanism for the rapid spread around the globe of infectious agents (bacteria, viruses, fungi, etc.), including drug-resistant strains of bacteria, vectors (organisms such as mosquitoes that move infectious agents from one individual to another), and animal reservoirs (animals that play host to diseases that also infect human beings). Furthermore, human-induced global climate change threatens to increase the range of the tropical vectors of serious diseases such as malaria and dengue fever.[58] And finally, but far from exhaustively,[59] a combination of widespread malnutrition, exposure to immune-suppressing chemical pollutants, and HIV infection has produced a human population with a very large subpopulation of immune-compromised individuals; as easy targets for pathogens, they increase humanity's vulnerability to epidemics. In rich nations such as the United States, infectious diseases are mostly relatively minor causes of death, but there is no guarantee that situation will continue.

☐ **Those who are concerned about world hunger are simply wrong.[60]**

The Population Bomb starts with these words: "The battle to feed all of humanity is over. In the 1970s the world will undergo famines—hundreds of millions of people are going to starve to death in spite of any crash programs embarked upon now."[61] In fact, some 250 million people, about as many as now live in the United States, have perished for lack of food since those words were written. Roughly 100 to 140 million of them died in the 1970s. But because the famines of the 1970s were less catastrophic than we predicted, we've probably been criticized more for the "battle is over" statement than any other. Our response is that partly because of *The Population Bomb* and similar warnings by food specialists,[62] global programs to improve food distribution were initiated and emergency systems set up to feed famine victims. Those programs were largely successful in heading off the massive famines we had thought would occur during that decade.[63]

Typical of the criticism directed toward us is an assertion in a brownlash book issued by the Heartland Institute, which claims that "None of [the Ehrlichs'] predictions has come true, or is ever likely to come true."[64] Lawyer Michael Fumento, author of *Science Under Siege,* also quotes our prediction of famine in his book, adding that it was "off by hundreds of millions."[65] But there were substantial food shortages and some acute famines in sub-Saharan Africa in the early 1970s,[66] which recurred throughout the 1980s. Even in the 1990s, the Refugee Policy Group estimated that roughly 150,000 to 200,000 people have starved in acute famines each year.[67] This estimate may be too high, but even if it is double the actual figure, it represents a tragic failure for our civilization.

The principal problem, of course, is not acute famines; it is chronic undernutrition of huge numbers of extremely poor people. Overall, since *The Population Bomb* was published, roughly 8 to 10 million people (mostly young children) have died each year from hunger and hunger-related diseases, according to studies by the World Bank and other international agencies.[68] And such numbers may well be underestimates. First of all, governments don't like to admit they can't feed their people; and second, starvation compromises the immune system, so often the proximate cause of death—the final blow—is not starvation per se but disease.[69]

Today some 700 to 800 million people, perhaps even as many as a billion, don't get enough food to support normal daily activities.[70] Even if the actual number of hungry people were only half as high, it would still indicate a level of human suffering that doesn't match the rosy views of the brownlash. The vast extent of chronic hunger, mainly in developing countries, reflects extreme poverty; hundreds of millions of poor people, largely in rural areas, simply cannot afford to buy sufficient food and lack the means to grow enough for themselves.

Acute famines are a different matter. Although crop failures and production shortfalls continue to occur frequently, modern communications and distribution mechanisms have enabled national and international agencies to prevent large-scale famines by rushing emergency food supplies to the hungry from areas of surplus production. Only when such assistance has been blocked by local wars or politics, as in the Sudan, or, earlier, in Ethiopia, have acute famines resulted. Of course, the severity of the famines and the consequences suffered by the people in these situations are intensified when they occur, as is usually the case, in societies that are already chronically underfed.

In short, we believe the statement that the battle to feed all of humanity is over was correct; we still think it unlikely that large-scale hunger will be banished. Should all human beings become well fed in the future, we shall be delighted to be proven wrong.

□ Feeding the world's population is a problem of distribution, not supply.[71] "Famine is a thing of the past for most of the world's people." (Dennis Avery, 1995)[72]

These are two of the most common assertions about food supplies made by the brownlash. There is some truth to the first statement. If there were no maldistribution, if everyone shared equally, and if no grain were fed to animals, all of humanity could be adequately nourished today.[73] Unfortunately, such claims are irrelevant. Although people in developed countries could eat lower on the food chain, it is as unrealistic to think we will all suddenly become vegetarian saints as it is to think we will suddenly trade in our cars for bicycles or go to bed at sunset to save energy.

Overpopulation and carrying capacity are calculated on the basis of animals—and people—as they are, not as we might wish them to be. Human carrying capacity is the *long-term* ability of an area to support human beings. When people are living on natural capital rather than what might be called "natural interest"—sustainable resource flows based on natural capital—then, by definition, carrying capacity is exceeded and the area is overpopulated. The circumstance of overpopulation sometimes can be remedied by changing patterns of behavior without changing the numbers of people—for instance, by adopting vegetarian diets or better soil husbandry practices. Overpopulation exists whenever people trying to produce food allow soil to erode faster than new soil can be generated, or drain aquifers faster than they can be recharged, or exterminate populations and species that are working parts of the ecosystems that support agriculture and fisheries faster than recolonization and speciation can reestablish them. Today overpopulation prevails worldwide.

But suppose everyone *were* willing to eat a largely vegetarian diet today, with only a small supplement from fish and range-fed animals. Suppose, in addition, that people were also willing to share food absolutely equitably, varying only according to the caloric and other nutritional needs of individuals of different ages, sizes, and levels of activity. Today's harvests could feed about 7 billion such vegetarians (assuming that crops to feed humans were planted in place of those now grown to feed livestock).[74] Since our population size is nearly 6 billion already, that is hardly a comforting number.

For comparison, assume that everyone in the world switched to the equivalent of an average Latin American diet, in which some 15 percent of calories are of animal origin (as opposed to 30 percent or more in rich countries). Under such a scenario, only about 4 billion would have enough food; almost 2 billion people—a third of today's population—would get no food at all. In contrast, if everyone were to eat something resembling a North American or northern European diet, only half of today's population could be fed. The other half would just be out of luck.

But humanity shows precious little sign of turning into a species of vegetarians. Indeed, if recent world trends are any indicator, equal sharing is likely to become less, not more, common.[75] So is it sensible to describe today's situation as "just" being caused by maldistribution? We don't think so. Wouldn't it be more sensible to work toward a world in which *everyone* could have a healthy, satisfying diet, regardless of food preferences? Those who say we shouldn't worry about the food situation because it's just a matter of sharing are being wildly overoptimistic about human social behavior.

The statement that famines are history was made by Dennis Avery of the Hudson Institute, a prominent technological optimist about agricultural prospects. We agree with him that most people may be safe from famine at the moment because improved distribution and emergency food programs can head off famine when local food shortages occur. But that says nothing about the future. So Avery's statement cannot be said with assurance to be either true or false. We think his confidence is unwarranted, considering that food production is being undermined by the depletion of natural capital—that is, by erosion and paving of farmland, draining of aquifers, loss of biodiversity, and destruction of marine fisheries. Per-capita yields from the sea are already dropping precipitously, and the prospects of turning that trend around are not encouraging.[76] Can the harvests from land be far behind? We still fear that the apprehensions of environmental scientists will be justified and that Avery's assurance is misplaced, for reasons that will become obvious in what follows.

□ **Even though millions of people are still inadequately nourished, advances in agriculture will eliminate the remaining pockets of hunger early in the next century.[77]**

The argument that technology will save us is a frequent theme of the brownlash, here applied to agriculture. The claim is rooted in past technological successes but is usually made without considering the totally unprecedented nature of today's situation. Technological optimism is nowhere more rampant than in connection with increasing food production.

In addition, agricultural optimists often exaggerate past successes by choosing a time scale for comparison that is congenial to the notion that hunger can be easily eliminated.[78] Thus they compare total food production in 1950 directly with that of the present, calling attention to the great increase in output over the intervening period. This is proof, they suggest, that hunger will be easily eliminated. But simply considering the increase over the entire period obscures the much less favorable trend that started about a decade ago, as we discuss later in this chapter.[79]

The optimists also ignore or understate the depletion of natural capital, biophysical limits beyond which yields simply cannot be increased, and other factors that make a repetition of the 1950–1985 food production surge very unlikely. They do not point out, moreover, that the institutions and infrastructure needed to translate technological developments into greater agricultural productivity are largely absent in food-short (i.e., less developed) regions and that financial support for those institutions has diminished in recent years. Furthermore, they either neglect to mention or dismiss the potential impacts of global change on food production. And, finally, they seem unaware of the principle advanced by the eminent demographer Nathan Keyfitz that "bad policies are widespread and persistent."[80]

Knowledgeable scientists are greatly concerned that these constraints on food production may soon result in serious food shortages. As Mahabub Hossain, head of the Social Sciences Division of the International Rice Research Institute (the organization that created the green revolution in rice, the grain that sustains more people than any other), stated in 1994:

> The race to avoid a collision between population growth and rice production in Asia goes on, amid worrying signs that gains of the recent past may be lost over the next few decades. . . . If [current] trends continue, demand for rice in many parts of Asia will outstrip supply within a few years.[81]

Since Hossain's comment appeared in the *International Herald Tribune,* the development of a new, higher-yielding variety of rice was announced, which is expected to increase rice production roughly 10 percent after full field testing and deployment.[82] This was good news following a period when agronomists feared they had encountered a "yield cap" on rice—that is, a biophysical limit beyond which increased seed production by a rice plant would be impossible. But this latest breakthrough is no guarantee that others will follow; on the contrary, there's every reason to think the limits aren't far off. Moreover, a 10 percent increase in rice production may sound impressive, but set against growing human numbers in Asia (where 90 percent of the world's rice is consumed), that increase would be barely sufficient to support five years of population growth.

We suspect agricultural optimism can be traced mostly to a great faith in the potential of science to pull technological rabbits out of a hat. An example of that optimistic attitude appeared recently in one of the world's best business journals, *The Economist.*[83] The article discussed the probable impact in China of both population growth and increasing per-capita demand for grain (accompanied by losses of farmland). After describing a pessimistic assessment by agricultural policy analyst Lester R. Brown, president of the Worldwatch Institute, and several Chinese scholars, the last paragraph exemplified this blind faith in technology: "Optimists counter the gloomy Malthusians by pointing to as yet unimagined scientific breakthroughs that will boost crop yields around the world. Economists add the simple point that China could then easily export other goods to pay for its imported grain."

The first statement, converted to a sports analogy, is like claiming that "unimagined breakthroughs in training will allow a runner to run a two-minute mile." The second sentence simply ignores the economics of supply and demand. If China's demand skyrockets, grain prices will be driven up, and global access of people to food will quite likely *decrease.* The agricultural scientists we know don't look to "unimagined breakthroughs" to solve their problems; that would hardly be a prudent strategy. Rather, they are deeply concerned about keeping humanity nourished. As for China's grain imports, what other countries produce enough surplus grain to fill the gap for over a billion consumers? China's need for imported grain by 2025 could exceed all the grain traded today on the world market.[84]

Analyses of food production trends over the past few decades suggest that there is indeed cause to worry about maintaining food supplies. It is certainly true that the most important indicator of human nutrition, world grain production, has roughly tripled since 1950. What the food optimists overlook is that the rate of increase has markedly slowed since the 1950s and 1960s. More sobering is that since 1985, grain production increases have failed to keep up with population growth, even though population growth itself has slackened; and since 1990 there has been no increase in absolute terms, causing severe shrinkage in grain reserves by 1996.

There are many reasons for this change. It's true, as Avery points out,[85] that some of the slowdown can be attributed to changes in agricultural policies and land use in rich countries—enacted in part to reduce surpluses. But far more relevant to future food production are tightening constraints such as degradation and losses of land, limited water supplies, and biophysical barriers to increased yields, all of which are increasingly evident.

The agricultural achievements of the past half-century did not come easily; they took a great deal of effort, cooperation, and investment. Even before the great post–World War II surge in agricultural productivity, the tools needed to do the job were in hand: fertilizer-sensitive crops, synthetic fertilizers, and irrigation technologies. Effecting such far-reaching changes required decades of lead time, and the result is now clear, in terms of both impressive success and growing constraints.

The green revolution has already been put in place in most suitable areas of the world, and most of the expected yield gains have been achieved. Farmers now are seeing diminishing returns from fertilizer applications on some major crops over much of the world,[86] and the biological potential for genetically increased yields in some crops may now be approaching the maximum.[87] Even if some unanticipated breakthrough were to be made, it would take many years, if not decades, to develop and deploy new crop varieties—years during which demand would continue rising as the population expands.

A global study by the United Nations Environment Programme found that significant degradation, ranging from slight to severe, has occurred on vegetated land on every continent just since 1945.[88] This deterioration is the result of human activities—chiefly overcultivation, overgrazing, and deforestation. Soils in many areas have deteriorated beyond the ability of fertilizers to mask the impacts of soil erosion. A subsequent study estimated that the capacity of all the world's productive land to supply food and other direct benefits has declined by about 10 percent.[89] And the degradation continues.

Land is not only being rapidly degraded; it is also increasingly being diverted to uses other than food production. Most commonly, land is taken over simply for living space.[90] As the population expands, more people need room for housing, stores, offices, industry, roads, and other infrastructure. Millions of acres of prime farmland are being lost to urbanization each year.[91]

Impending severe water shortages also threaten world food production.[92] Providing a dependable and abundant supply of water is essential for achieving the high yields of modern grain varieties; indeed, the great increase in grain production of past decades can be ascribed largely to the more than doubling of the amount of irrigated land since 1950. But today, most of the readily available sources of irrigation water have already been tapped, and the trend is beginning to reverse. More and more land is being taken out of production because of the rising costs of pumping water from depleted aquifers or because of the classic problems of irrigation: salting up or waterlogging of soils. In addition, urban demands for water often outbid farmers in water-short areas. By 1980, irrigated acreage was no longer expanding faster than the population,[93] and the day when it ceases to increase at all may not be far off.

More ominous, perhaps, is the possible impact of global climate change on agricultural ecosystems.[94] Rapid climate change could deliver the coup de grace to humanity's chances of even restricting hunger to the present levels. Frightening indeed is the possibility that long-standing climatic patterns could be disrupted by more frequent or severe floods or droughts, farming areas could experience too much or too little rainfall or temperatures higher or lower than those at which crops currently planted thrive, and so on. Such changes could be exceedingly disruptive to farming. They would necessitate adjusting to a new regime, during which time food production would likely drop. And since the climate is unlikely simply to shift to a new, stable regime overnight, farmers may suffer a protracted period of grappling with the vicissitudes of an unpredictable climate.

Climatologists on the International Panel on Climate Change think that climate-related agricultural problems will be most severe in low-latitude developing nations, where agriculture is less adaptable than it is in richer countries like the United States.[95] We suspect the reverse is true, for several reasons. First, modern intensive agriculture as practiced in rich countries centers on monocultures—large-scale plantings of a single genetic strain of a crop, usually a high-yielding variety. These strains are often more sensitive to adverse weather than are traditional crop strains. Second, the most agriculturally productive regions are in temperate zone areas where exceptionally good soils and climate coincide. Climate change, however, may decouple the favorable climate and the good soils, leaving farmers struggling to maintain food production with new handicaps—either poorer soils or a less benign climate.[96]

In contrast, traditional agriculture in developing nations depends less on monocultures and frequently involves planting several crops together to provide some insurance against failures. We would put our bets on the flexibility of traditional farmers. They not only might adapt more readily to changing conditions than can operators of large industrial farms, they also don't depend on recommendations of an agricultural administration to change crops or planting times. Nor are they constrained by government subsidies and restrictions on their crops. Furthermore, most global warming models project relatively little change in tropical climates from greenhouse gas buildups; more dramatic changes are likely in the temperate zones. In all food-growing regions, global climate change is expected to manifest itself in the short to medium term principally as abnormally severe storms, floods, droughts, and other disruptive weather factors, all of which are potentially catastrophic for agriculture.[97]

The impressive array of tools developed in the 1930s and 1940s to expand food production were deployed around the world in the 1960s and 1970s and did their job well. A new kit of tools is required to carry us into the future; yet no such kit appears to be on the horizon, although some help will be provided by genetic engineering. Meanwhile, the world's farmers must persist in their monumental struggle to increase production in the face of deteriorating natural capital and faltering ecosystem services (such as natural pest control being disrupted by misuse of pesticides), and they must win the battle year after year without doing irreparable damage to those services.[98] Continued success might be assured, but only if (among other things) the size of the human population can soon be stabilized and a gradual decline initiated. Yet even the most optimistic assumptions for success in reducing population growth suggest that at least 2 to 3 billion more people will need to be fed within a few decades.

A potentially powerful approach to ending and eventually reversing population growth more rapidly would be greatly increasing socioeconomic equity in opportunity between the sexes and among families, regions and nations—as we have discussed elsewhere.[99] To a large degree, past successes in raising crop yields have come from pushing back biophysical frontiers. Now humanity is faced with pushing back socioeconomic frontiers. That may be the toughest task of all. Confronted with such an enormous challenge, it is difficult to be complacent.

> There is no need to worry about any population-related problem. The human mind is the "ultimate resource," and growing populations will always be able to solve their resource problems. We need more people in order to have more geniuses; it would be immoral to keep them from being born.[100]

How typical of the brownlash to define away population problems as self-solving while arguing that limiting the number of people alive at any given time—something virtually all societies have tried to do to one degree or another[101]—is immoral! As Julian Simon put it, "What business do I have trying to help arrange it that fewer human beings will be born, each one of whom might be a Mozart or a Michelangelo or an Einstein—or simply a joy to his or her family or community, and a person who will enjoy life?"[102] The obvious response might be: What business does anyone have trying to help arrange it that more human beings will be born, each one of whom might be a Judas, an Attila the Hun, or a Hitler—or simply a burden to his or her family and community and a person who will live a life that is nasty, brutish and short?

Of course, having additional people to work on problems does not necessarily lead to solutions. Consider what happened to the people of Easter Island.[103] This triangular sixty-four-square-mile Pacific island, isolated some 2000 miles west of Chile, was colonized by Polynesians some 1500 years ago. When the first colonists landed, they found an island covered by a tall subtropical forest, with the commonest tree a palm that grew to some eighty feet in height and had a trunk up to six feet in diameter. Yet when the first European visitor, Dutch explorer Jacob Roggeveen, arrived on Easter Sunday, 1722, he found a grassy wasteland inhabited by perhaps 2000 people.

By then the island lacked firewood and had no mammals (not even bats), land birds, reptiles, or snails. The only domestic animals raised by the Easter Islanders were chickens. While their ancestors had hunted porpoises from seagoing canoes crafted from the trunks of the now-extinct palms, the islanders of Roggeveen's day had to make do with small, flimsy, leaky canoes put together from small planks.

During the time of the carving of the some two hundred giant stone statues that once lined the island's coast (ca. A.D. 1200–1500), archaeologists estimate that the island's population had exploded to between 7000 and 20,000 people. But all those minds couldn't solve the island's resource problems. The fate of the population has been reconstructed from pollen records, archaeological evidence, and legends. The large trees were harvested more rapidly than they could regenerate, particularly when rats (which arrived with the Polynesians) ate the seedlings. Once the trees were gone, there was no way to build canoes for porpoise hunting, and there were no materials for making ropes and rollers to drag statues to their places of erection. Without the forest to absorb and meter out rainfall, streams and springs dried up, unprotected soil eroded away, and crop yields dropped. Rival clans warred over resources, and famine struck the once-rich island.

Unlike most premodern peoples,[104] the Easter Islanders apparently didn't limit their fertility. Instead, as food supplies became short they switched to cannibalism, which turned out to be an effective—if not very attractive—method of population control.[105] A common curse became "The flesh of your mother sticks between my teeth."

Long ago, Robert Louis Stevenson commented on overpopulation in the South Pacific:

> Over the whole extent of the South Seas, from one tropic to another, we find traces of a bygone state of over-population, when the resources of even a tropic soil were taxed, and even the improvident Polynesian trembled for the future.... we may suppose, more soberly, a people of sea-rovers, emigrants from a crowded country, to strike upon and settle island after island, and as time went on to multiply exceedingly in their new seats.

> In either case the end must be the same; soon or late it must grow apparent that the crew are too numerous, and that famine is at hand.[106]

Ecologist Jared Diamond of the University of California, Los Angeles, drew similar conclusions but added a modern parallel: "Any islander who tried to warn about the dangers of progressive deforestation would have been overridden by vested interests of carvers, bureaucrats, and chiefs, whose jobs depended on continued deforestation. Our Pacific Northwest loggers are only the latest in a long line of loggers to cry, 'Jobs over trees!'"[107]

As Stevenson implied, Polynesia historically generated a lot of environmental refugees. So, obviously, did many ancient societies that suffered ecological collapse. Today such refugees remain a well-known problem related to imbalances between human numbers and resources, a problem that is totally ignored by the brownlash.[108] Of the more than 50 million refugees counted in 1995, at least 25 million were environmental refugees.[109] Ecologists Norman Myers and Jennifer Kent recently wrote:

> The total may well double by the year 2010 if not before, as increasing numbers of impoverished people press ever harder on over-loaded environments. Their numbers seem likely to grow still more rapidly if predictions of global warming are borne out, whereupon sea-level rise and flooding of many coastal communities, plus agricultural dislocations through droughts and disruption of monsoon and other rainfall systems, could eventually cause as many as 200 million people to be put at risk of displacement.[110]

But can't today's population, with its knowledge of the histories of past civilizations[111] and billions of working brains keep us from repeating the gigantic mistakes of the past? Surely we can avoid the fate of the Easter Islanders, the Henderson Islanders (a population that died out completely on an island of the Pitcairn group in the South Pacific),[112] the classic Maya,[113] the early inhabitants of the Tigris and Euphrates Valleys,[114] the Greeks,[115] the Anasazi (Native Americans who built the vast pueblos of Chaco Canyon),[116] and others who destroyed the environmental supports of their societies!

We wish the answer were yes. But the billions of human brains we have today are not stopping civilization from destroying its natural capital even faster than the Easter Islanders, Sumerians, or Anasazi destroyed theirs. Instead, an overpopulated global society is inflicting enormous, multifaceted damage on its life-support systems and simultaneously generated climate change—a situation eerily similar to the one analysts think may have faced the classic Maya civilization just before its collapse.[117] As archaeologist Jeremy Sabloff remarked:

> [R]esearch [on climate change and the Mayan collapse] also raises an anthropological question that is relevant not only to the ancient Maya but to the contemporary world as well, and is certainly deserving of continued attention—namely, how severe do internal stresses in a civilization have to become before relatively minor climate shifts can trigger widespread cultural collapse?[118]

There is no evidence that larger numbers of human beings translates into more talented or more humane individuals. Of course, there is a certain threshold—a community of 50 souls cannot have 100 geniuses. But arguably, Athens with perhaps 50,000 people in the year 425 B.C., had more geniuses than does San Francisco today, with fifteen times the number of citizens.

Of course, environmental rather than genetic differences determine what proportion of a population will display genius. Thus the San Francisco Bay Area has a far greater reputation for science, art, and education than, say, Kinshasa, Zaire, or Dallas–Fort Worth, although all three metropolitan areas have populations of the same magnitude. The point, of course, is that genius, like most human characteristics, results from an interaction between a genetic heritage and an environment—and there is no shred of evidence that any *group* of human beings has a greater genetic potential to produce geniuses than any other.[119] The Bay Area's advantage can be traced to its environment: among other things, the area has long supported education and the arts; it can claim some of the best universities and colleges in the world; and (not unconnected to the others) it hosts a concentration of forward-looking and high-tech industries. But as the population of the Bay Area keeps growing and California's financial situation becomes more precarious, school systems have gone into decline and many valuable programs are being cut back.

It is quite possible that Dallas–Fort Worth will soon surpass the San Francisco Bay Area as a cultural center—more evidence that it was not California genes but the intellectual and physical environment of the Bay Area that made it a center of excellence.

Whatever the causal relations, contrary to Julian Simon's expectations, as California's population has soared, its quality of life and intellectual potential have fallen. A state school system that ranked as one of the best in the nation now ranks thirty-eighth in expenditures per child and essentially ties with Utah for having the largest classes.[120] The University of California, Berkeley, has lost much of the financial support it needs to remain one of the world's best institutions of higher education, a development that may negatively influence California's economy and quality of life for generations.

In China's imperial past, the Chinese ruled a large part of East Asia while Europeans were living in caves and painting themselves blue. That makes it crystal clear that China has no lack of genes to produce talented administrators, scientists, artists, and others. Although there are many, many more Chinese today, and many of them are also highly talented, they live in a political milieu that often suppresses rather than promotes intellectual expression. Art and science also thrived in ancient India and still thrive in India today despite the handicap of poverty; Arabs many centuries ago invented the number system that made modern science possible. And who could doubt the genius of the people who produced Benin bronzes or the great ruined cities of Zimbabwe? African genius (aided by English incompetence) allowed the Zulus to destroy a British army at Islawanda in southern Africa more than a century ago. Extraordinarily smart administrators clearly lived in Mayan, Aztec, and Inca civilizations; and Native Americans on the Great Plains could boast the finest light cavalry in the world a few centuries after the Spanish reintroduced the horse into North America. Germany in World War II, despite its abominable and ignorant Nazi overlords, nearly beat a combination of nations with many times its population by being more clever militarily.

The point is that virtually all human individuals have enormous potential, and as soon as there are hundreds or thousands of them together, the appearance of genius of one sort or another is almost assured. Once there are tens of millions, the success of a society cannot be seriously constrained by a lack of brains, only by the environments in which those brains must develop and operate. Put another way, it's very hard to become the next Mozart if one is starving to death on the outskirts of Port-au-Prince! Having more people today is not the solution for generating more geniuses. Creating environments in which the inherent talents of people now disadvantaged—by race or gender discrimination, poverty, malnutrition, or whatever—can be fully expressed is. Indeed, there is every reason to believe that having *fewer* people would make it easier to create those environments. Thus Simon seems to have the genius-population relationship exactly backward: smaller, smoothly-functioning, nurturing societies are far more apt to give rise to geniuses than are large, debt-ridden, disintegrating, and inequitable societies.

If human resources are not necessarily increased by population growth, supplies of other resources—non-living and living—certainly are not enlarged by the explosion of human numbers. It's to those resource categories that we turn in the next two chapters.

CHAPTER 6

Fables about
Non-living Resources

□

CONFLICTS BETWEEN THE WISE-USE MOVEMENT and the environmental community—conflicts increasingly involving the government— are most often over resources and who will control them and for what ends. The environmentalists are interested in the use of resources in ways that enhance the common good, including the needs of future generations. This is (or should be) the government's goal as well. In contrast, the wise-use folks maintain that resources exist for the benefit of those seeking private, short-term gain. Unfortunately, they have been successful at convincing many conservative politicians that such exploitation is in the national interest.

Certainly, private property rights (the rights to do whatever one wants with one's property), although never absolute, have a long history. But today these rights are impinging more and more on the right of the public at large to retain access to resources in the future. The public seems increasingly concerned with environmental protection, and that protection often interferes with unrestricted exercise of property rights, especially with respect to land use and resource extraction. This conflict explains much of the brownlash's preoccupation with resources, property rights, and related issues. In this chapter, we focus on the fables the brownlash has offered to justify private overexploitation of resources; in the next, we discuss biological resources—a category that is little recognized and far undervalued by the brownlash.

Non-biological resources fall into two basic categories: non-renewable and renewable.[1] Minerals, for example, generally are non-renewable, although some can be recycled. Soils exploited for agricultural purposes and much groundwater are also non-renewable at current rates of consumption.[2] Solar energy, however, is renewable, as is most surface fresh water.

In turn, each of these resources can be classified as either essential or substitutable. For instance, water in most uses is an essential resource with no known substitute, whereas many metals have substitutes in the form of other metals or non-metallic materials. Resources can also be divided according to whether they are necessarily degraded or dispersed in use. Because fossil fuels degrade (are converted into other substances as they are burned), they are inevitably lost as fuels when they are used; most metals, however, are simply dispersed, although they may change form by combining with other elements (as when iron rusts).[3]

Environmental optimists like to point out that resources such as petroleum and copper are so abundant that one need not be concerned with their depletion. To a degree they are right. Technological advances have often led to the utilization of new deposits, the development of more efficient methods of extraction and use, and the discovery of substitutes—thus effectively expanding the supply. And so for many non-renewable mineral resources, the main problems in the next few decades will be not their exhaustion but rather the environmental costs (oil spills, acid mine drainage, etc.) of their mobilization. But the optimists miss the crucial point.[4]

Far more critical than supplies of those mineral resources are four "renewable" resources that are effectively being transformed into non-renewable ones because of current rates of use: rich agricultural soils, groundwater, biodiversity, and the recycling and absorbing capacity of Earth's lands, waters, and atmosphere.[5] These are among the most important components of the natural capital upon which civilization depends. That human beings are depleting this capital at a very high rate shows that *Homo sapiens* is well beyond the carrying capacity of Earth. Human carrying capacity, remember, is the *long-term* ability of an area to support human beings.

Today global overpopulation is a basic cause of the resource dimension of the human predicament. Here we'll focus on some of the distortions of the situation regarding mineral resources presented by the brownlash.

☐ **Human dependence on physical resources is an illusion. Depletion of resources is a non-issue; substitutes can be found for any and all physical substances.**

Brownlash author Ronald Bailey showed his support of this myth as follows: "Most people are beguiled by the 'resource illusion,' the notion that physical substances are the chief source of wealth in the world."[6]

Contrary to Bailey's view, how human beings manipulate physical substances, and the state of their supplies, are critical components of what we think of as "wealth." Just try to be wealthy without such "physical substances" as oxygen, stratospheric ozone, fresh water, soil, and nitrogen-fixing organisms! But these aren't the physical resources the brownlashers think about. They are fixated mostly on metals and fossil fuels, which are non-renewable and are mostly being depleted at ever-faster rates. The brownlash discounts their value because some are substitutable in various uses and some are partly recyclable.

The fable that one can find substitutes for any and all physical substances is one that the brownlash has inherited from outdated economics and has nothing to do with how the world actually functions.[7] That notion traces in part to a classic misunderstanding of a technical point in physics propagated in 1963 by two distinguished economists, Harold Barnett and Chandler Morse, who imagined one material could easily be tranformed into another because of the "uniformity of energy/matter."[8]

Needless to say, Barnett and Morse had the physics upside down. It is the *lack* of homogeneity that creates resources. That matter can be converted into energy and vice versa in some circumstances does not make these two entities "uniform" any more than a pile of shattered glass and a fine goblet are "uniform." Although under certain circumstances tiny quantities of one element can be converted into another, such transformations require so much energy as to be totally impractical for material quantities large enough to be of economic interest.

The problems commonly encountered in making substitutions, such as substituting nuclear power for fossil fuels, chlorofluorocarbons

(CFCs) for ammonia in refrigerators, or aluminum for copper wire, should have alerted everyone to the "unlimited substitution" fallacy. Once claimed to be the key to a clean, safe future of energy super-abundance, nuclear power is now a scorned technology, irrevocably scarred by accidents at Three Mile Island and Chernobyl as well as by high costs, scandals of careless and illegal operation, and unresolved issues of weapons proliferation and waste disposal.[9] CFCs, once believed to be totally benign substitutes for highly toxic ammonia, are now known to erode Earth's ozone layer. And the replacement of copper with aluminum has created unforeseen fire hazards. Sadly, too many economists have been lulled into complacency by some bona fide successes, such as, in some uses, substitutions of fiber optics for copper wire and plastics for metals and wood. In practice, they act as if they accept the unlimited substitution fallacy, dismissing substitution problems as minor technical complications.

If allowed to pursue "business as usual," energy industries can supply us with all that is necessary to power industrial civilization far into the future.[10]

This is a favorite theme of corporations that mobilize and market energy, especially that embodied in fossil fuels. Lobbyists working on behalf of energy suppliers and industry organizations vociferously argue that overregulation stifles exploration and often prevents access to new oil reserves. If the U.S. government would only allow unlimited drilling (even within protected areas), they say, we could have an energy-secure future. And while it is probably true that existing fossil fuel resources could power civilization well into the future, such thinking neglects the high and growing environmental costs of mobilizing and burning those fuels and the prospect of relatively early exhaustion of petroleum supplies that can be economically extracted.[11]

John Holdren, a Teresa and John Heinz Professor at the Kennedy School of Government, Harvard University and a member of the President's Committee of Advisors on Science and Technology, has spent his career studying the energy-environment interface.[12] Recently, John Holdren summarized the situation: we're not running out of energy, but "we're running out of environment, patience with inequity, money for sustainability, time for making a transition, and leadership to do what is required."[13] Let's examine each of these points.

Running out of environment simply means that the environmental damage from mobilizing and using energy is becoming unsustainable. Local damage occurs in the form of acute water pollution (including oil spills) and air pollution (including severe indoor air pollution from burning of traditional fuels in the developing world). Burning of fuels also causes regional problems, such as acid precipitation, and global ones exemplified by the injection of greenhouse gases into the atmosphere. Nuclear power presents another set of liabilities. And even hydropower, generally considered relatively benign, has already been deployed in most of the appropriate places and has taken its environmental toll by flooding many ecosystems and farm areas and decimating fish populations.

Running out of patience with inequity refers to the increased resentment (and decreased willingness to cooperate in resolving environmental problems) of the poor, who often have to suffer consequences that the rich can pay to avoid. On the global scene, the rich-poor gap has made developing nations distrustful of rich nations. The wealthier countries, which have about a fifth of the human population, have appropriated roughly three-quarters of the world's wealth and use about two-thirds of the energy. In the process, they cause the majority of environmental destruction, yet they have the audacity to call for reductions in greenhouse gas emissions while doing essentially nothing to limit their own.

Not surprisingly, many developing nations resent such behavior, which they see as threatening their own chances for development. But unless some solution to this energy dilemma is found, the goal of a sustainable global society may never be achieved. For example, China has already surpassed the United States as the biggest coal user in the world, and in its quest for economic development it plans to double its coal use by 2010. The consequences of burning such huge quantities of coal in terms of greenhouse gas emissions will be staggering. India, too, is poised for economic expansion powered by coal, but it has not progressed as far, so India's use of coal is still small relative to that of China.[14]

Running out of financial resources is one major reason why humanity is not further along the route to sustainable energy technologies. The

U.S. government, for example, has been increasingly unwilling to fund research and development in this area. Between 1978 and 1995, the Department of Energy's (DOE's) annual research and development funding for energy technology plunged more than $9 billion to less than $2 billion (in constant 1995 dollars).[15] DOE expenditures for renewable energy research and development fell from $1.5 billion in 1980 to $0.4 billion in 1995. Perhaps more important, capital is in very short supply in less developed countries, where most new energy facilities will need to be built.

Money for adequate research and development in an area such as energy, which is of critical importance to the nation's economic well-being, environmental health, and political security, shouldn't be hard to find in the United States. Doing so is a matter of political will and public attitudes. As strong advocates of a carbon tax, we were disappointed in 1993 when President Clinton bargained away the opportunity to put more than a few cents per gallon in additional tax on gasoline in exchange for votes he needed on the North American Free Trade Agreement (NAFTA). Even worse, when a temporary but substantial rise in gasoline prices occurred in spring 1996, the response by Congress was to try to rescind the 4.3 cents per gallon tax. What is really needed is a steep carbon tax on *all* fossil fuels.

Even a modest tax of twenty cents per gallon on gasoline would yield more than $20 billion annually, enough to fund a reasonable energy research and development program and help steer the United States toward sustainability. A larger energy tax—amounting to a dollar or two per gallon of gas—would encourage both conservation and recognition of the high social costs[16] of fossil fuel use (many of which are not captured in the market price of the fuels). We suspect, however, that such a tax remains unpalatable for a number of reasons, including Americans' love affair with cars, their resentment of taxes, and their lack of understanding of the diverse impacts of fossil fuel use, more than it indicates a cavalier attitude toward the environment. And because all the social costs of burning fossil fuels have not been incorporated in fossil fuels' prices,[17] they are so cheap that there is no demand for alternatives, which would certainly have stimulated more investment in developing them.

Running out of time is serious because research and development are only the beginning. It typically takes forty to fifty years from the beginning of development of an energy technology for it to be deployed widely enough to make a significant contribution to the energy economy. Worldwide, the infrastructure of this energy economy represents a $10 trillion investment, with an average lifetime of perhaps thirty years.[18] Thus making large-scale changes in how civilization mobilizes energy is practical only if done over a time scale of many decades. Those who favor a business-as-usual attitude should realize that now is the moment for long-term planning and for starting to wean ourselves from heavy dependence on fossil fuels in order to have a new structure by 2030 or so. And in any case, the transition will take several decades.

Running out of leadership may be the most serious of Holdren's points. Without political leadership, the world will continue drifting into the trap of depending on energy technologies that undermine humanity's life-support systems. Will the leadership needed to shift directions come from the U.S. administration or Congress? We would like to think so but fear that the power of the energy lobbies (now backed by the brownlash) is too great to make meaningful change in the United States possible. The best hope for leadership seems to lie with grassroots organizations, which with the help of their members will encourage politicians to move in the right directions.

Limits to Growth was "a spectacularly wrongheaded book [which] popularized the notion of non-renewable resources." (Ronald Bailey, 1993)[19] "Impending scarcity provokes people to search for substitutes and to improve technologies used to exploit natural resources." (Ronald Bailey, 1993)[20]

To a large degree, the Ronald Bailey–Cato Institute attack quoted here is directed against aged straw men—a favorite target for brownlash misinterpretation. The book *Limits to Growth*[21] was published in 1972. It was based on a pioneering computer study that came to the same conclusion as did we and other analysts in the same period—that continued expansion of the human enterprise on a business-as-usual trajectory would lead to disaster. The study may have underrated (as we once did) the amount of technological innovation and substitution that can be called forth in the short term by prices driven upward by scarcity—just as the brownlash habitually overrates, in our opinion, the power of prices to call forth resources perpetually. The *Limits to Growth* study could, in fact, be viewed as one of the sorts of signal counted upon by economists to encourage efficiency and substitution.

> ▣ **Resources are actually getting more abundant, as one can tell from their declining prices. "In the 1980s almost all raw materials declined in price." (Stephen Moore, 1995)**[22]

The prices of more raw materials are indeed dropping than are rising;[23] but those who cite this statistic as evidence that everything is rosy on the material resource front fail to recognize that market prices don't capture the full social costs of resource harvesting and consumption. Put another way, market prices reflect the costs of production, marketing, and distribution, as well as taxes and profits, but don't include external costs (negative externalities)—undesirable side effects of production or consumption that are not borne exclusively by the producer and consumer. For example, the market price of gasoline put into American cars does not reflect such negative externalities as the impact of tailpipe emissions on human health, forests, and crops or the prospects of climate change induced by the CO_2 in the exhaust. Were the external costs of gasoline use included in the price at the pumps, people would have to pay much more to drive their cars and might also understand much more clearly the impact of fossil fuel combustion on human well-being.

Similarly, the tropical hardwood that beautifies a home does not include in its price the pauperization of tropical forest peoples caused by the destruction of their environment; the CO_2 added to the atmosphere as waste wood is burned or decays and as fossil fuels are burned in the processes of timbering, transportation, and processing; the soil and biodiversity that are lost after clear-cutting, and so on. Adding all the social costs of harvesting the hardwood to the market price would make it very much higher.

Because market prices do not capture all social costs, market prices and social costs may move in opposite directions. If, for example, the Organization of Petroleum Exporting Countries (OPEC) should dissolve, the world market price of gasoline might well drop and people might drive even more, increasing the social cost of gasoline use. Similarly, a drop in the price of tropical timber may reflect mechanization that reduces direct costs of harvesting but increases environmental damage, makes the flow of wood unsustainable, and leaves local people inhabiting a wasteland.

The bottom line is: declining prices may not indicate increasing human welfare.

□ "For practical purposes [the supply of natural resources on Earth] is infinite...." (George Reisman, 1992)[24] "Even the total weight of the earth is not a theoretical limit to the amount of copper that might be available to earthlings in the future.... Only the total weight of the universe ... would be such a theoretical limit ... because copper can be made from other metals." (Julian Simon, 1980)[25]

With the above statement, George Reisman, Professor of Economics at Pepperdine University's School of Business and Management, allies himself with Julian Simon, Professor of Business Administration at the University of Maryland, who has long championed the view that resources are limitless. For example, Simon also asserts that "Our energy supply is non-finite, and oil is an important example. . . . the number of oil wells that will eventually produce oil, and in what quantities, is not known or measurable at present, and probably never will be, and hence is not meaningfully finite."[26]

Following Simon's logic, if Earth's entire supply of oil were contained in a dozen pint cans, it would be finite; but if those cans were dumped into the ocean and allowed to mix for a while, the twelve pints would no longer be countable and so not "meaningfully finite" and therefore would be infinite. One economist reviewing this chain of logic described it as "straightforward nonsense."[27]

This sort of elementary logical error is translated by Reisman into recommendations for social action that reflect the notion that resources are limitless: forget recycling, persist with wasteful packaging, and above all keep consuming so the economy can grow.[28]

□ Living a life that greatly reduces each American's impact on the environment means freezing in the dark and generally doing without.

This myth, implied in the quote that follows, is another brownlash favorite.

Let the ecologists [sic] adopt the poverty-stricken life-style of Eastern Europe if they choose. Let them go about like old Russian grandmothers in Moscow, with an ever-present

NORTHCOAST ENVIRONMENTAL CENTER
LIBRARY
822-6918

shopping bag and herring jar, if that is what they like. Let them pick through garbage pails while pretending that they live in a spaceship—"spaceship Earth," they call it—rather than in the richest country of the planet Earth. But there is absolutely no sane reason why anyone should or needs to live this way, and certainly not in modern America.[29]

Note the misuse of the term "ecologists" (scientists who study the interrelationships of animals, plants, and microorganisms with each other and the non-living portions of their environments). Presumably "extreme environmentalists" or something similar was intended.

Despite the brownlash line that reducing resource consumption means undergoing self-inflicted poverty, there is every reason to believe that a reduction in U.S. energy use per person from the present almost 12 kilowatts (kW)[30] to about 3 kW could be achieved with a *higher* quality of life than that of today. Enormous potential exists for increasing the efficiency of energy-using devices and for modifying structures and living patterns so that less energy is required to achieve the same, if not a more desirable, outcome.[31]

Those who doubt the potential for improvements in energy efficiency need only look at the nearly 40 percent increase in energy efficiency of the U.S. economy[32] in the seventeen years following the initial oil price shock of 1973. Moreover, dozens of detailed engineering-economic studies testify to the further efficiency improvements waiting to be harnessed in particular sectors of human activity, such as transportation, agriculture, housing, and manufacturing.[33]

□ **"In 1990 [Julian Simon] won a much publicized ten-year bet with ecologist Paul Ehrlich [and physicists John Harte and John Holdren] ...wagering correctly that the price of a basket of five metals would fall between 1980 and 1990 (meaning supplies became more plentiful)."(Norman Myers and Julian Simon, 1994)[34] "[The bet affirmed] cornucopian claims that the supply of resources is becoming more abundant, not more scarce." (Ronald Bailey, 1993)[35]**

In 1980, Julian Simon repeatedly challenged environmental scientists to bet against him on trends in prices of commodities, asserting that humanity would never run out of anything.[36] Paul and the other scientists knew that the five metals in the proposed wager were not critical indicators and said so at the time.[37] They emphasized that the depletion of so-called renewable resources—environmental resources such as soils, forests, species diversity, and groundwater—is much more indicative of the deteriorating state of society's life-support systems.

Nonetheless, after consulting with many colleagues, Paul and Berkeley physicists John Harte and John Holdren accepted Simon's challenge in late 1980, jointly betting a total of $1000 ($200 each on five metals),[38] rather than listen to him charge that environmental scientists were unwilling to put their money where their mouths were. Perhaps it was a mistake, but it can be quite satisfying to skewer an adversary on his own terms, and they thought they had a good chance of winning.

Prices of all five metals (chromium, copper, nickel, tin, and tungsten) had gone up between 1950 and 1975. But the prices of three of the five went down in the 1980s, in part because a recession in the first half of that decade slowed the growth of demand for industrial metals worldwide. Ironically, a prominent reason for the slower industrial growth was the doubling of world oil prices in 1979.[39] Indeed, the price of oil probably was a factor in the prices of metals in both years, being unprecedentedly high in 1980 and unprecedentedly low in 1990. Paul and his colleagues ended up paying a small sum on the bet, even though the price of a ton of copper (Simon's favorite example) had risen in constant 1980 dollars from $1970 per ton in 1975 to $2166 in 1989.[40]

Simon issued a challenge for a second bet in 1995. In an essay in the *San Francisco Chronicle,* he claimed that "*Every* measure of material and environmental welfare in the United States and in the world has improved rather than deteriorated. *All* long-run trends point in exactly the opposite direction from the projections of the doomsayers"[41] (our emphasis). Simon asserted that everything will get better; he wanted ecologists to bet that "any trend pertaining to material human welfare" will get worse.

Paul and Stephen Schneider, a climatologist at Stanford University, offered to bet Simon $1000 per trend that each of the following fifteen continental and global indicators "pertaining to material human welfare" will worsen over the next decade:[42]

1. The three years 2002–2004 will on average be warmer than 1992–1994. (Rapid climate change associated with global warming could pose a major threat of increasing droughts and floods.)

2. There will be more carbon dioxide in the atmosphere in 2004 than

in 1994. (Carbon dioxide is the most important greenhouse gas driving global warming.)

3. There will be more nitrous oxide in the atmosphere in 2004 than in 1994. (Nitrous oxide is another greenhouse gas that is increasing due to human disruption of the nitrogen cycle.)

4. The concentration of ozone in the lower atmosphere (the troposphere) will be greater in 2004 than in 1994. (Tropospheric ozone is a component of smog that has important deleterious effects on human health and crop production.)

5. Emissions of the air pollutant sulfur dioxide in Asia will be significantly greater in 2004 than in 1994. (Sulfur dioxide in the atmosphere becomes sulfuric acid, the principal component of acid rain, and it is associated with direct damage to human health, forests, and crops.)

6. There will be less fertile cropland per person in 2004 than in 1994. (Much of Earth's best farmland is being paved over, but even if it weren't, population growth will reduce per-capita acreage.)

7. There will be less agricultural soil per person in 2004 than in 1994. (Erosion virtually everywhere far exceeds rates of soil generation.)

8. There will be on average less rice and wheat grown per person in 2002–2004 than in 1992–1994. (Rice and wheat are the two most important crops consumed by people.)

9. In developing nations there will be less firewood available per person in 2004 than in 1994. (More than a billion people today depend on fuelwood to meet their energy needs.)

10. The remaining area of virgin tropical moist forests will be significantly smaller in 2004 than in 1994. (Those forests are the repositories of some of humanity's most precious living resources, including the basis for many modern pharmaceuticals worldwide.)

11. The oceanic fisheries harvest per person will continue its downward trend and thus in 2004 will be smaller than in 1994. (Overfishing, ocean pollution, and coastal wetlands destruction will continue to take their toll.)

12. There will be fewer plant and animal species still extant in 2004 than in 1994. (Other organisms are the working parts of humanity's life-support systems.)

13. More people will die of AIDS in 2004 than did in 1994 (as the disease takes its toll of already infected individuals, continues to spread in Africa, and takes off in Asia).

14. Between 1994 and 2004, sperm counts of human males will continue to decline and reproductive disorders will continue to increase. (Over

the past fifty years, sperm counts worldwide may have declined by as much as 40 percent. Paul and Steve bet this trend will continue due to the widespread use and environmental persistence of hormone-disrupting synthetic organic chemical compounds.)

15. The gap in wealth between the richest 10 percent of humanity and the poorest 10 percent will be greater in 2004 than in 1994.

We do not argue that all environmental trends are unfavorable, simply that many of the most important ones are *very* unfavorable and thus demand prompt attention. It is sensible to focus on the things that need fixing rather than on those that don't. Virtually all long-term trends have short-term fluctuations; thus in response to Simon's challenge, Steve and Paul picked fifteen trends to avoid having a statistical fluke decide this bet.[43]

Yet Simon refused to accept the wager, going back on his original challenge by saying he will gamble only on "direct" measures of human welfare such as life expectancy, leisure time, and purchasing power.[44] Steve and Paul refused to let Simon change his bet for several reasons. First, life expectancy is determined by a complex interaction of many factors, including infant and child nutrition, availability and sophistication of medical services, cleanliness of air and water, and other elements of environmental quality. Also, while life expectancies may temporarily (i.e., between 1995 and 2005) continue to rise, that increase may well not be sustainable.

Steve and Paul deliberately limited their list to negative environmental or social trends because *they are the ones that need to be fixed* regardless of whether other trends are positive. Policies and practices are established area by area. Life expectancy is more likely to increase (certainly over the long term) if negative trends such as those listed by Steve and Paul could be turned around by wise policy actions. No doubt it would be higher today if those trends had been reversed twenty years ago.

A second reason for not letting Simon off the hook is that he, not the "doomsayers," prominently declared "all trends" to be positive. Steve and Paul indulged in this betting foolishness in the first place in the hope of (1) getting Simon to retract his socially dangerous and scientifically ridiculous assertion that all material or environmental welfare trends were positive, (2) getting Simon to contribute $10,000–15,000 to the environmental charities they select in 2005 to receive the winnings, or (3) getting the public to see that Simon blusters and asserts but won't back up his own rhetoric when seriously challenged. The third outcome was the one obtained.

Bets, of course, are a poor way to settle disputes about the human future, but Paul and his colleagues have been compelled to make two of them in an effort to counter the inaccurate information spread by Simon and others.[45] Scientists in all nations must be ready to counter the arguments of brownlash spokespersons who misinterpret information on what is happening to the environment. Such misinformation gives aid and comfort to those who promote unrestrained population growth and reckless consumption and in so doing threaten society's life-support systems. Rational scholarly discourse is all very well, but it does not hold sway where controversies affecting public policies are concerned.

The fifteen wagers Paul and Steve offered Simon are ones we would love to lose. In fact, we will keep on doing everything in our power to make that happen. But the complacent outlook and inaccuracies spread by Simon tragically increase the chances that we will win the bet—while humanity loses. We can only hope the wagers will cause Simon and others to reconsider the risks they so blithely encourage the public to take by promoting the fantasy that indefinite growth is both possible and benign.

> If "the supply of resources is becoming more abundant, not more scarce" (Ronald Bailey, 1993),[46] why doesn't the brownlash talk more about supplies of water? Is it because water is superabundant?

A standard technique of anti-science, one used extensively by creationists, among others, is to ignore evidence that does not fit the writer's preconceptions. In this context, it is interesting that the one resource brownlashers shy away from is one of the most critical—water. Equally interesting, the only extensive treatment we've found of water in a brownlash book, a chapter by Terry L. Anderson in one of Ronald Bailey's books, is basically sound and sensible.[47]

It's no wonder the brownlashers largely ignore the issue of freshwater supplies. Not only does fresh water, a substance essential for life, have no substitutes in virtually all uses, but its supply is also strictly finite. About half of Earth's freshwater runoff is floodwater not presently captured, and another 20 percent is located far from population centers.

The most recent analysis estimates that humanity already uses more than half of all temporally and geographically accessible runoff.[48] Although new dam contruction may increase accessible runoff by about 10 percent over the next thirty years, the world's population is projected to grow by almost 50 percent during that time.

In our view, instituting many of the market-based solutions proposed by Anderson could help avoid widespread, devastating shortages—at least in the short term. In the longer term, however, the picture will depend heavily on what happens to the scale of the human enterprise— and vice versa. The apparent brownlash view that water is globally too abundant to limit the scale of the human enterprise is wrong.[49] Growing problems with supplying an expanding agriculture with water could make the issue of other resource constraints on food production largely moot.

Water, of course, not only is a resource that human beings must use directly but also is a resource critical to the maintenance of the living resources upon which humanity is utterly dependent. As we see next, the brownlash has been promulgating erroneous information about those resources too.

CHAPTER 7

Biological Diversity
and the Endangered Species Act

□

BIOLOGICAL DIVERSITY—the plants, animals, and microorganisms that are working parts of society's life support systems—is one of humanity's most essential resources. Although Americans think of society as dependent on inanimate resources such as coal, oil, copper, and iron ore, society in fact depends much more on those living resources. Many components of biological diversity (biodiversity) are dwindling, and attempts to conserve them in the United States through the Endangered Species Act (ESA) and other policies affecting land use and aquatic resources sometimes conflict with the short-term economic goals of individuals, firms, industries, or political entities. The ESA is a particular target of the brownlash, in part because it lends itself to a simplistic us-versus-them mentality. After all, what's more important—the economic well-being of people or the existence of a single species of owl, or snail, or butterfly?

As citizens, we are particularly incensed by attempts to derail the ESA because they strike at our love for our grandchildren and our love of nature in one blow. As biologists, we are outraged that the pioneering efforts by the United States to preserve biodiversity, primarily through the ESA, the National Forest Management Act, a variety of other national

107

and state laws, and participation in international conventions on Biodiversity, Forests, and International Trade in Endangered Species (such as CITES, the Convention on International Trade in Engangered Species of Wild Fauna and Flora), should be threatened by an outspoken minority of people who clearly do not realize what is at stake. We are generally proud of our government's record on conservation. Thanks to the ESA, the status of roughly 40 percent of the listed endangered species in the United States is considered stable or improving.[1] We are not proud, however, of the failure of the Senate to ratify the Biodiversity Convention, an important international tool for protecting living resources, or of the efforts of many politicians to reverse the progress that has been made.

Living predominantly in urban and suburban environments, most Americans never think about society's dependence on biological resources. Yet biological resources supply humanity with all crops and domestic animals, timber, many other industrial products, food from the sea, about half of all medicines, and, above all, those critical ecosystem services that are essential to producing food and supporting the economy.[2]

But many Americans are also aware—if only subconsciously—that those resources play a central role in maintaining their emotional equilibrium. Speaking for ourselves, Earth's biological riches greatly enrich our daily lives. Who can place a price on the pleasure of walking among wildflowers on the open hills behind the Stanford campus, seeing a kestrel or white-tailed kite hovering in search of prey, glimpsing a prowling coyote, or watching a fluttering female Bay checkerspot butterfly look for a suitable plant on which to lay her eggs? Like many people, we find that time spent in natural surroundings and with other organisms—be they pets or the birds we watch—restores our spirits as little else can. One of the great joys of our profession is being paid for doing what we love, working with animals and plants—and having the privilege of studying biodiversity across the globe. It is an inexhaustible source of inspiration.

Over the past two summers at the Rocky Mountain Biological Laboratory, 9500 feet high in Colorado, Paul switched his research focus from birds and butterflies to flies. With the help of Jennifer Hughes, now a graduate student at Stanford, he has been working on a project run by our colleague Gretchen Daily, examining one aspect of a mundane but basic and difficult question—what determines which organisms live where? The research involves sorting huge numbers of tiny animals taken from soil and vegetation in different habitats; and in that subalpine area, the dominant animals on the vegetation are flies—some 350 species of Diptera, the insect order that includes mosquitoes and the common housefly.

The chore of sorting all the flies and other tiny insects has fallen to Jennifer and Paul, and one might think it a boring way to spend a summer. It can be tedious, but their fascination with the incredible diversity of body form, the intricacy of the veins that support the wings, the modifications of legs for gripping prey or mates, typifies biologists' reactions to their chosen group of organisms. There's also beauty; scattered among the duller-colored flies are ones with coppery metallic bodies. To know a fly is to love one. And flies aren't the only beautiful insects in the samples. The sorting is always enlivened by the presence of tiny parasitic wasps. These, some of which are smaller than the letters on this page, under a microscope often look as though they were carved from blocks of metal—amazingly beautiful minute sculptures, some golden, that are among the most gorgeous products of evolution. Tedium? Yes, there's some of that. But only by looking at such seemingly mundane organisms as flies can scientists figure out how critical but little-appreciated working parts of the human life-support apparatus can be preserved. The flies, after all, help pollinate the profusion of wildflowers that carpet the area around the laboratory and aid in the crucial processes of controlling pests, disposing of wastes, and recycling nutrients.

The job of preserving biodiversity is going to be desperately difficult. Earth's biological capital is being hammered by direct destruction of habitats and by habitat alteration through mechanisms such as the addition of toxic substances (e.g., pesticides, acid rain) and the introduction of exotic organisms (e.g., rats, starlings, goats, and kudzu vines). Outside the environments in which they evolved, such invaders can be very destructive of other life-forms. A few types of organisms are superabundant: human beings, domesticated animals, and the pests, weeds, and other life-forms that thrive in response to the activities of *Homo sapiens.*

The concern of the biological community over the present spasm of mass extinction cannot be overestimated. The just-completed and monumental *Global Biodiversity Assessment,* commissioned by the United Nations Environment Programme (UNEP) and funded by the Global Environmental Facility (GEF), is a 1149-page, large-format, peer-reviewed document to which some 1500 scientists from all over the world contributed.[3] It clearly represents a consensus of the relevant scientific community, and its foreword is worth quoting:

> Biodiversity represents the very foundation of human existence. Yet by our heedless actions we are eroding this biological capital at an alarming rate. Even today, despite the destruction that we have inflicted on the environment and its natural bounty, its resilience is taken for granted. But the more we learn of the workings of the natural world, the clearer it becomes that there is a limit to the disruption that the environment can endure.
>
> Besides the profound ethical and aesthetic implications, it is clear that the loss of biodiversity has serious economic and social costs. The genes, species, ecosystems and human knowledge which are being lost represent a living library of options available for adapting to local and global change. Biodiversity is part of our daily lives and livelihood and constitutes the resources upon which families, communities, nations and future generations depend.[4]

Among the causes listed for the loss of biodiversity, the first is "increasing demands for biological resources due to increasing population and economic development." Another is a "failure of government policies to address the overuse of biological resources." These basic causes lead to "the loss, fragmentation, and degradation of habitats; the conversion of natural habitats to other uses; overexploitation of wild resources; the introduction of non-native species; the pollution of soil, water and atmosphere; and . . . signs of long-term climate change." The summary concludes: "Unless actions are taken now to protect biodiversity, we will lose forever the opportunity of reaping its full potential benefit for mankind."[5]

As one might expect, the brownlash sees biodiversity very differently from the way the scientific community sees it. The brownlash views Earth's biological capital pretty much as it does non-living resources: both sets of resources are essentially infinite, are in no danger of depletion, and exist just so people can exploit them without restraint—as the following positions related to biodiversity illustrate.

"[O]nly a small portion of Earth has been altered significantly by men and women . . . ." (Gregg Easterbrook, 1995)[6]

This statement by Gregg Easterbrook surely couldn't fool anyone. If you live in Los Angeles, London, Madrid, or New Delhi, how far do you need to go to find unaltered nature? Much of Earth's natural habitat has long since disappeared under cities, towns, roads, railways, farm fields, pastures, and so on. But Easterbrook implies that one needs to look hard to find a place that has been altered!

Significant alteration of habitat, the engine driving the current surge of extinctions, can, however, take place in subtle and thus easily over-looked ways. Habitat alteration is not restricted to paving over or plow-ing under of natural ecosystems. For example, Nevada has fewer than 1.4 million residents, the vast majority of them in two urban complexes that constitute less than one percent of the state's land area. Yet these urban complexes and the 3 percent of Nevada's land in crop agriculture co-opt virtually the entire water budget of the state plus a significant portion of the Colorado River's water, to the detriment of its natural habitats and biodiversity.

Even if one were to require a portion of Earth's surface to be cov-ered with skyscrapers, highways, wheat fields, or pastures to call it "al-tered significantly," the portion so affected is far from small. For decades, the Food and Agriculture Organization of the United Nations (FAO) has classified well over a third of all the land surface of Earth as cropland or permanent pasture.[7] The majority of the additional 35 per-cent or so that is forest and woodland, including the once-remote forests of Siberia and the Amazon basin, has also been highly modified by hu-manity.[8] A further 2 percent or so is under buildings, roads, and other human structures. Even much of the remainder, mostly "wasteland" such as deserts, mountaintops, and polar regions, has also been impacted by *Homo sapiens,* as anyone who has visited a desert area accessible to off-road vehicles can testify. And we're considering only such physical al-terations as deforestation, conversion to agriculture, grazing by non-na-tive domestic animals, dams and stream diversions, and construction. When global toxification (including releases of persistent organochlo-rine compounds such as DDT and long-lived radioactive fallout from nuclear weapons and power plants) and human-transplanted exotic or-ganisms are included, every square inch of Earth's surface, land and sea, has been "significantly altered."[9]

Some actual numbers can shed some light on the degree to which bi-ological communities have been transformed on a regional scale. San Diego County, California, a county not unlike many others being subjected to urban sprawl, exemplifies the process. Originally, the county contained some 750 square miles of coastal sage scrub, the habitat of a now-famous threatened species of bird, the California gnatcatcher. By 1988, only about 210 square miles of coastal sage scrub were left, a habitat loss of over 70 percent. More serious has been the loss of 85 to 97 percent of the native grassland, coastal mixed chaparral, maritime sage scrub, coastal salt marsh, freshwater marsh, and vernal pools that once dotted the county; today no measurable coastal strand vegetation persists.[10]

□ **Biological diversity and species diversity are the same thing.**[11]

Many people assume that preserving a few hundred or a few thousand representatives of each species is sufficient and that "extinction" means only the extinction of species.[12] This is a natural mistake, caused in part by the focus of biologists on species extinction,[13] a tendency that simply reflects the convenience of using species in communicating about the living world. But preserving different populations and the genetic variability within populations is critical both to the maintenance of ecosystem services and to the capacity of species to survive environmental changes and respond evolutionarily to them.[14]

A simple thought experiment shows how hopelessly inadequate it would be to save only a few members of each species. Suppose every non-human species on the planet were somehow reduced to a single minimum viable population (the smallest population that could persist for, say, 500 years), saved in a reserve, zoo, aquarium, botanical garden, bucket of soil, or culture dish. There would be no decline in species diversity, but virtually all human beings would soon die from starvation and loss of ecosystem services.[15] For instance, even if each crop species needed 10,000 individual plants to maintain its single population, that population would not provide food for more than a handful of people.[16] For their own survival and well-being, human beings need, not just a great variety of other species around them, but an abundance of ecosystems, populations, individuals, and genes—a richness of life—as well.[17]

Another unfortunate consequence of a focus on species extinction is that biologists don't know exactly how many species there are, what their precise relationships with one another are, or just how many are going extinct each year.[18] Such uncertainty makes an easy target for the brownlash, which can claim that in the absence of such information no one can be sure there is an extinction crisis.[19] But biologists don't need to know how many species there are, how they are related to one another, or how many disappear annually to recognize that Earth's biota is entering a gigantic spasm of extinction. All they need to know is that high rates of habitat destruction and alteration are occurring everywhere and that most species have quite limited distributions and are highly habitat specific. The conclusion is obvious.

To think otherwise is equivalent to believing no one can tell whether a beach is eroding away unless every grain of sand, seashell, piece of driftwood, and strand of seaweed has been counted, measured, and classified and a record kept of the ones that have disappeared. Nonetheless, biologists' honest attempts to estimate the dimensions of the extinction problem have been constantly attacked—as if showing the estimates to be inaccurate would make the problem disappear.[20]

> "[I]f one takes the admittedly very rough guesses at the numbers of species being made extinct and of the numbers that exist hazarded by the rightly eminent biologist Edward O. Wilson, less than 1% of species would become extinct in 30 years." (Wilfred Beckerman, 1995)[21]

Our old friend and colleague Ed Wilson was surprised to learn about this interpretation of his work by Wilfred Beckerman, an English economist. In his classic book *The Diversity of Life,* Wilson wrote of extinction among the conservatively estimated 10 million species living in rain forests: "Even with these cautious parameters, selected in a biased manner to draw a maximally optimistic conclusion, the number of species doomed each year is 27,000."[22] If we make another extremely optimistic assumption—that extinction rates in rain forests will not increase as the human enterprise expands and rain forests shrink—that amounts to $27,000 \times 30 = 810,000$ species, or 8.1 percent of Wilson's conservative estimate of 10 million. If, again conservatively, only half of all species occurred in rain forests, and there were no extinctions outside rain forests, over 4 percent of all species would go extinct in the next thirty years.

Note that even under the most wildly optimistic assumptions, Beckerman miscalculated by a factor of four. As Wilson wrote to *Wall Street Journal Europe* in response, "I used the most conservative parameter values allowed by the data. Additional extinction is certain to be caused by incursion of exotic species, edge effects following cutting, and other factors."[23]

> ☐ **"Almost ninety percent of the Atlantic coastal forests of Brazil have been cleared in the last five hundred years. . . . [But] a survey by Brazilian zoologists found that not a single known species could be declared extinct." (Stephen Budiansky, 1995)[24]**

On the basis of this evidence, brownlash journalist Stephen Budiansky suggests the techniques widely used by ecologists to evaluate the extinction process are flawed. While it is true that nearly 90 percent of the Atlantic forests of South America have been cleared, and that no species has been *proven* to be extinct, it isn't true that this demonstrates that the standard techniques for estimating extinction rates (mathematical models that relate areas of habitat to numbers of species supported) are flawed.[25] To the contrary, recent research has shown a close match between predicted extinctions based on area of deforestation and observed numbers of threatened species.

The lack of documented species loss along Brazil's Atlantic coast may reflect several factors. First, since much of the forest clearance occurred recently, many organisms may still persist but in dwindling numbers—that is, the flora and fauna are in the process of going extinct and are "relaxing" toward a new, lower equilibrium number of species. Second, because several species have not been seen for fifty years, they are quite likely already extinct. As one ecologist has noted, "that there is a time-lag between deforestation and extinction is [the] only explanation for the similarity between the observed number of threatened [thought likely to go extinct within a few decades] Atlantic forest endemics and the number expected from deforestation. Forest clearance is leading to mass bird extinctions in the Atlantic forests, at levels predicted by . . . species-area analyses."[26]

> ☐ **"[T]he Endangered Species Act . . . has become an unintended monument to the practical failure of this species-by-species approach." (Stephen Budiansky, 1995)[27]**

The United States has great advantages over poor nations like Brazil in attempting to preserve its living resources. First, the United States has documented the distribution and abundance of its resources much better. Second, it can relatively easily afford to take the necessary steps (although no country can afford not to) to protect its resources, and third, it posseses the farsighted Endangered Species Act (ESA). Passed in 1973, the act's purposes include "to provide a means whereby the ecosystems upon which endangered species and threatened species depend may be conserved, [and] to provide a program for the conservation of such endangered species and threatened species."[28] The act's inclusion of ecosystem preservation reflects truly enlightened thinking. When ecosystems are preserved, many or most co-occurring species enjoy protection as well. In that respect, the ESA does not take only a species-by-species approach.

But because of a number of high-profile, highly controversial species (most notably the northern spotted owl), the wise-use movement has been surprisingly successful in its campaign against the Endangered Species Act. A lawsuit aimed at destroying the habitat-preserving portions of the ESA went all the way to the U.S. Supreme Court. Fortunately, it lost. Rebuffed by the Court, wise-use advocates have turned to Congress to gut the law.

Despite claims of its failure by the brownlash, a review of the ESA by the National Research Council did not "uncover any major scientific issue that seriously hinders implementation of the act."[29] Overall, the council's review found the scientific underpinnings of the act sound and its stated goals appropriate and defensible.[30] One thing is certain: hundreds of individual species are in substantially better condition today than they would have been without the ESA.

☐ **The ESA shows that the government cares more about the well-being of animals no one has ever heard of than it does about human welfare.**[31]

To quote Dennis Murphy, President of Stanford University's Center for Conservation Biology:

> Never mind that most of the horror stories of the Endangered Species Act and agency excesses cannot be substantiated—particularly the really dramatic ones. You may have heard some of them. The hundred thousand jobs sacrificed to protections for the northern spotted owl in the Pacific Northwest. The ten thousand houses not built in Kern County because of the Mojave ground squirrel. The dozens of homes lost in Riverside

County when local fire abatement regulations were overridden by federal demands that habitat for the Stephen's kangaroo rat be protected. Or the thousands of farm acres lost to flooding in the Pajaro Valley in Monterey County for conservation measures for the Santa Cruz long-toed salamander. Well the salamander did not even reside in the flooded Pajaro Valley; and the other stories are equally unsupported. But heart-wrenching stories of hard-working citizens put out of work to save snakes and bugs remain the stuff of ongoing debate.[32]

Murphy is not a wild-eyed environmentalist—indeed, many in the environmental community might consider him too sympathetic to industry and developers. His carefully crafted guidelines for conservation of the coastal sage scrub community of southern California reflect attempts to balance species and ecosystem protection with responsible land development, an approach Secretary of the Interior Bruce Babbitt considers the "model" for avoiding future "environmental and economic train-wrecks" like that over the northern spotted owl in the Pacific Northwest.[33]

⬜   **"Probably no 'endangered species' has achieved so much notoriety as the Northern Spotted Owl, nor has any listing been so hypocritical and unjustified." (Dixy Lee Ray and Lou Guzzo, 1993)[34]**

The ESA has been at the top of the list of environmental statutes targeted by the 104th Congress to be weakened or outright eliminated— the result of serious lobbying by the wise-use movement. Some property owners, fearing that discovery of an endangered species on their land would prompt severe restrictions on their land-use decisions, hate the law. So do the folks whose idea of recreation is tearing up fragile desert surfaces by driving off-road vehicles over them. Groups such as loggers whose livelihoods are threatened when resources are put off-limits not surprisingly are outraged by the ESA. For almost a decade now, the struggles over logging in the Pacific Northwest's old-growth forests, focused on the endangered northern spotted owl, have spotlighted the problem—even though the forests in question are mostly on public lands.

To the public, the spotted owl symbolizes an ESA run amok.[35] Because saving the spotted owl meant saving large tracts of old-growth

forests (each breeding pair requires 600 to 2500 acres of old-growth forest),[36] there was an outcry, mostly from timber interests, over the ESA
provision that requires protection of the ecosystems supporting endangered species. Yet it is this aspect of the ESA that, in our view, makes it
most valuable. Because single species can serve as "umbrellas" to protect the biodiversity of entire ecosystems, can be indicators of ecosystem health or disruption, and can serve as symbols for the need to conserve living resources, they can gain significance far beyond their own
intrinsic value.

We won't attempt to review the complex science of the much-dis-
cussed spotted owl controversy here.[37] The claim that its listing was "unjustified" has no support among scientific experts in the field of conservation biology. That the species was in danger of becoming extinct was
an opinion *unanimously* shared by more than fifty members of government agencies, scientists from universities and research institutions,
and independent experts on wildlife who attended a December 1993
workshop in Fort Collins, Colorado. All government, academic, and private sector biologists who study the owl were present, along with sta-
tisticians and others to aid in their analysis.[38]

Not only was listing of the northern spotted owl as threatened entirely
justified, but also almost none of the local controversy was generated
over legitimate economic issues. Even in the short term, there never was
an issue of "owls versus jobs;" rather, the issue was "jobs versus jobs."
Timber interests won out over salmon fishing (which is heavily damaged by cutting the old-growth forests) and recreational interests because trees are harvested by big businesses with big lobbying capacity.
Fishing and recreational services are mostly businesses run by small, independent operators with little political clout. So jobs for loggers were
preserved at the cost of jobs for fishers and shopkeepers.

Five years after federal protection was extended to the northern spotted owl, the unemployment rate in Oregon had declined significantly
and was lower than the national average. Many of the loggers who have
lost their jobs are retraining for new careers—not being as inflexible and
slow to learn as timber industry lobbyists sometimes paint them.[39]

Rather than being a major block to development, the ESA has actually
been an overwhelming success, despite the handful of serious confrontations over its implementation. Between 1987 and 1992, the U.S.
Fish and Wildlife Service conducted 96,832 informal and formal consul-

tations regarding federal projects and permits that might affect endangered species. Only 54 (less than 0.06 percent) projects were ultimately blocked because of endangered species conflicts. The remaining projects went forward without objection or were modified to make some accommodation for the needs of endangered species.[40]

□ **Old-growth forests are not necessary to preserve northern spotted owls.** According to ecologist H. R. Pulliam, director of the National Biological Service, species have both source and sink habitats, and for the northern spotted owl second growth may be the source and old growth the sink, since the relevant studies to determine which is which have not been done.[41]

Philosopher Alston Chase, author of *In a Dark Wood,* one of the most recent brownlash books, has attempted to debunk the notion that the northern spotted owl's survival depends on old-growth forest. To support that notion, he cites one of the world's outstanding ecologists, H. Ronald Pulliam, who developed the area of "source-sink" dynamics.[42] Sinks are areas where a species cannot maintain itself by reproduction alone but survives only through continued immigration. Sources are areas where populations reproduce well enough to generate a flow of migrants to the sinks.

Pulliam corrected Chase as follows:[43]

> In fact, the thesis that northern spotted owls require old growth forest has been tested and the results strongly support the notion that old growth forests are source habitats and that excess production in this source results in immigration of surplus individuals into secondary growth forests,[44] just the opposite of Mr. Chase's contention. To complicate matters, northern spotted owls do breed in secondary growth areas, although their reproductive success in these sinks is not sufficient to balance mortality there. To make matters even more complex, recent studies in California have suggested that secondary forests there may indeed be source habitat for the California subspecies of the spotted owl.[45]

The foregoing example points out not only how complicated the natural world is but also how difficult our role as information providers can be. Scientific facts are frequently distorted to serve a political agenda. As if that were not bad enough, what is false in one place may be true elsewhere, and we have to explain all this to contentious policy makers and a confused public.

<table>
<tr><td>⬛</td><td></td></tr>
</table>

☐ **The Endangered Species Act is too strong and should be weakened.**

Crippling the ESA is a key goal of the wise-use movement and a popular refrain of the brownlash. In particular, it's the theme of the book *Noah's Choice* by Charles Mann and Mark Plummer.[46] That book claims that the Endangered Species Act is too rigid to permit the necessary compromises to be made between the preservation of biodiversity and other socially valued goals. The authors cite the conflict over the building of Tellico Dam by Tennessee Valley Authority,[47] saying, "Tellico has not proven a complete disaster."[48] A telling comment indeed, as Mann and Plummer might more accurately have described the dam as a completed disaster.

Politics and "pork" are such cozy bedfellows that the dam was completed by a special congressional mandate suspending the ESA in the Tellico case. It was completed despite the threat to the snail darter, a small fish then thought to be endangered, and even a "God committee" empowered to suspend the ESA, which instead ruled in favor of the darter![49] Moreover, it was completed despite several adverse economic analyses, appeals to prevent the desecration of a sacred Cherokee burial ground, and protests against the destruction of eastern Tennessee's last free-running trout stream. The dam has yet to justify its huge cost to taxpayers, quite apart from the environmental values it destroyed. Furthermore, most of the numerous promised economic benefits never materialized.[50] So we are at a loss to explain Mann and Plummer's defense of the project.

Of Mann and Plummer's account, ecologist Stuart Pimm of the University of Tennessee wrote:

> [Their] discussion of the Snail Darter is particularly fanciful. I cannot imagine that Mann or Plummer talked to anyone in Tennessee about this case. . . . What would we have saved if the [Endangered Species] Act had been upheld? First the family farm of one of my former undergraduates. Second, a fine trout stream—for trout fishermen tried to stop the dam long before environmentalists. Third, burial grounds sacred to Native Americans. And, yes, a river rich in species. . . . With very little imagination, one could easily write about the 1973 Act as being a great savior of individual rights.[51]

Another project Mann and Plummer describe is the development of beautiful Texas hill country west of Austin, site of a proposed Balcones Canyonlands Conservation Plan. The Balcones plan was designed to preserve two interesting species of birds—the black-capped vireo and the golden-cheeked warbler—but it failed when the interested parties could not get the local support needed to implement it. Mann and Plummer describe their reaction to the development site:

> Driving along the verdant slopes of the Hill Country, we found it hard to believe we were in a metropolitan area of three-quarters of a million people. Views of apparently untouched canyons, splendid in afternoon light, would make anyone want to have a home in those hills. The people who have those homes also want the other comforts of American civilization: banks and burger joints, diners and doughnut shops. . . . As roadside billboards attested, much of the land was owned by developers with visions of housing tracts and office parks. . . .[52]

Thus, according to Mann and Plummer, the ESA would deny future generations of Texans the right to enjoy a landcape of subdivisions and hamburger stands rather than a natural landscape complete with beautiful, interesting, and now-endangered species.

Mann and Plummer press their case for weakening the ESA, especially as it affects owners of private land, by focusing on some of the least successful applications of the act. They attempt to scare owners of private land into thinking they will lose their property rights because of some six-legged creatures. Much attention is given to the Karner blue butterfly[53] and the American burying beetle,[54] which are treated as prime examples of federal legislation gone awry. Yet Mann and Plummer describe the Karner blue so inaccurately that one ecologist referred to what they wrote as "more science fiction than science."[55] Attacking these species, however, had advantages for Mann and Plummer. Few people express much fondness for insects (certainly not burying beetles); fewer still are aware of their role in keeping civilization going.

Mann and Plummer's discussion of the burying beetle is based on the premise that such an organism certainly can't be worth much effort to preserve. "Is the beetle edible?" they ask. "Will it provide us with a cure for the common cold? If it becomes extinct, will Oklahoma be inundated with the carcasses of small mammals? On each count, [the burying beetle] seems expendable."[56]

But insects and other obscure animals are far from expendable. They provide essential ecosystem services, including ensuring that animal wastes are transformed into plant nutrients. Mann and Plummer may thus underrate the direct value of the burying beetle. Any insect that lives in carrion could be an important source of antimicrobial or anti-fungal substances or may have immunological capabilities that might be of great interest to medical researchers. The American burying beetle might have an unusual relationship with the mites it often carries; could they help it resist pathogens? The possibilities are endless; surely such a resource should not be discarded lightly.

Biologist Edward O. Wilson was absolutely correct when he called insects and other invertebrate animals (those without backbones) "the little things that run the world."[57] Every American should read his words:

> The truth is that we need invertebrates but they don't need us. If human beings were to disappear tomorrow, the world would go on with little change. . . . But if invertebrates were to disappear, I doubt that the human species could last more than a few months. Most of the fishes, amphibians, birds, and mammals would crash to extinction about the same time. Next would go the bulk of the flowering plants and with them the physical structure of the majority of the forests and other terrestrial habitats of the world. The earth would rot. As dead vegetation piled up and dried out, narrowing and closing the channels of the nutrient cycles, other complex forms of vegetation would die off, and with them the last remnants of the vertebrates. The remaining fungi, after enjoying a population explosion of stupendous proportions, would also perish. Within a few decades the world would return to the state of a billion years ago, comprised primarily of bacteria, algae, and a few other very simple multicellular plants.[58]

At the policy level, Mann and Plummer offer no in-depth discussion of the great successes of the ESA. No mention is made of the act's role in helping save the long-term future of the timber industry in the Pacific Northwest by preserving the genetic and ecological diversity of old-growth forests through the medium of the northern spotted owl. Nor do they mention the Natural Community Conservation Planning Program in California, engineered in no small part by Dennis Murphy and endorsed by Republican governor Pete Wilson and Democratic secretary of the interior Bruce Babbitt, a program centered on protection of the California gnatcatcher.[59] Would it surprise Mann and Plummer to know that the legacy of the Endangered Species Act in California is not one of chain saws silenced, small farmers displaced, and home builders denied? Rather it is one of regional ecosystem-based planning efforts involving cooperation between landowners and local governments. Close to 80 percent of California's public and private lands are now in locally driven multiple-species planning programs that respond to the needs of threatened and endangered species and other environmental challenges.[60]

Astonishingly, the word "ecosystem" doesn't even appear in the index to *Noah's Choice*. Overall, the book reflects the widespread brownlash attitude that saving insects, obscure plants, and the like is a pretty poor reason for slowing down "progress."[61]

The problems of protecting biodiversity are severe in the face of the rapidly expanding human enterprise.[62] They are also complex, involving federal and state agencies, industries, private citizens, courts, and so on. We concur with *Noah*'s authors that the ESA hasn't done as well as it might in conserving America's biological heritage and that its implementation has sometimes been less than ideal. Further, we are convinced that the costs of protection should be borne as equitably as possible by society.

But we also believe that the greedy, myopic land abuser described by Mann and Plummer as the ubiquitous landowner who wishes that the ESA and the U.S. Fish and Wildlife Service would simply disappear is far from typical. Many landowners understand the goals of the ESA and wish to help meet them. Most see their land as a long-term investment and want its values to remain undiminished generation after generation; preserving the biodiversity on it is one way to accomplish that goal. Landowners do, quite reasonably, want certainty in their planning, the ability to deal with a single agency, no surprises, and costs equitably shared. None of these expectations is antithetical to effective implementation of the ESA, contrary to the contentions of *Noah's Choice*.

We disagree totally with *Noah*'s notion that the ESA should be redrafted to make it easier to choose between "nature" and "human desires."[63] Our disagreement rests on a mix of science and belief. We do believe that human beings have an ethical obligation to protect their only known living companions in the universe,[64] although we don't believe that the right of other organisms to exist is unqualified. Human beings create rights and ethics; humanity clearly would be in deep trouble if it invented rights and ethics that forbade us to injure or kill other organisms.

Choices about biodiversity are all about human desires, among which are the collective desires to keep civilization going and to pass on Earth's biological resources as undiminished as possible to future generations. We see it as the ethical duty of anyone who appreciates biodiversity and understands the irreversible nature of its destruction (from a human perspective)[65] to fight hard against the forces that would continue to destroy it ad lib.

The choice today is between permitting the continued depletion of America's vital natural capital and making an all-out effort to save it. Science tells us that America's population cannot keep expanding perpetually, always demanding more and more from the nation's finite living and non-living resources. The Endangered Species Act at the very least acknowledges the preservation of living resources as a high priority, which was a historical first. By attempting to shield those resources from the piecemeal destruction that is ensured when each species is measured against some perceived immediate economic gain, it helps set the United States on a path toward sustainability.

The basic recommendations Mann and Plummer put forth in *Noah's Choice* would reverse that situation.[66] Along with other brownlash writers and conservatives in Congress, they would limit the actions prohibited under the ESA to those that cause direct injury to listed species and deny protection of the habitat essential to the survival of the species. If these individuals prevail, biodiversity once again will be hostage to every congressman's pork-barrel dam and each developer's "need" for profit maximization.

Contrary to the view put forward in *Noah,* we believe the ESA should be strengthened so that it can be a more effective tool for preserving the habitats—the ecosystems—that provide irreplaceable support both to the human enterprise and to the human spirit.[67] In the short run, it should be modified so developers and property owners can be compensated to some extent by society, through devices such as tax breaks, for financial losses they might suffer in order to preserve biodiversity and so they can be provided with a reasonable degree of certainty about their obligations.[68] Doing this will require considerable care. For example, some environmentalists fear that if compensation is built into the law and funding is inadequate, habitat destruction might be resumed because the government will not be able to compensate property owners.[69]

In the long run, though, it is clear that yesterday's kind of "development" must cease; the principal question remaining is, what will be left when it does? Americans need to take a close look at the scale of their collective activities: the number of American citizens, the amount an average person consumes, and the kinds of technologies that support that consumption. They should examine the implications of so large an enterprise for the sake of both biodiversity and the American future, and they should consider how much longer (in the words of Dennis Murphy) economic growth and conservation efforts can be "responsibly balanced." We are highly doubtful that any balance can be maintained for very much longer without extremely adverse consequences for society. We think the conclusion of such an examination might be that the scale of the enterprise is already much too large and that any further "development" on land not yet obviously scarred by human activities in the United States should be prohibited except on an emergency basis.

In the final analysis, the ESA can serve only as a safety net—as a last-ditch effort to save endangered habitats, species, and populations. The United States needs strong environmental laws that will preserve biological resources long before they need to be listed.

Just as economists and others tend to overestimate the ease with which society can find substitutes for inanimate resources, they largely remain blissfully unaware of the much greater difficulties of finding substitutes for ecosystem services. Of course, attempts have been made, such as building dams to replace the flood-control service of natural vegetation, or using ever more pesticides to replace the natural ecosystem controls destroyed when predators are killed off. But such attempts have generally been extremely expensive, environmentally damaging, or unsuccessful—and often all three.[70]

Let us emphatically repeat that our strong defense of the ESA doesn't mean human needs shouldn't be considered. Indeed, securing a world in which the human species will flourish for many more generations is a goal that drives us and other conservation biologists. We have always thought that making protection of biodiversity an ethical issue was the best way to achieve that very utilitarian end.[71] In our view, we have an ethical obligation to preserve Earth's biological resources for our children and future generations, and in this context we find the assault on them by the brownlash profoundly immoral.

CHAPTER 8

Fables about
the Atmosphere and Climate

□

IN FEW AREAS has the brownlash produced more inaccuracies and misinterpretations of science than in dealing with atmospheric issues. This is hardly surprising, since our society is based on fossil fuel use (the leading source of anthropogenic, or human-caused, greenhouse gas increase and acid precipitation), and the chlorofluorocarbons responsible for ozone depletion were once considered a triumph of the powerful chemical industry. Possible policy changes in response to scientific findings thus obviously could pose a huge threat to business as usual for some of the world's most powerful industries.

Yet environmental scientists have long been properly concerned about the potential effects of rapidly enhancing the greenhouse effect. They also cannot view with equanimity a thinning of the stratospheric ozone shield, which is a critical feature of the atmosphere that makes life on land possible. Nor can they be unconcerned about the impacts of acid precipitation on terrestrial and aquatic ecosystems. Let's take a look at what the producers of feel-good fables claim about human-induced atmospheric changes. The following statement encapsulates the message that has been conveyed in a half-dozen recent books and countless magazine articles, opinion pieces, and radio talk shows.

☐ **Global warming is not a major environmental problem and certainly is not an environmental crisis.**[1]

There has probably been more nonsense expounded on global warming than on any other topic in environmental science (population is a contender, though). Whether warming is contributing significantly to environmental problems today is uncertain. It is, of course, possible that humanity's alteration of the climate is not playing a role in droughts or more intense hurricanes or coral bleaching at present. But such phenomena are the sorts that many scientists believe will sooner or later accompany global warming. Therefore, the possibility that human activities have added to the severity of current events cannot be readily dismissed; it takes many rolls of a pair of dice to find out whether it has been slightly loaded.

As described in chapter 5, rapid climate change is a huge potential threat to agricultural productivity. Any significant disruption of food production could have catastrophic consequences in a world where the nutritional future of the still-growing human population seems less than secure in any case. Rapid climate change also could increase temperature-related direct public health threats[2] and encourage the spread of some of humanity's nastiest diseases.[3] A rising sea level would directly endanger human populations and ruin agriculture in low-lying coastal areas already vulnerable to large storm surges; it would also salinize coastal aquifers and destroy vital coastal wetlands.[4] Indeed, it would threaten the very existence of some island nations.

So today one might define global warming as "not a major environmental problem" in the same way as one might define a small breast or prostate cancer as "not a major medical problem." For most of us, though, having either of those cancers would qualify as a crisis—and humanity certainly "has" global warming.

☐ **There is little or no evidence that global warming is real.**[5]

Whether global warming should be labelled a "problem" or a "crisis" is largely a matter of personal opinion. What is incontrovertible is that humanity has begun to alter the climate of Earth by changing the composition of the atmosphere and also by influencing the reflectivity (albedo) of the planet. Elementary physics tells us that these factors govern the absorption, transmission, and reflection of the sun's radiant energy by Earth and its atmosphere and that this energy is the primary driver of the climate.

The climatic system is exceedingly complex and is not entirely understood.[6] But certain facts are indisputable. First, scientists have known for more than a century that there is a "greenhouse effect" caused by the gaseous composition of Earth's atmosphere.[7] The atmosphere contains an array of natural "greenhouse" gases—including water vapor, carbon dioxide, and methane—that are relatively transparent to the incoming short-wavelength energy of sunlight but relatively opaque to the long-wavelength infrared energy radiated upward by the sunlight-warmed Earth. The greenhouse gases and clouds together absorb most of this outgoing infrared energy and reradiate some of it back toward Earth. The greenhouse gases thus function as a heat-trapping blanket over the planet. The naturally occurring concentrations of these gases are enough to raise Earth's average surface temperature to about 59° Fahrenheit (15° Celsius); without greenhouse gases, it would be about 0°F (–18°C). The influence of this heat-trapping blanket is called the greenhouse effect, and there is no scientific dispute about its existence. None. Without the greenhouse effect the oceans would be frozen to the bottom, and life as we know it would be impossible.

Second, scientists know that humanity is adding to the greenhouse effect—that the atmospheric concentration of carbon dioxide in 1992 was some 30 percent above preindustrial levels,[8] and the concentration of methane had increased by 145 percent.[9] Both gases are natural atmospheric constituents whose concentrations have fluctuated substantially in geologic history. But from analyses of air trapped in ice cores from the Antarctic and Greenland ice caps, scientists know that today's levels are by wide margins the highest concentrations of these greenhouse gases in at least the past 160,000 years. Nitrous oxide, another greenhouse gas, has increased about 15 percent over its preindustrial level.[10] Chlorofluorocarbons (CFCs)—the ozone-destroying chemicals—also contribute to the greenhouse effect; these potent and long-lasting gases, unlike the others, are exclusively human additions to the atmosphere.

The human-caused emissions of all these greenhouse gases, except CFCs, can be traced mainly to fossil fuel burning, deforestation, and agricultural practices. They are affecting Earth-atmosphere energy flows globally, even if their consequences for weather patterns cannot yet be unambiguously distinguished from climatic fluctuations of natural origin.

While knowledgeable scientists do not dispute the basic mechanism of the greenhouse effect and the reality that society is augmenting global greenhouse gas concentrations, they also agree that there remains considerable uncertainty about the magnitude, timing, and geographic distribution of the climate change that will result. There also is nearly universal agreement in the scientific community that human activities will make the planet hotter[11]—that there will be "global warming"—but just how much there will be, how fast it will occur, and what its regional implications will be are much more uncertain. A great deal of the uncertainty traces to lack of knowledge about the balance between various positive and negative feedbacks in the climate mechanism.

Unfortunately, the atmospheric system's extraordinary complexity creates barriers to precise understanding. The evidence strongly indicates that increased evaporation of water in response to higher temperatures powerfully reinforces global warming because water vapor itself is a greenhouse gas. By nearly all accounts, this is a potent *positive feedback mechanism*—one in which a trend or disturbance reinforces itself. *Negative feedbacks,* on the other hand, tend to damp out the trends or disturbances with which they interact. Infrared radiation to space is a climatic negative feedback operating on Earth's surface temperature; as the temperature increases, more infrared energy is radiated to space, and this constrains the rise in surface temperature.

Only part of the warming that is predicted to result from gases added to the atmosphere by *Homo sapiens* would be directly caused by those gases—the bulk would come indirectly from the strong positive water vapor feedback just mentioned. But that additional water vapor would also change cloud cover, and whether clouds contribute more to warming or to cooling depends on their form and the altitude of their tops.[12]

The kinds of clouds produced by global warming will depend in part on what happens to patterns of atmospheric circulation, which in turn will depend on the warming or cooling effects of the clouds. Further uncertainties surround such factors as changes in the amounts of atmospheric aerosols and sea ice (both of which reflect solar radiation and inhibit heat exchange between the atmosphere and oceans); direct effects of CO_2 on heat exchange by vegetation; changes in the ability of the oceans to absorb CO_2; the possible release of large amounts of CO_2 from warmed soils; CO_2 fertilization of terrestrial ecosystems; rates of deforestation and reforestation; and the impacts of other pollutants that humanity is releasing into the atmosphere. Moreover, similar sets of uncertainties surround the effects of methane and nitrous oxide, and the contributions from chlorofluorocarbons (CFCs) are contingent on human decisions.

Little wonder scientists can't responsibly make definitive statements when asked about timing and regional manifestations of global warming. Nevertheless—and this is a point we will make many times—these uncertainties include a significant chance for big changes and thus are no excuse for avoiding action to ameliorate the potentially catastrophic consequences of rapid climate change.

□   Global warming "may exist only in computer simulations." (Dixy Lee Ray and Lou Guzzo, 1993)[13]

Dixy Lee Ray is wrong here. Let us reiterate that global warming is undeniably real; worldwide thermometers have documented nearly a 1°F rise since the nineteenth century. Indeed, a consensus has formed in the climatological community that a "discernable signal" of anthropogenic warming is beginning to emerge from the "noise" of natural climatic variation, despite such confounding factors as the atmospheric burden of sulfate aerosols.[14] Put in plain language, the effects of human activities that are increasing the greenhouse effect and causing global warming are just now being sorted out from the variation arising from natural changes in climate and the regional cooling effects of some forms of air pollution.

The 1995 report of the scientific committee of the Intergovernmental Panel on Climate Change (IPCC) stated that the warming recorded over the past century, and especially in recent decades, "is unlikely to be entirely natural in origin. . . . the balance of evidence suggests that there is a discernible human influence on global climate."[15] The IPCC is a conservative organization that includes scientists and policy makers working on behalf of governments. Its reports are written and reviewed by hundreds of scientists from all over the world, including the cream of the climatological community, without significant interference from governments—which are then obliged to confront the results.

The IPCC's conclusion was based primarily on a new generation of computer simulations and more detailed comparisons of the results with actual temperature records. These showed much closer agreement between predictions and observations than did earlier ones, not just for global average temperatures but also for climatic patterns.[16] That 1995 proved to be the warmest year ever at Earth's surface—a return to warming after the temporary cooling effect of the 1991 Mount Pinatubo volcanic eruption—certainly reinforces the IPCC's conclusions.[17]

The evidence that the planet *is* warming is gradually becoming overwhelming. For example, surface temperature records, when corrected for urban "heat island" effects (weather stations have increasingly been measuring temperatures in areas artificially heated by buildings, etc.), show that the ten warmest years in the past 140 have all occurred since 1980. In descending order of the highest average temperature, they were 1995, 1990, 1991, 1988, 1987, 1981, 1983, 1989, 1980, and 1993. Warming would be expected to cause a reduction in the area covered by Arctic sea ice. Most recent satellite measurements show that shrinkage in sea ice area, detected earlier for the period 1978–1987,[18] accelerated between 1987 and 1994,[19] although the scientific community has yet to find unambiguous indications of an overall warming trend in the polar regions.[20]

Further evidence comes from recent studies of precipitation and temperature patterns. Computer models have suggested that an enhanced greenhouse effect will cause an increased proportion of precipitation to come in downpours and heavy snowfalls, which can lead to floods and major disruptions of agriculture. They also predict smaller changes in temperature from day to day and from week to week. Recent analyses show signs that just such patterns are emerging.[21]

Despite such mounting evidence, the brownlash still attempts to deny the reality of global warming. When the *New York Times* reported the IPCC's conclusion that "a pattern of climatic response to human activities is identifiable in the climatological record,"[22] Massachusetts Institute of Technology physicist Richard Lindzen provided a contrary view. He stated that there is "no basis" yet for saying that any human influence on the climate has been detected.[23] Of course, the majority of the experts could be mistaken, and it is perfectly proper—indeed, essential— for scientists to take contrary positions they feel are justified. But it is important to distinguish off-the-cuff opinion from in-depth analysis. To say there is "no basis" for the current conclusions of the climatological community when the IPCC's report has a lengthy chapter that details the considerable amount of new evidence is both incorrect and irresponsible.[24]

🔲 "The earth's atmosphere has actually *cooled* ... since 1979, according to highly accurate satellite-based atmospheric temperature measurements." (Ronald Bailey, 1995)[25] "[T]he atmosphere is not warming—nor has it warmed in the past 16 years, ever since precise global data have become available for the first time from weather satellites." (S. Fred Singer, 1995)[26]

The erroneous notion that Earth is *not* warming (and may actually be cooling), here promulgated by Ronald Bailey and S. Fred Singer, has been rejected by the most recent report of the IPCC.[27] It originated in 1993 when a *Washington Post* reporter misunderstood a scientific paper on satellite measurements and drew wrong conclusions about its implications for global warming.[28] Unfortunately, the error has been widely disseminated by the brownlash.[29] Written by journalist Boyce Rensberger, the *Post* article emphasized that surface and satellite temperature readings had shown opposite trends. In fact, the satellite data[30] were only marginally different from those gathered by the surface temperature network of thermometers and actually *validated* surface measurements that showed about a 1°F (0.5°C) warming over the past century.

The satellite measurements had two important drawbacks. First, the satellite record is too short to show the general century-long warming trend. It goes back only to 1979, and over only a fifteen-year record, "noise" (random variation) would be expected to obscure any long-term trend. Second, satellites measure not the surface temperature (which is the critical one for life) but some sort of weighted average of mid-atmospheric temperatures. The exact mix is a matter of some dispute, so Singer's use of the word "precise" in his statement is itself imprecise.

Notable, too, is that in the same fifteen-year period the surface temperature record also did not show any significant warming. At the start, 1979 was a very, very warm year. Then the 1980s were the hottest decade of the century.[31] Finally, an unpredictable event, the volcanic eruption of Mount Pinatubo, caused a transient cooling in 1992–1994, at the end of the sequence. A partial analogy would be if your friends denied that you had a fever if your temperature was 102°F one day, climbed to 103° for the next week, and then dropped back to 101° after two weeks.

The similarity in trends of mid-atmospheric (satellite) and surface measurements is revealed by the year-to-year temperature fluctuations seen in each record. In both cases, the fluctuations are generally much larger than the expected overall trend of slowly increasing global temperatures over many decades. Adjacent years may differ in average temperature by several tenths of a degree Celsius, whereas the average surface warming trend per decade over the past thirty years has been only about 0.1°C. (To make this difference clear, a person might well have gained about half a pound in weight each year for a decade, since many people slowly gain weight as they age. At the same time, his or her weight may change by several pounds during a single day or from week to week, fluctuating around a gradually rising average.) Between 1979 and 1994, when yearly fluctuations in both satellite and ground temperatures are compared, the ups and downs of the satellite data for atmospheric temperatures actually tracked those of the surface temperature data quite closely.[32]

As University of Michigan geophysicist Henry Pollack put it in a letter to the *Washington Post* (which the newspaper declined to publish) attempting to correct Rensberger's error, "the two data sets are remarkably coherent, each showing departures from the average consistent with each other. Far from telling conflicting stories, the data are telling the same story about temperature fluctuations in the 1980s, and should build rather than undermine confidence in the ground-based temperatures measured in the century preceding the satellite era."[33] This strongly suggests that had there been satellite coverage during the past century, it would show a warming trend similar to that detected by conventional surface temperature measurements. When the story that 1995 had been the hottest year in history broke, the *New York Times* reported: "In the past, skeptics about global warming have cited the satellite data. But Dr. [John R.] Christy [of the University of Alabama and coauthor of the original satellite paper] said that even the rate of warming measured from the satellites has begun to move into the range scientists expect to result from human-caused warming."[34] So the data cited by Singer as showing there has been no global warming actually supported, and still supports, the opposite view when a fair examination of the records is made.[35]

☐ **Since carbon dioxide is responsible for only 1 percent of the greenhouse effect, why should we care if its concentration doubles?[36]**

In fact, CO_2 accounts for some 10 to 25 percent of the natural greenhouse effect.[37] By itself, a doubling of CO_2 would warm Earth by less than 1°C, but therein lies the power of positive feedbacks. A 1°C warming would cause more water to evaporate from the oceans and thus contribute additional water vapor to the greenhouse effect, resulting in a final warming most climatologists project to be a little less than 2°C. But if the complicating ice and cloud feedbacks are added in, models suggest that anywhere from a 1.5° to 4.5°C warming would result from a doubling in CO_2 levels. Scientists cannot make more accurate predictions at the moment because of uncertainties surrounding the feedback processes, yet most think the upper limit represents ecological disaster. For example, 5°C is about the difference in global average temperature separating today's climate from the last ice age, when New York City was visited by a mile-thick glacier. That's why all sensible scientists think that a doubling of CO_2 is something to be very concerned about.

 It is unlikely that human beings can "really influence the *overall climate* . . . [because] there are one million tons of air per capita for every person [sic] on earth." (Dixy Lee Ray and Lou Guzzo, 1993)[38]

This statement is almost like saying, "I doubt that a few micrograms of bacteria could make a 200-pound man sick" or "I don't believe the tiny electric current from a battery could set off a hydrogen bomb." It certainly shows a profound lack of understanding of the workings of the physical world.

Human additions of CO_2 to the atmosphere have actually been gigantic. Over the past two centuries, human activities have raised the concentration of that one greenhouse gas some 30 percent above the level of the previous ten millennia. Annual additions from human activities now total about 25 billion metric tons of CO_2 (or about 7 billion metric tons of carbon, as scientists tracing the global carbon cycle commonly express it).[39]

 "The less than one-half degree of temperature rise, which is all that global warming enthusiasts can find, is probably part of the slow recovery from the Little Ice Age of 1450–1850." (Dixy Lee Ray and Lou Guzzo, 1993)[40]

The so-called little ice age did indeed end in the nineteenth century—precisely when greenhouse gases began to build up. Whether this is cause and effect or coincidence is debated. What is not debated is that the last half of the twentieth century is as warm as or warmer than any century at least since 1400; data from before then are too sparse to make comparisons.

> ☐ "The eruption of Mount Pinatubo in the Philippines may well prove to be a source of frustration to the purveyors of disastrous global warming predictions." (Ben Bolch and Harold Lyons, 1993)[41]

Contrary to this excerpt from a book published by the Cato Institute, the cooling caused by Mount Pinatubo's eruption turned out precisely as predicted by computer models. The cooling helped to validate the models and provided part of the rationale for the much stronger warnings in the 1996 IPCC report than in its 1990 assessment. Those same models show that just as a reduction of a few watts per square meter of surface heating beneath a stratospheric dust cloud can cause a significant drop in global temperature, a few watts of heating from additions to the atmospheric stock of greenhouse gases can cause significant global warming.

> ☐ Even if global warming occurs, "[a]ny necessary adjustments would be small relative to the adjustments that we make during the year to temperature differences where we reside and as we travel." (Julian Simon, 1994)[42] If the average mean temperature of the world were to rise a few degrees in the next century, "the only appropriate response would be to be sure that more and better air conditioning were available." (George Reisman, 1992)[43] "If postponing action for ten years means that in the long run average global temperature would be 0.2C [sic] higher than it otherwise would be, well that gives us plenty of time to change into a lighter shirt." (Wilfred Beckerman, 1995)[44]

The idea expressed here by economists Julian Simon, George Reisman, and Wilfred Beckerman, that the primary reason to be concerned over global warming is that our backyards will be a little hotter during the summer barbecue season, is as pervasive as it is wrong. The ability of individuals to deal with variations in temperature associated with daily or seasonal differences or during travel is totally irrelevant. Indeed, it has been called "the traveler fallacy."[45]

Warming could make the temperate zones less healthy places to live[46] and probably would make life uncomfortable for more people than it would make comfortable—since more people live in warm climates that are likely to get hotter than in cold climates likely to get warmer. A glimpse into the future was made possible on July 13, 1995, when Chicago experienced its hottest day in history, an event that resulted in more than 600 deaths—most of them among the elderly poor.[47]

More serious, though, is the potential for rapid climate change to disrupt a food production system that already is showing signs of stress. Other potential problems include sea-level rise and its associated impacts (coastal flooding, salinization of groundwater, etc.) as well as the possibility of more intense storms with their costly consequences. And natural ecosystems—our life-support systems—will have great difficulty adjusting to rapid climate change.[48] The trees of the Washington, D.C., area can't just fly up to Boston or put on a lighter shirt when the heat becomes too much for them.

> "The annual cost to the world as a whole of global warming associated with a doubling of CO_2 concentrations is likely to be almost negligible by comparison with the value of world output over the period in question." (Wilfred Beckerman, 1995)[49]

This statement probably ought to be modified to substitute "private costs" for "cost" since in this case economist Wilfred Beckerman is ignoring full social costs, which could include widespread starvation, epidemics, and millions of deaths and enormous destruction from severe storms. The most famous statement bearing on this issue was made by William Nordhaus, a serious, smart economist who expressed his own lack of concern about global warming's impact on agriculture and forestry because those economic sectors contribute only 3 percent to the U.S. gross national product (GNP).[50] Our friend John Holdren riposted, "Yeah, and the heart is only 3 percent of the body's weight, too." The response of an economist colleague of our daughter's, following a similar statement at a seminar by another distinguished economist, was simply, "What does he think we're going to eat?"

And that is precisely the point. There is considerable uncertainty about how much and what kind of climate change we are facing, and this uncertainty will probably persist for some time.[51] The critical point is that many analysts consider the world's food situation already pre-carious;[52] further destabilization by climate change would be a serious risk. We prefer to be conservative and favor the adoption of at least the most obvious "no regrets" strategies to slow down the flow of green-house gases into the atmosphere. One strategy, especially for the United States, would be to impose substantial increases in gasoline taxes (or, better yet, carbon taxes). Doing so would encourage energy efficiency, which would help reduce emissions of pollutants directly harmful to human and ecosystem health, as well as those that alter the climate, without imposing bothersome pollution-control regulations. More gen-erally, the public needs to understand that climate change could do enough damage to render economic forecasts wrong, whereas the costs of evasive action would slow expected economic growth only a little. But the amount of "insurance" to take out is an issue for social decision, not scientific determination.

□   *"It's getting colder in Greenland?* Isn't the Earth supposed to be **warming?" (Gregg Easterbrook, 1995)[53] "Though it surely was hot in North American [sic] in summer 1988, at the same time central Asia experienced a cold wave. The cold Asian area was roughly equiva-lent in size to the warm North American region." (Gregg Easter-brook, 1995)[54]**

These quotes from Gregg Easterbrook's *A Moment on the Earth* illustrate the common confusions between global and regional climates and be-tween climate and weather. "Global warming" refers to what may be happening to the average temperature of Earth (global), not the tem-perature of any particular area of its surface (regional). Global warming refers to trends perceptible on a time scale of decades or more (climate), not to atmospheric events in a specific area at a certain time (weather). It is quite possible for the average temperature of Earth to rise and for Greenland to cool simultaneously. And since climate always fluctuates, one would not expect weather in any region to show what scientists call "monotonic trends"—that is, an unbroken increase or decrease in rain-fall, temperature, or average wind velocity.

Moreover, several recent computer model runs that include both CO_2 and sulfate aerosols (particulate matter with both direct and indirect in-fluences on climate)[55] show Greenland cooling while the globe overall warms.[56] Indeed, computer models that take into account the regional scattering of radiation by sulfate aerosols (a cooling effect) predict patterns of temperature change closer to those actually observed than did previous models.[57]

☐ **Global warming can be ignored as a threat, since climatologists a couple of decades ago were concerned about *global cooling*.**[58]

This statement in various forms has been made by a legion of brownlash writers and speakers. "Climatologists" here refers primarily to Stephen Schneider, a careful, world-class atmospheric scientist who is anathema to the anti-scientific brownlash and to some of his colleagues who lack his wit and television presence. For more than two decades, Schneider has tried to explain the complexities of climate to intelligent laypeople in books, public addresses, and the print and electronic media. For his efforts, he has been criticized by journalists, including Michael Fumento: "It should be disconcerting to hear that Stephen Schneider wrote a book back in the 1970s warning that the world might be facing—and must take steps to prepare for—a 'Little Ice Age.' "[59]

Since Schneider has been such a repeated target of the brownlash, this attack is worth examining in some detail. By showing concern first for cooling and then later for warming, Schneider was doing exactly what good scientists should be doing—changing his views as new data are gathered to test hypotheses. George Will, in a 1992 *Washington Post* column, derided Schneider, who was then with the National Center for Atmospheric Research: "Today Schneider is hot about global warming; 16 years ago [1976] he was exercised about global cooling."[60]

Will's statement is, first of all, false. Schneider's cooling concerns were expressed in 1971.[61] In the early 1970s, the contribution of greenhouse gases other than CO_2, such as methane, nitrous oxide, and chlorofluorocarbons, had not been recognized. As a result, the climatological community was more concerned about possible cooling of the planet by the particulate pollution humanity was injecting into the atmosphere than about CO_2-induced warming. But by the mid-1970s, the role of other greenhouse gases was just being assessed. Schneider reported this in his 1976 book (co-authored with Lynn Mesirow), *The Genesis Strategy: Climate and Global Survival*.[62] The section referred to by Fumento (and the source of many citations of Schneider's "wrong predictions") actually deals primarily with climatic variability and Schneider's worries (which are central to the book) about the impact of climate change on food production. His concern was the danger posed to agriculture and natural ecosystems of a rapid *rate* of climate change—in any direction.

Schneider wrote: "I have cited many examples of climatic variability and repeated warnings of several well-known climatologists that a cooling trend has set in—perhaps one akin to the Little Ice Age—and that climatic variability, which is the bane of reliable food production, can be expected to increase along with the cooling."[63] But with regard to human impacts on climate, early in *The Genesis Strategy* Schneider wrote: "A consensus among scientists today would hold that a *global* increase in atmospheric aerosols would probably result in the cooling of the climate; however a smaller but growing fraction of the current evidence suggests that [a global aerosol increase] may have a warming effect. A few climatologists believe that the 0.5°C warming observed in the first half of this century may have resulted in part from the increase of CO_2 in the atmosphere and in part from the relative absence of aerosols due to little volcanic activity."[64] His basic conclusion: "If concentrations of CO_2, and perhaps of aerosols, continue to increase, *demonstrable* climatic changes could occur by the end of this century."[65] This is precisely what the IPCC reported in 1996—a "discernable" signal from CO_2 and aerosols combined.[66] Schneider was as right as it was possible to be given all the unknowns in the 1970s.

The ability of human activities to increase greenhouse gases other than carbon dioxide (methane, chlorofluorocarbons, nitrous oxide) and thus trap a significant amount of the sun's energy near Earth's surface was uncovered several years after Schneider published an article on aerosol cooling,[67] and what was known by the mid-1970s was reported in *The Genesis Strategy*. With the discovery of the significance of the other gases, the concerns of the climatological community (including Schneider) began to shift toward warming, where they are focused today.[68] Schneider would have been an irresponsible scientist indeed had he not revised his opinion in the late 1970s as new evidence was found. And aerosols now have come back into the picture as a regional problem—as Schneider suggested in 1976—and provided a missing factor that has helped to reconcile modeling results with observed climate changes.

Will's confusion in this case rests on his misunderstanding of science. As we pointed out in chapter 3, science never "proves" anything. Scientists can't even be certain that the second law of thermodynamics (which states that all physical processes lead to a decrease in the availability of the energy involved) is correct. But because all physical processes observed on this planet are consistent with the second law and no exception has ever been shown, scientists ordinarily *act* as though it were certain. In matters like climate change, where the problem is in predicting the behavior of extremely complex systems, scientists know better than to project particular outcomes as absolutely certain.

The best science can do in situations in which uncertainties are large is give an estimate of the odds of certain outcomes, and those odds often must be based on combinations of observation, theory, computer modeling, and, yes, informed intuition.

"Paul Ehrlich [has made] incredible claims in connection with the 'greenhouse effect.' . . . In the first wave of ecological hysteria, this 'scientist' declared: 'At the moment we cannot predict what the overall climatic results will be of our using the atmosphere as a garbage dump. We do know that very small changes in either direction in the average temperature of the Earth could be very serious. With a few degrees of cooling, a new ice age might be upon us, with rapid and drastic effects on the agricultural productivity of the temperate regions. With a few degrees of heating, the polar ice caps would melt, perhaps raising sea levels 250 feet. Gondola to the Empire State Building, anyone?' " (George Reisman, 1992)[69]

George Reisman, Professor of Economics at Pepperdine University's School of Business and Management, attacked this passage in *The Population Bomb* twenty-four years after the *Bomb* was published, yet the statement remains correct except for the reference to sea-level rise. Although the amount of sea-level rise that Paul indicated so long ago— 250 feet—remains essentially correct,[70] most scientists now think such a total meltdown, which would liquefy the Antarctic and Greenland ice caps as well as all smaller glaciers, would likely take thousands of years and would happen only if warming were sustained at a much greater level than 5°C.[71]

Still, even a few feet of sea-level rise would constitute a vast disaster, costing many hundreds of billions of dollars through flooding of cities, destruction of coastal wetlands essential to oceanic fisheries, salinization

of aquifers, aggravation of shoreline erosion, and increased vulnerability to storm damage.[72] Current estimates actually project a rise of somewhere between 10 centimeters and 1.2 meters (4 inches to 4 feet) by the
end of the next century, rising to at least a meter (3.3 feet) in the twenty-
second century.[73] A 1-meter rise would, given the *present* population
size and distribution, increase the number of people exposed to coastal
storm surges each year from 46 million to 118 million. Land losses in
deltas and small island nations would be substantial: 1 percent of Egypt
would be submerged, including a substantial proportion of its best farmland; 6 percent of the Netherlands would be under water, as would 17
percent of Bangladesh. Only about 20 percent of the Marshall Islands
would remain above water.[74] The Maldives would disappear.

□   **If global warming *is* occurring, there's probably not much we can
    do about it anyway.**

We have long agreed with Steve Schneider's basic contention that humanity should take steps to protect its food supply from rapid climate
change—natural or anthropogenic. Many potential steps, such as
putting much more effort into maintenance of the genetic diversity of
crops and conserving the genetic resources that exist in crop relatives,
increasing the amount of food that can be stored as insurance against
crop failures, and educating the public about how agricultural systems
work and the potential impacts on them of climate change, would be
beneficial regardless of the outcome of the global climate change debate. Reducing the use of fossil fuels by encouraging conservation and
efficiency is another "no regrets" strategy—and one that could help forestall the most serious potential damage if the majority of the climatological community is correct.

  The possibility exists, of course (however unlikely), that all the feedbacks will be strongly favorable to humanity and our descendants will
not suffer, or might even gain, from global climate change. There is,
however, roughly an equal chance the feedbacks will all go in the
"wrong" direction and humanity will face a climatic catastrophe—widespread crop failures, seaside cities flooded, island nations disappearing,
tropical diseases invading previously temperate areas, colossal damage
and loss of life from megastorms, and the like. We believe society would
be wise to take out insurance against such contingencies. The recom-

mendations of Richard Lindzen and other greenhouse contrarians like Patrick Michaels and Fred Singer to follow a "what, me-worry?" strategy are grounded in disagreement with what the bulk of the scientific community believes. Such a posture strikes us as a very dangerous gamble and thus a poor basis for public policy.

Ozone Myths

Misunderstandings about the atmosphere are not confined to global warming. A rich supply of misconceptions also exists concerning ozone depletion, another problem of great concern to the scientific community. The discovery that freons, or chlorofluorocarbons (CFCs), a class of synthetic chemicals containing chlorine, could destroy the ozone shield that protects life on land was one of the most unpleasant scientific surprises of all time.[75] When first synthesized in the early 1930s, freons were heralded as one of the great inventions of the chemical industry—stable, non-toxic compounds that were ideal replacements for the toxic cooling agents then used in refrigerators.

One source of confusion is that ozone (a molecule consisting of three oxygen atoms) occurs in two different places in the atmosphere. The primary shield protecting life against a lethal ultraviolet component of solar radiation is a thin layer of ozone in the stratosphere—the upper part of the atmosphere extending from roughly 13 to 50 kilometers (8–30 miles) above Earth's surface. The ozone layer is formed by the action of ultraviolet light on oxygen molecules. But ozone also exists nearer the surface—that is, in the troposphere (0–13 kilometers, or up to 8 miles, above Earth's surface)—where it is formed primarily by ultraviolet light acting on atmospheric pollutants emitted by transport and industry. Tropospheric ozone in high concentrations can damage crops, forests, and human health. Thus ozone both helps and hinders the human enterprise, depending on its altitude.[76]

The leading culprits in stratospheric ozone depletion are the CFCs, which, though being phased out, are still used in refrigeration and air-conditioning units and in a variety of industrial applications, and compounds called halons. Halons are human-made compounds containing bromine (an element in the same group as chlorine) that are used in fire extinguishers and to fumigate soil and stored grain. Both CFCs and halons are chemically inert in the troposphere, but they eventually diffuse upward into the stratosphere, where ultraviolet radiation decomposes them. Their breakdown releases chlorine and bromine, which in turn catalyze the destruction of ozone, allowing more ultraviolet radiation to reach Earth's surface. Synthetic compounds releasing chlorine and bromine were and are the main threat to the stratospheric ozone layer;[77] a strong scientific consensus has formed about the danger posed by them.[78]

And while many people may associate ozone depletion only with a need for more sunscreen, the phenomenon is in fact profoundly dangerous. Life was able to leave the oceans and colonize land some 450 million years ago, only after a sufficiently protective ozone layer had been formed as oxygen accumulated in the atmosphere from the activities of photosynthetic organisms in the oceans.[79] The land surface had previously been bathed in lethal ultraviolet radiation. Substantial further depletion of the ozone layer today could be catastrophic for terrestrial life.

Despite such high stakes and a consensus among scientists about anthropogenic ozone depletion, the brownlash has persisted in claiming that ozone depletion is not a problem—that humanity is not threatening the crucial ozone shield.

> "The regular, annual ozone 'hole' that appears over Antarctica was first measured and described in 1956–57, long before CFCs were in common use." (Dixy Lee Ray and Lou Guzzo, 1993)[80]

This statement is blatantly incorrect; the ozone hole was not detected until more than two decades later. Sherwood Rowland, who, with Mario Molina, was codiscoverer of the chemistry of ozone depletion (for which they shared with Paul Crutzen the 1995 Nobel Prize in chemistry),[81] put it succinctly in his presidential address in 1993 to the American Association for the Advancement of Science (AAAS):[82] "[V]ery large losses of ozone over Antarctica during October—now exceeding 60% each Southern Hemisphere spring—first became noticeable around 1980 in measurements conducted continually since 1956 and became public knowledge in 1985." The ozone hole became public knowledge because of the work of British scientist Joe Farman and his colleagues in the British Antarctic Survey. Using well-established instruments, they documented the thinning of the ozone shield over Halley Bay and Argentine Island.[83] This thinning had previously been missed by a NASA satellite, due to a series of errors in computer programming and data analysis.[84]

☐ "Two French scientists recently republished data showing pronounced ozone decreases . . . during the Antarctic spring in 1958. These measurements were taken years before CFCs could have caused any such decline." (Ronald Bailey, 1993)[85]

This statement by Ronald Bailey illustrates the perils of quoting articles from scientific literature that one thinks pertinent but doesn't understand. It also emphasizes the importance of having conclusions reviewed by scientists competent in the relevant area. Mistakes, misinterpretations, and irrelevancies do appear in the scientific literature, and even scientists in related disciplines often need the help of specialists to evaluate a paper properly.

It turns out that the data referred to by the French do show ozone decreases, but they were obtained with unreliable instruments. Still, the issue raised by the French paper in question[86] is a complex one, and when we saw it cited in Ronald Bailey's book, we asked Sherry Rowland about it. According to Rowland,[87] the French participated in the International Geophysical Year and attempted to measure ozone in the Antarctic from their station at Dumont d'Urville. The state of the art of ozone measurement involved two competing instruments—the Dobson instrument (the kind used by Joe Farman's team) and another identified as a "filter instrument," of which one was used by the French and another by the Soviets. Both types measure ozone by comparing the ratio of two types of ultraviolet radiation from the sun: ultraviolet-A (UV-A), which essentially is not absorbed by ozone, and ultraviolet-B (UV-B), which is partially absorbed. Thus the UV-B/UV-A ratio decreases as the amount of ozone between the instrument and the sun increases. The instruments, however, must be carefully calibrated according to the sun's position, since obviously, when the sun is very low on the horizon, its radiation travels a much longer path through the atmosphere (and through any gas in the atmosphere) than when it is higher in the sky. In Antarctica, so near the South Pole, the sun is never very high in the sky.

The calibrations could not be done properly with the filter instruments, which proved to be quite useless under Antarctic conditions. The French apparently never used their instrument again. The Soviets, however, established a network of filter instruments across the entire Soviet Union, and they had to replace them because they did not work well at any latitude. So the basis of the fable represented by the quoted excerpt is poor instrumentation.[88] (For further details on the science of this point, see the notes at the end of the book.)

☐   **Chlorofluorocarbons (CFCs) can't rise into the stratosphere and deplete ozone.** "CFCs are heavy, complex molecules. . . . It is especially difficult to see how they can rise as high as 30 km, where the greatest concentration of ozone is located." (Rogelio Maduro, 1989)[89] "How does CFC rise when its molecules are four to eight times heavier than air?" (Dixy Lee Ray and Lou Guzzo, 1993)[90] "If CFCs are responsible for the destruction of the ozone layer, why has their presence never been detected in the stratosphere?" (R. Bennett, 1993)[91]

This array of statements reveals outrageous misconceptions about the dynamics of the atmosphere. Gases of the atmosphere are not layered like a lasagne. If they were, the lowest few feet of atmosphere would consist of krypton, ozone, nitrous oxide, carbon dioxide, and argon. Above that would be a thick layer of pure oxygen, and above that an even thicker layer of pure nitrogen followed by water vapor, methane, neon, helium, and hydrogen. The lack of a hydrological cycle alone would preclude the existence of any life on land. Earth can sustain life because to an altitude far above the ozone layer, the atmosphere undergoes dynamic mixing, dominated by motions of large air masses, which thoroughly mixes light and heavy gas molecules.[92]

Because of this mixing, CFCs have been detected in, as Rowland put it, "literally thousands of stratospheric air samples by dozens of research groups all over the world."[93] Thus the brownlash notion that CFC molecules are simply too heavy to rise into the stratosphere has no basis in reality. In fact, the only significant mechanism for cleansing the atmosphere of CFCs is decomposition by ultraviolet light in the stratosphere—with associated ozone depletion.

☐   **Chlorofluorocarbons are not likely to be the source of the chlorine that is depleting the ozone layer because volcanoes are a much more prolific source of chlorine.** "Mount Erebus [in Antarctica] . . .

pumps out 50 times more chlorine annually than an entire year's production of CFCs." (Dixy Lee Ray and Lou Guzzo, 1993)[94] "Conclusion: mankind can't possibly equal the output of even one eruption from Pinatubo, much less a billion years' worth, so how can we destroy ozone?" (Rush Limbaugh, 1992)[95]

Mount Erebus *does* pump out fifty times more chlorine per year than humanity adds in CFCs. Unfortunately, the statement is irrelevant to depletion of the ozone layer. Good scientists have long carefully considered volcanoes, which emit hydrogen chloride (HCl), as sources of stratospheric chlorine. In 1980, a paper in *Science* by David Johnston of the U.S. Geological Survey raised the issue to some prominence, suggesting that "volcanic sources of stratospheric chlorine may be significant in comparison with anthropogenic sources."[96] Following publication of his paper, a series of investigations ruled out volcanic eruptions as the chief source of stratospheric chlorine.[97] It is likely that much of the HCl released by volcanoes is dissolved in the abundant steam they also emit and thus is quickly rained out. This is not surprising; before Johnston's paper appeared, atmospheric scientists knew that HCl is water soluble and rains out. But CFCs are insoluble. As Rowland said in his AAAS presidential address: "The working atmospheric science community has . . . rejected volcanoes as an important source of chlorine (and fluorine) for the stratosphere, at least for the past 15 years during which significant ozone depletion has been observed."[98] Nonetheless, perennial contrarian Fred Singer wrote in the *National Review* in 1989, "[E]vidence is firming up that volcanoes . . . contribute substantially to stratospheric chlorine, and thus dilute the effects of CFCs."[99] It wasn't until four years later that he finally recanted this assertion in a statement to *Science* magazine.[100]

In 1990, Dixy Lee Ray and her assistant Lou Guzzo declared in *Trashing the Planet:* "[T]he eruption of Mount St. Augustine (Alaska) in 1976 injected 289 billion kilograms of hydrochloric acid directly into the stratosphere. That amount is 570 times the total world production of chlorine and fluorocarbon compounds in the year 1975. . . . So much is known."[101] Ray and Guzzo confused a *hypothesis* about the results of a gigantic eruption 700,000 years ago (which left the Long Valley crater in California) with measurement of a 1976 event. Rowland referred to Ray's gaffe in his AAAS presidential address:

Incidentally those same authors have identified as one of the major contributing factors to scientific misinformation the unwillingness of respected scientists to speak out on such subjects through their professional organizations.[102] I am pleased to attempt the correction of a major source of such misinformation, although it will be difficult for my message to catch up with their misstatements of the atmospheric facts. Their erroneous conclusions about the stratospheric importance of volcanic chlorine [are] now being widely quoted in other magazine articles and books, including one of the current national best sellers. . . . [A] plausible, but fallible, hypothesis subsequently disproved by stratospheric observation has been elevated . . . into purported fact and then into gross exaggeration of the faulty conclusion."[103]

It is instructive to note that the scientific community did not criticize David Johnston for having drawn a tentative conclusion about volcanoes that turned out to be wrong after the gathering of further data. Johnston was doing exactly what good scientists are expected to do—make the best possible interpretation on the basis of available information.

What amounts to the final word on the issue of the source of stratospheric chlorine appeared in an article in *Nature* magazine as this book goes to press.[104] The article's abstract tells the story very well:

Here we report a four-year global time series of satellite observations of hydrogen chloride (HCl) and hydrogen fluoride (Hf) in the stratosphere, which shows conclusively that chlorofluorocarbon releases—rather than other anthropogenic or natural emissions—are responsible for the recent global increases in stratospheric chlorine concentrations. Moreover, all but a few per cent of observed stratospheric chlorine amounts can be accounted for by known natural and anthropogenic tropospheric emissions. Altogether, these results implicate the chlorofluorocarbons beyond reasonable doubt as dominating ozone depletion in the lower stratosphere.

"The doubled [UV-B] radiation [over the Antarctic] worked out to only about the natural increase a person would experience by traveling south from Chicago to New Orleans." (Gregg Easterbrook, 1995)[105] The increase in ground-level UV-B near Cape Horn "works

out to the natural UV-B increase a person would experience by moving north, the warm direction of the southern hemisphere, from Cape Horn to Buenos Aires." (Gregg Easterbrook, 1995)[106]

Gregg Easterbrook here perpetuates the traveler fallacy noted earlier, one endemic to the brownlash. The critical question is how ecosystems would react if they were suddenly transported from the vicinity of Cape Horn to that of Buenos Aires. There is also little doubt (as Easterbrook recognizes)[107] that any long-term increase in exposure to ultraviolet radiation, whether by a change in geographical location to where the sun is more directly overhead or by a thinning of the ozone shield, increases a person's risk of developing skin cancer.[108]

☐ "[I]f there were in fact some reduction in the ozone layer, the appropriate response, to avoid the additional cases of skin cancer that would allegedly occur from exposure, to more intense sunlight, would be to be sure that there were more sunglasses, hats, and suntan lotion available. . . . It would *not* be to seek to throttle and destroy industrial civilization." (George Reisman, 1992)[109]

What an appallingly limited and shortsighted understanding of the benefits of the ozone layer! The direct health effects of increased ozone depletion are potentially very serious—increased rates of skin cancer (possibly including lethal melanomas) and possible disruption of the immune system. These direct effects, of course, could be partially avoided by increased use of hats, sunglasses, and sunscreen, but rubbing sunscreen lotions on Earth's plants and animals would be required as well, since the most important threat from ozone depletion is to natural and agricultural ecosystems.[110] Even small increases of UV-B radiation could significantly reduce yields of major crops. Little is known yet of specific impacts of UV-B exposure on other organisms, but significant effects have been noted in a wide variety of plants, animals, and microorganisms.[111]

Not all attempts to minimize the role of CFCs in thinning the ozone layer have been as transparent as Reisman's statement. A more subtle attack was launched by a leading brownlash writer, the late political scientist Aaron Wildavsky, and his student Robert Rye,[112] who jointly concluded: "[I]f someday we find out that CFCs really are not all that bad, we will look back and wonder why we put ourselves through the pain of banning them. . . . Ozone depletion should be effectively monitored; but it does not deserve to be ranked as a global disaster toward whose alleviation huge resources should be devoted."[113]

Needless to say, the banning of CFCs never had the slightest chance of "throttling," let alone "destroying," industrial civilization, and "huge resources" have not been devoted to solving the problem of ozone thinning. Indeed, most of the chemical companies most affected by the phaseout of CFCs are thriving by making CFC substitutes.[114] We will return to the issue of the environment and capitalism in chapter 10.

The Wildavsky-Rye effort can best be summarized as a case of complex obfuscation—the mistakes are too numerous and too subtle to be sorted out by anyone but an expert. Sherry Rowland was kind enough to send us some comments on its errors, some of which are quoted in the notes.[115] Anyone inclined to read Wildavsky and Rye and then read Rowland's comments will understand how difficult it can be for those without technical training to deal with such obfuscation.

Acid rain is only a minor environmental problem.

Complex confusion has also frequently appeared on the subject of acid precipitation and acid dry deposition, usually collectively referred to simply as "acid rain."

As any tropical fish enthusiast who has tried to breed neon tetras in alkaline water or black mollies in acidic water knows, organisms are sensitive to the level of acidity or alkalinity (pH) of their environments. So are the ecosystems that support our economy. Increasing the acidity of soils, for example, can cause changes that damage the roots of plants; acidification of lakes and streams can wipe out valuable fish species such as trout and salmon and starve predators dependent on fishes,[116] and breeding bird populations may be injured by eggshell thinning traceable to acid deposition.[117] In addition, evidence is accumulating that acidification of forests retards the critical process of nutrient cycling and annual resupply of nutrients by macroinvertebrates (especially earthworms).[118] The scientific community is properly concerned about the long-term effects on ecosystems—especially forests—from precipitation containing sulfuric and nitric acids. The acid precipitation is a result of atmospheric releases of oxides of sulfur and nitrogen from power plants, automobile exhaust, and the burning of grasslands, savannas, and forests.[119] Acid precipitation doubtless combines with other anthropogenic stresses to disrupt the functioning of our life-support systems.[120]

Because attempts to control acid rain have direct consequences for industry, brownlash writers frequently try to minimize the issue.[121] Discussing the Adirondack Mountains, Wildavsky and Rye state that "90 percent of all acid lakes in that region were acidic before the industrial revolution. Thus most of the acidity in that region is not the result of human activities."[122] The paper they cite to support their assertion, however, states that only seven out of the forty-eight Adirondack lakes studied were acidified before industrialization[123]—15 percent rather than the misreported 90 percent! One of the saddest things about the Wildavsky book (which contains the chapters coauthored by Wildavsky and Rye) is that it was issued by Harvard University Press, a publisher usually thought to have high standards. The press knew, as Wildavsky states in his introduction,[124] that the book was written largely by undergraduate and graduate students in political science who had little or no scientific background or expertise on the issues covered, yet there is no evidence that it was technically reviewed.

Other attempts to minimize the importance of acid rain have been even more ridiculous. One writer for *Fortune* magazine went so far as to try to implicate bird droppings as a contributor to acidity in lakes![125] Of course, recently acidified lakes have been made more acid primarily by sulfuric and nitric acids, not by the readily decomposed *uric* acid found in bird droppings. Furthermore, bird populations have not exploded in the past half-century as the lakes acidified, while sulfur dioxide and nitrogen oxide emissions have. Nor do birds seem to be defecating more or concentrating their populations around the acidified lakes in the Adirondacks.

Despite the scientific consensus that acid rain was and is a serious problem,[126] confusion surrounds the issue in part because it was the subject of a gigantic, somewhat politicized, and readily misrepresented government study, the National Acid Precipitation Assessment Program (NAPAP).[127] The assessment was a mixed bag.[128] Although it contributed some important research to scientists' understanding of acid rain, it also produced some reports from which misleading conclusions can be drawn.[129] For example, NAPAP is often erroneously quoted as showing acid rain not to be a problem, although it also provides evidence that acid rain poses a very serious threat to soils and forests, as well as to human health.

In 1990, shortly before the final NAPAP report was released but after preliminary drafts had circulated widely on Capitol Hill, Congress passed amendments to the Clean Air Act that included provisions designed to control acid rain. Ecologist Gene Likens of the Institute of Ecosystem Studies, one of the leading scientific authorities on the problem, has calculated what will happen even under the new provisions. By the year 2000 at Hubbard Brook, the New Hampshire site of his classic ecosystem studies with F. H. Bormann, "the estimated sulfur loading from the atmosphere will still be 2.7–3.3 times higher than values recommended for protection of sensitive forest and associated aquatic ecosystems like those found at Hubbard Brook."[130] The recommended levels are those that "will not cause chemical changes leading to *long-term* harmful effects on essential ecosystem properties"[131] (our emphasis).

In other words, the 1990 amendments to the Clean Air Act will help improve the health of ecosystems, but they will not be sufficient to achieve the desired goal of ensuring the long-term viability of the forest ecosystems needed to support the human enterprise. Hubbard Brook is a surrogate for significant portions of the land surface of the planet, especially Europe, eastern North America, and parts of southern China, all of which are now being subjected to acidification.[132]

> **"With regard to [climate affecting pH readings] . . . it may be that the more alkaline results reported by Coghill and Likens for the northeastern United States in the 1950s were related to the drought conditions that prevailed during those years. By contrast the 1960s were rainy." (Dixy Lee Ray and Lou Guzzo, 1990)[133]**

This statement shows a deplorable carelessness with facts. Actually, the 1960s were relatively dry; 1963–1965 were severe drought years, with 1964–1965 the driest year on record at the Hubbard Brook Experimental Forest, where the work was done.[134]

Ray spends several pages arguing that "an indisputable trend toward higher acidity in the rainfall of the northeastern United States" does not exist.[135] Part of her evidence, however, rests on a misinterpretation of data from studies of the Global Precipitation Chemistry Project (which perhaps she did not realize was set up by Gene Likens, whom she attacked earlier). That project, in fact, supported the view that acid rain was connected to the growth of industrial production. For example, the project showed that the components that make rain acidic at a remote site in northern Australia averaged "about an order of magnitude lower than those in eastern North America."[136]

In general, there is growing evidence that forests are in trouble from overcutting (primarily in tropical and boreal forests)[137] and from a combination of environmental stresses, one of which is acid rain. Death rates in trees in midwestern U.S. forests showed a dramatic rise during the 1980s. This, and similar problems in European forests, appears to be due to interactions of air pollution effects (acid rain and excess deposition of nitrogen are altering soil chemistry and water quality, and high ozone concentrations at ground level are damaging foliage) with natural stresses, such as insect attacks, diseases, and drought.[138]

Leaching of the critical nutrient calcium from forest soils in the eastern United States is occurring at an unsustainable rate.[139] That loss, which appears to be caused by a combination of short-rotation harvesting of the forests and acid precipitation,[140] could result in a roughly 50 percent drop in both calcium and forest biomass (timber yield) in about 120 years.[141]

The interaction between atmospheric pollution and ecosystem function was well summarized in 1989 by Orie L. Loucks, Ohio Eminent Scholar of Applied Ecosystem Studies and professor of zoology at Miami University in Ohio:

> While uncertainty remains regarding many details of productivity loss from regional air pollutants or of CO_2 enhancement, one conclusion is clear: . . . the destabilizing factors are entirely attributable to human activities. The most serious impacts appear to derive from an assumption that the atmosphere is a global "commons" to be used as a sink, when in fact it is the living system at the surface of the Earth that is presently functioning as a sink.[142]

We ourselves are part of that "sink," and its continued proper functioning is crucial to the persistence of civilization.

This brings us to the close of a far from exhaustive tour of how the brownlash has tried to convince the public that there is no need to try to rein in the gigantic experiments *Homo sapiens* is running on Earth's atmosphere and itself. It is noteworthy that in 1995 the attacks of the brownlash on the science surrounding ozone depletion had been sufficiently successful that a concerted effort was made in the United States Congress to pass legislation postponing the phaseout of production and sale of CFCs.[143] We hope we have provided enough of a scientific framework to counterbalance the fables that have no basis in reality yet are having a malign influence on public policy in an area of crucial importance.

CHAPTER 9

Fables about
Toxic Substances

☐

EVALUATING THE CONSEQUENCES of releasing toxic substances into the environment is one of the most difficult tasks facing people in general and environmental scientists in particular. Not only are cause-and-effect relationships difficult to establish, but the flood of chemicals entering the environment also remains largely invisible and therefore is all too easily overlooked. Human beings are "sight animals"; our vision overwhelms the other senses in informing us about our surroundings. But much of the living world is tuned in to a vivid, complex environment in which most perception takes place through the detection of chemicals. That environment is almost as unknown to human beings as would be the lively electromagnetic environment full of news, gossip, music, drama, and sports to a hermit lacking a radio or television receiver. If people were equipped with "chemical receivers" much more sensitive than human noses and tongues, we would be stunned to discover how ubiquitous toxic substances have become as the result of an annual release into our environment of millions of tons of synthetic chemical compounds.

Despite this handicap, environmental science has uncovered enough information about the invisible chemical world to raise warning flags.

Direct impacts on human health are known for many toxins, such as lead, asbestos, some pesticides, and various components of air pollution. And numerous synthetic chemicals that have been added to food and other consumer products, or have been purposely released into the environment (insecticides, fungicides, etc.), are suspected of being carcinogenic (causing cancer) or teratogenic (causing birth defects) or both.[1] Scientists know that people may be exposed to toxic substances in several ways: inhaled with air, ingested with food or water, or absorbed through the skin. In some cases, exposure occurs because a substance is widely dispersed in the environment, as are air pollutants and pesticides, and preventing exposure is virtually impossible. In others, exposure occurs in conjunction with certain activities, such as using household pesticides or cleaning compounds, or through occupational exposure.

Cancer is very frightening to all of us, and for good reason; it is the second leading cause of death in the United States, exceeded only by cardiovascular disease, and a major one in most other developed nations as well. The proportion of those cancers that result from exposure to toxic substances produced by industrial society is unknown and may never be measurable, but it probably is no more than a third. (Smoking, by far the leading cause of cancer, alone accounts for nearly a third of all diagnosed cancers in the United States.) Unfortunately, cancers don't carry labels saying "I was caused by exposure to dioxin in 1973" or "by a sunburn in 1967." Moreover, because cancer mostly strikes older people, curing all cancers would extend the life expectancy of the average American by only a little more than three years.[2]

But human deaths and illness from cancer are by no means the only consequences of exposure to toxic substances. Numerous other problems have been traced to such exposures, from black lung disease in coal miners to chloracne and birth defects from dioxin and subtle impairment of children's brain development and function from lead. Overall, environmental toxins can cause a wide range of health effects, including hypertension, impairment of immune function, reduced fertility, birth defects, skin lesions, and neurological disorders.[3] Yet people seldom consider such hazards when buying new clothes, which may be treated with formaldehyde to reduce wrinkling, when storing food in certain types of plastic, or when sitting in a brand-new car with the windows rolled up. The growing impacts of toxins on human health are underscored by the emergence of a new and rapidly growing field of environmental medicine.

Thousands of new chemicals are introduced by industry every year in the United States and other developed nations. So, not surprisingly, pinning down the effects of any particular compound is extraordinarily difficult. Not only will individuals respond differently to a given substance, but often they are also exposed to more than one at a time, thus complicating the diagnosis. Apart from pesticides, medicines, and substances added to foods, new chemicals are not carefully tested or regulated. The Environmental Protection Agency (EPA) may require testing of a new compound if it has some reason to suspect toxicity (such as its being chemically similar to a known toxin), but most are not subjected to regulatory action.

Yet toxic substances, frightening as they might be, are generally viewed as threats to individuals, not to societies. They have not ordinarily been seen as posing the same sort of threat to the future of humanity as do essentially irreversible environmental impacts such as land degradation, loss of biodiversity, and climate change, each of which could jeopardize the continuance of civilization itself. Cancer deaths and disabilities from toxins surely are tragedies for individuals and families; collapses of agricultural and natural ecosystems could be tragic for entire societies.

In recent years, that assessment has been changing as scientists have learned more and more about the effects of various substances both on human health and on the environment.[4] Investigations of toxicity continue to indicate that most chemicals are more toxic than originally thought; none has been found to be less so.[5] A fair amount of what has been learned about toxicity and its implications for human well-being was first discovered through studies of effects on wildlife. There is no question that globally distributed toxins (for instance, some chlorinated hydrocarbons such as DDT breakdown products, endosulfan, and PCBs)[6] can kill or injure many kinds of wildlife and seriously disrupt natural ecosystems.[7]

Now a growing body of evidence indicates that some synthetic chemicals have molecular structures similar to naturally occurring hormones and may affect—in ways both subtle and insidious—normal development in both animals and human beings.[8] As discussed in greater detail later, these hormone-mimicking chemicals may pose a potentially gigantic threat to humanity, both directly and indirectly. The direct threats are in causing or exacerbating reproductive disorders, including infertility, and triggering behavioral changes in some people. Indirectly, since these chemicals are known to interfere with behavior and reproduction of many kinds of animals, significant disruption of ecosystem services could result.

Why, if toxic synthetic chemicals are so dangerous to human beings, does our industrial society continue to churn out billions of pounds of them each year? There are several reasons. First, toxicology, the branch of science devoted to studying toxic chemicals and their impacts on the living world, is extremely complex.[9] Not all chemicals are harmful by any means, and many, even though toxic under some circumstances, provide significant benefits. Establishing harmfulness may take years of research involving both laboratory models and actual systems, a far from easy process for any single compound, let alone thousands. When the possible harmful interactions between two or more different chemicals are considered, the uncertainties about risks escalate enormously.

Risk assessment, an integral part of toxicity studies, is itself a complex science with a large personal component.[10] Scientists generally view risks in statistical terms from a long-term, epidemiological perspective, asking questions such as, how many people in an exposed population are likely to have which adverse effects within X years from chemical Y? But the public mostly sees the risks from an individual's point of view. For instance, most people view risks taken voluntarily (such as smoking or driving a car) very differently from those imposed involuntarily (exposure to environmental toxins), especially if no particular benefit is associated with them. This difference is at the heart of many disputes about risk.

Finally, the financial stakes are huge for some powerful industries, including petrochemical, pulp and paper, and tobacco companies. Not coincidentally, toxic chemicals and regulations to control them are frequent targets of campaigns of misinformation. In some cases, major national controversies have raged over hazardous chemicals. A case in point is that of Alar. No dispute over a toxic substance in recent memory has been the subject of so much bombast and erroneous information as the great Alar flap of 1989. It is a favorite target of the brownlash and has been featured in recent books by Ronald Bailey, Michael

Fumento, Ben Bolch and Harold Lyons, and Dixy Lee Ray, among others. As an illustration of how complex science-society interactions can be, and how anti-science writings can influence even the perceptions of scientists, the Alar story deserves examination in some detail.

□ "Science by press release has also been used to publicize lesser 'crises' such as the carefully choreographed Alar scare in which the Natural Resources Defense Council used a public relations firm to promote the bogus 'story' of poisoned apples to CBS's *60 Minutes*." (Ronald Bailey, 1993)[11] "This was the great apple scare of 1989, the result of one of the slickest, most cynical fear campaigns in recent American history." (Michael Fumento, 1993)[12] "The coverage of this 'story' was professionally orchestrated by the Fenton Communications Company, which had been retained for this purpose by the Natural Resources Defense Council (NRDC), an activist organization noted more for the excellence of its lawyers than for the quality of its science." (Ben Bolch and Harold Lyons, 1993)[13]

These quotes are a sample of the brownlash view of the Alar controversy. The Alar story is instructive not because of the fundamental seriousness of the problem but for the way it has been treated by the brownlash. One especially ironic aspect is the professed outrage of brownlash writers over the use of a public relations firm by the Natural Resources Defense Council (NRDC)—when brownlash rhetoric is so often disseminated by public relations firms and right-wing think tanks. The political right has found a gold mine in Alar; the issue would have dropped from public view long ago if the brownlash hadn't kept it alive. Indeed, the brownlash version has been repeated so often that even many pro-environmental people now vaguely—and incorrectly—remember it as a case in which environmentalists were wrong. So what actually happened?

Alar is the brand name for daminozide, a chemical that was used until 1989 to keep ripening apples from falling off the trees. During the 1980s, scientific studies produced mounting evidence that Alar (more accurately, one of its breakdown products, UDMH)[14] was significantly carcinogenic, a verdict that was confirmed by subsequent testing.[15] Given that young children, who in general are physiologically more vulnerable to toxic agents,[16] commonly consume large amounts of apple products (especially juice), removal of Alar from the market seemed justified.[17]

The EPA was moving ponderously toward banning use of the chemical in food production in February 1989 when the NRDC launched a public campaign to draw attention to the inadequacy of the EPA's procedure for regulating pesticides. Having investigated some twenty-three pesticides then under evaluation by the EPA, the NRDC claimed that the process was too slow and regulators were too complacent about risks to children. The CBS television program *60 Minutes* aired a segment, based on the NRDC study, on the general problem of inadequate pesticide regulation, with heavy emphasis on Alar because of its evident dramatic potential.[18]

The nationwide publicity about hazards to children from Alar and other pesticides caused an immediate public furor. Although the actual risk to an individual of developing cancer from consuming apples containing Alar (or UDMH) is tiny, the EPA's assessment had indicated that the hazard was twenty to fifty times higher than the agency's permissible standards for cancer-causing substances in food (one cancer per one million lifetime exposures).[19] Most likely, the public's reaction was so powerful because children were particularly threatened, because the threat was cancer, and because apples are such an icon for healthful food in American culture (in contrast to a "poisoned" apple, which evokes all sorts of negative images from Adam and Eve to Snow White's evil stepmother).

People were outraged to learn that the risks from Alar had been known for years but the government had failed to ban it, largely because of the industry's efforts to delay action against it. That Alar was undetectable by consumers, so they had no way of controlling the risks personally (other than giving up apples), doubtless contributed to the public's indignation. Most consumers also viewed Alar in apples as an unnecessary risk, since its main contribution was to prolong ripeness and reduce spoilage in storage and marketing. Clearly, the principal beneficiaries of Alar's use were farmers, distributors, and food retailers, not consumers, although consumers may have benefitted from slightly lower apple prices.

Uniroyal Chemical Corporation, Alar's manufacturer, finally withdrew its product from the market, realizing a ban by the EPA was imminent, based on new test data showing that UDMH caused cancer in mice. By then, even the apple producers wanted the product off the market, as sales of apples and apple products began dropping. Apple farmers and processors suffered losses estimated at about $100 million in 1989, a fact not lost on Alar's defenders. But a more careful reading shows that prices were depressed for only a few months and that the losses were due mainly to an oversupply caused by a bumper harvest the year before, not to the furor over Alar.[20] The latter exacerbated but did not cause the industry's economic woes.

Long-term foes of environmental regulation quickly exploited the Alar dispute to advance their claim that "bad science" and irresponsible behavior by the NRDC had created an economic disaster. In an attempt to allay public fears, leaders of government agencies jumped into the fray, declaring (correctly) that the risks from eating apples were vanishingly small but undermining their own case by understating both the level of risk from Alar and the proportion of apples on the market that contained it. These errors were widely carried in the press and even repeated by Daniel Koshland Jr., then editor of the journal *Science,* who asserted that the risks from Alar had been grossly exaggerated.[21] Other scientists chimed in with complaints that the publicity was heavy-handed and that the actual risks from Alar were not solidly established and were at least debatable.[22]

A group of wise-use activists in Washington State, some of whom were apple growers, filed suit against both the NRDC and CBS News, claiming they had spread "false, misleading, and scientifically unreliable statements" about apples, and sought compensation to the tune of $200 million.[23] The suit lost in court, but it may have succeeded in intimidating the media.

Ironically, apple products were off the shelves for barely four months, and growers had bumper crops (without the use of Alar) in each of the next two years. In some ways, both consumers and apple growers have benefited; partly because of the Alar controversy, the Washington apple industry is more diversified and less dependent on a single apple variety (red delicious) than before. Thus consumers have more choices and growers have less economic risk.[24]

Much of the backlash involved friends and members of the chemical industry who rushed to Uniroyal's defense. Uniroyal had succeeded in delaying the ban on Alar twice previously—delays that had aroused substantial public anger over Alar as early as 1986.[25] That had been part of a more general campaign by the industry to roll back regulations on its products and to convince the public that chemical residues in food are harmless—a campaign that has, if anything, intensified since then.

Biochemist Bruce Ames of the University of California, Berkeley, and his collaborator Lois Gold led the charge against the NRDC–*60 Minutes* indictment of Alar. Ames and Gold claimed in a letter to *Science* magazine that Alar's carcinogenicity was insignificant because human beings live in a sea of natural pesticides that are ubiquitous in food and against which people have natural defenses.[26] Against Alar's risks, they contrasted the potential economic and health consequences of increased apple spoilage and the hypothetical presence of other, more dangerous natural toxins that might be in apples unprotected by Alar.

Ames and Gold also cast grave doubt on the credibility of animal testing as a means for gauging carcinogenicity, calling such findings "speculative," then far more speculatively suggested that human beings would be protected against Alar by their natural defenses. With an irrelevant and distracting digression into the supposed benefits of very low doses of radiation in strengthening DNA repair, they pooh-poohed the dangers of low doses of chemical carcinogens. While quite properly noting that some high-dose exposures such as tobacco use and occupational exposures to toxic substances pose much greater threats than low-dose exposures to chemicals like Alar, they in effect dismissed low exposures as not needing regulation because there are millions of them (if the natural chemicals are included) and "it is not feasible to test all of them."[27]

Ames has consistently used such arguments in the cause of deregulation.[28] He is a respected scientist at the University of California, Berkeley, who we believe overrates the potential role of physiological defense mechanisms, which presumably have evolved in human beings and their ancestors over countless millennia as responses to toxic and mutagenic (inducing mutation, possibly causing birth defects) substances that occur *naturally* in foods. Ames and Gold assume that such mechanisms will be equally effective against human-made, novel chemicals—despite a lack of evidence that they are. Moreover, the strategy of trying to reduce the odds of getting cancer by minimizing exposures to some portion of the host of chemicals that people may be exposed to, especially exposures that are both involuntary and unnecessary, apparently isn't persuasive to them.

But Ames and Gold have scientific credentials and are voices of reason compared with others who picked up on the Alar controversy and ran with it. One, Elizabeth Whelan, president of the American Council on Science and Health (ACSH), promptly began defending Alar in the press and on television.[29] Author of *Toxic Terror: The Truth behind Cancer Scares,* she is a long-time stalwart fighter for deregulation of chemicals.[30] Not surprisingly, her organization derives a large part of its financial support from the food and chemical industries.[31]

Three years later, the EPA issued a statement reaffirming the sound scientific basis for banning Alar. Meanwhile, Whelan's organization was still trying to persuade CBS News to disavow its *60 Minutes* story. At the behest of the ACSH, Stephen Symms, senator from Idaho, wrote to William Reilly, then head of EPA, and Samuel Broder, director of the National Cancer Institute, as part of a campaign to reopen the case against Alar.[32] One of the ACSH's goals was to obtain statements from qualified officials that Alar was "safe," an effort that largely failed. A cautious statement was eventually elicited from Richard H. Adamson, director of the National Cancer Institute's Division of Cancer Etiology (to whom the letter to Broder had been referred):

> Nothing is completely "safe." There are risks with everything we do in life. But I feel that the alleged role of pesticide residues in the causation of human cancer has been grossly overstated. Indeed, we know of no evidence that suggests that pesticide residues at or below approved tolerances contribute to the toll of human cancer. I would compare the cancer risks associated with eating an apple containing trace amounts of Alar™ with the lifetime risk of eating half a peanut butter sandwich or smoking one cigarette.[33]

Who could quarrel with this statement? The problem with Alar-containing apples (as with cigarettes and peanut butter sandwiches) is that most people who consume them don't stop with one in a lifetime. Obviously, risks escalate with multiple exposures. The risk from peanut butter is from a natural carcinogenic contaminant, aflatoxin, caused by a mold; that from cigarettes is well known. The peanut butter risk is tiny, and largely unavoidable by consumers (although processors can and do minimize aflatoxin in their products), and peanut butter provides some benefits. Cigarettes do not, of course, so people usually don't allow children to smoke. But apples are assumed to be safe. A typical American three-year-old may drink apple juice or eat applesauce virtually every day; before 1989, that could have meant hundreds of exposures to UDMH during a single year. In our view, a risk to a small child equivalent to smoking even a few cigarettes is hardly negligible!

Even so, the ACSH issued a press release in 1992, using Adamson's statement to support its view. One of his sentences was rephrased to read: "I am unaware of evidence that suggests that regulated and approved pesticide residues in food contribute to the toll of human cancer in the U.S."—a subtle but interesting shift of emphasis.[34] Similar brief statements reflecting a lack of information by respected individuals such as former Surgeon General C. Everett Koop and *Science* editor Daniel Koshland, Jr. appeared in the release. The ACSH also pointed out that environmental regulators in the United Kingdom and the World Health Organization (which use different criteria from those used by the EPA) had approved the use of Alar. Whelan was still trying in 1994 with another special report and news release, presenting a "Pinocchio Prevaricator's Award" to the NRDC.[35]

Dixy Lee Ray commented on Alar in her 1990 book *Trashing the Planet:* "The technique of making unsubstantiated charges, endlessly repeated, has since been used successfully against asbestos, PCBs, dioxin, and, of course, Alar."[36] The discussion leaned heavily on Ames and Gold's argument about natural toxic chemicals in foods and blamed the growers' "$200 million" losses (nearly twice what was originally claimed) on the "Alar scare."[37] She denied that Alar had been shown to cause cancer, using a familiar brownlash argument: "[A] person would have to eat 28,000 pounds of apples every day for 70 years to produce tumors similar to those suffered by mice exposed to megadoses of Alar."[38]

It is, of course, not logistically feasible, even with laboratory animals, to test for carcinogenicity at doses comparable to average exposures. Gigantic numbers of mice would have to be exposed to various low doses to determine the level of exposure that would cause, say, one cancer in 1000 mice. There are reasonable arguments about the validity of testing a chemical with high doses on animals to see whether it can cause cancer, and, by inference, might cause it in humans. But most scientists accept animal testing as a legitimate procedure that yields useful data when interpreted with appropriate caution.[39]

Ray, who was a marine biologist (but not a chemist or epidemiologist), should have known better. Her followers are free of any such qualifications but have no hesitation in interpreting scientific conclusions. A 1990 book, *Fear of Food* by Andrea Arnold, carried the Alar backlash a few steps further.[40] In an introduction by Senator Symms and a foreword by William Perry Pendley, president of the Mountain States Legal Foundation, as well as in Arnold's text, the book accuses the NRDC not just of conducting "irresponsible science" but also of deliberately generating the whole controversy just to raise money and recruit members.

Senator Symms virtually portrayed the events of February 1989 as a vast conspiracy by the NRDC and the television industry to victimize American farmers and warned forebodingly: "By spreading false and misleading scare stories of exaggerated dangers from pesticides, the 'instigators' could very well cause public panic and ill-conceived political measures that would destroy America's farm productivity—and the American farmer."[41] And they call environmentalists "alarmists"!

▢ **Without heavy use of pesticides, starvation would stalk the planet.**[42]

This statement paraphrases a message offered by a host of brownlash writers. It is a classic case of exaggeration that neatly sidesteps the real issue with regard to pesticides, a class of often dangerous chemicals used to suppress organisms that eat or compete with our crops. The central question is: exactly what benefits are gained from the large-scale release of pesticides, and do they outweigh the costs to human health and environmental stability?

The pests include plant-eating insects and rodents, microbes that cause plant diseases, and weeds. Natural ecosystems have evolved an extensive web of checks and balances among organisms that largely prevent outbreaks of "pests." To a very large degree, this natural ecosystem service operates in agriculture also, and it has been estimated to have a current maximum value (worldwide) of about $1.4 trillion annually.[43] But modern agriculture is based on large-scale monocultures, which are especially vulnerable to pest attack.[44] So it has become heavily dependent on the use of synthetic chemicals to control pests, whose populations could otherwise build up to very destructive levels.

Humanity now uses about 2.5 million tons of synthetic pesticides worldwide each year,[45] and pesticide production is a multibillion dollar industry. Yet despite both natural and human controls, pests and spoilage still destroy about 25 to 50 percent of crops before and after harvest.[46] That proportion is, if anything, *higher* than average crop losses before synthetic pesticides were widely introduced after World War II. The strategy of large-scale broadcast spraying of pesticides has proven a poor one—except from the standpoint of petrochemical company profits.

An important reason for this lack of success is the rapidity with which pest populations evolve resistance to the pesticides. Almost as soon as a new pesticide is deployed, resistance appears in the targeted population. Aided by short generation times and large populations, the bugs, rats, weeds, fungi, and plant diseases are generally winning this coevolutionary race.[47] More than 500 species of insects and mites have become resistant to insecticides and miticides, and resistance to herbicides has been noted in more than 100 species of weeds. In addition, about 150 species of plant pathogens show resistance to the chemicals used to attack them.[48]

Unquestionably, much too great a tonnage of pesticides is used for the results achieved. Only a very small proportion of the pesticides applied to fields ever actually reaches the target pest. For instance, of those delivered by aerial crop dusters, some 50 to 75 percent miss the target area[49] and less than 0.1 percent may actually reach the pest. The remainder by definition is an environmental contaminant that can injure people and non-target species and in some cases can migrate to the far reaches of the globe.[50]

DDT is probably the best known of the persistent pesticides in the latter category.[51] Residues of DDT and its more toxic breakdown products have been found literally everywhere on the planet. Since DDT was banned in the United States and most industrialized nations in the early 1970s, populations of some severely affected wildlife species such as eagles and falcons have partially recovered. DDT concentrations in human tissues also have fallen significantly (but haven't disappeared) in most developed countries. Yet DDT is still manufactured and exported to many developing countries, where it continues to be widely applied. Although it is less directly dangerous to human health than originally feared, DDT now is a suspect in a new category of hormone-mimicking compounds.[52] And because its effects on wildlife, especially birds, can be serious, DDT remains a threat to non-target organisms in many countries.

The banning of DDT and some other persistent organochlorine compounds led to increased use of shorter-lived pesticides instead, especially organophosphates such as parathion. Many of these are acutely toxic and dangerous to farm workers and non-target organisms, including predators of the pests. In developing countries, pesticides often don't bear labels in the local language. Since many farmers and farm workers are illiterate and untrained in the proper handling of these materials, pesticide poisonings are a common occurrence, and abuse of the chemicals is widespread.

Yet in most cases, pests can be effectively controlled without heavy application of pesticides by using more biologically based methods. Known as integrated pest management (IPM),[53] this approach involves various strategies such as encouraging natural enemies of pests, developing and planting pest-resistant strains of crops, fallowing, mixed cropping, destroying crop wastes where pests shelter, and so on. IPM is generally vastly superior to chemical-based pest-control methods from both economic and environmental perspectives; and it is gradually spreading despite a variety of socioeconomic and political problems impeding its progress.[54]

Indonesia has had remarkable success with IPM. In 1986, responding to the failure of chemical control of the brown plant hopper, a presidential decree banned fifty-seven of sixty-six pesticides used on rice.[55] Pesticide subsidies, which were as high as 80 percent, were phased out over two years, and some of the resources saved were diverted into IPM.[56] Since then, more than 250,000 farmers have been trained in IPM, insecticide use has plunged by 60 percent, and the rice harvest has risen more than 15 percent. Farmers and the Indonesian treasury have saved a total of more than $1 billion.

Equally impressive was a four-year study in New Zealand that compared chemical-dependent farming methods with "biodynamic" farming. Like organic farming, biodynamic farming uses no synthetic chemical fertilizers or pesticides; instead, soil quality is improved with additions of compost and manure, and pests are managed through crop rotation and crop diversification. Not only did the biodynamic farms in the New Zealand study have better soil quality than the industrial farms but they were equally successful financially.[57]

Pesticide use no doubt could be greatly reduced everywhere by wider adoption of IPM, which uses synthetic pesticides as a scalpel only when needed rather than as a bludgeon. Relaxing cosmetic standards on foods (such as allowing signs of minor insect damage) might well also lead to reductions in pesticide use without causing any harm.[58] Strong incentives to change pest-control practices could result from a continuation of the recent shift in public preferences toward "organically grown" foods—foods grown without pesticides or synthetic fertilizers.[59] Clearly, Americans increasingly distrust toxic chemicals, as is indicated by soaring sales of organically grown fruits and vegetables, which doubled from 1989 to $7.6 billion in 1994.

Overall, pesticide use in the United States could be reduced by an estimated 50 percent for a negligible increase (less than 1 percent) in food prices.[60] Such a reduction in use could prove to be a great bargain if, as some scientists think, exposure to pesticide residues can impair the immune system.[61] In view of today's deteriorating epidemiological environment, in which new diseases are emerging and drug-resistant strains of bacteria are causing resurgences of diseases once believed conquered, any loss of immune function should be taken seriously.[62]

Of course, many synthetic chemicals greatly enhance human well-being; pesticides, when properly used, could be in that category. Nevertheless, the risks that accompany various uses of these compounds are potentially so serious (even if difficult to evaluate) that it seems only prudent to minimize inefficient use of them and unnecessary exposures to them. Once pesticides are widely dispersed in the environment, humanity has no choice but to accept the risks. The social costs and benefits of all uses should be subjects of open public discussion backed by careful analyses and a frank airing of uncertainties.

But with a multibillion-dollar business at stake, it is no surprise that pesticide-producing firms have often supported brownlash scientists, writers, and activists to defend their products against criticism—a strategy they have employed since Rachel Carson published *Silent Spring* in 1962 and was treated to a firestorm of denial and personal attack.[63] By lulling the public into complacency about pesticides and downplaying any adverse information about them that may surface, these companies do an effective job of protecting their business-as-usual operations. Unfortunately, what might make sense for a petrochemical company makes no sense ecologically.

☐ **Dioxin is vastly overrated as a dangerous chemical.**[64] **Exposure to dioxin "is now considered by some experts to be no more risky than spending a week sunbathing." (Keith Schneider, 1991)**[65]

Of course, with the increase in ultraviolet radiation reaching Earth's surface because of depletion of the ozone shield, a week of sunbathing is hardly a risk-free activity! More seriously, despite a recent barrage of misinformation, there is plenty of evidence that dioxins are very dangerous chemicals, especially one of their more common forms, known by its chemical shorthand as TCDD.

Dioxin is a toxic contaminant—a by-product of the combustion of chlorine-containing substances—that commonly forms when plastics are burned in incinerators. It also forms during the manufacture of the herbicide 2,4,5-T and when chlorine is used in some industrial processes such as bleaching paper.[66] People can absorb tiny amounts of dioxin by eating contaminated food, by breathing air polluted by emissions from waste incineration, or through skin contact. Dioxin also leaches into food stored in paper or cardboard containers (such as milk cartons) and finds its way into fish taken downstream from paper pulp mills. Intake through the skin can come from contact with herbicides and possibly with household bleached paper products such as diapers and toilet tissue.

Dioxin not only is easily absorbed and persists in the body, it is also an extremely potent toxin. As little as one billionth of an ounce can cause chloracne (a severe form of acne) and various generalized complaints such as headaches, dizziness, digestive upsets, and pain.[67] Animal studies and some epidemiological investigations indicate that larger doses of dioxin can cause some kinds of cancer. Other effects that have been found include liver and kidney problems, stillbirths, birth defects, and immune suppression. And prenatal exposure to dioxin appears to have a variety of effects on hormone expression, sometimes feminizing, sometimes masculinizing.[68]

Similar effects have also been seen in wildlife exposed to TCDD, as well as in laboratory animals. But species vary in their sensitivity to dioxin, so the applicability of laboratory findings to human beings is a matter of scientific dispute—a circumstance that provides the brownlash with ammunition for their denunciations of toxics regulations.

Nonetheless, most scientists are extremely wary of dioxins. One 1995 study concluded:

> The available data indicate that high-level human exposure to dioxins produces adverse health effects and that humans are a sensitive species to the toxic effects of dioxins. Whether . . . low-dose effects are occurring in the general population or the more highly exposed subpopulations remains to be determined.[69]

We think an earlier (1991) editorial in the *New England Journal of Medicine* stated the situation quite fairly:

> There is abundant and convincing evidence that TCDD (dioxin or 2,3,7,8-tetrachlorodibenzo-*p*-dioxin) is an extremely potent carcinogen and general toxin in rodents, perhaps the most potent yet tested. Human exposure is therefore regulated strictly and at considerable cost, both direct and indirect. . . . Despite widespread low-level human exposure to TCDD, however, direct evidence of effects on humans is equivocal. No biologic reasons for a marked difference in sensitivity between humans and rodents have been established, so additional efforts to confirm or deny human risk are needed"[70]

That editorial appears in the same issue with a paper describing a careful study of dioxin's role in causing cancers among workers with occupational exposure.[71] Although its results were equivocal on the crucial question of small-dose effects of dioxin, an excess of cancers showed up "just at the points at which earlier research or intuition would lead one to expect an excess." The editorial concluded: "[T]he hypothesis that low exposures are entirely safe for humans is distinctly less tenable now than before."[72] Recent research indicating that TCDD is another potent hormone disrupter during early development only underlines the truth of that statement.[73]

Uncertainty about the exact risks of low-dose exposure to dioxin is likely to persist. Whatever the risks turn out to be, we have little choice in running them, since dioxin is both widespread in the environment and virtually immortal.[74] But containing it and minimizing its creation are possible, and federal regulation aims to do both. Some progress has already been made by strengthening controls of municipal waste incinerators. Moreover, the amount of dioxin now present in the herbicide 2,4,5-T is 1000 times less than it was when Agent Orange (which was half 2,4,5-T) was used to defoliate tropical forests and expose the enemy during the Vietnam War. The use of 2,4,5-T in the United States is now heavily restricted.[75] Since 1990 the EPA has regulated TCDD as a hazardous air pollutant, and paper-bleaching processes have been altered to minimize dioxin in milk cartons.

Much of the current brownlash effort to downplay the health risks of dioxin arises from the pulp and paper industry's reluctance to stop using chlorine-based bleaches, although several companies have already switched to more benign processes. Some other industry groups have also been active in trying to forestall further regulation by the EPA, insisting on a detailed study by the agency with exhaustive review and public comment.[76] Among these are the Chlorine Chemistry Council and the National Cattleman's Association (the latter was stirred up because dioxin had been detected as a contaminant in meat). Some scientists connected with the chemical industry have also claimed that natural causes such as wood burning and forest fires are major sources of dioxin in the environment.[77]

One telling example of how brownlash writers can mislead the public through bungled reasoning comes from Dixy Lee Ray, who displayed her lack of scientific acumen most thoroughly on the subject of dioxin. Discussing nine flounder specimens contaminated with 1.5 parts per trillion of dioxin, she stated:

> Note that the 1.5 parts per trillion of dioxin were dispersed among the nine flounder, and that the test included the internal organs, which nobody ever eats, and the skin which nobody ever eats. . . . On the basis of a trivial 1.5 parts per trillion—not per flounder but in the total of nine flounder mashed up together, guts and all—the EPA proposed a national program to examine the aqueous environment around every pulp mill in the country![78] . . . On whose expertise did the EPA rely to decide that *one-ninth of 1.5 parts per trillion* was a sufficient risk to human health to undertake an expensive and extensive nationwide program? *It begs repetition of a question I have asked so often and have been trying to answer for many years: Who*

speaks for science? Or, to put it another way: On whom does the
press rely to speak for science? [our emphasis][79]

Obviously, Ray didn't understand how concentrations are determined
or the meaning of "parts per trillion." As a rough parallel, consider a
case of wine with an alcohol content of 12 percent (twelve parts per
hundred). If you poured the wine from a dozen bottles into a vat, would
the vat then have an alcohol content of only 1 percent? In this case, the
late Dr. Ray also judged that parts per trillion were so infinitesimal as to
be trivial, although dioxin accumulates in the body and, as noted earlier, one billionth of an ounce has measurable consequences.[80] Ray, incidentally, served one term as governor of Washington State, where her
performance paralleled her scientific accomplishments.[81]

> ☐ **Too many chemicals such as DDT have been overregulated. If
> there's no evidence they are serious causes of cancer, why can't we
> use them as much as we want?[82]**

Cancers are only one class among a variety of potential health consequences resulting from exposure to toxic substances. Many effects are
subtle and difficult to detect. After several decades of creating and releasing into the environment thousands of synthetic and naturally occurring chemicals, scientists are only now discovering unexpected effects of those releases on human beings. In tiny quantities, a variety of
compounds can disrupt the endocrine system—the complex communication system that uses chemical messengers (hormones) to control the
development and much of the functioning of animal bodies. The problems were first noted among fish and wildlife exposed to pesticides and
PCBs; recent research indicates that people are being affected as well.
Chlorinated hydrocarbons such as DDT and PCBs rank high among the
suspects, as do dioxins, certain breakdown products of plastics and de-
tergents, and many other compounds that have been implicated as hormone mimics or blockers.[83]

Sensitivity to these compounds is especially high in early stages of development, and reproductive systems, both male and female, seem to
be particularly affected. Among the potentially disastrous consequences
that may result from prenatal exposure to female hormone–mimicking
chemicals are marked decline in male fertility, including very low sperm

counts, and abnormal development of sexual organs in either sex. DDE, a ubiquitous and durable breakdown product of DDT, and vinclozolin, a fungicide, have been shown to cause such problems in reptiles and rodents.[84] Some other compounds, by contrast, seem to have an opposite effect: they block the action of female hormones, in effect masculinizing the individual. Prenatal exposure to dioxin, as mentioned earlier, can exert both feminizing and masculinizing effects.[85]

Some other undesirable effects apparently linked to prenatal exposure to these compounds include behavioral and developmental problems in children such as hyperactivity and learning problems, associated mainly with PCBs.[86] Some hormone mimics may predispose people to depression, anxiety, and other neurological problems.[87] And exposure to estrogen mimics may cause breast cancer in women, and prostate and testicular cancer in men.[88]

Since the process of development, especially sexual development, in human beings is both extremely complex and not fully understood, tracing the pathways and effects of these hormone mimics is very difficult. But the more scientists look for such effects, the more they find. Even more worrisome, levels of toxins that have no apparent ill effects on older children and adults may seriously affect prenatal development in ways that can carry lifetime consequences. Concentrations as small as a few parts per trillion may induce unwelcome changes.[89] Toxicologists (including a team at the EPA) are now developing a system for identifying potential hormone mimics and blockers among industrial chemicals.[90] Since there are many thousands of candidates, the job is a massive one.

With regard to the special vulnerability of fetuses to environmental chemicals that mimic estrogens (female sex hormones), Howard A. Bern, a distinguished embryologist, wrote: "It seems evident that epidemiological, histopathological, biochemical and behavioral studies on human and animal populations and experimental analyses . . . must continue *in order to allow potentially disastrous problems to be defined and confronted* (our emphasis).[91]

A fine new book for a general audience, *Our Stolen Future,* written by two excellent scientists, Theo Colborn and J. P. Myers, and a leading science journalist, Dianne Dumanoski, offers a balanced view of hormone mimics and their impacts on human health.[92] Even though exhibiting due caution, given the complexity and subtlety of the effects, the book provides a strong indictment of hormone-mimicking chemicals. We expect *Our Stolen Future* to receive substantial negative attention from the brownlash.

Because research often leads to discoveries such as the risks from hormone-mimicking chemicals, which in turn lead to a demand for more regulation, it is hardly surprising that industrial groups are supporting efforts to slash funds for research on toxic substances as well as to impede regulatory action. Sometimes this effort is indirect, such as pushing for more lengthy epidemiological research or adding cost-benefit studies, which use up the EPA's limited budget and delay regulation. They also have pushed to divert research on carcinogenicity away from testing substances on animals to examining the mechanisms of cancer induction, which could delay results and reduce the number of chemicals that can be tested.[93]

But ignorance is not safety. Instead of an attack on research and regulation, what is needed is a broad public dialogue on the costs and benefits of creating and using toxic chemicals—a dialogue that frankly recognizes the enormous difficulties of assaying the risks posed by synthetic chemicals both singly and in combination. Such a dialogue must also recognize issues of social justice (since low-income groups and minorities are often disproportionately victims) and the concerns of individuals, whose views of risks necessarily will influence policy. Encouraging the trend toward reducing the use of toxins and developing less hazardous substitutes in industrial processes is also important.[94]

The explosive production and use of novel chemicals by industrial societies in the past half-century may have bestowed on all of us a multitude of problems for the future, many of which we may not yet even suspect. Surely the prospect of an accumulating burden of damaged genetic material being passed down through generations (which seems at least possible, given the mutagenic effects of many toxins) is a matter for concern.

And, apart from cancer and possible genetic defects caused by toxic exposures, numerous other effects are known, such as lower IQs and neurological problems from lead poisoning; lung damage, asthma, and emphysema from air pollutants and other compounds; skin and bone disorders from excess selenium; liver, kidney, or nerve damage, miscarriages, and stillbirths from mercury poisoning, and on and on.[95] And hormone-mimicking chemicals may be causing widespread developmental problems in human populations, a possibly dramatic drop in human sperm counts at least in some areas,[96] and serious difficulties in at least some ecosystems.[97]

Even though illnesses and cancers can be caused by other factors, from genetic predispositions to naturally occurring or otherwise unavoidable exposures to potent chemicals, most reasonable observers would prefer to lower the risks to individuals and to future generations posed by dangerous chemicals created and dispersed by society. Cancers, illnesses, disabilities, and early deaths caused by unnecessary exposures to toxic chemicals impose huge costs on society, both in medical expenditures and in lost productivity.

Similarly, subjecting the ecosystems that support human life and the economy to a constant toxic assault by chemicals, many of which are very persistent in the environment, is hardly wise. There are too many possible interactions, and too many chances for threshold effects that can allow serious problems to build up until it is too late, for the toxification of Earth to be accepted complacently. Attempting to suppress scientific research and interfere with government efforts to regulate toxic chemicals not only is socially irresponsible, it is economic folly as well.

CHAPTER 10

Fables about
Economics and the Environment

□

I F MAINTAINING ENVIRONMENTAL QUALITY were completely without economic consequences, the state of the environment and actions for
keeping it healthy would not be contentious issues. But as we have
shown throughout this book, obstructionism and controversy reign.
Many businesspeople see environmental regulations as both financially
crippling and mindlessly bureaucratic, designed more to drive a stake
through the heart of free enterprise than to improve human well-being.
In their view, overconcern about the environment has spawned regulations so costly that they have seriously slowed economic growth in the
United States and other rich nations and are hindering globalization of
the economy.[1] Such anti-regulatory sentiment, driven by the desire to
protect short-term economic interests and to continue operating according to a business-as-usual regimen, fuels the wise-use movement
and the generation of the brownlash fables described throughout this
book.

Such fables should always be discussed with several things in mind.
First, although poor nations clearly need economic growth and development, the scope of that growth may be constrained by severe environmental consequences generated largely by continued growth among

the rich.[2] Second, just how much genuine economic growth (if any) is actually taking place at present is difficult to ascertain because the depreciation of natural capital (non-renewable resources such as petroleum and renewable resources such as forests)[3] is not captured in standard economic statistics such as gross national product (GNP).[4]

Third, as we discussed in chapter 6, prices are often a poor index of human welfare, since they generally do not reflect negative environmental externalities. Air pollution from a power plant is a classic example—the costs of damage to lungs and property caused by noxious emissions are paid by the public in the form of higher medical bills, home painting costs, taxes for maintenance of public structures, and so on; those costs are not reflected in the market price of the electricity sold to consumers.[5] Another example can be found in the Pacific Northwest, where logging has had a devastating impact on forest ecosystems. Not only do taxpayers help pay for construction of logging roads, but society also pays higher prices for fishes whose stocks are depleted by runoff from logged areas and bears the less tangible costs of lost esthetic values and diminished ecosystem functioning, none of which is included in the price of the timber.

And finally, front-line economists increasingly are coming to understand the ecological constraints on economic growth and development—constraints that could spell disaster if the scale of the economy outstrips its environmental base. As a result, they have begun to realize that conventional economic growth per se is not a desirable goal. Consider the recent consensus statement issued by a group of leading economists and ecologists at a meeting in Askö, Sweden, sponsored by the Beijer Institute of Ecological Economics of the Royal Swedish Academy of Sciences. It said in part:

> The economists agreed that GNP is not an ideal measure of human welfare and that it is all too often misinterpreted in the popular and business press and by politicians. The economists also shared the ecologists' concern on the importance of global-scale issues, since they agree we now have a "full" world where natural capital is increasingly becoming scarce. They agreed that there is a need for a careful reconsideration of where and how economic growth *and shrinkage* should be pursued [our emphasis].[6]

The coming together of specialists from such traditionally disparate fields presents hope, although as the following brownlash fables indicate, short-term economic interests are a powerful hindrance to environmental progress.

▣ Unregulated capitalism is good for the environment.[7]

This viewpoint gained popularity following the collapse of the Soviet empire. As westerners gained access to former Soviet bloc countries and began to consider commercial ventures there, it quickly became clear that those nations constituted an ecological disaster area.[8] Far from creating a sustainable society, communism had allowed air and water pollution to reach nightmarish levels, a situation that was accompanied by a decline in human health and ecosystem functioning. At first glance, the idea that markets will automatically protect the environment is certainly an attractive companion to Adam Smith's idea that the marketplace will act as an "invisible hand" leading to maximum economic efficiency and greater good for all.[9] But an ideal laissez-faire economy is one in which there are no externalities. When there are significant negative externalities (as in the market for coal, which is used in power generation), unregulated markets are not efficient.[10] Buyers and sellers, remember, consider only their direct (private) costs,[11] and prices therefore do not reflect an economic good's full social cost.

To put it a different way, most companies have no economic incentive to address external costs and may even put themselves at a competitive disadvantage by doing so. Why, for example, should a company reduce its sulfur dioxide (SO_2) emissions—at great cost to itself—when its competitors do not and when doing so offers no benefits in sales or profits? Although pollution control may be morally correct, in the absence of uniform regulatory standards (a "level playing field") it may also lead to the bankruptcy of moral firms. Thus the notion that unregulated capitalism will protect the environment might be accurate if key environmental goods and services—such as climatic stability, the ozone layer, biodiversity, or minimal exposure to mercury or lead—were traded in markets and therefore were assigned monetary value.

But these amenities are not now, and are not likely to be, traded in markets. To preserve environmental benefits, collective action in the form of regulation is required. Wherever possible, of course, regulations should aim to internalize externalities and minimize social costs within a market context.[12] With incentives supplied by enlightened regulation, markets can step in and provide manufacturers with incentives to compete with one another in providing such goods as ozone-friendly CFC substitutes and unleaded, no-knock gasolines. Thus when brownlash advocates indiscriminately oppose all regulation, they often are in effect hindering the attainment of efficient market-based outcomes.

Still, not all negative environmental externalities can be internalized. Above all, markets are an inadequate mechanism for imposing the constraints on human activities that are necessary to keep civilization's life-support systems functioning. At present they do not come close to including the costs of unsustainability. A British professor of accounting, Robert Gray, put the issue of the flaw in using conventional measures of growth as measures of well-being another way. He stated that the costs of sustainability must be calculated in terms of the investment required to restore society's natural capital—to undo the ecological damage created in the course of doing business. Corporate accounting does not now include those costs. If it did, "[i]t may be that no company could report a profit for the last fifty years."[13] While such a dismal revision may be unlikely, it is clear that proper accounting for environmental costs would substantially lower reported profits.

We would also like to point out that although Adam Smith was a great proponent of self-interested action, he also firmly believed that such actions had to have a moral basis. His notions of morality included being helpful to other people and being good to nature.[14] Indeed, he considered the market so dangerous that he saw it as functioning properly only when operating within the contraints of shared community values.[15] As the environmental record of communist governments clearly indicates, central planning is not a key to maintaining environmental quality; but neither is unrestrained capitalism. Whereas market forces must be harnessed to work effectively on behalf of the environment and human well-being, they should also be restrained by the least intrusive types of regulations that will do the job. A sensible strategy generally combines a mix of free-market and regulatory controls.

☐ **The United States can't afford stronger environmental protection; it would interfere with growth of the GNP.**

In 1990, William K. Reilly, then head of the EPA, reported that the direct cost of compliance with federal environmental regulations was more than $90 billion per year—about 1.7 percent of the nation's GNP. But Reilly also pointed out that, during the two decades when the United States made the substantial environmental progress described in chapter 4, "the GNP increased by more than 70 percent."[16] At worst, it seems that environmental regulation may slightly slow growth in the most commonly used measure of economic progress. One reason is that the dollars paid to control or prevent pollution are factored into the GNP—and they replace dollars lost to the GNP because of reduced expenditures on repair of pollution-induced illness and property damage. The difference is in whose ox is gored. Taxpayers and businesses pay for pollution controls; citizens and insurance companies pay for damages to health and property—and often suffer losses that cannot be compensated. And all of society "pays" for the loss of environmental quality.

Analyses of the costs, benefits, and economic significance of environmental protection to the United States suggest that the overall environmental benefits outweigh the costs. The costs are debated, but a respected economist at Harvard University, Dale Jorgenson, estimates that economic growth has been only slightly slowed (by perhaps 0.2 percent per year) by allocation of resources for environmental protection.[17] We believe—and most recent polls support our claim—that most citizens value environmental quality highly enough to accept such a small cost. When one considers that investments in environmental protection are absolutely essential to the long-term economic well-being of the nation, two or three times the price might seem cheap indeed—although we are sure that with greater cleverness and more market-based environmental controls, more effective protection per dollar could be attained.

One should note there is a growing general distrust of the ability of GNP and the related GDP to mirror social well-being (GNP is the total value of the goods and services produced by factors of production—machinery, labor, land, and so on—owned by Americans; GDP—gross domestic product—represents production inside the United States, including that by factors owned by foreigners). Much of what most Americans *don't* like about their society contributes to the growing GDP: crime, divorce, costs of health care and pollution cleanup, and production and sales of weapons and cigarettes (as well as treatment of gunshot wounds and lung cancer). Once a nation has reached a certain level of individual material comfort, further growth in per-capita GDP does not seem to enhance people's subjective feelings of well-being. Between 1957 and 1992, for example, U.S. per-capita income doubled, while the percentage of people considering themselves "very happy" declined from about 35 percent to 32 percent.[18]

One of the most prominent critics of GDP (or GNP) as an indicator of well-being has been economist Herman E. Daly of the University of Maryland, formerly with the World Bank. Daly has suggested a new measure of economic well-being, the index of sustainable economic welfare (ISEW), which attempts to incorporate negative environmental externalities in its calculation. Between 1951 and 1990, the U.S. per-capita GNP in inflation-adjusted dollars more than doubled, whereas the ISEW grew considerably less than 20 percent and actually declined slightly between 1980 and 1990. Daly's explanation: "Economic welfare has been deteriorating for a decade largely as a result of growing income inequality, the exhaustion of resources and unsustainable reliance on capital from overseas to pay for domestic consumption and investment."[19]

Other nations are actively seeking better indicators of human satisfaction,[20] especially ones that include the critical factor of depreciation of natural capital.[21] As mentioned earlier, natural capital includes Earth's vast array of life-supporting resources, from the microbes that maintain soil fertility to fresh water stored in aquifers. Norway has started calculating balances for mineral and living resources; France now has "natural patrimony accounts," which track the status of all resources influenced by human activity. Economist Roefie Hueting of the Netherlands' Central Bureau of Statistics has pushed the Dutch government to institute an accounting system that includes environmental damage and the costs of repairing it. Sweden and Germany are moving in the same direction. The United States government also has shown interest in such calculations; in fact, the Department of Commerce is currently attempting to develop a "green gross domestic product." In short, recognition is growing that "[b]oosting the GDP is no longer a sufficient aim for a great nation, nor one that America can continue to endure."[22]

☐ The burden of environmental regulations is reducing the competitiveness of American industry.

Some analysts have claimed, contrary to this brownlash dogma, that the system of environmental protection in the United States actually has given American companies a competitive edge as environmental standards tighten globally.[23] Environmental protection surely has significantly bolstered conventional economic indicators by having become an important industry, rivaling General Motors or Exxon (the two biggest U.S. corporations) in aggregate size and accounting for some 4 million jobs and over $150 billion in sales per year in the early 1990s.[24] In addition, U.S. businesses have assumed a leadership role in the development of environmental technologies, in many cases enhancing American competitiveness in the world market and helping to improve our trade balance.[25]

The "green technology" market is now worth roughly $200 billion annually in rich countries and is poised for dramatic growth in the developing world, where pollution problems are becoming so severe that some countries, such as Mexico, are already trying to put controls in place, and others, such as China and India, seem certain to adopt emissions standards. Having been forced by legislation such as the Clean Air and Clean Water Acts and regulation of toxic chemicals to meet stringent American standards, U.S. industries are in a powerful competitive position to introduce to global markets such pollution-control technologies as catalytic converters and in-factory recycling. Already American manufacturers have captured the largest single share of the green-technology market, worth more than $100 billion per year.[26]

Driven by a variety of forces—including regulations, the desire to preempt government regulation, consumer demand, competitive pressures, opportunities for profit, public image concerns, and a willingness to act responsibly, many businesses are shifting to more environmentally benign technologies.[27] One strategy is to switch from using regulated (i.e., toxic) chemicals to using others not thought to present serious hazards. One of many such examples is Union Carbide Corporation's decision to change its bleaching process by substituting relatively harmless ozone for toxic chlorine.[28]

Another strategy is to design products for easier disassembly and recycling—a practice pioneered by automakers in Germany, where complete recyclability is required by 2000.[29] Xerox Corporation is redesigning its copiers for easier upgrading and recycling; it considers its leased equipment as part of its inventory and is concerned about problems of disposal at the end of a copier's useful life. Along with Hewlett Packard, Canon, and other companies, Xerox has established recycling programs for spent copier cartridges.

A third strategy is to institute environmental management and internal assessment programs to guide environmental practice. Some companies are now openly adhering to the principles of "Total Quality Environmental Management" (TQEM), based on "Total Quality Management" (TQM), a widely instituted business practice that calls for continuous upgrading of manufacturing operations. Others have designed their own environmental management systems with similar goals in mind.

Some large companies, especially in Europe, have realized that cleaning up pollution is not enough and that they have a responsibility to help steer the world toward sustainability. Consider, for example, the 1994 environmental report of Electrolux, a Swedish company. It stated:

> Researchers all over the globe are analyzing and discussing environmental issues. They are trying to work out how much acid rain the forests can tolerate, how much heavy metals can be stored in the soil. Trying to determine exactly where nature draws the line. We believe this is the wrong road. Nowadays we don't need to guess what nature's limits are. Scientific consensus has been created (in Sweden by the environmental foundation, *The Natural Step*) around the framework which is superior to all other frameworks, namely the conditions of the ecological system. This frame determines the absolute boundaries for civilization and every living thing. And it is not negotiable.
>
> Electrolux is an industrial company, not a green business. We continue our industrial operations; the only change is that we now carry out our activities increasingly in accordance with ecological demands.[30]

A group of powerful international business leaders called the Business Council for Sustainable Development, organized by Swiss billionaire Stephan Schmidheiny, has bluntly said that business executives must start addressing environmental issues if their businesses are to survive. The council also embraces the idea of internalizing externalities—that is, gradually adjusting the prices of all goods and services to reflect the environmental costs of production, use, recycling, and disposal.[31]

Multinational corporations that understand the need for sustainability have an extraordinary opportunity to brighten humanity's future. Among American companies that recognize this relationship and have started to act on it is Monsanto, a St. Louis–based multinational corporation with diversified interests from food and agriculture to pharmaceuticals and transport. With a vision not often seen in large corporations, Monsanto undertook a comprehensive corporate overhaul of its environmental policies.[32] The result was a pledge to manage its own property sustainably, open its plants to community scrutiny, and carefully review its environmental impacts.

What prompted such enlightened steps? Like other companies that have undertaken similar programs, Monsanto's leaders saw a need to respond to the public's growing environmental concerns and also to stay ahead of environmental regulations. It was deemed better to anticipate regulation and meet its goals in a way that worked best for the company than to be forced to follow government mandates in ways that might disrupt operations.

With operations and employees on every continent, Monsanto set out to examine the global ecological context in which all those operations take place. After all, its profitability depends, among other things, on ecosystem services: dependable flows of fresh water; maintenance of the topsoil and nutrient cycling that provide biological productivity; reasonably stable climatic patterns; protection from ultraviolet radiation; and the biodiversity that is the ultimate source of many pharmaceuticals. The company also depends on political and economic stability; healthy, educated people able to purchase things; and a diverse, intelligent (and well-fed) population from which to attract good employees. Since there is abundant evidence that many ecosystems are in decline and also that Monsanto's business depends on their continued functioning, the company viewed taking action as inevitable. It recognized that having enormous inefficiency in the top fifth of world economies and enormous deprivation in the bottom fifth is hardly a recipe for stability. Therefore, investing in a stable future, when the prospects are clearly for rapid destabilization, made excellent business sense.[33]

To help in the task, Monsanto has sought the advice of scientists, ecological economists, and business environmentalists.[34] Sustainability is a core theme for the company; to pursue this goal, it has established a "sustainability team" composed of more than 100 members, most of whom have volunteered to join the effort. Some of the team's projects include developing an accounting system that includes all social costs of operations and a "map" of the energy and raw material throughputs of Monsanto's manufacturing processes. In addition, the company encourages employees to join in the sustainability effort and to search for opportunities for Monsanto to have a positive impact on global issues such as world hunger and water quality and availability.

Obviously, even progressive businesses have a long way to go in fulfilling their potential to help resolve the human predicament. They suffer a series of handicaps inherent in modern manufacturing in even taking the first steps. These include inadequate systems for providing information on social costs, difficulties in assessing demand for alternative products and in developing uses for the company's waste streams in other parts of the industrial ecosystem, and so on. The National Academy of Engineering is aware of these and related problems and has begun to outline solutions to them.[35]

Huge questions remain about the environmental consequences of the globalization of corporations and loosening of restrictions on trade. Many analysts believe that the exact opposite of today's trends—a return to much more local control of resources and environment—is the only path to sustainability.[36] We are afraid that could prove true but hope it will not, since it appears that the trend toward globalization would be very difficult to reverse. Globalization also may be the best way to knit societies together closely enough to prevent war and establish the international cooperation necessary to solve humanity's problems. We do find it hopeful that more and more people in the business community express concern about the environment's future and are taking steps to safeguard it. We hope they soon will become a powerful pro-environmental force.[37]

☐ **Stricter environmental regulations will cost American jobs by forcing industries to relocate in nations with weaker standards.**

Certainly environmental regulations can cost some jobs, especially in extractive industries or in the manufacturing sector when outdated plants are forced to close because the costs of installing emissions controls exceed the factories' value. It should be noted, though, that some of the industries (e.g., logging and mining) that complain most loudly about jobs being lost because of environmental regulation are of the boom-and-bust variety—set to move on when local resources are depleted.

Some companies pressed by regulations may choose to relocate to nations with weaker environmental laws (and cheaper labor). But at the same time, new jobs are created in, say, the recreation sector and in high-tech industries that favor settling in areas where environmental quality is high, both because clean air and water are essential for their operations and because a healthy local environment helps them attract skilled labor. And whenever there is a shift in the economy, whether driven by regulations or by changing consumer preferences, jobs are both created and destroyed. Some factories that are required to install pollution-control equipment will close down and throw their employees out of work. But others will purchase smokestack scrubbers, thus helping create jobs in factories where pollution-control equipment is made. Overall, environmental protection seems not to be a major cause of job losses[38] and can in fact be a significant source of new jobs.

Economist Robert Repetto of the World Resources Institute dealt concisely with this issue:

> The real issue is not "environment vs. jobs," but what we want our economy to produce. If we want it to produce a clean environment along with other goods and services, the industries that contribute to that end will have a higher output and employment, and those that damage the environment will have less. What we want the economy to produce is continually changing, and industries expand and contract to keep pace. When personal computer sales boomed, typewriter sales declined, but no politician or lobbyist has said "Our economy can't afford to have personal computers because it will destroy jobs in the typewriter industry." Yet they routinely claim that we can't afford clean air because it will destroy jobs in the coal-mining or some other industry.[39]

☐ **Economics, not ecology, should guide policy decisions.**[40]

A politician who says something like "The time has come to put the economy ahead of the environment" clearly doesn't understand that the economy is a wholly owned subsidiary of natural ecosystems and that the natural environment supplies humanity with an indispensible array of good and services. He or she undoubtedly also does not understand key threats to those ecosystems such as population growth and rapid climate change. Such a lack of understanding about matters fundamental to our existence highlights not only a failure of our educational system but also the failure of professional ecologists to communicate their knowledge to the general public.

Expressed in standard economic terms, the value of ecosystem services is enormous.[41] The pest-control service alone could be worth $1.4 trillion annually, since without natural pest control there could be no production of agricultural crops.[42] The total value of ecosystem services might be reckoned in dollar terms as about $20 trillion per year—almost equal to the gross global product. But these valuations give only a small hint of the actual value of the services, for without them there would be no human society to enjoy their unsung benefits.

All economists understand that economics is supposed to seek wise ways to allocate resources to meet human needs. As traditionally practiced, however, economics has been overly restrictive in the resources it has considered, ignoring many natural resources. It has also addressed only a narrow domain of human needs, often considering only the delivery of conventional material goods and services while ignoring the delivery of environmental goods and services. That economics is not a wise guide for policy decisions dealing with environmental issues is underlined by statements of economists themselves that they detect few "signals" of serious environmental problems.[43] They are, of course, waiting for price signals of shortages in resources while remaining ignorant of the depletion of many of the most critical resources, such as biodiversity, water quality, and the atmosphere's capacity to absorb greenhouse gases without catastrophic consequences, which are not priced by markets. In this respect, those economists are like blind men claiming there is no difference between a Rembrandt and a child's scribble because they cannot discern it.

Given the built-in blinders of traditional economics, we are much encouraged by the growing cadre of academic economists who realize that the proper definition of economics embraces ecological phenomena.[44] A reciprocal realization is needed by many ecologists. The economy can be viewed as the metabolism of Earth's dominant organism, and all of the planet's surface has been altered by that metabolism. Ecologists can no longer afford to act (as they often do) as if they were studying systems uninfluenced by human activities; they must pay much closer attention to the environmental impacts of the economic system. Indeed, an argument could be made that economics and ecology can no longer be sensibly considered separate disciplines.[45]

In closing, we reiterate the key themes of this chapter: first, because the economic system is embedded in and supported by the ecosphere, any major disruption to the ecosphere could spell economic disaster; and second, not only will environmental protection not damage the economy, it will, in fact, allow the economy to persist.

CHAPTER 11

Faulty Transmissions

T HE MOTIVES OF INDIVIDUALS who dispense erroneous information about science and the environment vary widely, ranging from a simple urge to challenge conventional thinking to a desire to spread right-wing ideology or further some economic or political goal. The first is perfectly acceptable; the latter clearly isn't when it could jeopardize the public's well-being. Despite the differing agendas, however, the brownlash has been remarkably effective in advancing its views with what appears to be one voice. As a result, it has succeeded in at least confusing many issues and at worst setting into motion efforts to change public policy through legislation based on faulty information.

How does the body of misinformation produced by the brownlash get transmitted to the public and become part of the policy dialog? Brown-lash messages reach the public through the same channels that most information does: through newspapers, magazines, radio, and television; that is, through journalism. Journalists by tradition are the objective observers and guardians of our free society; an important part of their job is distilling complex information and reporting essential facts that enable people to make informed choices in their lives.

Society, of course, ultimately gains its knowledge of environmental problems from the scientists who carry out the research. The scientific community thus clearly must bear part of the blame when citizens cannot tell where the weight of scientific opinion on a matter lies. Environmental scientists have failed to educate the public adequately about what is known in disciplines such as ecology, evolutionary biology, and climatology.

But interpretation and presentation of scientific findings to the public (outside the classroom) are done mostly by journalists. Without them, the information would languish in technical journals, unintelligible to most non-scientists. And this dependence on journalists to inform the public is growing as scientific information becomes an increasingly important factor in guiding public policy and in building public support for appropriate policy decisions. So both scientists and journalists have a heavy responsibility to transmit information accurately and objectively.

Unfortunately, this process doesn't always work perfectly. Clearly, reporters are expected to rise above their own biases and portray information and events as accurately and honestly as possible, and the vast majority of them strive to do so. But not all reporters have the background for dealing with scientific or environmental issues. And many other circumstances can affect the way a story is reported.

For instance, a journalist's background, location, or personality may influence the overall tone or direction of a news report or even the choice of topic—just as personal views may inadvertently enter into a scientist's work. Thus a reporter with a background in biology might be inclined to write about the Endangered Species Act, whereas one with a degree in economics might prefer to write about the costs of environmental regulations. Geography plays a role too. There aren't many endangered species in Minnesota, so the *Minneapolis–St. Paul Star Tribune* doesn't give as much coverage to the reauthorization of the Endangered Species Act as do California, Texas, and Florida newspapers.[1] Ted Turner's cable network programs cover environmental issues more thoroughly and in greater depth than do those of the competition because Turner cares about the environment.[2]

A more serious, if subtle, problem is that some journalists and editors may share some of the brownlash's views, and those views may shade their work. And editors can contribute to a political atmosphere simply through their decisions on which stories or articles to print (for example, is the population issue something that should be discussed or ig-nored?). And not uncommonly, reporters simply pass on information, correct or not, without examining it critically, for a variety of reasons.

Moreover, reporters are subject to certain pressures that can be ex-plained by the economics of the news business. Controversy, exagger-ation, and scandal sell; stories about the gradual deterioration of our en-vironment do not. Reporters are under pressure from editors to write ever-punchier stories and to infuse their prose with colorful anecdotes. The result can be a loss of accuracy or a change of emphasis, especially when the underlying science is complex, as it often is. When anecdotes are repeated, they may take on a self-perpetuating life of their own. These problems can be magnified when environmental matters are pre-sented by reporters with no scientific background.

One such instance was related in a recent issue of the journal of the Society of Environmental Journalists (SEJ) by Randy Lee Loftis and Kevin Carmody,[3] who acknowledged that reporters are susceptible to a good story (which explains the proliferation of spin doctors, especially in pol-itics). They described a press conference called by Chicago's mayor, Richard Daley, to denounce a regulatory order to test the city's drinking water. Daley claimed that regulations had become so outrageous that the city was being forced to test for a pesticide used only on pineap-ples, which of course are grown in Hawaii, not in Illinois. Loftis and Carmody wrote: "News coverage mirrored the mayor's spin, and Chi-cagoans may have been left with the impression that environmental 'wackos' in the EPA had struck again."

Unfortunately, the pineapple story wasn't true; the pesticide in ques-tion is widely sprayed on farms throughout the Midwest. Yet no reporter challenged Mayor Daley's account, so a bogus environmental anecdote was dutifully—if inadvertently—passed along by the press. Unhappily, people tend to remember the pineapples and the original message and not to recall or even notice subsequent corrections.

In this case, the story may have been covered by city reporters rather than science reporters, so the scientific "facts" weren't questioned. But where were the editors and fact checkers? Clearly, some erroneous in-formation gets through because of deadline pressures and competition. With declining sales and rising paper costs, newspaper publishers in-creasingly press their reporters to write more stories in less time and in fewer column inches. And reporters are always under pressure to break a story first. A catchy item from the steps of city hall, delivered close to deadline, could be the perfect piece to liven up the daily news.

Another explanation is that news coverage, like many social phenomena, is subject to trends. People want to read about what's fashionable, whether the topic is clothing, sports, technology, or politics. Thus, as Loftis and Carmody noted, "Instead of picking apart the claims of partisans, many journalists are spreading them unchallenged. In newsrooms throughout the country it is trendy to ask whether environmental laws, not polluters, are the real public enemy. The politics of the day dictate that most of the current whoppers come from opponents of existing environmental laws—partisans trying to turn public opinion."[4]

One journalist has reported being told by an editor, "We don't want anything scary." Readers, she said, are "tired of bad news, scary facts, and being held responsible for things."[5] It's easier to shoot the messenger than to take corrective action. And while there is good news about the environment (as we pointed out in chapter 4), it's not very new, and much that is new—about global warming, population growth, and deforestation, to name a few topics—isn't good. Tim Noah of the *Wall Street Journal* observed: "Five years ago, environmental issues were subjected to far too little skepticism in the press. Journalists were faddish and unthinking in their coverage of some stories. Now there is a faddish, unthinking, knee-jerk reaction in the other direction."[6]

In addition, because journalism often thrives on controversy, reporters sometimes let its appeal override their judgment. For example, a journalist once telephoned Peter Raven (a world-renowned evolutionist, Director of the Missouri Botanical Garden, and Home Secretary of the National Academy of Sciences) and told him that he was going to write a story about Julian Simon's statement that there was no extinction crisis. Peter asked why. The reporter replied: "Everyone else, Ed Wilson at Harvard, Tom Eisner at Cornell, Paul Ehrlich at Stanford, says there is a crisis. So when Simon says there isn't one, that's news."[7] That Simon is a business economist with no background in biology and thus might not have known what he was talking about apparently was irrelevant.

Such "balanced" coverage clearly is not required for all topics. Every time the space shuttle is launched, the press doesn't feel obliged to give space to the ideas of flat-earth believers who claim the whole thing is a hoax. Flat-earthers think the sun circles Earth, but that isn't "news." Astronomers are not expected to respond to the views of astrologers, and the purported invention of perpetual-motion machines isn't "news" because all physicists agree that they can't work. Yet the public is regularly exposed to statements such as "greenhouse warming is just a theory"[8] or that the ozone hole is a hoax. Biologists are often confronted with assertions that population growth has no connection to environmental deterioration or that there is no upsurge in the rate of extinctions.

This is not to say that all reporting of scientific and environmental information is flawed. Indeed, one bright spot is the large number of responsible electronic and print journalists who regularly offer dependable information to the public on the environmental situation. These include, among many, many others: Tom Brokaw (NBC), Dianne Dumanoski (*Boston Globe*), Laurie Garrett (*Newsday*), Ross Gelbspan (formerly of the *Boston Globe*), Mary Hager (*Newsweek*), Sam Hurst (Buffalo Gap Productions and CNN), Richard Kerr (*Science*), Jim Mayer (*Sacramento Bee*), Tom Meersman (*Minneapolis–St. Paul Star Tribune*), Janet Raloff (*Science News*), Phil Shabecoff (formerly of the *New York Times,* now with *Greenwire*), Bill Stevens (*New York Times*), and Robyn Williams (Australian Broadcasting Company). In addition, the thriving Society of Environmental Journalists, with more than 1000 members, endeavors to uphold high standards in environmental reporting. The society's meetings are regularly addressed by environmental scientists, and its members are exposed to the latest scientific thinking.

But there certainly have been cases of reporting, even by otherwise respected journalists, that were less than careful. In 1992, *Washington Post* columnist George Will wrote an especially ill informed column, "Al Gore's Green Guilt,"[9] attacking Gore (then a senator) for his concern about the state of the environment. He wrote that Gore's former mentor, Roger Revelle, who died in 1991, had concluded: "The scientific base for greenhouse warming is too uncertain to justify drastic action at this time. There is little risk in delaying policy responses." But Revelle had a long history of concern about greenhouse gases; indeed, he had been instrumental in getting measurement of atmospheric CO_2 under way as early as 1959.

Revelle's wife and children replied to Will in a letter published in the *Post,* declaring that Revelle's position had been completely misinterpreted and listing his concerns and the actions he had recommended.

Of Will's implication that Revelle was unconcerned about global warming, they said, "Nothing could be farther from the truth."[10]

In the same column, Will had sniped at Stephen Schneider for his concern about global warming, referring to him as a "panic monger" who had once been concerned about global cooling. Schneider also sent a letter to the *Washington Post,* pointing out that scientists were expected to change their views as new data came in. He summarized his position in a metaphor: "What doctor would be in practice if he or she doggedly stuck to a preliminary diagnosis after all the lab tests and X-rays the physician had responsibly ordered pointed to a different disease?"[11] A member of Will's staff later acknowledged their errors to Schneider, explaining that their information system had "broken down."[12] But the damage had been done; anyone who had read Will's column would have been left with the impression that leading atmospheric scientists were both in doubt and in dispute over the seriousness of global warming.

It is important to note that there is a big difference between misquoting or misrepresenting scientific literature and making predictions that turn out to be wrong. The first is not part of the scientific process; the second frequently is. Scientists are trained to make predictions that can later be falsified by experiment or events—indeed, specifying and falsifying hypotheses is one major way that science advances. But environmental anti-science advances differently, as we have seen.

Some news stories originate with a press release. Again, most journalists check their sources carefully and seek independent verification of the information in press releases. But some press releases seem relatively unbiased and authoritative, so it is possible to be misled. For instance, on February 3, 1995, a public relations firm, E. Bruce Harrison, released a draft report by Accu-Weather, a commercial weather forecasting firm, on the question of whether there had been any recent increase in extreme weather, which might be a sign of global warming.

Although scientists would be hard-pressed at present to reach a conclusion one way or another, Accu-Weather came up with an answer. After examining data from a sample of only three sites, all in the United States, it announced in the press release that "the data show that hurricane frequency is not increasing, the number of violent tornados is not increasing, and temperature and precipitation extremes are no more common now than they were 50 to 100 years ago."[13] This is roughly equivalent to pronouncing on Mickey Mantle's lifetime batting average after observing his performance for the month of August in a single year.

The press release, however, did not mention that Accu-Weather's study had been funded by the Global Climate Coalition, which reportedly "has spent more than a million dollars to downplay the threat of climate change."[14] Moreover, the report described in the press release misstated the views of several climatologists whose opinions of global warming were included in a study by Granger Morgan of Carnegie Mellon University and David Keith of Harvard University.[15] It is worth quoting an e-mail message (slightly edited) from Keith to Steve Schneider, one of the scientists whose views were misstated:

> Accu-Weather Inc. has released a report titled "Changing Weather? Facts and Fallacies about Climate Change," which cites our Carnegie Mellon study and mentions your name along with those of the other experts. It states you all agree that "a doubling of carbon dioxide would result in temperature increases of 0.5° to 1.0°C sometime well into the next century." This is, of course, false. We have received a written apology from the report's senior author and have received assurances that all references to us or our study will be removed in future versions.
>
> However, the "pre-publication draft" which includes the error was released to the press by a Washington PR firm, E. Bruce Harrison Co., under contract from the "Global Climate Coalition" (which I believe to be an energy industry lobby group). I first learned about the trouble on Wednesday [February 8] when I was contacted by a reporter from Business Week. Don Rheen of E. Bruce Harrison Co. has agreed to circulate a retraction to all who received the document. I have no way of knowing if he will honor that commitment.[16]

If such a retraction was ever circulated, it would have made little difference. Retractions ordinarily are the equivalent of locking the barn door after the horse is out.

As scientists, we often wonder why journalists sometimes continue presenting contrary views of issues that the scientific community considers resolved. A good example is that of ozone depletion. The vast majority of atmospheric chemists, including Mario Molina and F. Sherwood Rowland, who were awarded a Nobel Prize for their work on stratospheric ozone, concur that the issue is clear-cut: scientists now know in essence how ozone depletion occurs, what causes it, what many of the consequences of its loss might be, and how to remedy the problem. Thus most scientists would regard a newspaper account that quoted as credible someone advocating a repeal of the phaseout of CFCs and other ozone-depleting chemicals as misguided if not irresponsible.

But one aspect of journalism that can inadvertently lead to repetition of errors is the reliance of many reporters on a computer database known as the Nexis News Service. Like any reference material, including the many other databases to which reporters have access, Nexis is only as good as its sources.[17] Any news story written on a given topic, correct or not, enters the Nexis database, where it is often found and copied by other journalists looking for background information on a story. Thus a reporter looking for something written about extinction might well pull up the story about Julian Simon's view of extinction and present it as scientifically valid. Although most reporters rely on Nexis only as a starting point and independently check their sources, some (perhaps under time pressure) might not. Thus a chain reaction is set off; instead of an error being eliminated from the system, it is amplified as more and more journalists uncritically pick up and use it. In this way Nexis accidentally can serve as a potent positive feedback system for inaccuracy.

Most egregiously, in stark contrast to the majority of reporters, a handful of journalists and writers, many of whom have no scientific training, apparently feel qualified to write authoritatively about numerous complex scientific issues. The problem is that they draw conclusions based on their own or others' misrepresentations of the facts and repeat ill-founded claims that they then set forth as scientific truths.

The power of the press in influencing the public opinion on scientific and environmental issues can hardly be overstated. For example, journalist Keith Schneider of the *New York Times* almost single-handedly succeeded in changing the public view on the dangers of dioxin (chapter 9).[18] In 1991, Schneider published a very influential article in which, as one writer noted, he quoted some experts to the effect that exposure to dioxin was "no more risky than spending a week sunbathing," but in fact did not have scientific evidence to back his claims.[19] Nonetheless, his reporting led to a cascade of articles and many editorials throughout the United States questioning the expenditure of public funds to control the release of dioxin and clean up the dioxin already in the environment.

In 1993, Schneider was one of three writers of a series of five articles attacking federal environmental policies for wasting billions of dollars trying to solve problems that weren't all that dangerous.[20] These articles too have been very influential and doubtless have contributed to the efforts of conservative legislators to roll back environmental regulations. Not only were many of Schneider's claims simply incorrect, they also no doubt underestimated public concerns about toxic substances. Keith Schneider is an experienced science reporter; how he fits into the brownlash is unclear, but his recent work is an example of how powerful brownlash messages transmitted by the media and press can be.

To our distress and that of many of our colleagues, brownlash messages seem to be having a measurable effect on the general public. A Roper Starch Worldwide poll conducted in May 1995 for Times-Mirror magazines revealed that 51 percent of those polled believed the media's coverage of environmental issues was biased and 35 percent thought the media made environmental issues seem worse than they really are.[21] These opinions also are favorite themes of brownlash writers; now they are trying to discredit journalists as well as scientists.

In early 1996, the Union of Concerned Scientists ran an advertisement on the editorial page of the *New York Times* denouncing what it called "junk science": the "'data' and 'research' that some corporate interests and radio talk show hosts have been force-feeding America."[22] The advertisement pointed out the danger from such erroneous messages, which conflict with, and even threaten to drown out, the voices of scientists whose work has been carefully reviewed and approved by their peers.

Although the dissemination of junk science is multifaceted, its spread clearly has been facilitated by some journalists, among them Gregg Easterbrook, journalist and contributing editor for *Newsweek* and the *Atlantic Monthly*.[23] Easterbrook gained wide recognition with the publication of his book *A Moment on the Earth: The Coming Age of Environmental Optimism,* in 1995.[24] Tedious, tendentious, and, with 698 pages, too long to be reviewed quickly, the book's publication was accompanied by snappy one-line notices such as "Smoothly and vividly written . . . often highly persuasive" and "Long overdue, challenging fundamental assumptions about our role in Earth's future."

Yet careful examination of the book's contents reveals multitudinous mistakes combined with startlingly little documentation. Easterbrook not only acknowledges the lack of documentation but also rationalizes it in two ways. First, he writes, "Environmental books contain such a confluence of facts that footnoting every reference would cause little carrot [sic] marks to take over the pages."[25] Second, he claims a precedent was set by Rachel Carson when she wrote *Silent Spring*. More than thirty years have passed, of course, since *Silent Spring* was published, during which time environmental science has bloomed as a distinct subdiscipline and scientific knowledge has increased exponentially, doubling in volume roughly every ten years. What might have been appropriate documentation in Rachel Carson's day would hardly be acceptable today.

The scarcity of footnotes in *A Moment on the Earth* has been noted by several reviewers, including Michael Specter of the *New York Times,* who asserted that the dearth of documentation made it nearly impossible for readers to check the honesty of Easterbrook's allegations. Among those who know the arguments, inaccuracy emerges as a serious concern. Population biologist Peter Raven commented, ". . . Gregg Easterbrook, concealing his know-nothingness under the guise of 'eco-realism,' offers a much more effective poison pill . . . [than] Dixy Lee Ray, Julian Simon, [or] the editorial staff of the *Wall Street Journal* . . . to those who are either poorly informed about the areas he treats so superficially or those who are simply anxious to forget about them as rapidly as possible."[26] Kathy Sagan, book review editor for the *SEJournal,* wrote, "Only by half-reporting some issues, and misrepresenting others, can [Easterbrook] draw some of the conclusions he does."[27]

Unfortunately, Easterbrook's book not only is full of errors of fact and interpretation, it also attacks a wide range of environmental scientists in ways typical of brownlash writers. For instance, in it he refers to distinguished atmospheric scientists such as Stephen Schneider, John Firor (National Center for Atmospheric Research), and James Hansen (director of NASA's Goddard Institute for Space Studies) as "greenhouse true believers."[28] Not only was this petty, but it also wrongly implied that these respected scientists had traded in objectivity for a form of theology.

A stunning contrast to *A Moment on the Earth* is Laurie Garrett's lengthy and heavily documented 1994 book, *The Coming Plague: Newly Emerging Diseases in a World Out of Balance.*[29] That volume shows what a superb job a good journalist can do with a complex scientific topic when backed up by careful technical reviewing. Another example is *Our Stolen Future,* the result of a highly effective collaboration by two scientists, Theo Colborn and J. P. Myers, and a journalist, Dianne Dumanoski, science writer for the *Boston Globe.*

We are also concerned about a small subset of journalists (mostly in the electronic media) whose objectivity has been questioned. Sam Donaldson of ABC News has come under attack for remarking that he would sooner kill a wolf than watch it cross his New Mexico ranch.[30] At the 1995 annual national conference of the Society of Environmental Journalists, John Stossel of ABC's *20/20* was pressed by a reporter about whether he still considered himself a journalist in view of the tens of thousands of dollars he receives in speaking fees from chemical companies and other business groups. Stossel replied, "Industry likes to hire me because they like what I have to say." He then added that he supposed he was no longer a journalist in the traditional sense but rather a reporter with a perspective.[31]

Perhaps no one is more up-front about having a perspective than Rush Limbaugh, purportedly America's top talk show host. At least he's honest about his biases; as he says in his book *The Way Things Ought to Be,* "My views on the environment are rooted in my belief in Creation."[32] It's hard to imagine that readers could swallow such brash Limbaugh assertions as "The fact is, we couldn't destroy the earth if we wanted to," "The key to cleaning up our environment is unfettered free enterprise," or "With the collapse of Marxism, environmentalism has become the new refuge of socialist thinking."[33] But somehow a lot of people apparently have.

More dangerous, though, are statements that suggest a certain familiarity with scientific findings. When Limbaugh writes (and says) such things as "Despite the hysterics of a few pseudo-scientists, there is no reason to believe in global warming,"[34] he sends a message that reaches millions of Americans who are in no position to evaluate the truth of his remarks. But a layperson with a gift for gab casually passing judgment on the qualifications of scientists is, to say the least, offensive.

How does our country's most popular talk show host get away with such erroneous and potentially damaging commentary? Limbaugh makes no attempt to adhere to journalistic standards of objectivity and accuracy; he has even denied being a journalist. When errors are pointed out to him, he rarely admits or retracts them. He is an extreme case of ignorance parading as informed discussion. The danger lies in his influence on millions of readers and listeners who accept his often outrageous pronouncements as the truth.

Part of the blame for this unquestioning acceptance must lie with our educational system and the failure of the scientific community to create a scientifically literate populace. Scientists should have a role in informing citizens about scientific issues. But most scientists, who are trained to be cautious, accurate, and comprehensive in describing and interpreting their work, cannot compete with the flamboyant Rush Limbaughs of the world. Some reporters have gone so far as to accuse scientists of not wanting to be understood, saying they dwell too much on details and refuse to speculate on the longer-term implications of their research.[35] Scientists need to respond to this frustration.

Rather than stonewalling, scientists should actively help journalists translate complex issues into material understandable to a lay audience. They need to learn how to communicate scientific findings in a sound bite–oriented, media-dominated world, with an understanding of the need for simplification and the constraints on journalists in time and space. They must learn to play the media game, realizing that those who furnish the strongest and most provocative copy often receive the most attention. They must, in one-on-one interviews, ask at the start about a reporter's needs in order to meet those needs as well as possible. If environmental scientists fail to convey effectively the critical importance of ecology, evolutionary biology, atmospheric chemistry, or climatology, how can they expect to evoke interest from the press?

To their credit, professional organizations such as the American Association for the Advancement of Science, the American Institute of Biological Sciences, and the Ecological Society of America have begun to incorporate into their annual meetings special sessions on media communications. At the Ecological Society of America's 1995 meeting, for instance, scientists attended a communications workshop led by Carl Benscheidt, a former producer of *CBS News with Dan Rather*.

The extent to which our society depends on electronic media for information is indicated by the growing preference for television news (instead of newspapers) and the popularity of investigative newsmagazine shows such as *20/20* and *60 Minutes*. In this competitive journalistic arena, controversy obviously has much appeal. Brownlash spokespeople, who gain recognition more often through exaggeration than through the cogency of their arguments, take advantage of the media's appetite for controversy.

Nevertheless, we feel strongly that the stakes are much too high to allow the brownlash to go unchallenged. Not only do brownlash messages confuse and mislead the public on the importance of the environmental situation, they are being adopted and used as a basis for critical policy decisions—often without careful examination of the potential consequences of those decisions. Brownlash commentary needs to be exposed for what it is: polemics based on a fundamental misinterpretation of scientific knowledge and the scientific process.

Still, it must be remembered that the great majority of journalists are thoughtful, objective, and responsible transmitters of information. Without their dedication, our democracy would be in a sorry state indeed. Rather than rejecting communication with the media because of concerns about inaccurate reporting, scientists need to recognize journalists as potential allies in educating and communicating with the public.

We hope that scientists and journalists can learn to work together to present environmental science accurately and clearly to the public and to decision makers in a timely fashion. The state of the environment and the implications for the future deserve to be at the top of the public agenda. Better yet, we hope environmental problems can fairly soon be moved downward on the agenda through successful efforts to resolve them—without huge battles over whether the problems are real. If that doesn't happen, then we're doomed to continue earning the label of "doomsayers."

CHAPTER 12

How Can Good Science Become Good Policy?

□

O NE ESPECIALLY UNPALATABLE CONSEQUENCE of the brownlash's attempts to disseminate erroneous information is the undue influence its rhetoric has on public policy. Brownlashers try to convince
not only policy makers but also the public at large that their view is the
right one—a moderate, scientifically justified position on environmental
matters. But we have seen that much of the propaganda is seriously at
variance with informed scientific opinion on many critical issues. How
can decision makers and the general public be made more aware of the
actual findings of environmental science, and thus of the increasingly
grave threats posed by environmental deterioration?

Obviously, public education must play a paramount role in helping
disseminate the real conclusions of environmental science (indeed, of
science in general). A better understanding of the brownlash, its goals,
and its tactics could also help environmental scientists communicate
their findings more effectively to the rest of society. We hope this book
provides some of that understanding. We also want to offer some suggestions on how to communicate environmental science to the public,
based on our own thirty years of experience and that of some colleagues. We divide our suggestions into things we think environmental

scientists can and should do and things that concerned citizens, especially environmental activists, can and should do, although the goal in both cases is the same: to push public policy more into line with the realities of environmental science as the turn of the century approaches.

What Can Scientists Do?

Simplistic as it sounds, the first thing that environmental scientists—indeed, probably all scientists—should do is get involved. Educating the public should be an integral part of every scientist's career; if something is worth discovering, it is worth communicating. If those of us who are most familiar with the beauty and intricacy of nature, and its essential role in supporting humanity, will not come to nature's—and thus humanity's—defense, who will? How can we complain about the lack of action by politicians or the ignorance of talk show hosts, Sunday morning television pundits, or even brownlash reporters, if we don't help them get the facts straight?

Any scientist who sees a scientific issue being mangled in the media should write a letter to the editor or news director. In addition, the incident could be selected for classroom analysis, included as an example of misinformation in a textbook, or developed into a high school curriculum unit. Why not give a speech on the topic and get out a press release beforehand? Other options include volunteering to give environmental organizations technical advice, calling in to a talk show, discussing the matter with colleagues or administrators, ranting about it to your tennis partner, and waxing eloquent in front of your favorite bartender.

Yet we recognize that scientists are loath to leave their laboratories and get involved in the public arena. We can sympathize somewhat with that view—especially when some political event interrupts our field research! Part of the reason may be a certain reticence among scientists that helps them focus on the details and the frequent tedium of their research. But all too often, public involvement is avoided because it isn't likely to contribute to gathering professional perks: tenure, promotion, salary raises, or intradisciplinary recognition. That's something senior scientists have a special responsibility for changing, particularly in fields like ecology that are so essential to dealing with the human dilemma. The system of professional rewards needs to be changed so that public outreach is counted as an important, positive element of high-caliber professional behavior. At the very least, scientists can support their colleagues, especially junior colleagues, who do first-rate science *and* choose to join the fray. Scientists, like all citizens, should at least "tithe to society"—spend 10 percent of their time trying to make the human endeavor more sustainable.

Many scientists in fields like ecology, earth sciences, epidemiology, and economics will want to devote much more time than that. They also will want to initiate interdisciplinary work, since virtually all significant problems affecting society fall within the domains of more than one discipline. One of our great pleasures in recent years at Stanford has been participating in interdisciplinary research with economists and attending seminars in which we can discuss the human predicament with agriculturalists, engineers, earth scientists, professors of business and law, and so on.

Paul has also greatly enjoyed serving on the board of the Royal Swedish Academy of Science's Beijer Institute of Ecological Economics. There he has interacted with some of the world's best economists, as well as a superb group of ecologists. Anne, in her work with organizations like the Sierra Club and the Pugwash Movement, has been impressed by how well scientists, engineers, attorneys, physicians, educators, and other professionals can communicate and work together in a common cause. In our view, the growing unity of scientists from different disciplines who are working to solve environmental problems is one of the most heartening intellectual developments of the past decade.

All scientists who teach, of course, can introduce critical issues wherever they are pertinent to their courses—and can give pertinent courses to as wide a variety of students as possible. On many campuses, there are journalism schools or workshops for working reporters; establishing contact with journalists and participating in programs for them can be especially effective. Among other benefits, such involvement allows journalists to see scientists as approachable and knowledgeable people who—for all the right reasons—care passionately about the issues. The same goes for activities at business schools, which often conduct educational programs for junior executives.

But above all, academic scientists must see to it that college curricula ensure that students have a basic understanding of the workings of science, its principal findings, and how these relate to their own lives. Too many students graduate from college or university knowing next to nothing about the planet they inhabit and how human beings fit into the panoply of life. Some of the key topics we always try to include in courses and workshops at Stanford University and in our public lectures are the following:

1. How the scale of the human enterprise critically affects the environment, that scale being determined by population size, per-capita consumption, and choices of technologies to serve the consumption. This is the material subsumed in the $I = PAT$ identity: a population's impact (I) on the environment is a product of the number of people (P), their per-capita consumption (affluence, A), and a measure of the environmental damage done by the technologies that supply each unit of consumption (T).[1]

2. The nature and importance of ecosystem services.

3. Basic evolutionary theory and its applications to agriculture and public health.

4. The major characteristics and environmental impacts of agricultural ecosystems.

5. How the atmosphere-ocean-climate-weather system operates and how it interacts with the agricultural system.

6. Geologic history, including the history of climate changes.

7. Major features of the epidemiological environment.[2]

8. The central role of energy in environmental affairs and the characteristics of energy systems.

9. An overview of the links between ecology and economics (ecological economics).

10. An overview of social (especially equity) issues as they influence the human dilemma.

11. The influence of environmental change in human history.

12. Problems of scale: the concept that what is safe locally or in the short term may be catastrophic globally or in the long term. For example, chlorofluorocarbons are safe in the kitchen and in the short term, but they represent large-scale disaster in the long term. The depletion of local biodiversity in downtown New York or in Stanford, California, gives no hint of the disastrous consequences of its depletion globally.

13. Risk assessment: how to deal with uncertainty.[3]

Of course, a major challenge for scientists is how to educate the general public and decision makers about these complex issues, especially when the brownlash misinformation campaign has already shaped public opinion. Obviously, improving environmental education from elementary school through university would be a substantial help in the long term, but it is of little help in the short term. A more powerful approach in the short term is to work with the media—especially the electronic media.

But this is not the place for a dissertation on how scientists can be effective on television; there are professionals who can help with that, although relatively few scientists take advantage of them now. For instance, the Safe Energy Communication Council, based in Washington, D.C.,[4] conducts workshops on interviewing effectively, developing media strategies, writing press releases, and so on. And many environmental organizations conduct workshops and distribute advisory literature. Still, a few hints for scientists seem in order:

1. When speaking with the media, one should avoid the standard "introduction, materials and methods, results" format of scientific papers. The camera will be on someone else or the reporter will have gone home before you have reached even the materials and methods. *Conclusions must come first.* After all, a television appearance may consist of only a ten-second "sound bite," and the most important part of one's message needs to get aired.

2. Scientists need to be direct and succinct when dealing with the electronic media. One could talk for hours about the uncertainties associated with global warming. But a statement like "Pumping greenhouse gases into the atmosphere could lead to large-scale food shortages" is entirely accurate scientifically and will catch the public's attention. So would "One of the most environmentally damaging activities of human beings begins in the bedroom."

3. Many excellent scientists are, by disposition or training, not comfortable in dealing with the press. Those who aren't, shouldn't. But those who are willing to "go public" need the support of their colleagues. When Paul first started his campaign of public education using the media, he was afraid he would lose the respect of his colleagues. Instead, the enthusiastic support of the vast majority of them, at Stanford and around the world, has made our lives infinitely more enjoyable. If science is to have the support it needs to help solve the most pressing environmental problems, "popularizer" needs to become a compliment in all disciplines.

4. Anyone who writes for a general audience should avoid scenarios—stories to help people picture the future. Scenarios are attractive because they can help dramatize the potential consequences of soci-

ety's present trajectory. But, as we have learned,[5] they are almost certain to be misrepresented as "predictions" rather than fictions. No matter how attractive or illustrative, scientists should eschew them.

5. Before going public at all, one's analyses and positions—especially in multidisciplinary areas—should be reviewed by knowledgable colleagues. Peer review is as important in communication as it is in technical work—and even more important when educational efforts span disciplinary boundaries. Mistakes are inevitable in any human endeavor, but scientists are obliged to take extra care to avoid them. We consult with colleagues about questionable publications outside our areas of expertise all the time. We also pester them to review our work, including chapters of this book. For instance, we wanted Susan Solomon to review our chapter on atmospheric issues because we and her other colleagues know that she is a world-class scientist and a stickler for scientific accuracy and that she wouldn't bend a scientific opinion for a friend or a cause. We selected all our scientific reviewers (see the acknowledgments) on the same basis.

6. Practical and optimal policies should be clearly differentiated. Scientists should present what they think is ideal, but then also present what they think is feasible. In that way, citizens have a practical target to work toward in the future. Scientists should make clear, however, that policy advice, though often based on in-depth studies and years of experience, is a value judgment, not a scientific proposition.

Brownlash writers seem to have a great deal of difficulty not only in accurately reporting the views of others but also in separating what would be the *best* policy from what would be a *practical* policy. Consider the following statement from journalist Stephen Budiansky:

> Biologists who have led the fight to save in toto the tropical rain forests and other species-rich habitats of the world have a strange habit of not grasping the political implications of their calls to arms in the name of wilderness. In an article in *Science* magazine, overpopulation guru Paul Ehrlich and Harvard biologist Edward O. Wilson, the man who made *biodiversity* a household word, issued a manifesto calling upon mankind to "reduce the scale of human activities" in order to save the planet's biodiversity. The "first step," they said, would be to cease "developing" any more relatively undisturbed land.[6]

Budiansky points to Paul's and Ed's "naïveté" in suggesting that "development can simply be made to cease." He then loftily explains the statistics of population growth as if Paul and Ed were unaware of them. What Paul and Ed actually said was, "Many steps can be taken to preserve biodiversity, *if the political will is generated*. Perhaps the first step, *which would be seen as especially extreme by Americans,* would be to cease 'developing' any more relatively undisturbed land"[7] (our emphasis).

Politically naïve? Of course, Paul and Ed don't expect their personal preferences to be followed, but redeveloping and restoring already badly disturbed areas is clearly one way to preserve both farmland and biodiversity—and thus our civilization. Budiansky obviously confuses what, sadly, is likely to be with what should be.

▣ What Can Concerned Citizens Do?

There is simply no substitute for spending time getting acquainted with the issues. Determining the best possible scientific position on an issue can be a non-trivial problem even for scientists in related fields. But clearly the more informed a person is, the better able she or he will be to weigh the issues. For those with some technical background, much can be learned from reputable scientific journals—magazines such as *Science, Nature, BioScience, Chemical and Engineering News, Technology Today, Ambio, Conservation Biology, Climatic Change, Ecological Economics,* and *Ecological Applications.* Many of the articles in these publications are accessible to laypersons as well, especially in the "News and Views" or "Forum" sections, which are often found up front.

Less technical magazines such as *Scientific American, Discover, Natural History, Pacific Discovery, Environment, Science News,* and *New Scientist* often cover environmental issues well. Some magazines published by environmental organizations print informative articles designed for non-specialists, including *The Amicus Journal, Audubon, Sierra, Wilderness,* and *World Watch.*

It is important to recognize that even the scientific literature isn't totally objective; all scientists bring their cultural values to their science. As we discussed at length in chapter 3, what sets science apart from most other ways of finding out about the world are the rather rigid requirements for investigative protocols and testing of hypotheses, backed by an adversarial system in which scientists can advance their careers by showing that well-accepted ideas are false.

Identifying the author of a suspicious environmental story requires access to a substantial library. If the author is labeled a "scientist," is he or she included in *American Men and Women of Science?*[8] Does the individual have recent publications referred to in the *Science Citation Index*,[9] which lists both a scientist's current publications (source indices) and citations of those publications by other scientists (citation indices)? The *Index* can help determine whether the author is a regular contributor to the pertinent scientific literature—and whether those contributions have generally dealt with environmental issues and their relation to the human predicament.

If the item in question is a book authored by a non-scientist, the acknowledgments can often reveal a lot about its credibility. Have a substantial number of scientists been credited with reviewing the contents for accuracy? Are at least some of the reviewers from major universities? There are many fine scientists in four-year colleges and in other non-university positions, but in highly technical areas one would expect to see some reviewing by prominent people at research universities or at leading research institutions or laboratories. There are, of course, a very few scientists at major universities ready to sell out to the highest bidder—but the vast majority are honest scientists to begin with, and all are under considerable peer pressure to give scientifically sound judgments. Like almost everyone else, scientists want the approval of their colleagues. Of course, an author can submit a book to scientific reviewers and then neglect their advice.

Perhaps the simplest way to gain a balanced view of an environmental problem is to consult the national and international assessment literature. Included in this category are reports from the U.S. National Research Council (NRC), the research-conducting arm of the National Academy of Sciences; the Intergovernmental Panel on Climate Change (IPCC); the World Meteorological Organization (WMO); the U.S. Office of Technology Assessment (eliminated, sadly, by Congress in 1995); Australia's Commonwealth Scientific and Industrial Research Organization (CSIRO); the United Nations Environment Programme (UNEP); and so on. Such groups always represent the scientific consensus and provide cautious, conservative evaluations of problems.

All these steps can help you gauge whether someone is trying to get you to believe some anti-science, but in the end some impromptu analysis may be needed. With highly technical issues such analysis often won't be possible; but in many cases, a little work on a calculator or even some mental arithmetic can supply an answer. Checking a person's conclusions may require looking at relatively unbiased data, which often can be found in statistics from the United Nations, the *World Almanac* or *U.S. Statistical Abstract,* and various government agencies.

The Food and Agriculture Organization of the United Nations (FAO), for example, supplies the estimate that Earth has roughly 3.6 billion acres of arable land (about 0.6 acres per person). Suppose someone claims that human population growth can continue at current rates for 1000 years. That's more than twenty doublings. For mathematical ease, assume there are only 5 billion people now instead of almost 6 billion. Doubling ten times starting with 5 gives you 5 → 10 → 20 → 40 → 80 → 160 → 320 → 640 → 1280 → 2560 → 5120, or roughly 1000 times the current population—some 5 trillion people about five hundred years in the future. Doubling ten more times gives another roughly thousandfold increase—to *one million times* the current population. Getting out the old calculator, you discover that agricultural production for each of some 5 million billion persons will necessarily come from only 0.7 millionth of an acre—roughly four square inches—per person. Even if we learned to farm all of Earth's surface, land and sea, we'd need to feed each person from a plot of about one square foot (arable land is about one-thirty-sixth of the total surface).

That would be a clever trick—but, of course, a brownlasher will say we'll be farming Mars or planets of other stars. We'll leave you and your calculator to figure out the likelihood of that.[10] Should you be at all mathematically inclined, there is a wonderful book to guide you in making such informative approximations and solving other environmental problems: John Harte's *Consider a Spherical Cow.*[11]

Plain common sense can also help you determine where the dependable views lie in most brownlash debates. Given that the nations of the world were willing to negotiate a treaty banning CFCs, the manufacturers were willing to go along with it, the National Academy of Sciences elected F. Sherwood Rowland and Mario Molina as members, and the very conservative Royal Swedish Academy of Sciences gave them Nobel Prizes, it doesn't take too much discernment to evaluate the credibility of Rush Limbaugh's view that concern over stratospheric ozone is "Poppycock. Balderdash."[12]

Similarly, claims that population isn't a problem simply don't stand up to casual scrutiny. One has only to visit a large city and drive around at rush hour to get some insight into the problems human numbers can create. As to the claim that people can always move to that "empty" space in Iowa or Nevada, ask whether the space is really empty in Iowa and why people are not already living in the open areas in Nevada. Anyone who says that some substance that is carcinogenic in mice "has never given any person cancer," should be asked how anyone could possibly know that. And since scientists agree that adding greenhouse gases to the atmosphere leads to changes in climate, is it sensible to be unconcerned when humanity's activities are releasing large quantities of such gases into the atmosphere and food production is heavily climate dependent?

If there is no world population-food problem, why did Norman Borlaug, "father of the green revolution," state in 1995: "Twenty-five years ago, in my acceptance speech for the 1970 Nobel Prize . . . I warned that unless the frightening power of human reproduction was curbed, the success of the green revolution would be only ephemeral"?[13] Why would the newspapers be full of discussions of fishing fleets idled in port for lack of fish to catch?[14] Anyone who claims that cleared rain forests will "grow back" (as an Australian forester once said to us) should have to explain where the unique animals that inhabited them will live in the meantime.[15]

In short, people should have faith in their own judgment when they've taken the time to examine different views of an issue and taken into account their own predispositions and prejudices. Then they can become activists—devote as much of their time as possible to improving the human condition. The scientific community needs help in re-plotting humanity's trajectory toward a sustainable future.

CHAPTER 13

One Planet, One Experiment

A quick review of some compelling statistics reveals how wrong—and indeed how threatening to humanity's future—the brownlash can be. The roughly fivefold increase in the number of human beings over the past century and a half is the most dramatic terrestrial event since the retreat of ice-age glaciers thousands of years ago. That explosion of human numbers has been combined with about a fourfold increase in consumption per person and the adoption of a wide array of technologies that needlessly damage the environment.

The result has been something like a twentyfold escalation since 1850 of the pressure humanity places on its environment—an unprecedented assault on natural ecosystems. The symptoms of this assault, all clearly linked to overpopulation, include the following:

1. Land degradation, with Earth having already lost some of the potential value of more than 40 percent of its land surface;

2. Deforestation, with about a third of the original forest cover having been removed without replacement since the invention of agriculture and much of the remaining forest highly modified and disrupted;

3. Ecosystem toxification, with thousands of synthetic chemicals being poured into the environment and disturbing signs emerging that

213

many of them interfere with ecosystem functioning, human developmental processes, and human resistance to disease;

4. Loss of biological diversity, with populations and species, which are working parts of our life-support systems, being exterminated at rates unprecedented since the mass extinction 65 million years ago that finished off the dinosaurs;

5. Depletion of Earth's vital ozone shield, which may be corrected by the Montreal Protocol but which still must be considered a potential threat;

6. The prospect of rapid climate change threatening agricultural productivity, causing coastal flooding, and altering the epidemiological environment, made more credible by the news that 1995 was the warmest year on record and the consensus of the scientific community that global warming has arrived;

7. Crop and fisheries production already lagging behind population growth, with little prospect of a new "green revolution" to produce increases in agricultural yields that soon may be desperately needed; and

8. Deterioration of the human epidemiological environment, with causal connections to all of the above, which threatens humankind with great epidemics, the potential seriousness of which is only hinted at by AIDS, recent outbreaks of the Ebola virus, and rapid proliferation of antibiotic-resistant strains of bacteria.

The symptoms also may include increasing social disruption, although the connection of the latter to the increased scale of the human enterprise is more controversial.[1]

That the planet as a whole is overpopulated, as are virtually all nations, is clear. Today's 5.8 billion people cannot be supported on "income"— only by the destruction and dispersal of a one-time inheritance of natural capital. The most important elements of that capital are deep, rich agricultural soils, fossil groundwater deposited during glacial periods, and biological diversity.

Population growth is also a key factor in the deterioration of humanity's epidemiological environment. Large populations are needed to maintain many infectious diseases and also are more likely to be invaded by pathogens previously restricted to non-human organisms—especially populations that contain many hungry and thus immune-compromised people. The AIDS epidemic is likely to be just the first of many.

Despite such ominous trends, the brownlash continues to hammer away in print and over the airwaves, sowing confusion and doubt in the minds of many citizens about the seriousness—if not the very existence—of environmental deterioration. Meanwhile, politicians, pundits, and other leaders focus narrowly on political issues such as conflict in the Balkans and central Africa (without examining underlying causes), short-term economic trends, and the morality of birth control and abortion as the very foundations of our civilization are being ripped away. And while on one hand we applaud the grassroots efforts on behalf of environmental protection (such as curbside recycling, ecotourism, and enthusiasm for things "organic"), we can't help but fear that these useful but utterly insufficient steps may also help to distract attention from much more basic issues. Society needs to recognize that to be sustainable, the economy must operate in harmony with rules set by Earth's ecosystems—and needs to act accordingly.

Civilization's highest priority must be given to lowering the pressure on those vital ecosystems, seeking a sustainable food-population balance, and safeguarding human health against global toxification and emerging pathogens alike. Achieving this will require humanely reducing the size of populations worldwide (by lowering birthrates to below death rates)—especially populations in rich nations. It will also mean reducing per-capita consumption among the rich, which will make room for needed growth in consumption among the poor and can be achieved while *enhancing* the quality of life; adopting more environmentally benign technologies; and establishing *a general increase in equity*.[2] It is important to note that the sticky issue of population policy cannot be avoided. Whatever your cause, it's a lost cause if humanity doesn't solve its population problem.

Scientists in general, and environmental scientists in particular, have grown more and more troubled by the grim trends just described. So it seems appropriate to finish this book with a summary of the views expressed in 1993 by the scientific community as a whole. Those views were presented in two historic statements, both of which are reprinted in full in appendix B. The first is a joint statement by fifty-eight of the world's scientific academies, including those of Australia, Brazil, Canada, China, Denmark, France, Germany, Great Britain, India, Kenya, the Netherlands, Norway, Russia, Sweden, and the United States, issued following a scientific summit on world population held in New Delhi, India, on October 24–27, 1993. The second is the *World Scientists' Warning to Humanity,* which was sponsored by the Union of Concerned Scientists[3] in 1993 and has been signed by more than 1700 of Earth's leading scientists, including 104 Nobel laureates—more than half of the living recipients in the sciences. Sadly, neither statement received significant coverage in the press or the electronic media.

As you will see, there is substantial overlap between the two statements and between them and our views. Of course, no scientist is likely to agree with every word in the statements—or in this book—and some scientists would take major exception to portions of all three. But we believe those two statements and this book express a clear consensus of the global scientific community about the precariousness of humanity's position. It is a consensus totally at variance with the views promoted by the brownlash. And, we reiterate, consensus—the judgment arrived at by most of those most knowledgeable—should form the basis of scientific input to public policy.

The consensus of the scientific community is as follows:

- Earth is finite.
- Declining supplies of good agricultural land, soils, and biodiversity are matters of great concern. So are overexploitation of fisheries and forests and growing demand on limited supplies of fresh water.
- The life-support systems of civilization are being pushed ever closer to their limits and are in danger of being damaged beyond repair.
- Toxification of the planet (including acidification and exposure to dangerous ultraviolet radiation) are threats to human well-being and the stability of natural and agricultural ecosystems.
- Global warming has the potential to change the world's climates and further destabilize civilization's life-support systems.
- Population growth is a major factor in the deterioration of local, regional, and global ecosystems.
- Overconsumption is also a major factor in that deterioration.
- People in both developed and less-developed nations must change their own behavior and cooperate with one another to solve these overarching problems.

The world's scientific community is now pointing out that we have only one Earth and that our global society is running a vast and dangerous experiment on it. If the experiment goes wrong, there will be no way to rerun it. In the end, we can only hope that the voices of science and reason will prevail over the brownlash and that the public and political leaders, who enjoy the many benefits that have been provided by the scientific community, will heed its warnings.

Brownlash Literature

□

Here we provide some comments on a sample of the brownlash literature we have used in our survey for those interested in more detail on this genre. We focus first on three brownlash books that are very troubling because they purport to contribute seriously to the scientific dialogue: Gregg Easterbrook's *A Moment on the Earth*, Stephen Budiansky's *Nature's Keepers,* and Charles Mann and Mark Plummer's *Noah's Choice.* The sample underlines an important point—that the errors we've cited are not just random mistakes in otherwise valuable attempts to describe the environmental situation; in aggregate, these books portray current environmental issues as relatively unimportant to the public's health and well-being and suggest that the policies and conclusions supported by environmental scientists are misguided. Following this discussion we comment on a few of the more routine brownlash efforts that seem simply to be broadsides against environmental science and environmentalism. Readers who have a scholarly interest should investigate this literature for themselves.

☐   **Gregg Easterbrook, 1995, *A Moment on the Earth: The Coming***
      Age of Environmental Optimism

We start with a relatively detailed look at Gregg Easterbrook's much-praised book[1] because doing so reveals more of the nature of the sources we have frequently quoted piecemeal throughout this book. This 745-page tome is a broad-gauge attack on environmental scientists (Paul in particular, but he is in good company with Rachel Carson and E. O. Wilson, among others) and the environmental movement. Its basic claim is that a doomsaying orthodoxy has greatly inflated the environmental threat to civilization, a claim it shares with the rest of the brownlash. It calls for what Easterbrook terms "ecorealism," the "next wave of environmental thinking." *Moment* is a mélange of truth, important factual errors, silly mistakes, pop philosophy, and attacks on straw men. Even here it is possible to give only a very small sample of what's wrong with *Moment*.[2]

Easterbrook's basic messages are simple. First, environmental impacts of human beings are minor compared with natural catastrophes such as collisions with asteroids, and therefore concern about them by a "green orthodoxy" is overblown.[3] Second, that concern is overblown largely because environmental problems either have been fixed (by a set of laws in the United States of which Easterbrook, to his credit, mostly approves), are in the process of being fixed, or are readily fixable. The environment is growing steadily cleaner, and within a few decades pollution will be a thing of the past. Overall, therefore, humanity need not pay heed to the doomsayers but can continue expanding the scale of its activities. This is the essence of Easterbrook's "ecorealism."

Contrary to the strong impression Easterbrook gives,[4] many of the points in *Moment* would be agreed with by most if not all environmental scientists and many "doctrinaire environmentalists"[5]—even though the book is presented as a counterbalance to their views that will make the debate on "environmental protection clearheaded and rational." The praise given to William Reilly for his valiant and often successful efforts as head of the Environmental Protection Agency during the Bush administration is a case in point. Too often Reilly was attacked by the environmental community for doing or trying to do sensible things.

Environmental scientists and environmentalists can agree with many other points made in *Moment*. Crop production in the United States is generally up and the acreage in production is generally down.[6] The expansion of the human enterprise has been greatly aided by unusually favorable climatic conditions, and this calls for "ecological caution."[7] There are many actions that should be taken to counter the threat of global warming "that are justified in and of themselves"[8]—what environmental scientists today call "no regrets" strategies. Carbon taxes and marketable trading permits are promising tools for limiting the flow of carbon dioxide into the atmosphere.[9] There has often been a problem of misplaced priorities in the reactions of the public, the environmental community, and the government to environmental threats.[10] The trend away from heavy dependence on pesticides and toward integrated pest management (IPM) is desirable.[11] The original compromise on the preservation of the California gnatcatcher and the coastal sage scrub was a good one.[12]

We and most other environmental scientists also agree with many other of Easterbrook's positions. The Endangered Species Act would indeed be more effective if it focused on protection of habitats rather than individual species[13] (although there could be real problems in doing so, as we noted earlier). "Population growth is indeed the core environmental problem for most of the world."[14] We too believe that capitalism is superior to communism, although there may be other candidates for "the worst social organizing principle ever devised."[15]

These, we repeat, are points that environmental scientists and other analysts—the "green orthodoxy" (or those supporting an "environmental credo") that Easterbrook repeatedly attacks[16]—have been making for years. For example, they have long been discussing institution of carbon taxes, tradeable emission permits, and "no regrets" strategies for countering enhancement of the greenhouse effect.[17] And we and others of the "green orthodoxy" have long crusaded for IPM.[18] The much-praised compromise on preservation of the California gnatcatcher and coastal sage scrub, one of Easterbrook's examples of ecorealism, was engineered by Paul's student and colleague Dennis Murphy, then Director and now President of Stanford University's Center for Conservation Biology, with our full support.[19] In short, the things that are correct in *Moment* come as no surprise to environmental scientists, nor, we expect, to most environmentalists. They are not new.

What does come as a surprise is the many errors in the book. Easterbrook states: "When no source for a fact is indicated in the text or these notes, this is because the assertion is not generally in dispute among specialists."[20] On that point he is repeatedly wrong. Some of the errors are minor—significant only in that they plainly show that many of his assertions are, in fact, disputed by specialists. Thus Easterbrook tells us that the "genus *Homo* [is] 'panmictic' to biologists."[21] Panmictic means exhibiting random mating, and *Homo sapiens* is an outstanding example of a species that is not—indeed, few if any of its *populations* are—panmictic. For *Homo sapiens* to be panmictic, each human being would have to have exactly the same chance of mating with every other human being of the opposite sex. For instance, each resident of Beijing would have to be equally likely to mate with a resident of Berlin as with another resident of Beijing.

A few other examples of such mistakes in *Moment* include the following: Lepidopterans are "insects in the moth family."[22] There are dozens of families of moths, which, together with a few families of butterflies, make up the great insect order Lepidoptera. "Myrmecophilous" is not the name of a caterpillar, as Easterbrook supposes.[23] A myrmecophilous caterpillar is any one (such as many species of the butterfly family Lycaenidae) that forms a mutually beneficial association with ants. Whether plants are "green-stemmed"[24] does not define them as vascular. Vascular plants are those (like most familiar plants) that have evolved efficient conducting systems (xylem and phloem) for moving water and nutrients about internally. Trees with brown or gray stems are very vascular.

"The United States is the most carefully studied biosphere in the world. . . ."[25] But, of course, the United States by definition cannot be a biosphere, since there is only one known biosphere—"the 'thin film' of life that occurs near the surface of Earth and the physical-chemical environment in which it is embedded."[26] "Less than one-tenth of one percent of the sun's power output falls on Earth."[27] A lot less—less than a millionth of a percent. Finally, one would hope that some knowledgeable reviewer would have gotten rid of the expression "the ecology," which in phrases like "bioaccumulative threat to the ecology"[28] translates as "bioaccumulative threat to the branch of science concerned with the relationships of organisms to their environments." Asteroids are not threats to "the physics."

Other factual errors are much more serious and would be vigorously disputed by specialists. For instance, one could easily gain the impression from the book that life has somehow overcome the second law of thermodynamics. "Perhaps one purpose of humankind is to expand complexity in defiance of the second law. . . ."[29] But neither human beings nor other organisms have the option of defying the all-important second law. They operate entirely according to its dictates. Whatever order and complexity they generate is overmatched by disorder and simplification created elsewhere in the system—just as refrigerators release more heat into a room than they extract from water in the process of ice-making. When volcanic activity creates order in the form of deposits of relatively pure minerals, it does not violate the second law of thermodynamics. On the other hand, carrying out Julian Simon's notion of converting the entire universe into copper[30] *would* require violating the second law. Ignorance of the second law is what gives hope to those trying to invent perpetual-motion machines or discover planets on which human activities can expand forever.

We are also told in *Moment* that "east of San Francisco" and "in all directions around Atlanta, and Denver and Warsaw and Madrid, and in many similar locations worldwide, extensive tracts of habitat that have known only occasional human intervention abut centers of mechanistic human excess."[31] Habitat for what? House sparrows, cockroaches, and cows, which are specialists in living where human intervention is substantial? Paul well remembers the day that he and Dennis Murphy spent trying to find anything remotely resembling undisturbed habitat around Madrid. East of San Francisco one finds the highly modified San Francisco Bay, followed by Oakland, Alameda, San Leandro, and other cities and suburbs and the completely agriculturalized Central Valley of California. Virtually all the areas Easterbrook mentions are utterly devoid of habitats "that have known only occasional human intervention."

The entire discussion that follows rests heavily on this incorrect assumption about habitats virtually unaffected by human disturbance. "At the small scale level upon which most earthly creatures dwell hardly anything has transpired."[32] Yet study after study has shown that small organisms are dramatically affected—more so than some larger creatures such as coyotes and red-tailed hawks. In particular, numerous populations of native plants are displaced by urbanization and agriculture, and with them go the insects that have a coevolved dependence on them.[33]

This is one of the most pernicious errors in *Moment,* one especially favorable to the view of the wise-use movement that development does not harm biodiversity.

Chapter 8 of this book describes many of the serious scientific errors that, taken together, deeply flaw Easterbrook's treatment of global warming.[34] Among the pervasive mistakes, *Moment* incorrectly assumes that the problems of forecasting climate and the problems of forecasting weather are the same,[35] confuses the "greenhouse effect" (which has been around for billions of years) with the human-caused enhancement of that effect usually known as "global warming,"[36] mixes up temperatures in Celsius and Fahrenheit,[37] and repeatedly confuses regional effects, in which cooling may accompany a gradual increase in the *average* temperature of Earth, with global effects.[38] *Moment*'s treatment of ozone issues is of similar quality.[39] Significantly, it shares many mistakes in atmospheric issues with brownlash publications.

In addition, *Moment* misstates the results of many scientific studies[40] and the work of outstanding scientists such as James Hansen and Stephen Schneider. Easterbrook's treatment of Schneider is especially egregious: "Even Schneider at Stanford, a prominent greenhouse believer, acknowledges, 'It's possible that everything in the last 30 years of temperature records is no more than noise.' "[41] Easterbrook displays his ignorance here—he presumably meant that Schneider believes human activities are enhancing the greenhouse effect, causing global warming (all scientists are "greenhouse believers," knowing full well that they'd all be frozen stiff if the greenhouse effect somehow ended!). Schneider, as we have already pointed out, is a cautious scientist who is noted for following the data or modeling results wherever they lead.[42] In the same sentence, Easterbrook labels Schneider a "believer" in global warming and then quotes him honestly explaining that the most important data set then available may not have shown warming at all. A little later,[43] Easterbrook snidely attacks Schneider for thinking that recent expansion of Greenland glaciers could be due to a cooling of Greenland, underlining Easterbrook's erroneous assumption that global warming means everyplace must get hotter.

Moment continually attacks "orthodoxy," "green orthodoxy," "green doctrine," "environmental credo," and so forth.[44] Easterbrook makes it clear that he considers ecologists to be part of that orthodoxy in general,[45] and that Paul (and by association, Anne) is among the prime examples, if not *the* prime example, of an orthodox ecologist doomsayer.[46] The book is crowded with claims (often erroneous) about what we and our colleagues think, but there is essentially no documentation of those views because of Easterbrook's disclaimer that they are generally accepted by specialists.[47]

Untruths and misstatements abound. For example, Easterbrook falsely states that in *The Population Bomb,* Paul "predicted that general crop failures would 'certainly' result in mass starvation in the United States by the 1980s."[48] Paul has never raised the possibility of mass famine in the United States.[49] His statement, almost three decades ago, was: "If the optimists are correct, today's level of misery will be perpetuated for perhaps two decades into the future. If the pessimists are correct, massive famines will occur [in "UDCs"—underdeveloped countries] soon, possibly in the early 1970s, certainly by the early 1980s. So far most of the evidence seems to be on the side of the pessimists, and we should plan on the assumption that they are correct."[50] The "optimists" proved more correct: "only" some 250 million people have died from hunger-related causes since Paul made that statement.

Others are similarly misrepresented in *Moment.* Donella Meadows points out that *Moment* falsely asserts that the book she coauthored in the early 1970s, *Limits to Growth,*[51] projected that petroleum would be exhausted by the 1990s. Like *The Population Bomb, Limits to Growth* is misrepresented by those too lazy to read it. As Meadows wrote in one of her newspaper columns:

> Gregg Easterbrook is one of the journalists who regularly repeat the *Limits to Growth* fable. A few years ago I met him at a conference and told him about my problem. I don't like being infamous for something I never said, I told him, and the rumor doesn't serve society. What can I do to stop it?
>
> Not much he said. Journalists use a computerized data base, where they can look up everything that's been printed about a book or person or event. Whenever a rumor is repeated, it builds another entry, so it strengthens itself. All you can do, he said, is wait for someone to repeat the myth, write a correction, and get it into the data base.[52]

Easterbrook asserts that the orthodox view of ecology is that there is a balance of nature "of an ecology that shatters at the lightest touch."[53] The orthodoxy is nothing of the sort and never has been. Ecologists have for decades recognized that natural systems are in constant flux. The older idea that the process of succession (orderly change in disturbed ecological communities) led to a stable, unchanging climax has long been recognized as being approximated only in certain situations and over certain time scales. The degree to which current ecosystems are resilient to perturbations over dozens or hundreds of years, and the characteristics that tend to enhance or degrade their stability, have long been, and remain, an active area of investigation.[54] That ecosystems change dramatically over millennia is well established and well accepted.[55] No ecologist thinks that any normal community (a collection of organisms living together in a defined physical location) or ecosystem (a community plus its physical-chemical environment) will "shatter at the lightest touch."[56] And, of course, no ecologist would think of "an ecology" doing anything.

Easterbrook also claims that the "orthodoxy wants the [Endangered Species] Act renewed much as it is, in its effective but panic-oriented form. For this a continuing owl emergency is a political essential."[57] Yet neither we nor our colleagues believes that this is an ideal solution. Rather, every ecologist we know would prefer the act to be modified into one that focuses protection on entire ecosystems, if there were a practical way to do that. But establishing a practical way represents a gigantic "if." Ecologists support the existing Endangered Species Act because it is the best available tool in the United States for protecting America's biological capital, but they know it is far from ideal.

Easterbrook's coverage of ESA issues typically reflects inadequate attention to details. For instance, he states that the "environmental orthodoxy" requires that a bush lupine be protected in Monterey County, California, where it is native, and eradicated in Humboldt County, where it is not native.[58] Easterbrook is probably talking about *Lupinus arboreus* var. *eximius,* endemic to Montara Mountain, San Mateo County, which is not protected under the ESA but is listed as of conservation concern. It is not protected under any law. Another variety, *Lupinus arboreus* var. *arboreus*, is widespread along the California coast and native in Humboldt County, where owing to disturbance it is crowding out native vegetation. A distinguished botanist commenting on Easterbrook's error said, "All in all, it's a classical case of reading something quickly and superficially, and then jumping to whatever conclusions one wants, rather like a junior high school project by a mediocre student."[59]

"Agricultural green doctrine," Easterbrook asserts, praises "labor-based low technology farming" in the Sahel,[60] even though it is environmentally destructive. Ecologists do favor labor-based farming in many areas because of catastrophic unemployment problems in poor countries; they always favor appropriate technologies, ones that cause the least possible environmental destruction and social disruption and are within the means of local farmers.[61]

"In environmental orthodoxy fear of nuclear power has gone beyond irrational: it has entered a category that might be called transrational, in which the logical aspects of an issue are not merely misconstrued but actively shunned."[62] Since we're presumably part of that "orthodoxy," the reader is invited to peruse our discussion of nuclear power in *Healing the Planet,* which is based largely on the views of our close colleague John Holdren, who is at present a member of the President's Committee of Advisors on Science and Technology. It says in part:

> . . . for fission to be candidate as an important power source in the future . . . several hurdles must be overcome [which we then discuss]. . . . The world would have been better off if the first deployment of nuclear power had featured reactors designed from scratch to run electric grids rather than nuclear submarines. It seems unlikely to us now that the arguments on safety will ever be fully resolved until and unless a new nuclear technology has been fully deployed on a large scale—that is to say, unless society decides to run what may be a very risky experiment.[63]

Some years ago we argued hard with members of Congresswoman Claudine Schneider's staff to permit funds for research on nuclear power to remain in Senator Tim Wirth's proposed energy bill. These "transrational" positions, we assert, represent a consensus of the segment of the scientific community that is competent to judge the potential benefits and costs of nuclear power without having a vested interest in its expansion.

Moment's Pollyannish view of the world is greatly enhanced by what it omits. Perhaps the most ominous of all environmental trends is that of land degradation. Yet Easterbrook provides only a brief discussion of desertification, in which he confuses the problem of productive land being degraded to desert with efforts to keep natural desert ecosystems intact.[64] He overlooks the fact that over 40 percent of Earth's vegetated land surface "has diminished capacity to supply benefits to humanity, because of recent, direct impacts of land use."[65] The book further fails to recognize that the most serious resource constraint on further expansion of the human enterprise may be the availability of fresh water— its chapter on water deals only with water quality.

Stephen Budiansky, 1995, *Nature's Keepers: The New Science of Nature Management*

This addition to the brownlash literature does not contain quite the density of errors and misrepresentations found in *Moment,* but it is in the race. For instance, on page 182 *Nature's Keepers* claims that the rivet popper analogy comes from "a grade B science fiction story." The rivet popper analogy comes from our book *Extinction,* pages xi–xii, and Budiansky obviously has never read it. It is instructive to compare the real thing with his version. The following is from *Extinction:*

> As you walk from the terminal toward your airline, you notice a man on a ladder busily prying rivets out of its wing. Somewhat concerned, you saunter over to the rivet popper and ask him just what the hell he's doing.
>
> "I work for the airline—Growthmania Intercontinental," the man informs you, "and the airline has discovered that it can sell these rivets for two dollars apiece."
>
> "But how do you know you won't fatally weaken the wing doing that?" you inquire.
>
> "Don't worry," he assures you. "I'm certain the manufacturer made this plane much stronger than it needs to be, so no harm's done. Besides, I've taken lots of rivets from this wing and it hasn't fallen off yet. Growthmania Airlines needs the money; if we didn't pop the rivets, Growthmania wouldn't be able to continue expanding. And I need the commission they pay me—fifty cents a rivet!"
>
> "You must be out of your mind!"
>
> "I told you not to worry; I know what I'm doing. As a matter of fact, I'm going to fly on this flight also, so you can see there's absolutely nothing to be concerned about."
>
> Any sane person would, of course, go back to the terminal, report the gibbering idiot and Growthmania Airlines to the FAA, and make reservations on another carrier.
>
> Rivet-popping on Spaceship Earth consists of aiding and abetting the extermination of species and populations of

nonhuman organisms. . . . Some of these species supply or could supply important direct benefits to humanity, and all of them are involved in providing the public services without which society could not persist. . . .

Ecosystems, like well-made airplanes, tend to have redundant subsystems and other "design" features that permit them to continue functioning after absorbing a certain amount of abuse. *A dozen rivets, or a dozen species, might never be missed* [our new emphasis]. On the other hand, a thirteenth rivet popped from a wing flap, or the extinction of a key species involved in the cycling of nitrogen, could lead to a serious accident.

In most cases an ecologist can no more predict the consequences of the extinction of a given species than an airline passenger can assess the loss of a single rivet. But both can easily foresee the long-term results of continually forcing species to extinction or of removing rivet after rivet. No sensible airline passenger today would accept a continuous loss of rivets from jet transports. Before much more time has passed, attitudes must be changed so that no sane passenger on Spaceship Earth will accept a continuous loss of populations or species of nonhuman organisms.[66]

That's what we wrote. This is how Budiansky, a "senior writer at *U.S. News and World Report*,"[67] characterized by Gregg Easterbrook as "an astute observer,"[68] described what we wrote:

Are there certain species or certain processes or certain characteristics of "natural" or managed ecosystems that are more important for the long-term well-being of an ecological community than others?

To doctrinaire environmentalists this question is, of course, heresy. *It is given that all species are equally vital strands in the web of life* [our emphasis]; to remove one is to risk the collapse of all. Paul Ehrlich often invokes the metaphor (it comes from a grade B science fiction story) of the madman pulling rivets out of an airplane in mid-flight; finding that nothing happens each time he pulls one out, he keeps at it until, loosening the thirteenth rivet, the plane splits apart and crashes."[69]

The truth is that neither we nor any other environmental scientist we know has ever claimed that all species (or populations) are equally important, from the viewpoint of either direct economic benefits to humanity or the delivery of ecosystem services. We would not even make

the claim that all species should be equally valued for moral reasons—
quite the opposite, although assigning values tends to be a deeply personal and vexing problem. We don't miss "wild" smallpox virus a bit, for
example. We recognize that there are reasonable arguments for preserving a few samples of the virus for research purposes, but would suffer no great angst if it were exterminated.

The problem for ecologists in 1981, when we wrote the analogy, and
the problem now, is that we have *no way of judging the value* of most
species, to say nothing of populations, which also can be extremely important. When Budiansky states that there are "many cases in which extinctions of one species have had no consequences whatsoever,"[70] he's
talking nonsense. All extinctions have further consequences; some have
no known consequences for human society. The issue of the importance of extinctions in the short and long term to the delivery of ecosystem services is becoming an active area of ecological research; the hypothesis that diversity is not important to the functioning of ecosystems
appears less and less likely all the time.[71]

Budiansky's book is replete with other mistakes, contradictions, and
irrelevancies. A small sample from Budiansky's chapter 7, "Waiting for
Newton," includes the following excerpts.[72]

"It says much about the state of ecology as a predictive science that
one of the few clear-cut applications of ecological theory to the real
world in the scientific literature is a disproof of the existence of large
mythical monsters."[73] Ecological theory actually has been applied to a
host of real-world situations, successfully predicting such things as the
dynamics of populations; the spread of diseases; patterns of foraging;
life history strategies; competition; predation; the composition, structure,
and assembly of communities; and island biogeography. This has produced a huge technical literature, including dozens of books and thousands of articles, which apparently have escaped Budiansky's notice.[74]

"Indeed, the most well-publicized effort of late to apply basic ecological theory to conservation and ecosystem management is, upon closer
inspection, little more than a bomb thrower's polemic masquerading as
science. The effort in question is principally that of one man, Harvard
biologist Edward O. Wilson, a relentless popularizer of the theory that
'we are in the midst of one of the great extinction spasms of geological
history.'[75] . . . Wilson uses different numbers in different contexts—low
numbers in scientific journals, high numbers in his popular books and

magazine articles, and the highest numbers in newspaper interviews and other carefully orchestrated media events . . ."[76] The current extinction spasm is not just theoretical (in lay terms) but is the sort of thing knowledgeable scientists treat as fact—based simply on what is known of the distribution of species and the amount of habitat destruction and conversion that is occurring. A detailed analysis of Wilson's estimates by ecologist Thomas Brooks of the University of Tennessee found that all of the estimates lie within two orders of magnitude as a result of the two orders of magnitude of uncertainty about the number of extant species: "Rather than a 'publication effect,' I would suggest that if anything [there is] a 'date effect,' with the higher extinction rates being more recent as it has become more obvious how many species there really are on Earth."[77] In each case, Wilson carefully gives the basis for his estimates, and his are in accord with those made by other scientists.[78]

"The predictions are based on what is rather grandly termed the theory of island biogeography . . . [which] consists of but a single equation."[79] Actually, both Wilson's estimates and the theory of island biogeography are based on F. W. Preston's species-area relationship.[80] The theory contains many equations, was first published as a long scientific paper and then as a monograph,[81] and has subsequently been analyzed very extensively. Budiansky then follows his error with a parade of mistakes or untruths about the theory and about the Endangered Species Act.[82]

Ecologist Thomas Brooks summarizes Budiansky's chapter as follows:

> In conclusion, the chapter can be divided into four parts, which are connected together very poorly, if at all. The first is a broad, interesting but irrelevant discussion of the failures of historical game management policies. The second is an attack on large-scale conservation biology, mainly a personal attack on E. O. Wilson, masquerading as a "critique" of the species-area relationship, for not taking individual species into account. The third, in direct contradiction, is an attack on species-based conservation (in particular, the Endangered Species Act) for not considering the large scale. Budiansky compromises with medium-scale population and community biology, concluding with a sensible discussion of the application of these sciences to conservation, but failing completely to recognize that all scales must be considered in "nature management" or, indeed, in any science.[83]

☐   Charles C. Mann and Mark L. Plummer, 1995, *Noah's Choice:*
The Future of Endangered Species

This book attacks the Endangered Species Act (see chapter 7) and may
well influence reauthorization of the ESA. It is more subtle, better organized, more interesting, and better written than *A Moment on the Earth.*
It does not contain the high density of outright errors found in *Moment*
or in *Nature's Keepers.*[84] *Noah's Choice* does, however, misstate our
views,[85] and it contains a totally made-up statement that it attributes to
Paul and E. O. Wilson.[86]

Yet *Noah's Choice* is more dangerous than the others in its narrower
arena. Its approach is to give a few examples of instances in which the
ESA has not done a good job, ignoring its triumphs. The authors say
they omitted the story of the old-growth forests of the Pacific Northwest,
where the ESA may actually have preserved the long-term viability of
the timber industry, because Plummer's wife happens to work for the
Weyerhaeuser Company.[87] Mann and Plummer don't point out that Weyerhaeuser is one of the companies that might benefit in the short term
from their recommendation to reduce "our duties to biodiversity to the
barest of bare bones"[88] and their recommendation that the ESA be restricted to prohibiting only "direct, intentional harm."[89] If such modifi-
cation became law and the ESA lost the power to prevent habitat destruction, the act would be close to useless. No one, of course, will
benefit in the long term from destruction of the Endangered Species Act.

The remaining brownlash books are perhaps best exemplified by
Ronald Bailey's 1993 *Eco-Scam: The False Prophets of Ecological Apocalypse.*[90] This publication is a standard product of the Cato Institute's propaganda mill, written by someone described in the jacket copy (in total)
as follows: "has covered science as a writer for *Forbes* and as a producer
for PBS. He lives in Virginia." The book is of precisely the quality one
would expect of environmental coverage in *Forbes,* as the many references given in earlier chapters in this book indicate.[91] In quality it is similar to Dixy Lee Ray's two volumes and several others that are cited in
our main text, which merit no further discussion here.

Wilfred Beckerman's 1995 *Small Is Stupid: Blowing the Whistle on the
Greens*[92] deserves special mention. The book is an ideal candidate for
the review line "What's good in it is not new, and what's new in it is
not good." Mainstream economists such as Kenneth Arrow, Partha Das-

gupta, Walter Falcon, Lawrence Goulder, Karl-Goran Maler, Charles Per-
rings, and others are now meeting and working with ecologists in an effort to combine the powers of the two disciplines to deal with the
human predicament. Thus it's a shame that Beckerman's book, which
emphasizes tension between the two disciplines, had to be published.
It claims, for example, that "greens" believe "rising income levels are inevitably and at all times and in all circumstances associated with a deterioration in the environment."[93] It also asserts there are "no environmental limits to the total scale of world output."[94]

The brownlash literature is not, of course, restricted to books. We
have read hundreds of brownlash magazine and newspaper articles.
The editorial pages of the *Wall Street Journal* print a great deal of environmental anti-science. We are dismayed that the leading business
newspaper in the United States fails to inform the business community
accurately about environmental issues. Although the main part of the
Wall Street Journal is highly competent, its editorial pages regularly
publish completely erroneous material. Those businesspeople with an
interest in their children's future would be well-advised to subscribe to
the magazine *The Economist*. We sometimes disagree with it, but it does
an accurate and quite thorough job of covering the environment.

The left-wing counterpoint to the *Wall Street Journal*'s editorial pages
could be considered the *New York Review of Books,* which claims to be
the leading intellectual journal in the United States. Maybe it is, but its
coverage of environmental issues generally ranges from absent to poor
(see, for example, the 1994 article by economist Amartya Sen, "Population: Delusion and Reality," which, among other errors, badly underestimates the serious environmental impacts of population growth).[95]
Maybe many intellectuals think, as Rush Limbaugh apparently does, that
they are exempt from the laws of nature, but we doubt it. The intellectual community, like the business community, deserves better.

The Scientific Consensus

Statement by Fifty-Eight
of the World's Scientific Academies[1]

IN 1993, FIFTY-SIX of the world's scientific academies (including the U.S. National Academy) came together in a "Science Summit" on world population. The conference was an outgrowth of two earlier meetings, one by the Royal Swedish Academy of Sciences, the other by the Royal Society of London and the U.S. National Academy of Sciences. At both meetings, urgent concern was expressed for the expanding world population and a commitment was made to continue discourse on matters related to population growth. The resulting 1993 Science Summit—the first large-scale collaborative activity ever undertaken by the world's scientific academies—set as its primary goal the formulation of a statement to be presented at the International Conference on Population and Development in 1994. The statement, reprinted below, underscores the need for government policies and initiatives that will help achieve "zero population growth within the lifetime of our children."

The Growing World Population

The world is in the midst of an unprecedented expansion of human numbers. It took hundreds of thousands of years for our species to reach a population level of 10 million, only 10,000 years ago. This number grew to 100 million people about 2,000 years ago and to 2.5 billion by 1950. Within less than the span of a single lifetime, it has more than doubled to 5.5 billion in 1993.

This accelerated population growth resulted from rapidly lowered death rates (particularly infant and child mortality rates), combined with sustained high birth rates. Success in reducing death rates is attributable to several factors: increases in food production and distribution, improvements in public health (water and sanitation) and in medical technology (vaccines and antibiotics), along with gains in education and standards of living within many developing nations.

Over the past 30 years, many regions of the world have also dramatically reduced birth rates. Some have already achieved family sizes small enough, if maintained, to result eventually in a halt to population growth. These successes have led to a slowing of the world's rate of population increase. The shift from high to low death and birth rates has been called the "demographic transition."

The rate at which the demographic transition progresses worldwide will determine the ultimate level of the human population. The lag between downward shifts of death and birth rates may be many decades or even several generations, and during these periods population growth will continue inexorably. We face the prospect of a further doubling of the population within the next half century. Most of this growth will take place in developing countries.

Consider three hypothetical scenarios[2] for the levels of human population in the century ahead:

- Fertility declines within sixty years from the current rate of 3.3 to a global replacement average of 2.1 children per woman. The current population momentum would lead to at least 11 billion people before leveling off at the end of the twenty-first century.

- Fertility reduces to an average of 1.7 children per woman early in the next century. Human population growth would peak at 7.8 billion persons in the middle of the twenty-first century and decline slowly thereafter.

- Fertility declines to no lower than 2.5 children per woman. Global population would grow to 19 billion by the year 2100, and to 28 billion by 2150.

The actual outcome will have enormous implications for the human condition and for the natural environment on which all life depends.

Key Determinants of Population Growth

High fertility rates have historically been strongly correlated with poverty, high childhood mortality rates, low status and educational levels of women, deficiencies in reproductive health services, and inadequate availability and acceptance of contraceptives. Falling fertility rates and the demographic transition are generally associated with improved standards of living, such as increased per capita incomes, increased life expectancy, lowered infant mortality, increased adult literacy, and higher rates of female education and employment.

Even with improved economic conditions, nations, regions, and societies will experience different demographic patterns due to varying cultural influences. The value placed upon large families (especially among underprivileged rural populations in less-developed countries that benefit least from the process of development), the assurance of security for the elderly, the ability of women to control reproduction, and the status and rights of women within families and within societies are significant cultural factors affecting family size and the demand for family planning services.

Even with a demand for family planning services, the adequate availability of and access to family planning and other reproductive health services are essential in facilitating slowing of the population growth rate. Also, access to education and the ability of women to determine their own economic security influence their reproductive decisions.

Population Growth, Resource Consumption, and the Environment

Throughout history, and especially during the twentieth century, environmental degradation has primarily been a product of our efforts to secure improved standards of food, clothing, shelter, comfort, and recreation for growing numbers of people. The magnitude of the threat to the ecosystem is linked to human population size and resource use per person. Resource use, waste production, and environmental degradation are accelerated by population growth. They are further exacerbated by consumption habits, certain technological developments, and particular patterns of social organization and resource management.

As human numbers further increase, the potential for irreversible changes of far-reaching magnitude also increases. Indicators of severe environmental stress include the growing loss of biodiversity, increasing greenhouse gas emissions, increasing deforestation worldwide, stratospheric ozone depletion, acid rain, loss of topsoil, and shortages of water, food, and fuelwood in many parts of the world.

While both developed and developing countries have contributed to global environmental problems, developed countries with 85 percent of the gross world product and 23 percent of its population account for the largest part of mineral and fossil-fuel consumption, resulting in significant environmental impacts. With current technologies, present levels of consumption by the developed world are likely to lead to serious negative consequences for all countries. This is especially apparent with the increases in atmospheric carbon dioxide and trace gases that have accompanied industrialization, which have the potential for changing global climate and raising sea level.

In both rich and poor countries, local environmental problems arise from direct pollution from energy use and other industrial activities, inappropriate agricultural practices, population concentration, inadequate environmental management, and inattention to environmental goals. When current economic production has been the overriding priority and inadequate attention has been given to environmental protection, local environmental damage has led to serious negative impacts on health and major impediments to future economic growth. Restoring the environment, even where still possible, is far more expensive and time consuming than managing it wisely in the first place; even rich countries have difficulty in affording extensive environmental remediation efforts.

The relationships between human population, economic development, and the natural environment are complex. Examination of local and regional case studies reveals the influence and interaction of many variables. For example, environmental and economic impacts vary with population composition and distribution, and with rural-urban and international migrations. Furthermore, poverty and lack of economic opportunities stimulate faster population growth and increase incentives for environmental degradation by encouraging exploitation of marginal resources.

Both developed and developing countries face a great dilemma in reorienting their productive activities in the direction of a more harmonious interaction with nature. This challenge is accentuated by the uneven stages of development. If all people of the world consumed fossil fuels and other natural resources at the rate now characteristic of developed countries (and with current technologies), this would greatly intensify our already unsustainable demands on the biosphere. Yet development is a legitimate expectation of less-developed and transitional countries.

The Earth Is Finite

The growth of population over the past half century was for a time matched by similar worldwide increases in utilizable resources. However, in the past decade food production from both land and sea has declined relative to population growth. The area of agricultural land has shrunk, both through soil erosion and reduced possibilities of irrigation. The availability of water is already a constraint in some countries. These are warnings that the earth is finite, and that natural systems are being pushed ever closer to their limits.

Quality of Life and the Environment

Our common goal is improving the quality of life for all people, those living today and succeeding generations, ensuring their social, economic, and personal well-being with guarantees of fundamental human rights, and allowing them to live harmoniously with a protected environment. We believe that this goal can be achieved, provided we are willing to undertake the requisite social change. Given time, political will, and intelligent use of science and technology, human ingenuity can remove many constraints on improving human welfare worldwide, finding substitutes for wasteful practices, and protecting the natural environment.

But time is short and appropriate policy decisions are urgently needed. The ability of humanity to reap the benefits of its ingenuity depends on its skill in governance and management, and on strategies for dealing with problems such as widespread poverty, increased numbers of aged persons, inadequate health care and limited educational opportunities for large groups of people, limited capital for investment, environmental degradation in every region of the world, and unmet needs for family planning services in both developing and developed countries. In our judgment, humanity's ability to deal successfully with its social, economic, and environmental problems will require the achievement of zero population growth within the lifetime of our children.

Human Reproductive Health

The timing and spacing of pregnancies are important for the health of the mother, her children, and her family. Most maternal deaths are due to unsafe practices in terminating pregnancies, a lack of readily available services for high-risk pregnancies, and women having too many children or having them too early and too late in life.

Millions of people still do not have adequate access to family planning services and suitable contraceptives. Only about one-half of married couples of reproductive age are currently practicing contraception. Yet as the director-general of UNICEF put it, "Family planning could bring more benefits to more people at less cost than any other single technology now available to the human race." Existing contraceptive methods could go far toward alleviating the unmet need if they were available and used in sufficient numbers, through a variety of channels of distribution, sensitively adapted to local needs.

But most contraceptives are for use by women, who consequently bear the risks to health. The development of contraceptives for male use continues to lag. Better contraceptives are needed for both men and women, but developing new contraceptive approaches is slow and financially unattractive to industry. Further work is needed on an ideal spectrum of contraceptive methods that are safe, efficacious, easy to use and deliver, reasonably priced, user-controlled and responsive, appropriate for special populations and age cohorts, reversible, and at least some of which protect against sexually transmitted diseases, including AIDS.

Reducing fertility rates, however, cannot be achieved merely by providing more contraceptives. The demand for these services has to be addressed. Even when family planning and other reproductive health services are widely available, the social and economic status of women affects individual decisions to use them. The ability of women to make decisions about family size is greatly affected by gender roles within society and in sexual relationships. Ensuring equal opportunity for women in all aspects of society is crucial.

Thus all reproductive health services must be implemented as a part of broader strategies to raise the quality of human life. They must include the following:

- Efforts to reduce and eliminate gender-based inequalities. Women and men should have equal opportunities and responsibilities in sexual, social, and economic life.

- Provision of convenient family planning and other reproductive health services with a wide variety of safe contraceptive options, irrespective of an individual's ability to pay.

- Encouragement of voluntary approaches to family planning and elimination of unsafe and coercive practices.

- Development policies that address basic needs such as clean water, sanitation, broad primary health care measures and education, and that foster empowerment of the poor and women.

"The adoption of a smaller family norm, with consequent decline in total fertility, should not be viewed only in demographic terms. It means that people, and particularly women, are empowered and are taking control of their fertility and the planning of their lives; it means that children are born by choice, not by chance, and that births are better planned; and it means that families are able to invest relatively more in a smaller number of beloved children, trying to prepare them for a better future."[3]

Sustainability of the Natural World As Everyone's Responsibility

In addressing environmental problems, all countries face hard choices. This is particularly so when it is perceived that there are short-term trade-offs between economic growth and environmental protection, and where there are limited financial resources. But the downside risks to the earth—our environmental life support system—over the next generation and beyond are too great to ignore. Current trends in environmental degradation from human activities combined with the unavoidable increase in global population will take us into unknown territory.

Other factors, such as inappropriate governmental policies, also contribute in nearly every case. Many environmental problems in both rich and poor countries appear to be the result of policies that are misguided even when viewed on short-term economic grounds. If a longer-term view is taken, environmental goals assume an even higher priority.

The prosperity and technology of the industrialized countries give them greater opportunities and greater responsibility for addressing environmental problems worldwide. Their resources make it easier to forestall and to ameliorate local environmental problems. Developed countries need to become more efficient in both resource use and environmental protection, and to encourage an ethic that eschews wasteful consumption. If prices, taxes, and regulatory policies include environmental costs, consumption habits will be influenced. The industrialized countries need to assist developing countries and communities with funding and expertise in combating both global and local environmental problems. Mobilizing "technology for environment" should be an integral part of this new ethic of sustainable development.

For all governments it is essential to incorporate environmental goals at the outset in legislation, economic planning, and priority setting; and to provide appropriate incentives for public and private institutions, communities, and individuals to operate in environmentally benign ways. Trade-offs between environmental and economic goals can be reduced through wise policies. For dealing with global environmental problems, all countries of the world need to work collectively through treaties and conventions, as has occurred with such issues as global climate change and biodiversity, and to develop innovative financing mechanisms that facilitate environmental protection.

What Science and Technology Can Contribute toward Enhancing the Human Prospect

As scientists cognizant of the history of scientific progress and aware of the potential of science for contributing to human welfare, it is our collective judgment that continuing population growth poses a great risk to humanity. Furthermore, it is not prudent to rely on science and technology alone to solve problems created by rapid population growth, wasteful resource consumption, and poverty.

The natural and social sciences are nevertheless crucial for developing new understanding so that governments and other institutions can act more effectively, and for developing new options for limiting population growth, protecting the natural environment, and improving the quality of human life.

Scientists, engineers, and health professionals should study and provide advice on:

- Cultural, social, economic, religious, educational, and political factors that affect reproductive behavior, family size, and successful family planning.

- Conditions for human development, including the impediments that result from economic inefficiencies; social inequalities; and ethnic, class, or gender biases.

- Global and local environmental change (affecting climate, biodiversity, soils, water, air), its causes (including the roles of poverty, population growth, economic growth, technology, national and international politics), and policies to mitigate its effects.

- Strategies and tools for improving all aspects of education and human resource development, with special attention to women.

- Improved family planning programs, contraceptive options for both sexes, and other reproductive health services, with special attention to needs of women; and improved general primary health care, especially maternal and child health care.

- Transitions to economies that provide increased annual welfare with less consumption of energy and materials.

- Improved mechanisms for building indigenous capacity in the natural sciences, engineering, medicine, social sciences, and management in developing countries, including an increased capability of conducting integrated interdisciplinary assessments of societal issues.

- Technologies and strategies for sustainable development (agriculture, energy, resource use, pollution control, materials recycling, environmental management and protection).

- Networks, treaties, and conventions that protect the global commons. Strengthened worldwide exchanges of scientists in education, training, and research.

In 1992, some 1,575 scientists signed *The World's Scientists' Warning to Humanity,* which calls attention to the pressing environmental issues facing the natural world and emphasizes the need for immediate action in order to avert disaster. Coordinated by Dr. Henry Kendall, Nobel laureate and chairman of the Union of Concerned Scientists, the following document represents the consensus of many of the world's most distinguished scientists, including more than half of all living scientists awarded the Nobel Prize.

World Scientists' Warning to Humanity[4]

Introduction

Human beings and the natural world are on a collision course. Human activities inflict harsh and often irreversible damage on the environment and on critical resources. If not checked, many of our current practices put at serious risk the future that we wish for human society and the plant and animal kingdoms, and may so alter the living world that it will be unable to sustain life in the manner that we know. Fundamental changes are urgent if we are to avoid the collision our present course will bring about.

The Environment

The environment is suffering critical stress:

The Atmosphere

Stratospheric ozone depletion threatens us with enhanced ultraviolet radiation at the earth's surface, which can be damaging or lethal to many life forms. Air pollution near ground level, and acid precipitation, are already causing widespread injury to humans, forests, and crops.

Water Resources

Heedless exploitation of depletable groundwater supplies endangers food production and other essential human systems. Heavy demands on the world's surface waters have resulted in serious shortages in some 80 countries, containing 40 percent of the world's population. Pollution of rivers, lakes, and groundwater further limits the supply.

Oceans

Destructive pressure on the oceans is severe, particularly in the coastal regions, which produce most of the world's food fish. The total marine catch is now at or above the estimated maximum sustainable yield. Some fisheries have already shown signs of collapse. Rivers carrying heavy burdens of eroded soil into the seas also carry industrial, municipal, agricultural, and livestock waste—some of it toxic.

Soil

Loss of soil productivity, which is causing extensive land abandonment, is a widespread by-product of current practices in agriculture and animal husbandry. Since 1945, 11 percent of the earth's vegetated surface has been degraded—an area larger than India and China combined—and per capita food production in many parts of the world is decreasing.

Forests

Tropical rain forests, as well as tropical and temperate dry forests, are being destroyed rapidly. At present rates, some critical forest types will be gone in a few years, and most of the tropical rain forest will be gone before the end of the next century. With them will go large numbers of plant and animal species.

Living Species

The irreversible loss of species, which by 2100 may reach one-third of all species now living, is especially serious. We are losing the potential they hold for providing medicinal and other benefits, and the contribution that genetic diversity of life forms gives to the robustness of the world's biological systems and to the astonishing beauty of the earth itself.

Much of this damage is irreversible on a scale of centuries or permanent. Other processes appear to pose additional threats. Increasing levels of gases in the atmosphere from human activities, including carbon dioxide released from fossil fuel burning and from deforestation, may alter climate on a global scale. Predictions of global warming are still uncertain—with projected effects ranging from tolerable to very severe—but the potential risks are very great.

Our massive tampering with the world's interdependent web of life—coupled with the environmental damage inflicted by deforestation, species loss, and climate change—could trigger widespread adverse effects, including unpredictable collapses of critical biological systems whose interactions and dynamics we only imperfectly understand.

Uncertainty over the extent of these effects cannot excuse complacency or delay in facing the threats.

Population

The earth is finite. Its ability to absorb wastes and destructive effluent is finite. Its ability to provide food and energy is finite. Its ability to provide for growing numbers of people is finite. And we are fast approaching many of the earth's limits. Current economic practices that damage the environment, in both developed and underdeveloped nations, cannot be continued without the risk that vital global systems will be damaged beyond repair.

Pressures resulting from unrestrained population growth put demands on the natural world that can overwhelm any efforts to achieve a sustainable future. If we are to halt the destruction of our environment, we must accept limits to that growth. A World Bank estimate indicates that world population will not stabilize at less than 12.4 billion, while the United Nations concludes that the eventual total could reach 14 billion, a near tripling of today's 5.4 billion. But, even at this moment, one person in five lives in absolute poverty without enough to eat, and one in ten suffers serious malnutrition.

No more than one or a few decades remain before the chance to avert the threats we now confront will be lost and the prospects for humanity immeasurably diminished.

Warning

We the undersigned, senior members of the world's scientific community, hereby warn all humanity of what lies ahead. A great change in our stewardship of the earth and the life on it is required if vast human misery is to be avoided and our global home on this planet is not to be irretrievably mutilated.

What We Must Do

Five inextricably linked areas must be addressed simultaneously:

1. We must bring environmentally damaging activities under control to restore and protect the integrity of the earth's systems we depend on.

We must, for example, move away from fossil fuels to more benign, inexhaustible energy sources to cut greenhouse gas emissions and the pollution of our air and water. Priority must be given to the development of energy sources matched to Third World needs—small-scale and relatively easy to implement.

We must halt deforestation, injury to and loss of agricultural land, and the loss of terrestrial and marine plant and animal species.

2. We must manage resources crucial to human welfare more effectively. We must give high priority to efficient use of energy, water, and other materials, including expansion of conservation and recycling.

3. We must stabilize population. This will be possible only if all nations recognize that it requires improved social and economic conditions, and the adoption of effective, voluntary family planning.

4. We must reduce and eventually eliminate poverty.

5. We must ensure sexual equality, and guarantee women control over their own reproductive decisions.

The developed nations are the largest polluters in the world today. They must greatly reduce their overconsumption if we are to reduce pressures on resources and the global environment. The developed nations have the obligation to provide aid and support to developing nations, because only the developed nations have the financial resources and the technical skills for these tasks.

Action on this recognition is not altruism, but enlightened self-interest: whether industrialized or not, we all have but one lifeboat. No nation can escape from injury when global biological systems are damaged. No nation can escape from conflicts over increasingly scarce resources. In addition, environmental and economic instabilities will cause mass migrations with incalculable consequences for developed and undeveloped nations alike.

Developing nations must realize that environmental damage is one of the gravest threats they face and that attempts to blunt it will be overwhelmed if their populations go unchecked. The greatest peril is to become trapped in spirals of environmental decline, poverty, and unrest, leading to social, economic, and environmental collapse.

Success in this global endeavor will require a great reduction in violence and war. Resources now devoted to the preparation and conduct of war—amounting to over $1 trillion annually—will be badly needed in the new tasks and should be diverted to the new challenges.

A new ethic is required—a new attitude toward discharging our responsibility for caring for ourselves and for the earth. We must recognize the earth's limited capacity to provide for us. We must recognize its fragility. We must no longer allow it to be ravaged. This ethic must motivate a great movement, convincing reluctant leaders and reluctant governments and reluctant peoples themselves to effect the needed changes. The scientists issuing this warning hope that our message will reach and affect people everywhere. We need the help of many.

> We require the help of the world community of scientists—natural, social, economic, political;
>
> We require the help of the world's business and industrial leaders;
>
> We require the help of the world's religious leaders; and
>
> We require the help of the world's peoples.
>
> We call on all to join us in this task.

The following is an abridged list of signatories of the Warning. Over 1,670 scientists, including 104 Nobel laureates—a majority of the living recipients of the Prize in the sciences—have signed it so far. These men and women represent 71 countries, including all of the 19 largest economic powers, all of the 12 most populous nations, 12 countries in Africa, 14 in Asia, 19 in Europe, and 12 in Latin America.

Walter Alvarez, Geologist, National Academy of Sciences, USA

Philip Anderson, Nobel laureate, Physics; USA

Christian Anfinsen, Nobel laureate, Chemistry; USA

Werner Arber, Nobel laureate, Medicine; Switzerland

Michael Atiyah, Mathematician; President, Royal Society; Great Britain

Mary Ellen Avery, Pediatrician, National Medal of Science, USA

Julius Axelrod, Nobel laureate, Medicine; USA

Howard Bachrach, Biochemist, National Medal of Science, USA

John Backus, Computer Scientist, National Medal of Science, USA

David Baltimore, Nobel laureate, Medicine; USA

David Bates, Physicist, Royal Irish Academy, Ireland

Georg Bednorz, Nobel laureate, Physics; Switzerland

Baruj Benacerraf, Nobel laureate, Medicine; USA

Sune Bergstrom, Nobel laureate, Medicine; Sweden

Hans Bethe, Nobel laureate, Physics; USA

Konrad Bloch, Nobel laureate, Medicine; USA

Nicholaas Bloembergen, Nobel laureate, Physics; USA

Bert Bolin, Meteorologist, Tyler Prize, Sweden

Norman Borlaug, Agricultural Scientist; Nobel laureate, Peace; USA & México

E. Margaret Burbidge, Astronomer, National Medal of Science, USA

Adolph Butenandt, Nobel laureate, Chemistry; Former President, Max Planck Institute; Germany

Ennio Candotti, Physicist; President, Brazilian Society for the Advancement of Science; Brazil

Georges Charpak, Nobel laureate, Physics; France

Paul Crutzen, Chemist, Tyler Prize, Germany

Jean Dausset, Nobel laureate, Medicine; France

Margaret Davis, Ecologist, National Academy of Sciences, USA

Gerard Debreu, Nobel laureate, Economics; USA

Paul-Yves Denis, Geographer, Academy of Sciences, Canada

Thomas Eisner, Biologist, Tyler Prize, USA

Mohammed T. El-Ashry, Environmental scientist, Third World Academy, Egypt & USA

Mahdi Elmandjra, Economist; Vice President, African Academy of Sciences; Morocco

Richard Ernst, Nobel laureate, Chemistry; Switzerland

Dagfinn Follesdal, President, Norwegian Academy of Science, Norway

Otto Frankel, Geneticist, Australian Academy of Sciences, Australia

Konstantin V. Frolov, Engineer; Vice President, Russian Academy of Sciences; Russia

Kenichi Fukui, Nobel laureate, Chemistry; Japan

Robert Gallo, Research scientist, Lasker Award, USA

Murray Gell-Mann, Nobel laureate, Physics; USA

Donald Glaser, Nobel laureate, Physics; USA

Sheldon Glashow, Nobel laureate, Physics; USA

Marvin Goldberger, Physicist; Former President, California Institute of Technology, USA

Stephen Jay Gould, Paleontologist, Author, Harvard University, USA

Stephen Hawking, Mathematician, Wolf Prize in Physics, Great Britain

Dudley Herschbach, Nobel Prize, Chemistry; USA

Dorothy Crowfoot Hodgkin, Nobel laureate, Chemistry; Great Britain

Roald Hoffman, Nobel laureate, Chemistry; USA

Nick Holonyak, Electrical Engineer, National Medal of Science, USA

Sarah Hrdy, Anthropologist, National Academy of Sciences, USA

Kun Huang, Physicist, Chinese Academy of Sciences, China

Hiroshi Inose, Electrical Engineer; Vice President, Engineering Academy; Japan

Francois Jacob, Nobel laureate, Medicine; France

Carl-Olof Jacobson, Zoologist; Secretary-General, Royal Academy of Sciences; Sweden

Daniel Janzen, Biologist, Crafoord Prize, USA

Harold Johnston, Chemist, Tyler Prize, USA

Robert Kates, Geographer, National Medal of Science, USA

Frederick I. B. Kayanja, Vice-Chancellor, Mbarara University, Third World Academy, Uganda

Henry Kendall, Nobel laureate, Physics; Chairman, Union of Concerned Scientists; USA

Gurdev Khush, Agronomist, International Rice Institute, Indian National Science Academy, India & Philippines

Klaus von Klitzing, Nobel laureate, Physics; Germany

Aaron Klug, Nobel laureate, Chemistry; Great Britain

E. F. Knipling, Agricultural Researcher, National Medal of Science, USA

Walter Kohn, Physicist, National Medal of Science, USA

Torvard Laurent, Physiological chemist; President, Royal Academy of Sciences; Sweden

Leon Lederman, Nobel laureate, Physics; Chairman, American Association for the Advancement of Science; USA

Wassily Leontief, Nobel laureate, Economics; USA

Luna Leopold, Geologist, National Medal of Science, USA

Rita Levi-Montalcini, Nobel laureate, Medicine; USA & Italy

William Lipscomb, Nobel laureate, Physics; USA

Jane Lubchenco, Zoologist; President-Elect, Ecological Society of America; USA

Lynn Margulis, Biologist, National Academy of Sciences, USA

George Martine, Institute for Study of Society, Population, & Nature; Brazil

Ernst Mayr, Zoologist, National Medal of Science, USA

Digby McLaren, Past President, Royal Society of Canada; Canada

James Meade, Nobel laureate, Economics; Great Britain

Jerrold Meinwald, Chemistry, Tyler Prize, USA

M. G. K. Menon, Physicist; President, International Council of Scientific Unions; India

Gennady Mesiatz, Physicist; Vice President, Russian Academy of Sciences; Russia

César Milstein, Nobel laureate, Medicine; Argentina & Great Britain

Franco Modigliani, Nobel laureate, Economics; USA

Walter Munk, Geophysicist, National Medal of Science, USA

Lawrence Mysak, Meteorologist; Vice President, Academy of Science, Royal Society of Canada; Canada

James Neel, Geneticist, National Medal of Science, USA

Louis Néel, Nobel laureate, Physics; France

Howard Odum, Ecologist, Crafoord Prize, USA

Yuri Ossipyan, Physicist; Vice President, Russian Academy of Sciences; Russia

Autar Singh Paintal, Physiologist; Former President, Indian National Science Academy; India

Mary Lou Pardue, Biologist, National Academy of Sciences, USA

Linus Pauling, Nobel laureate, Chemistry & Peace; USA

Roger Penrose, Mathematician, Wolf Prize in Physics, Great Britain

John Polanyi, Nobel laureate, Chemistry; Canada

George Porter, Nobel laureate, Chemistry; Great Britain

Ilya Prigogine, Nobel laureate, Chemistry; Belgium

Edward Purcell, Nobel laureate, Physics; USA

G. N. Ramachandran, Mathematician, Institute of Science, India

Peter Raven, Director, Missouri Botanical Garden; National Academy of Sciences, USA

Tadeus Reichstein, Nobel laureate, Medicine; Switzerland

Gustavo Rivas Mijares, Engineer; Former President, Academy of Sciences, Venezuela

Wendell Roelofs, Entomologist, National Medal of Science, USA

Miriam Rothschild, Biologist, Royal Society, Great Britain

Sherwood Rowland, Chemist; Past President, American Association for the Advancement of Science; USA

Carlo Rubbia, Nobel laureate, Physics; Italy & Switzerland

Albert Sabin, Virologist, National Medal of Science, USA

Carl Sagan, Astrophysicist & Author, USA

Roald Sagdeev, Physicist, Russian & Pontifical Academies, Russia & USA

Abdus Salam, Nobel laureate, Physics; President, Third World Academy of Sciences; Pakistan & Italy

José Sarukhan, Biologist, Third World Academy, México

Richard Schultes, Botanist, Tyler Prize, USA

Glenn Seaborg, Nobel laureate, Physics; USA

Roger Sperry, Nobel laureate, Medicine; USA

Ledyard Stebbins, Geneticist, National Medal of Science, USA

Janos Szentgothai, Former President, Hungarian Academy of Sciences; Hungary

Jan Tinbergen, Nobel laureate, Economics; Netherlands

James Tobin, Nobel laureate, Economics; USA

Susumu Tonegawa, Nobel laureate, Medicine; Japan & USA

James Van Allen, Physicist, Crafoord Prize, USA

Harold Varmus, Nobel laureate, Medicine; USA

George Wald, Nobel laureate, Medicine; USA

Gerald Wasserburg, Geophysicist, Crafoord Prize, USA

James Watson, Nobel laureate, Medicine; USA

Victor Weisskopf, Wolf Prize in Physics, USA

Fred Whipple, Astronomer, National Academy of Sciences, USA

Torsten Wiesel, Nobel laureate, Medicine; USA

Geoffrey Wilkinson, Nobel laureate, Chemistry; Great Britain

Edward O. Wilson, Biologist, Crafoord Prize, USA

Solly Zuckerman, Zoologist, Royal Society, Great Britain

Notes

□

□ Chapter 1: A Personal Odyssey

1. Aldo Leopold, 1966, *A Sand County Almanac: With Essays on Conservation from Round River,* Ballantine Books, New York, p. 197. The quote is from "Round River," which was originally written in 1953.

2. Growing support in the scientific community can be seen in recent documents such as the *Sustainable Biosphere Initiative* of the Ecological Society of America; the *Global Biodiversity Assessment* of the United Nations Environment Programme, generated by hundreds of scientists; and *Systematics Agenda 2000,* produced by a consortium of societies dealing with biodiversity. All these illustrate a growing involvement among biologists. More and more, professional organizations like the American Institute of Biological Sciences and the Ecological Society of America have become active where science and society meet and interact. The Society for Conservation Biology and the International Society for Ecological Economics were both founded in the mid-1980s specifically to deal with aspects of the human predicament. They are now among the world's fastest-growing scientific societies.

3. See appendix B.

4. Here we adopt the definition of folly proposed by Barbara W. Tuch-

man (1984, *The March of Folly: From Troy to Vietnam,* Alfred A. Knopf, New York).

5. F. Osborn, 1948, *Our Plundered Planet,* Little, Brown, Boston; W. Vogt, 1948, *Road to Survival,* William Sloan, New York.

6. E. Cohen and J. Gooch, 1990, *Military Misfortunes: The Anatomy of Failure in War,* Free Press, New York, p. 202.

7. See, e.g., P. Ehrlich and R. Holm, 1962, Patterns and populations, *Science* 137:652–657; P. Ehrlich, 1964, Some axioms of taxonomy, *Systematic Zoology* 13:109–123; P. Ehrlich and R. Holm, 1964, A biological view of race, in A. Montague, *The Concept of Race,* Free Press, New York, pp. 153–180.

8. See, e.g., P. Ehrlich, R. White, M. Singer, S. McKechnie, and L. Gilbert, 1975, Checkerspot butterflies: A historical perspective, *Science* 188:221–228; S. Weiss, D. Murphy, P. Ehrlich, and C. Metzler, 1993, Adult emergence phenology in checkerspot butterflies: The effects of macroclimate, topoclimate, and population history, *Oecologia* 96:261–270. For a popular account of the more technical side of Paul's interests, see P. Ehrlich, 1987, *The Machinery of Nature: The Living World Around Us and How it Works,* Simon and Schuster, New York.

9. P. Ehrlich and P. Raven, 1964, Butterflies and plants: A study in co-evolution, *Evolution* 18:586–608; this area is also covered in Ehrlich, 1987.

10. See, e.g., L. Gilbert and P. Raven, 1975, *Coevolution of Plants and Animals,* University of Texas Press, Austin; J. Harborne (ed.), 1978, *Biochemical Aspects of Plant and Animal Coevolution,* Academic Press, London; J. Thompson, 1982, *Interaction and Coevolution,* Wiley, New York; M. Nitecki, 1983, *Coevolution,* University of Chicago Press, Chicago; D. Futuyma and M. Slatkin (eds.), 1983, *Coevolution,* Sinauer, Sunderland, MA; A. Stone and D. Hawksworth (eds.), 1986, *Coevolution and Systematics,* Clarendon Press, Oxford; J. Thompson, 1994, *The Coevolutionary Process,* University of Chicago Press, Chicago.

11. P. Ehrlich, 1968, *The Population Bomb,* Ballantine, New York.

12. Paul's letter to the USDA on the issue is reprinted in P. Ehrlich and A. Ehrlich, 1970, *Population, Resources, Environment: Issues in Human Ecology,* W. H. Freeman, San Francisco, pp. 347–348.

13. R. Carson, 1962, *Silent Spring,* Houghton Mifflin, Boston.

Chapter 2: "Wise Use" and Environmental Anti-Science

1. See, e.g., C. Holden, 1995, Alabama schools disclaim evolution, *Science* 270:1305.

2. Dunlap, G. Gallup Jr., and A. Gallup, 1993, Of global concern: Results of the Health of the Planet Survey, *Environment* 35 (9): 7–15, 33–39.

3. R. Ornstein and P. Ehrlich, 1989, *New World/New Mind: Moving Toward Conscious Evolution,* Doubleday, New York.

4. G. Daily (ed.), in press, *Nature's Services,* Island Press, Washington, DC.

5. A. Kinzig and R. Socolow, 1994, Human impacts on the nitrogen cycle, *Physics Today,* 24–31 November; J. Holdren, 1995, The Coming Energy-Environment Train Wreck, lecture, Woods Hole Research Center, Massachusetts, 11 October.

6. P. Vitousek, P. Ehrlich, A. Ehrlich, and P. Matson, 1986, Human appropriation of the products of photosynthesis, *BioScience* 6:368–373.

7. S. Postel, G. Daily, and P. Ehrlich, 1996, Human appropriation of renewable fresh water, *Science* 271:785–787.

8. R. Douthwaite, 1993, *The Growth Illusion,* Council Oak Books, Tulsa, OK. There are also serious issues of increasing maldistribution of wealth that call into doubt the notion that the system is making everyone better off (e.g., S. Pearlstein, 1995, The winners are taking all, *Washington Post Weekly,* 11–17 December, pp. 6–8; B. Schwartz, 1995, American inequality: Its history and scary future, *New York Times,* 19 December.

9. D. Helvarg, 1994, *The War Against the Greens: The "Wise Use" Movement, the New Right, and Anti-environmental Violence,* Sierra Club Books, San Francisco, pp. 458–459.

10. C. Deal. 1993. *The Greenpeace Guide to Anti-Environmental Organizations,* Odonian Press, Berkeley; J. Fritsch, 1996, Friend or foe? Nature groups say names lie, *New York Times,* 25 March. Ironically, as the *Times* pointed out, that these organizations resort to phony environmental names underscores the appeal of the environmental movement.

11. *Consumer Reports,* 1994, The ACSH: Forefront of science, or just a front?, May, p. 319.

12. Fritsch, 1996.

13. Quoted in Helvarg, 1994, p. 429.

14. B. Babbit, 1995, Springtime for polluters, *Washington Post,* 22 October.

15. Deal, 1993.

16. Quoted in ibid., p. 58.

17. M. Hager, 1993, Enter the contrarians, *Tomorrow,* October–December, pp. 10–19.

18. Helvarg, 1994, p. 32.

19. K. Boulding, 1966, The economics of the coming spaceship Earth, in

H. Jarrett (ed.), *Environmental Quality in a Growing Economy,* Johns Hopkins University Press, Baltimore.

20. See, e.g., D. Bromley, 1991, *Environment and Economy: Property Rights and Public Policy,* Blackwell, Oxford.

21. Quoted in Helvarg, 1994, p. 302.

22. The impossibility of business as usual is most evident in areas of environmental science that the brownlash hasn't discovered yet. The best example of this is the ignoring of the importance of ecosystem services in maintaining civilization. We have yet to find a single brownlash book that even indexes ecosystem services.

23. Helvarg, 1994, p. 13.

24. T. Williams, 1996, Defense of the realm, *Sierra,* January–February, pp. 34–39, 121–123.

25. T. Egan, 1996, Court puts down rebellion over control of federal land, *New York Times,* 16 March.

26. Dunlap, Gallup, and Gallup, 1993.

27. The late Republican senator John Heinz of Pennsylvania was a member of that tradition, as is Republican Tom Campbell, who represents a California district in the House of Representatives.

28. See, e.g., G. Durnil, 1995, *The Making of a Conservative Environmentalist,* Indiana University Press, Bloomington.

29. L. Divall, 1996, The environmental counterattack (editorial), *New York Times,* 5 February.

30. See, e.g., B. Allenby and D. Richards (eds.) (National Academy of Engineering) 1994, *The Greening of Industrial Systems* (National Academy of Engineering) Washington, DC.

31. Gary Sprung, High Country Citizens Alliance, Crested Butte, Colorado, personal communication, July 1994.

32. Consider the following from our 1977 environmental science textbook: "As a theoretical example, Steel Company X . . . is pouring filth into [a] lake at a horrendous rate. A study shows it would cost two dollars per share of common stock to build the necessary apparatus for retaining and processing the waste. Should the company be forced to stop polluting and pay the price?

"Certainly it must be forced to stop, but it seems fair that society should pay some of the cost. When Company X located on the lake, everyone knew it would spew pollutants into the lake, but no one objected. The local people wanted to encourage industry. Now, finally, society has changed its mind, and the pollution must stop. But should Company X be forced into bankruptcy by pollution regulations, penalizing stockholders and putting its employees out of work? Should the local politicians who lured the company into locating there and the citizens who encouraged them not pay a cent? Clearly society should order the pollution stopped *and pick up at least part of the bill.* . . . [When jobs are lost in such situations, society] must find mechanisms to compensate people . . . and it must retrain and, if necessary, relocate them." (P. Ehrlich, A. Ehrlich, and J. Holdren, 1977, *Ecoscience: Population, Resources, Environment,* W. H. Freeman, San Francisco, p. 848.)

33. D. Pirages and P. Ehrlich, 1974, *Ark II: Social Response to Environmental Imperatives,* Viking, New York, p. 287.

34. Deal, 1993, p. 58, quoting thirty-nine leading conservatives writing in *Policy Review.*

Chapter 3: In Defense of Science

1. M. Browne, 1995. Scientists deplore flight from reason, *New York Times,* 6 June; C. Holden, 1995, Reason under fire, *Science* 268:1853.

2. Browne, 1995.

3. Culture is the body of non-genetic information that is passed from individual to individual and from generation to generation.

4. M. Shamos, 1995, *The Myth of Scientific Literacy,* Rutgers University Press, New Brunswick, NJ. Shamos estimates that "the fraction of Americans who might qualify as true scientific literates . . . is 4 to 5 percent of the adult population, nearly all being professional scientists or engineers." Another scientist estimates that about 30 percent of Americans possess a "minimal" understanding of scientific terms and concepts (J. Miller, 1989, Scientific Literacy, paper presented at the annual meeting of the American Association for the Advancement of Science, January).

5. M. Zimmerman, 1990, Newspaper editors and the creation-evolution controversy, *Skeptical Inquirer* 13:182–195.

6. M. Lemonick, 1996, Dumping on Darwin, *Time,* 18 March, p. 81.

7. See chapter 9 of this book; also M. Cohen, 1992, Epidemiology of drug resistance: Implications for a post-antimicrobial era, *Science* 257:1050–1055; S. Levy, 1992, *The Antibiotic Paradox,* Plenum, New York; H. Neu, 1992, The crisis of antibiotic resistance, *Science* 257:1066–1077; A. Russell, 1993, Microbial cell walls and resistance of bacteria and fungi to antibiotics and biocides, *Journal of Infectious Diseases* 168:1339–1340; L. Garrett, 1994, *The Coming Plague: Newly Emerging Diseases in a World Out of Balance,* Farrar, Straus, and Giroux, New York; *New York Times,* 1995, Sharp rise in drug-resistant bacteria (25 August); and, for an overview and extensive bibliography, G. Daily and P. Ehrlich, 1996, Development, global change, and the

epidemiological environment, *Development and Environment,* in press.

8. This is purely a convention—it is the probability level that is the key, and the conclusion a scientist deems significant is a non-scientific decision that involves judgments about the question asked. Thus we might well accept a 5 percent chance of being wrong if the question concerned differences in the lengths of butterfly wings in two different populations but demand less than a 0.1 percent chance of being in error if it involved the safety of a medicine to be given to sick babies.

9. J. Harte, C. Holdren, R. Schneider, and C. Shirley, 1991, *Toxics A to Z: A Guide to Everyday Pollution Hazards,* University of California Press, Berkeley.

10. See, e.g., D. Tilman and J. Downing, 1994, Biodiversity and stability in grasslands, *Nature* 367:363–365; S. Naeem, L. Thompson, S. Lawler, and J. Lawton, 1994, Declining biodiversity can alter the performance of ecosystems, *Nature* 368:734–737.

11. J. Harte and R. Shaw, 1995. Shifting dominance within a montane vegetation community: Results of a climate-warming experiment, *Science* 267:876–880.

12. See, e.g., Intergovernmental Panel on Climate Change (IPCC), 1996, *Climate Change 1995*—The Science of Climate Change: Contribution of Working Group I to IPCC Second Assessment Report, Cambridge University Press, Cambridge, U.K.

13. These feedbacks are discussed further in chapter 8.

14. A. Ehrlich, 1990, Agricultural contributions to global warming, in J. Leggett (ed.), *Global Warming: The Greenpeace Report,* Oxford University Press, New York, pp. 400–420.

15. P. Ehrlich, 1968, *The Population Bomb,* Ballantine, New York; P. Ehrlich and A. Ehrlich, 1990, *The Population Explosion,* Simon and Schuster, New York.

16. See, e.g., M. Swaminathan, 1995, videotaped interview with S. Hurst, Madras, India, December.

17. Chlorofluorocarbons are the "freons" that were discovered also to cause destruction of the stratospheric ozone shield—see chapter 8.

18. See P. Ehrlich and A. Ehrlich, 1991, *Healing the Planet,* Addison-Wesley, Reading, MA, for an account of these discoveries and references to the scientific literature; see also S. Schneider, 1989, *Global Warming: Are We Entering the Greenhouse Century?,* Sierra Club Books, San Francisco.

19. For the classic description of how scientific change takes place, see T. Kuhn, 1962, The structure of scientific revolutions, *Foundations of the Unity of Science* 2:1–72.

20. Information on financial support of the contrarians is from R. Gelbspan, 1995, The heat is on, *Harper's Magazine,* December; correspondence with Gelbspan (9 April 1996); and a telephone conversation with him (11 April 1996).

21. Gelbspan, 1995. In actuality, the manufacturers were participants in the international negotiations leading to the phaseout of CFCs, and the timing was settled partly in response to their needs and ability to get more benign substitute products on the market.

22. Gelbspan, 1995.

23. R. Gelbspan, 1996. Living on Earth, Commentary, National Public Radio, January.

24. Such attacks have often resulted whenever a scientific organization has issued a statement on a politically sensitive subject; see, e.g., D. Ray (with L. Guzzo), 1990, *Trashing the Planet,* HarperCollins, New York, p. 163.

25. S. Singer, 1994, Climate claims wither under the luminous light of science, *Washington Times,* 29 November.

26. The greenhouse brownlash is international, no doubt stimulated in part by nations like Saudi Arabia, which, understandably, are fearful of any trend away from fossil fuel use. The same misstatements that appear in North America and Europe appear in places as distant as Australia, where one Andrew McIntyre, "a freelance writer and teacher," produced a compendium of error called "Propaganda breeds greenhouse panic" (*The Age,* 9 September 1994). In Europe, a film titled *The Greenhouse Conspiracy* was broadcast in British Channel 4's *Equinox* series in August 1990. The film attempted to show that evidence for past greenhouse warming was unreliable, that climate models are so seriously flawed that they deny the Sahara is a desert, and so on (V. Hutchings, 1990, The greenhouse war, *New Statesman and Society,* 21 September, pp. 20–21).

27. S. Kellert, 1995, *The Value of Life: Biological Diversity and Human Society,* Island Press, Washington, DC.

28. S. Budiansky, 1995. Unreason, red in claw, *New Scientist,* 23–30 December, pp. 66–67.

29. S. Kellert, 1996, letter to *New Scientist,* 7 January.

30. G. Easterbrook, 1995, *A Moment on the Earth: The Coming Age of Environmental Optimism,* Viking, New York.

31. *Wall Street Journal,* 1995, The Good Earth, (26 May).

32. See, e.g., P. Raven, 1995, review of *A Moment on the Earth* by Gregg Easterbrook, *The Amicus Journal* 17 (1): 42–45; J. Harte, 1995, Optimism about the environment, *Chemical and Engineering News,* 3 July, pp. 26–27; D. Meadows, 1995, Depressing case of environmental optimism, *Valley News,* 10 June; D. Davis, 1995, A "dead-body" approach to health, *Environmental Science and Technology,* August, pp.

370A–371A; J. Schultz, 1995, When nature writers get it wrong, *Natural History,* August, pp. 64–66; R. Noss, 1995, The perils of Pollyannas, *Conservation Biology* 9 (4): 701–703; L. Haimson and B. Goodman (eds.), 1995, *A Moment of Truth: Correcting the Scientific Errors in Gregg Easterbrook's "A Moment on the Earth,"* Environmental Defense Fund, New York; World Resources Institute, 1995, *A Thoughtful Reader's Guide to "A Moment on the Earth,"* World Resources Institute, Washington, DC; T. Lovejoy, 1996, Rethinking green thoughts, *Scientific American,* February, pp. 127–129.

33. Schultz, 1995, p. 64.

34. Lovejoy, 1996, p. 127.

35. Harte, 1995, p. 26.

36. See, e.g., R. Limbaugh, 1992, *The Way Things Ought to Be,* Pocket Books, New York, p. 155.

37. G. Taubes, 1993, The ozone backlash, *Science* 260:1580–1583. Material in this paragraph is based on that article.

38. D. Ray (with L. Guzzo), 1990, *Trashing the Planet,* HarperCollins, New York.

39. Ibid., p. 177, n.18.

40. R. Maduro and R. Schauerhammer, 1992, *The Holes in the Ozone Scare: Experimentalists vs. Modelers,* Twenty-first Century Science Associates, Washington, DC.

41. World Meteorological Organization, 1995, *Scientific Assessment of Ozone Depletion: 1994,* National Oceanic and Atmospheric Administration, National Aeronautics and Space Administration, United Nations Environment Programme, and World Meteorological Organization (available from the World Meteorological Organization, Global Ozone Observing System [GO$_3$OS], P.O. Box 2300, 1211-Geneva-2, Switzerland).

42. D. Helvarg, 1994, *The War against the Greens: The Wise Use Movement, the New Right, and Anti-Environmental Violence,* Sierra Club Books, San Francisco, p. 243.

43. Limbaugh, 1992, p. 155.

44. D. Ray (with L. Guzzo), 1993, *Environmental Overkill: Whatever Happened to Common Sense?,* HarperCollins, New York, pp. 35, 47. This is discussed further in chapter 8.

45. Taubes, 1993, p. 1583.

46. Ibid.

47. Ibid., p. 1580.

48. Ibid., p. 1581.

49. Ibid.

50. Our colleague Sam Hurst of Buffalo Gap Productions first made this explicit comparison (personal communication).

51. What follows is based on R. Ornstein and P. Ehrlich, 1989, *New World/New Mind: Moving Toward Conscious Evolution,* Doubleday, New York. This book should be consulted for details on this necessarily brief summary.

52. Ibid.

Chapter 4: The Good News ... in Perspective

1. See, e.g., G. Easterbrook, 1995, *A Moment on the Earth: The Coming Age of Environmental Optimism,* Viking, New York.

2. U.S. Department of Energy, 1995, *Sustainable Energy Strategy* (National Energy Policy Plan), U.S. Government Printing Office, Washington, DC.

3. J. Lents and W. Kelly, 1993, Clearing the air in Los Angeles, *Scientific American,* October, pp. 32–39.

4. *The American Almanac, Statistical Abstract of the United States, 1993–1994* (113th ed.), 1993, Reference Press, Austin, TX.

5. *American Almanac,* 1993; C. Flavin and N. Lensson, 1994, *Power Surge,* W. W. Norton, New York.

6. Flavin and Lensson, 1994; P. Portney, 1990, Air pollution policy, chapter 3 in P. Portney (ed.), *Public Policies for Environmental Protection,* Resources for the Future, Washington, DC.

7. Portney, 1990; World Bank, 1992, *World Development Report 1992,* World Bank, Washington, DC.

8. Portney, 1990.

9. P. Ehrlich, A. Ehrlich, and J. Holdren, 1977, *Ecoscience: Population, Resources, Environment,* W. H. Freeman, San Francisco, chapter 10.

10. Edward Groth III, Consumers Union, personal communication, 26 November 1995.

11. Portney, 1990, pp. 75–76.

12. J. Alper, 1993, Protecting the environment with the power of the market, *Science* 260:1884–1885. By 1996, reductions reportedly were ahead of schedule.

13. Sen. T. Wirth and Sen. J. Heinz, 1988, Project 88: Harnessing market forces to protect our environment, unpublished. Washington, DC.

14. A. Freeman III, 1990, Water pollution policy, chapter 4 in Portney, *Public Policies.*

15. R. Adler, J. Landman, and D. Cameron, 1993, *The Clean Water Act Twenty Years Later,* Island Press, Washington, DC, p. 2.

16. Freeman, 1990.

17. Ehrlich, Ehrlich, and Holdren, 1977.

18. World Resources Institute, 1992, *The 1992 Information Please Environmental Almanac,* Houghton Mifflin, Boston.

19. T. Colborn, D. Dumanoski, and J. P. Myers, 1996, *Our Stolen Future,* Dutton, New York.

20. R. Patrick, E. Ford, and J. Quarles (eds.), 1987, *Groundwater Contamination in the United States* (2nd ed.), University of Pennsylvania Press, Philadelphia.

21. S. Shulman, 1992, *The Threat at Home: Confronting the Toxic Legacy of the U.S. Military,* Beacon Press, Boston.

22. S. Terry, 1993, Drinking water comes to a boil, *New York Times Magazine,* 26 September, pp. 42–45ff.

23. L. Garrett, 1994, *The Coming Plague: Newly Emerging Diseases in a World Out of Balance,* Farrar, Straus, and Giroux, New York, p. 430.

24. Freeman, 1990.

25. In early 1996, the EPA announced that it was launching a program for trading permits for release of water pollutants (Pollution credits: EPA announces effluent trading program, *Greenwire,* 5:182, no. 8, 31 January 1996).

26. Freeman, 1990.

27. R. Dower, 1990. Hazardous wastes, chapter 5 in Portney, *Public Policies*; J. Lewis, 1991, Love Canal legacy—where are we now?, *EPA Journal,* July–August, pp. 7–14; M. Russell, E. Colglazier, and B. Tonn, 1992, The U.S. hazardous waste legacy, *Environment* 34 (6): 12–15, 34–39.

28. Shulman, 1992, appendix B.

29. T. Grumbly, 1995. Lessons from Superfund, *Environment* 37 (3): 33–34.

30. Colborn, Dumanoski, and Myers, 1996; J. Harte, C. Holdren, R. Schneider, and C. Shirley, 1991, *Toxics A to Z: A Guide to Everyday Pollution Hazards,* University of California Press, Berkeley; National Research Council, 1993, *Pesticides in the Diets of Infants and Children,* National Academy Press, Washington, DC.

31. Grumbly, 1995.

32. Dower, 1990.

33. M. Shapiro, 1990, Toxic substances policy, chapter 6 in Portney, 1990.

34. Ibid.

35. Ibid.

36. F. Cairncross, 1993, Old horrors, *The Economist,* 29 May, pp. 15–16 of a special section, Environment Survey: Waste and Environment.

37. Russell, Colglazier, and Tonn, 1992.

38. C. de Saillan, 1993, In praise of Superfund, *Environment* 35 (8): 42–44.

39. Ibid.; J. Acton and L. Dixon, 1992, *Superfund and Transaction Costs: The Experiences of Insurers and Very Large Industrial Firms,* RAND Institute for Civil Justice, Santa Monica, CA.

40. Dower, 1990; Russell, Colglazier, and Tonn, 1992; de Saillan, 1993.

41. Dower, 1990; de Saillan, 1993.

42. Acton and Dixon, 1992.

43. World Resources Institute, 1992, pp. 126–27.

44. R. Gottlieb, 1995, *Reducing Toxics: A New Approach to Policy and Industrial Decisionmaking,* Island Press, Washington, DC; B. Allenby and D. Richards (eds.), 1994, *The Greening of Industrial Ecosystems,* (National Academy of Engineering), National Academy Press, Washington, DC.

45. K. Oldenburg and J. Hirschhorn, 1987, Waste reduction: A new strategy to avoid pollution, *Environment* 29 (2): 16–20, 39–45; U.S. Congress, Office of Technology Assessment, 1986, *Serious Reduction of Hazardous Waste,* OTA-ITE-317, U.S. Government Printing Office, Washington, DC; R. Frosch and N. Gallopoulos, 1989, Strategies for manufacturing, *Scientific American,* September, pp. 144–153. F. Cairncross, 1992, *Costing the Earth,* Harvard Business School Press, Boston.

46. Groth, 1995; C. Frankel, 1996, Monsanto breaks the mold, *Tomorrow* 6 (3): 62–63.

47. *P&G 1995 Environmental Progress Report,* Procter & Gamble Company, Cincinnati, OH.

48. Frosch and Gallopoulos, 1989; Allenby and Richards, 1994.

49. P. Sinsheimer and R. Gottlieb, Pollution prevention voluntarism, chapter 12 in Gottlieb, 1995, pp. 389–420.

50. S. Schmidheiny, 1992, *Changing Course,* MIT Press, Cambridge, MA.

51. Du Pont recently announced a goal of zero wastes, zero emissions (*Greenwire,* 5:185, 5 February 1996).

52. I. Amato, 1993. The slow birth of green chemistry, *Science* 259: 1538–1541; E. Marshall, 1993, Is environmental technology a key to a healthy economy?, *Science* 260:1886–1888.

53. R. Frosch, 1995, Industrial ecology: Adapting technology for a sustainable world, *Environment* 37 (10): 16–24, 34–37.

54. J. MacKenzie and M. El-Ashry, 1989, *Air Pollution's Toll on Forests and Crops,* Yale University Press, New Haven, CT.

55. M. Feshbach and A. Friendly, 1992, *Ecocide in the USSR,* Basic Books, New York.

56. M. Specter, 1995, Plunging life expectancy puzzles Russia, *New York Times,* 8 August.

57. Quoted in A. Lewis, 1996, Marx and Gingrich, *New York Times,* 1 January.

58. For details on population policies, see chapters 3 and 4 in P. Ehrlich, A. Ehrlich, and G. Daily, 1995, *The Stork and the Plow: The Equity Answer to the Human Dilemma,* Grosset/Putnam, New York.

59. Marshall, 1993.

60. See, e.g., 1995 Nobel Prize–winning atmospheric chemists Sherwood Rowland, Mario Molina, and Paul Crutzen (W. Stevens, 1995, 3 win Nobel Prize for work on threat to ozone, *New York Times,* 12 October, pp. 1ff). See also the work of the Intergovernmental Panel on Climate Change (IPCC): J. Houghton, G. Jenkins, and J. Ephraums, 1990, *Climate Change: The IPCC Scientific Assessment Report of the Intergovernmental Panel on Climate Change,* Intergovernmental Panel on Climate Change [IPCC], World Meteorological Organization, and United Nations Environment Programme, Geneva. For a description of some of these science-policy interactions, see S. Schneider, 1989, *Global Warming: Are We Entering the Greenhouse Century?,* Sierra Club Books, San Francisco.

61. See, e.g., R. Barnet and J. Cavanagh, 1994, *Global Dreams: Imperial Corporations and the New World Order,* Simon and Schuster, New York; D. Korten, 1995, *When Corporations Rule the World,* Kumarian Press, West Hartford, CT.

62. R. Benedick, 1991, *Ozone Diplomacy,* Harvard University Press, Cambridge, MA.

63. J. Birks, J. Calvert, and R. Sievers (eds.), 1992, *The Chemistry of the Atmosphere: Its Impact on Global Change,* CHEMRAWN VII: Perspectives and Recommendations, Agency for International Development, Washington, DC. Sponsored by the International Union of Pure and Applied Chemistry and the American Chemical Society, this symposium brought together scientists from academic institutions, government laboratories, and industry to discuss problems of atmospheric chemistry. Such collaborative efforts are of enormous value in solving problems of global significance.

64. A. Ehrlich and P. Ehrlich, 1992, Ecosystem risks associated with the population explosion, in J. Cairns, B. Neiderlander, and D. Orvos (eds.), *Predicting Ecosystem Risk,* Princeton Scientific Publishing, Princeton, NJ.

65. United Nations Fund for Population Activities (UNFPA), 1995, *State of the World's Population 1995,* United Nations, New York.

66. C. Haub and M. Yanagashita, 1995, *1995 World Population Data Sheet,* Population Reference Bureau, Washington DC; for earlier estimates see the Population Reference Bureau's *World Population Data*

Sheet for various years or the United Nations' *Population Yearbook* for various years (United Nations, New York).

67. P. Ehrlich and A. Ehrlich, 1990, *The Population Explosion,* Simon and Schuster, New York; Ehrlich, Ehrlich, and Daily, 1995.

68. B. Wattenberg, 1987, *The Birth Dearth,* Pharos Books, New York.

69. Specter, 1995.

70. Study Committee of the Office of Foreign Secretary, National Academy of Sciences, 1971, *Rapid Population Growth: Consequences and Policy Implications,* Johns Hopkins University Press, Baltimore.

71. Ehrlich, Ehrlich, and Daily, 1995, chapter 4.

72. S. Horiuchi, 1992. Stagnation in the decline of the world population growth rate during the 1980s, *Science* 257:761–765 (7 August).

Chapter 5: Fables about Population and Food

1. T. Malthus, 1798, *An Essay on the Principles of Population,* reprinted: Modern Library, New York, 1960.

2. P. Ehrlich, 1968, *The Population Bomb,* Ballantine Books, New York.

3. P. Ehrlich, A. Ehrlich, and G. Daily, 1995, *The Stork and the Plow: The Equity Answer to the Human Dilemma,* Grosset/Putnam, New York.

4. Catholic bishops assembled for the anniversary of the encyclical Humanae Vitae announced that "the world's food resources theoretically could feed 40 billion people" *Washington Post,* 19 November 1988, p. C-15); this estimate is based on R. Revelle's estimate (1974, Food and population, *Scientific American,* September, pp. 165–178) of 38-48 billion as the absolute limit. Revelle (personal communication) considered this a theoretical upper bound and realized the assumptions on which it was based were utterly unrealistic.

5. N. Myers and J. Simon, 1994, *Scarcity or Abundance: A Debate on the Environment,* W. W. Norton, New York, p. 65. That this is not a typo is attested to by Simon's repeating of the statement in the introduction to a volume he edited (1995, *The State of Humanity,* Blackwell, Oxford, p. 26) and adding "Even if no new knowledge were ever invented . . . we would be able to go on increasing our population *forever* while improving our standard of living" (our emphasis).

6. The mathematically inclined can easily show that the doubling time for an entity growing at X percent per year (when X is less than 5 percent) is roughly equal to $70/X$ years. Hence the doubling time corresponding to a growth rate of 1.6 percent per year is $70/1.6 = 43$ years.

7. Even 200 years of growth at the 1994 rate produces preposterous numbers. The human population in 2194 would consist of about two

dozen individuals for everyone alive in 1994—137 billion people—a number that even the vast majority of technological optimists would agree would be unlikely to be supportable.

8. Each ten doublings increases a quantity by about a thousandfold (since 2^{10} = 1024). Twenty doublings thus produces about a million-fold increase (1024 × 1024 = 1,048,576). Eighteen doublings makes an increase of 2^{10} × 2^8 or about 250,000-fold, and 250,000 × 5.6 billion = 1400 trillion. The ice-free land of the Earth covers 133 million square kilometers, or 133 trillion square meters. The mass of the Earth is about 6 × 10^{24} kilograms, which is equivalent to 10^{23} people at an average mass of 60 kilograms per person. This number is 17.5 trillion times bigger than the 1994 population of 5.6 billion; a 17.5-trillionfold increase corresponds to about forty-four doublings, which at 43 years per doubling would take 1892 years. The mass of the universe is perhaps 2 × 10^{53} kilograms (based on an estimate of 10^{80} nucleons—protons and neutrons—which at 1.67 × 10^{-27} kilograms/nucleon would be 1.67 × 10^{53} kilograms). So the mass of the universe is about 3 × 10^{28} times the mass of Earth, which corresponds to ninety-five doublings, or another 95 × 43 = 4085 years beyond the 1892 years required for the mass of the human population to reach that of Earth. The figures for ice-free land area, the mass of Earth, and the number of nucleons in the universe are from J. Harte, 1985, *Consider a Spherical Cow: A Course in Environmental Problem Solving,* William Kaufmann, Los Altos, CA. Those interested in these sorts of numbers games should consult physicist John Fremlin's classic article (1964, How many people can the world support?, *New Scientist* 29 Ocober, pp. 285–287) which with great humor describes a theoretical limit of the human population on Earth at 10^{16} to 10^{18} people.

9. If the growth rate were 1 million times smaller, the mass of 2 x 10^{53} kilograms would be reached after 6 billion years instead of after 6 thousand.

10. See, e.g., J. Bast, P. Hill, and R. Rue, 1994, *Ecosanity: A Common-sense Guide to Environmentalism,* Madison Books, Lanham, MD, p. 231: ". . . predictions of a 'population explosion' and eventual resource depletion were wrong because they were based on past trends." See also Myers and Simon, 1994, and other works by Simon.

11. G. Daily and P. Ehrlich, 1992, Population, sustainability, and Earth's carrying capacity, *BioScience* 42:761–771.

12. We don't go into the question of reduction of future capacity to support guppies in this simplified example.

13. W. Catton, 1980, *Overshoot: The Ecological Basis of Revolutionary Change,* University of Illinois Press, Urbana.

14. P. Ehrlich and A. Ehrlich, 1990, *The Population Explosion,* Simon and Schuster, New York. See chapter 2 and the references cited there.

15. For a fine overview of some of the critical trends, see R. Naylor, 1996, Energy and resource constraints on intensive agricultural production, *Annual Review of Energy,* in press; and N. Myers, 1995, *Ultimate Security: The Environmental Basis of Political Stability,* W. W. Norton, New York.

16. See, e.g., H. Colby, F. Crook, and S.-E. Webb, 1992, Agricultural statistics of the People's Republic of China, 1949–1990, *Statistical Bulletin* no. 844, U.S. Department of Agriculture, Washington, DC; M. Imhoff et al., 1986, Monsoon flood boundary delineation and damage assessment using space-borne imaging radar and Landsat data, *Photogrammatic Engineering and Remote Sensing* 53:405–413. For an overview, see pp. 171–180 of Ehrlich, Ehrlich, and Daily, 1995.

17. For an overview, see chapter 6 of Ehrlich, Ehrlich, and Daily, 1995.

18. See, e.g., P. Gleick (ed.), 1993, *Water in Crisis,* Oxford University Press, New York; M. Reisner, 1986, *Cadillac Desert,* Viking, New York; S. Postel, 1990, *Water for Agriculture: Facing the Limits,* Worldwatch paper no. 93, Worldwatch Institute, Washington, DC; S. Postel, G. Daily, and P. Ehrlich, 1996, Human appropriation of renewable fresh water, *Science* 271:785–788.

19. P. Ehrlich, A. Ehrlich, and J. Holdren, 1977, *Ecoscience: Population, Resources, Environment,* W. H. Freeman, San Francisco, chapters 3, 4, 6, and 11; N. Myers, 1979, *The Sinking Ark,* Pergamon Press, New York; P. Ehrlich and A. Ehrlich, 1981, *Extinction: The Causes and Consequences of the Disappearance of Species,* Random House, New York; E. Wilson (ed.), 1988, *Biodiversity,* National Academy Press, Washington, DC; P. Ehrlich and E. Wilson, 1991, Biodiversity studies: Science and policy, *Science* 253:758–762; E. Wilson, 1992, *The Diversity of Life,* Harvard University Press, Cambridge, MA; J. Lawton and R. May (eds.), 1995, *Extinction Rates,* Oxford University Press, Oxford; S. Pimm, G. Russell, J. Gittleman, T. Brooks, 1995, The future of biodiversity, *Science* 269:347–350; E. Hoyt, 1988, *Conserving the Wild Relatives of Crops,* International Union for the Conservation of Nature, Gland and Rome; C. Fowler and P. Mooney, 1990, *Shattering: Food, Politics, and the Loss of Genetic Diversity,* University of Arizona Press, Tucson.

20. See, e.g., L. Oldeman, V. Van Engelen, and J. Pulles, 1990. The extent of human-induced soil degradation, annex 5 of L. Oldeman, R. Hakkeling, and W. Sombroek, *World Map of the Status of Human-Induced Soil Degradation: An Explanatory Note* (rev. 2nd ed.), International Soil Reference and Information Centre (ISRIC), Wageningen, Netherlands; R. Repetto, 1994, *The "Second India" Revisited: Population, Poverty, and Environmental Stress over Two Decades,* World Resources Institute, Washington, DC; G. Daily, 1995, Restoring value to the world's degraded lands, *Science* 269:350–354; National Research

Council, Committee on the Role of Alternative Farming Methods in Modern Production Agriculture, Board on Agriculture, 1989, *Alternative Agriculture,* National Academy Press, Washington, DC.

21. P. Vitousek, P. Ehrlich, A. Ehrlich, and P. Matson, 1986, Human appropriation of the products of photosynthesis. *BioScience* 36:368–373.

22. Oldeman, Van Engelen, and Pulles, 1990; P. Ehrlich, A. Ehrlich, and G. Daily, 1993. Food security, population, and environment, *Population and Development Review* 19:1, pp. 1–32; Daily, 1995.

23. Postel, Daily, and Ehrlich, 1996.

24. Ehrlich, Ehrlich, and Holdren, 1977; Myers, 1979; Ehrlich and Ehrlich, 1981; Wilson, 1988; Ehrlich and Wilson, 1991; Wilson, 1992; Lawton and May, 1995; Pimm et al., 1995; P. Raven and J. McNeely, 1996, Biological extinction: Its scope and meaning for life, in L. Guruswamy and J. McNeely (eds.), *Their Seed Preserves: Strategies for Preserving Global Biodiversity,* Duke University Press, Durham, NC, in press. This is a conservative estimate; see, for example, R. May, 1988, How many species are there on Earth?, *Science* 241:1441–1449, 16 September.

25. G. Daily (ed.), in press, *Nature's Services,* Island Press, Washington, DC.

26. P. Ehrlich and P. Raven, 1965, Butterflies and plants: A study of coevolution, *Evolution* 18:586–608.

27. C. Spedding, J. Walsingham, and A. Hoxey, 1981, *Biological Efficiency in Agriculture,* Academic Press, New York.

28. L. Brown, 1995, *Who Will Feed China?,* W. W. Norton, New York.

29. M. Forbes, 1989, Fact and comment II, *Forbes,* 20 March.

30. P. Ehrlich and J. Holdren, 1971, Impact of population growth, *Science* 171:1212–1217; see also P. Ehrlich and A. Ehrlich, 1972, *Population, Resources, Environment: Issues in Human Ecology* (2nd ed.), W. H. Freeman, San Francisco, p. 257.

31. N. Eberstadt, 1995, Population, food, and income, in R. Bailey (ed.), *The True State of the Planet,* Free Press, New York, pp. 14–15.

32. R. Bailey, 1993, *Eco-Scam: The False Prophets of Ecological Apocalypse,* St. Martin's Press, New York, p. 71.

33. B. Bolch and H. Lyons, 1993, *Apocalypse Not: Science, Economics, and Environmentalism,* Cato Institute, Washington DC, p. 26.

34. Bolch and Lyons, 1993, p. 27.

35. In 1989–1991, the Netherlands had average net imports of more than 3 million metric tons of cereals and 800,000 metric tons of pulses (peas and beans, including soybeans) (World Resources Institute, 1994, *World Resources 1994–95,* Oxford University Press, New York).

36. M. Wackernagel, 1993, *How Big Is Our Ecological Footprint? A Handbook for Estimating a Community's Carrying Capacity,* discussion

draft, Task Force on Planning Healthy and Sustainable Communities, University of British Columbia, Department of Family Practice, Mather Building, 5804 Fairview Avenue, Vancouver, B.C., Canada V6T 1Z3, 15 July. The Netherlands' "ecological footprint" or "appropriated carrying capacity" is defined as "the aggregate land (and water) area in various categories required by the people in a region (a) to provide continuously all the resources they presently consume, and (b) to absorb continuously all the waste they presently discharge, using current technology" (p. 10).

37. Bast, Hill, and Rue, 1994, p. 231.

38. D. Ray with L. Guzzo, 1993, *Environmental Overkill*, HarperCollins, New York, p. 79.

39. P. Ehrlich and A. Ehrlich, 1970, *Population, Resources, Environment,* W. H. Freeman, San Francisco, p. 338.

40. Ehrlich, Ehrlich, and Holdren, 1977, pp. 964–966.

41. D. Ahlburg, 1993. The Census Bureau's new projections of the U.S. population, *Population and Development Review* 19:159–174.

42. Whether they do or not is discussed in G. Easterbrook, 1995, *A Moment on the Earth: The Coming Age of Environmental Optimism,* Viking, New York, p. 480.

43. Ehrlich and Ehrlich, 1990, p. 170.

44. Easterbrook, 1995, p. 480.

45. We have made this point in literally dozens of speeches and in print; see, e.g., P. Ehrlich, 1991, Canaries in the global mine, *Audubon,* Autumn, p. 12; P. Ehrlich and A. Ehrlich, 1992, The most overpopulated nation, in L. Grant (ed.), *Elephants in the Volkswagen,* W. H. Freeman, New York, p. 133. This point is not original with us; it is a favorite of economist Herman Daly, among others. Daly describes the "people-hating" neo-Malthusians as having the goal of "maximizing cumulative lives ever lived." He adds "As far as we know God is not impatient for all lives to be lived soon"! (H. Daly, 1982, review of *The Ultimate Resource* by Julian Simon, *Bulletin of the Atomic Scientists,* January; reprinted in H. Daly, 1991, *Steady-State Economics,* Island Press, Washington, DC; and H. Daly and J. Cobb Jr., 1989, *For the Common Good,* Beacon Press, Boston, p. 239.)

46. J. Robb, 1995, How many immigrants does Vatican City take? Actually none, *The Social Contract,* 5 (4): 281.

47. See the discussion and references in Ehrlich, Ehrlich, and Daily, 1995, especially chapters 3 and 4.

48. See, e.g., E. Schlosser, 1995, In the strawberry fields, *Atlantic Monthly,* November, p. 106.

49. Brownlash writers don't entirely overlook the problem. See, for instance, an attempt to downplay the seriousness of deterioration of the

epidemiological environment by Stephen Budiansky (1995, Plague fiction, *New Scientist,* 2 December, pp. 28–31).

50. Ehrlich, 1968, pp. 70–71; similar statements appear in Ehrlich and Ehrlich, 1970, pp. 148–151; Ehrlich, Ehrlich, and Holdren, 1977, pp. 148–151; and Ehrlich and Ehrlich, 1990, pp. 143–150.

51. G. Easterbrook, 1991, Propheteers, *Washington Monthly,* November, p. 43.

52. Ehrlich, 1968, p. 71.

53. World Health Organization, 1991, *In Point of Fact,* World Health Organization, Geneva.

54. Quoted in L. Garrett, 1994, *The Coming Plague: Newly Emerging Diseases in a World Out of Balance,* Farrar, Straus, and Giroux, New York, p. 6.

55. Details on the deterioration of the epidemiological environment, with extensive references to the technical literature, can be found in G. Daily and P. Ehrlich, 1996, Global change and the epidemiological environment, *Environment and Development Economics,* in press.

56. K. De Cock and J. McCormick, 1988, HIV infection in Zaire, *New England Journal of Medicine* 319:309.

57. British biochemist J. Cairns, unpublished, quoted in Garrett, 1994, p. 235.

58. See, e.g., R. Shope, 1991, Global climate change and infectious diseases, *Environmental Health Perspectives* 96:171–174; P. Martin and M. Lefebvre, 1995, Malaria and climate: Sensitivity of malaria potential transmission to climate, *Ambio* 24:200–207.

59. For example, loss of biodiversity and agricultural intensification also cause deterioration of the epidemiological environment (Daily and Ehrlich, 1996).

60. See, e.g., R. Bailey, 1993; J. Simon, 1995, Betting on the Future, Australian Broadcasting Company (ABC) television, 30 November.

61. Ehrlich, 1968, p. 11.

62. See, e.g., W. and P. Paddock, 1967, *Famine—1975,* Little, Brown, Boston.

63. M. Swaminathan, personal communication, December 1994.

64. See, e.g., Bast, Hill, and Rue, 1994, p. 19; see also R. North, 1995, *Life on a Modern Planet,* Manchester University Press, Manchester, p. 14ff.

65. M. Fumento, 1993, *Science Under Siege: Balancing Technology and the Environment,* William Morrow, New York, p. 349.

66. See, chapter 7 in Ehrlich, Ehrlich, and Holdren, 1977, for a description of the situation in the mid-1970s and references.

67. S. Hansch, 1995, *How Many People Die of Starvation in Humanitar-*

ian Emergencies?, Refugee Policy Group, Center for Policy Analysis and Research on Refugee Issues (June), Washington, DC.

68. In 1980, there were about 36 million deaths in developing nations, about 16 million of them among children under age five (World Bank, 1993, *World Development Report 1993: Investing in Health,* Oxford University Press, Oxford). The estimate assumes that since 1968 about half of the infant-child deaths were from hunger or hunger-related diseases (see the discussion in World Bank, 1993, ch. 4, especially pp. 75–79 for the current situation, which is an improvement over previous decades). See also World Health Organization, 1995, *The World Health Report 1995; Bridging the Gaps,* World Health Organization, Geneva; and *International Health News,* September 1987, which estimated that over 14 million children were dying annually of hunger and hunger-related disease.

69. See, e.g., W. Beisel, 1984, Nutrition, infection, specific immune responses, and non-specific host defenses: A complex interaction, in R. Watson (ed.), *Nutrition, Disease Resistance, and Immune Function,* Marcel Dekker, New York, pp. 21–30; G. Harrison and J. Waterlow (eds.), 1990, *Diet and Disease in Traditional Developing Societies,* Cambridge University Press, Cambridge; P. Ellner and H. Neu, 1992, *Understanding Infectious Disease,* Mosby–Year Book, St. Louis, MO.

70. Estimates of the number of chronically malnourished people range from about half a billion (United Nations, 1993, *Report on the World Social Situation 1993,* United Nations, New York, chapter 2; World Food Council, 1992, *The Global State of Hunger and Malnutrition,* WFC/12, World Food Council, New York) to more than a billion (United Nations Children's Fund, 1992, *State of the World's Children 1992,* United Nations, New York; and World Bank estimates cited in R. Kates and V. Haarmann, 1992, Where the poor live: Are the assumptions correct?, *Environment* 34 (4): 5–11, 25–28). The Food and Agriculture Organization of the United Nations (FAO) estimated that 786 million people in developing regions were undernourished in 1988–1990 (Food and Agriculture Organization, 1992, *The State of Food and Agriculture, 1992,* Food and Agriculture Organization, Rome); for a more conservative estimate of hunger in one area, see P. Svedberg, 1991, Undernutrition in sub-Saharan Africa: A critical assessment of the evidence, in J. Dreze and A. Sen (eds.), *The Political Economy of Hunger,* vol. 3, *Endemic Hunger,* Oxford University Press, Oxford, pp. 155–193.

71. Many writers on the food problem have made this assertion in one form or another; some examples include F. Lappé and J. Collins, 1977, *Food First,* Houghton Mifflin, Boston; M. Swaminathan and S. Sinha (eds.), 1986, *Global Aspects of Food Production,* Tycooly International, Riverton, NJ; R. Lee, W. Arthur, A. Kelley, G. Rodgers, and T. Sri-

navasan, 1988, *Population, Food, and Rural Development,* Clarendon Press, Oxford; and G. Norton and J. Alwang, 1993, *Introduction to the Economics of Agricultural Development,* McGraw-Hill, New York. These writers focus strongly on the poverty and underdevelopment of rural areas and sometimes on the exploitation of the rural poor by the rich, factors that are important in explaining hunger. But they usually discount the roles of population growth and environmental deterioration in generating the problems and hindering solutions.

72. D. Avery, 1995, Saving the planet with pesticides. In Bailey (ed.), *The True State of the Planet,* Free Press, New York, p. 51.

73. R. Chen (ed.), 1990, *The Hunger Report: 1990,* The Alan Shawn Feinstein World Hunger Program, Brown University, Providence RI; M. Alberti, D. Layton, G. Daily, and P. Ehrlich, 1997, in preparation.

74. Chen, 1990; Alberti et al., 1997.

75. L. Brown, 1995, Facing food scarcity, *World Watch* 8:6, November–December, pp. 10–21.

76. P. Weber, 1994, *Net Loss: Fish, Jobs, and the Marine Environment,* Worldwatch paper no. 120, Worldwatch Institute, Washington, DC; Ehrlich, Ehrlich, and Daily, 1995, pp. 163–167; J. McGoodwin, 1990, *Crisis in the World's Fisheries,* Stanford University Press, Stanford, CA.

77. Avery, 1995, p. 51; see also A. Wildavsky, 1995, *But Is It True? A Citizen's Guide to Environmental Health and Safety Issues,* Harvard University Press, Cambridge, which asserts that climatologist Stephen Schneider in 1976 "is mistaken in his belief that the existing world food production system is inadequate" (p. 443).

78. Avery, 1995, p. 50; Eberstadt, 1995, p. 26.

79. Ehrlich, Ehrlich, and Daily, 1995, chapter 5.

80. N. Keyfitz, 1991. Population and development within the ecosphere: One view of the literature, *Population Index* 57:1, pp. 5–22.

81. M. Hossain, 1994. Asian population growth is overtaking rice output, *International Herald Tribune,* 18 March; see also J. Walsh, 1991, Consultative Group on International Agricultural Research (CIGIAR), Preserving the options: Food productivity and sustainability, *Issues in Agriculture* no. 2.

82. B. Holmes, 1994, Super rice extends limits to growth, *New Scientist,* 4 October, p. 29.

83. Malthus goes east, *The Economist,* 12 August 1995.

84. Brown, 1995, *Who Will Feed China?*

85. Avery, 1995, p. 50.

86. Brown, 1995, Facing food scarcity.

87. Hossain, 1994; Walsh, 1991.

88. Oldeman, Van Engelen, and Pulles, 1990; Ehrlich, Ehrlich, and Daily, 1993.

89. Daily, 1995.

90. M. Imhoff, W. Lawrence, M. Privalsky, E. Levine, and V. Brown, 1996, Can urban sprawl reduce human carrying capacity? Evaluating land use change with nighttime views of the Earth, manuscript.

91. More than a million acres per year are lost in east Asia alone (FAO estimate cited in L. Brown et al., 1990, *State of the World 1990,* W. W. Norton, New York).

92. Gleick, 1993; Reisner, 1986; Postel, 1990.

93. S. Postel, 1990; S. Postel, 1992, *The Last Oasis: Facing Water Scarcity,* W. W. Norton, New York.

94. D. Dudek, 1991, The nexus of agriculture, environment, and the economy under climate change, in R. Wyman (ed.), *Global Climate Change and Life on Earth,* Routledge, Chapman, and Hall, New York, pp. 180–200; M. Parry, 1990, *Climate Change and World Agriculture,* Earthscan, London.

95. Intergovernmental Panel on Climate Change (IPCC), 1996, *Climate Change 1995—The Science of Climate Change: Contribution of Working Group I to the Second Assessment Report of the Intergovernmental Panel on Climate Change,* Cambridge University Press, New York.

96. Ehrlich, Ehrlich, and Daily, 1995.

97. Intergovernmental Panel on Climate Change (IPCC), 1996.

98. All these topics are covered with references in chapter 6 of Ehrlich, Ehrlich, and Daily, 1995.

99. Ehrlich, Ehrlich, and Daily, 1995.

100. See, e.g., J. Simon, 1981, *The Ultimate Resource,* Princeton University Press, Princeton, NJ, p. 347.

101. A. Carr-Saunders, 1922, *The Population Problem: A Study in Human Evolution,* Oxford University Press, London; J. Neel, 1970, Lessons from "primitive" people, *Science* 170:816–817; Ehrlich, Ehrlich, and Daily, 1995, chapter 2.

102. Simon, 1981, p. 10.

103. Much of what follows is based on P. Bahn and J. Flenley, 1992, *Easter Island, Earth Island,* Thames and Hudson, London; J. Diamond, 1995, Easter's end, *Discover,* August, pp. 63–69.

104. N. Himes, 1936, *Medical History of Contraception,* Gamut Press, New York; M. Harris and E. Ross, 1987, *Death, Sex, and Fertility: Population Regulation in Preindustrial and Developing Societies,* Columbia University Press, New York; Ehrlich, Ehrlich, and Daily, 1995, chapter 2.

105. This interpretation is not considered established by some archaeologists—see J. Van Tilburg, 1994, *Easter Island: Archaeology, Ecology, and Culture,* Smithsonian Institution Press, Washington, DC.

106. R. Stevenson, 1925, *In the South Seas,* Charles Scribner's Sons, New

York. Note that Stevenson (1850–1894), like most of his contemporaries, incorrectly assumed tropical soils were the richest.

107. Diamond, 1995, p. 68.

108. See, e.g., E. El-Hinnawi, 1985, *Environmental Refugees,* United Nations Environment Programme, Nairobi; N. Myers, 1986, The environmental dimension to security issues, *The Environmentalist* 6:252–257; N. Myers, 1991, *Population, Resources and the Environment: The Critical Challenges,* Bantam Books, New York; Myers, 1995, *Ultimate Security,* W. W. Norton, New York.

109. N. Myers and J. Kent, 1995, *Environmental Exodus: An Emergent Crisis in the Global Arena,* Climate Institute, Washington, DC.

110. Ibid., p. 1.

111. J. Diamond, 1994, Ecological collapses of past civilizations, *Proceedings of the American Philosophical Society* 138 (3): 363–370.

112. D. Steadman and S. Olson, 1985, Bird remains from an archaeological site on Henderson Island, South Pacific: Man-caused extinctions on an "uninhabited" island, *Proceedings of the National Academy of Sciences USA* 82:6191–6195.

113. T. Culbert, 1973, *The Classic Maya Collapse,* University of New Mexico Press, Albuquerque; M. Coe, 1984, *The Maya,* (3rd ed.), Thames and Hudson, London; E. Abrams and D. Rue, 1988, The causes and consequences of deforestation among the prehistoric Maya, *Human Ecology* 16:377–395; J. Sabloff, 1990, *The New Archaeology and the Ancient Maya,* W. H. Freeman, New York; D. Hodell, J. Curtis, and M. Brenner, 1995, Possible role of climate in the collapse of classic Maya civilization, *Nature* 375:391–394.

114. See, e.g., T. Jacobsen and R. Adams, 1958, Salt and silt in ancient Mesopotamian agriculture, *Science* 128:1251–1258.

115. J. Hughes, 1975, *Ecology of Ancient Civilizations,* University of New Mexico Press, Albuquerque. See also T. van Andel and C. Runnels, 1987, *Beyond the Acropolis,* Stanford University Press, Stanford, CA. The latter authors doubt the importance of ecological factors but concede that human activity has brought the Mediterranean basin to its present degraded state.

116. J. Betancourt, J. Dean, and H. Hull, 1986, Prehistoric long-distance transport of construction beams, Chaco Canyon, New Mexico, *American Antiquity* 51:370–375; S. Lekson, T. Windes, J. Stein, and W. Judge, 1988, The Chaco Canyon community, *Scientific American,* July.

117. Hodell, Curtis, and Brenner, 1995.

118. J. Sabloff, 1995, Drought and decline, *Nature* 375:357.

119. The vast majority of the genetic variability in human beings occurs

among individuals within populations, not between populations. Contrary to some popular beliefs, there is no reason to believe that different races have significant differences in their hereditary intellectual endowments (see, e.g., P. Ehrlich and S. Feldman, 1977, *The Race Bomb: Skin Color, Prejudice, and Intelligence,* New York Times Books, New York). In other words, there is no reputable evidence that African Americans are on average one bit more or less "genetically intelligent" than European or Asian Americans. This means that any two metropolitan areas, even in very different areas of the world, with the same size population will have essentially the same hereditary talents available to it. There is no evidence that the San Francisco Bay area has more genetic resources than Kinshasa, Zaire, or Dallas–Fort Worth.

120. Yvonne Burtness, Palo Alto School System, personal communication, 3 January 1996. The decline has continued in recent years. In 1992–1993, California was the thirty-sixth state in expenditures per child; it dropped to thirty-eighth by 1994–1995.

Chapter 6: Fables about Non-living Resources

1. What follows is based in part on G. Daily and P. Ehrlich, 1992, Population, sustainability, and Earth's carrying capacity, *BioScience* 42:761–771.

2. Groundwater in some aquifers is being pumped at rates that make it non-renewable.

3. All materials are dispersed very gradually over time according to the second law of thermodynamics but at rates so slow as not to be pertinent to this discussion.

4. Julian Simon seems especially fascinated with copper (see, e.g., N. Myers and J. Simon, 1994, *Scarcity or Abundance? A Debate on the Environment,* W. W. Norton, New York, pp. 10–11). Other examples of resource optimism can be found in S. Moore, 1995, The coming age of abundance, in R. Bailey (ed.), *The True State of the Planet,* Free Press, New York, pp. 109–139; J. Bast, P. Hill, and R. Rue, 1994, *Ecosanity: A Common-Sense Guide to Environmentalism,* Madison Books, Lanham, MD, pp. 121–124; and R. Bailey, 1993, *Eco-Scam: The False Prophets of Ecological Apocalypse,* St. Martin's Press, New York, pp. 67–69.

5. All resources are probably ultimately renewable, of course, but on time scales of many hundreds to many millions of years.

6. Bailey, 1993, p. 69.

7. See, e.g., P. Ehrlich, 1989, The limits to substitution: Meta-resource de-

pletion and a new economic-ecological paradigm, *Ecological Economics* 1:9–16.

8. H. Barnett and C. Morse, 1963, *Scarcity and Growth: The Economics of Natural Resource Availability,* Johns Hopkins University Press, Baltimore, p. 11. Their complete statement was: "Advances in fundamental science have made it possible to take advantage of the uniformity of energy/matter—a uniformity that makes it feasible without preassignable limit, to escape the quantitative constraints imposed by the character of the earth's crust. . . . Nature imposes particular scarcities, not an inescapable general scarcity. Man is therefore able, and free, to choose among an indefinitely large number of alternatives. There is no reason to believe that these alternatives will eventually reduce to one that entails increasing cost—that it must sometime prove impossible to escape diminishing quantitative returns. Science, by making the resource base more homogeneous, erases the restrictions once thought to reside in the lack of homogeneity . . . the particular resources with which one starts increasingly become a matter of indifference."

9. J. Holdren, 1992, The transition to costlier energy, in L. Schipper and A. S. Myers (eds.), *Energy Efficiency and Human Activity,* Cambridge University Press, Cambridge.

10. J. Davis, 1950, Energy for Planet Earth, *Scientific American,* September.

11. World Energy Council, 1993, *Energy for Tomorrow's World,* St. Martin's Press, New York; A. Nur, 1996, The coming energy crisis, *Stanford Report,* 28 February, p. 4.

12. J. Holdren and P. Herrera, 1971, *Energy,* Sierra Club Books, San Francisco; P. Ehrlich, A. Ehrlich, and J. Holdren, 1977, *Ecoscience: Population, Resources, Environment,* W. H. Freeman, San Francisco, chapter 8 and references; J. Holdren, 1990, Energy in transition, *Scientific American,* September.

13. Lecture at Woods Hole Research Center, Massachusetts, 11 October 1995. The material that follows is based on his publications and the lecture.

14. For details and references, see P. Ehrlich and A. Ehrlich, 1991, *Healing the Planet,* Addison-Wesley, Reading, MA, pp. 67–69.

15. U.S. Department of Energy, Task Force on Strategic Energy Resources and Development, 1995, *Energy R&D: Shaping Our Nation's Future in a Competitive World,* U.S. Department of Energy, July. The figures given are the totals for all energy supply research and development, including fossil fuels, nuclear fission, nuclear fusion, renewable energy sources, and energy conservation.

16. The costs of a product reflected in the market price are the private

costs; those costs not captured by the price are the external costs (externalities). The sum of private and external costs is the social cost.

17. That is, the negative externalities have not been internalized.

18. J. Holdren and R. Pachauri, 1992, Energy, in International Council of Scientific Unions, *An Agenda of Science for Environment and Development into the 21st Century,* Cambridge University Press, Cambridge.

19. Bailey, 1993, p. 64.

20. Ibid., p. 69.

21. D. H. Meadows, D. L. Meadows, J. Randers, and W. Behrens III, 1972, *The Limits to Growth,* Universe Books, Washington, DC.

22. Moore, 1995, p. 126.

23. U.S. Department of Commerce, Bureau of the Census, 1994, *Statistical Abstracts of the United States,* U.S. Government Printing Office, Washington, DC.

24. G. Reisman, 1992, The toxicity of environmentalism, in J. Lehr (ed.), *Rational Readings on Environmental Concerns,* Van Nostrand Reinhold, New York, p. 632.

25. J. Simon, 1980, Resources, population, environment: An oversupply of false bad news, *Science* 208:1435–1436. If copper were to be made from other metals, that could be done most easily by changing nickel-62 into nickel-63 in a nuclear reactor and then allowing the nickel-63 to decay slowly (half-life 100 years) into copper-63. Under ridiculously optimistic assumptions, copper so produced would cost about $2 billion per pound (A. Bartlett and J. Kraushaar, 1982, in L. Grant [ed.], *The Cornucopian Fallacies,* TEF Reports, The Environmental Fund, Washington, DC).

26. J. Simon, 1981, *The Ultimate Resource,* Princeton University Press, Princeton, NJ, pp. 47, 49.

27. H. Daly, 1982, review of *The Ultimate Resource,* by Julian Simon, *Bulletin of the Atomic Scientists,* January, pp. 39–42.

28. Reisman, 1992, p. 635.

29. Ibid., p. 636.

30. Note that the energy flow is measured here in kilowatts—1000 watts (a rate of energy use, as in the flow through a 100-watt lightbulb—and not in kilowatt-hours (quantities of energy; a kilowatt-hour is the amount of energy that would be used keeping a 100-watt lightbulb burning for ten hours).

31. A. Fickett, C. Gellings, and A. Lovins, 1990, Efficient use of electricity, *Scientific American,* September, pp. 65–74.

32. As measured by inflation-corrected dollars of gross domestic product per gigajoule of primary energy.

33. For summaries of these results and guides to the detailed literature,

see, e.g., National Academy of Sciences, Committee on Nuclear and Alternative Energy Systems, 1980, *Energy in Transition 1985–2010,* W. H. Freeman, San Francisco; J. Goldemberg, T. Johansson, and A. Reddy, 1987, *Energy for a Sustainable World,* World Resources Institute, Washington, DC; H. Kelly, P. Blair, and J. Gibbons, 1989, Energy use and productivity: Current trends and policy implications, *Annual Review of Energy* 14:321–352; and L. Schipper and S. Meyers (eds.), 1992, *Energy Efficiency and Human Activity: Past Trends and Future Prospects,* Cambridge University Press, Cambridge.

34. Myers and Simon, 1994, back flap copy.

35. Bailey, 1993, p. 54.

36. See, e.g., Simon, 1981, p. 27.

37. J. Holdren, J. Harte, P. Ehrlich, and A. Ehrlich, 1980, Bad news: Is it true?, *Science* 210:1296–1297.

38. The bet was made on real (adjusted for inflation) prices.

39. Simon himself admitted he was lucky in a letter to Ehrlich, Harte, and Holdren in October 1989. Crowing in advance about his victory, he said, "I have been lucky that this particular period coincided so nicely with my argument."

40. World Resources Institute, 1992, *World Resources Report 1992–1993,* Basic Books, New York.

41. J. Simon, 1995, Earth's doomsayers are wrong, *San Francisco Chronicle,* 12 May.

42. P. Ehrlich and S. Schneider, 1995, Wagering on global environment, *San Francisco Chronicle,* 18 May.

43. In the first bet, prices increased for two metals and fell for three, an outcome that easily could have been changed by chance. On the direction of the trends in 2005, Paul and Steve agreed to accept the verdict of a panel of scientists chosen by the president of the National Academy of Sciences. Referees would have been necessary in some cases, since terms like "significantly" (e.g., in item 10 of the proposed wager) and estimates of such things as losses of agricultural soils involve questions of judgment. But there is an empirical basis on which competent scientists could make reasonable judgments. The bet would have been binding on Ehrlich's and Schneider's heirs, and their winnings would have gone to non-profit organizations dedicated to preserving environmental quality and human well-being.

44. Simon now tells reporters that he wants to bet only that the net effects of human activities will be positive, such as an increase in life expectancy, and accuses Steve and Paul of being unreasonable for not accepting this new kind of bet (see, e.g., C. Petitt, 1995, 2 Stanford scholars take on rosy economist, *San Francisco Chronicle,* 18 May). He claims that the Ehrlich-Schneider list dwells on aspects of our en-

vironment for which the connection to human welfare is questionable. Of course, the scientific community (of which he claims to represent the consensus) doesn't seem to find the list so "questionable"— see appendix B.

45. The wager has been taken quite seriously by the media and the public in western countries; see, e.g., J. Tierney, 1990, Betting the planet, *New York Times Magazine,* 2 December; *New Scientist,* 1995, Apocalypse tomorrow . . . 3 June, p. 3; R. Mestel, 1995, Doomsters take on global bet, *New Scientist,* 3 June, p. 5.

46. Bailey, 1993, p. 54.

47. T. Anderson, 1995. Water options for the blue planet, in R. Bailey, (ed.), *The True State of the Planet,* Free Press, New York, pp. 267–294.

48. S. Postel, G. Daily, and P. Ehrlich, 1996, Human appropriation of renewable fresh water, *Science,* 271:785–788.

49. Postel, Daily, and Ehrlich, 1996.

Chapter 7: Biological Diversity and the Endangered Species Act

1. National Research Council, Committee on Scientific Issues in the Endangered Species Act, 1995, *Science and the Endangered Species Act,* National Academy Press, Washington, DC; Defenders of Wildlife, 1995, *Saving America's Wildlife: Renewing the Endangered Species Act,* Defenders of Wildlife, Washington, DC.

2. N. Myers, 1979, *The Sinking Ark,* Pergamon Press, New York; P. Ehrlich and A. Ehrlich, 1981, *Extinction: The Causes and Consequences of the Disappearance of Species,* Random House, New York; N. Myers, 1983, *A Wealth of Wild Species,* Westview Press, Boulder, CO; E. Wilson, 1992, *The Diversity of Life,* Harvard University Press, Cambridge.

3. V. Heywood (ed.), 1995, *Global Biodiversity Assessment* (United Nations Environment Programme), Cambridge University Press, Cambridge.

4. E. Dowdeswell, 1995, foreword in Heywood, 1995, p. vii; also slightly modified in R. Watson, V. Heywood, I. Baste, B. Dias, R. Gámez, T. Janetos, W. Reid, and G. Ruark, 1995, *Global Biodiversity Assessment: Summary for Policy-Makers,* (United Nations Environment Programme), Cambridge University Press, Cambridge, p. iv.

5. R. Watson et al., 1995, p. 3.

6. This is a direct quote from G. Easterbrook, 1995, *A Moment on the Earth: The Coming Age of Environmental Optimism,* Viking, New York, p. 21.

7. Food and Agriculture Organization of the United Nations, 1993, *1992*

FAO Production Yearbook, vol. 47, Food and Agriculture Organization, Rome; a recent estimate is that over 40 percent of Earth's ice-free land surface is used for agriculture, including cropland, pasture, and tree plantations (M. Alberti, D. Layton, G. Daily, and P. Ehrlich, 1996, Ecological and economic measures of food security, in preparation).

8. See, e.g., N. Myers, 1989, *Deforestation Rates in Tropical Forests and Their Climatic Implications,* Friends of the Earth, London; S. Pimm and R. Askins, 1995, Forest losses predict bird extinctions in eastern North America, *Proceedings of the National Academy of Sciences USA* 92:9343–9347.

9. See, e.g., S. Simonich and R. Hites, 1995, Global distribution of persistent organochlorine compounds, *Science* 269:1851–1854.

10. Data are from Thomas A. Oberbauer, Regional Planner, Department of Planning and Land Use, County of San Diego, April 1994, based on a 1988 analysis.

11. There is great confusion in the brownlash about how the uncertainties and conflicts within the science of taxonomy reflect on the issue of preserving biological resources. For an especially unfortunate discussion, see A. Chase, 1995, *In a Dark Wood: The Fight over Forests and the Rising Tyranny of Ecology,* Houghton Mifflin, New York, pp. 109–110. Chase confuses the minimal utility of the subspecies concept for understanding evolution with the great utility of subspecies, under the Endangered Species Act, for protecting critical population diversity.

12. See, e.g., C. Mann and M. Plummer, 1995, *Noah's Choice: The Future of Endangered Species,* Alfred A. Knopf, New York, pp. 28–29.

13. We did not pay sufficient attention to the problem of preserving population diversity in our early book (Ehrlich and Ehrlich, 1981), but we tried to make up for that in later publications, such as P. Ehrlich and G. Daily, 1993, Population extinction and saving biodiversity, *Ambio* 22:64–68.

14. Ehrlich and Daily, 1993.

15. We say "virtually" because some critics might construct a scenario in which a minimum viable population of *Homo sapiens* might be preserved with the others.

16. The thought experiment obviously omits little complications like how animal species would eat, what would happen to nutrient cycles with key bacteria limited to single petri dishes, and so forth.

17. Ecologists don't know precisely how much species diversity is required to ensure the continuance of vital ecosystem services. See Heywood, 1995, chapters 5 and 6.

18. See, e.g., P. Raven and J. McNeely, 1996, Biological extinction: Its scope and meaning for us, in L. Guruswamy and J. McNeely (eds.),

Their Seed Preserves: Strategies for Preserving Global Biodiversity, Duke University Press, Durham, NC.

19. See, e.g., J. Simon and A. Wildavsky, 1993, Facts, not species are periled, *New York Times,* 13 May.

20. See, e.g., Easterbrook, 1995, pp. 556–562.

21. W. Beckerman, 1995, Why worry about the weather?, *Wall Street Journal Europe,* 25–26 August.

22. Wilson, 1992, p. 280.

23. E. Wilson, 1995, letter, *Wall Street Journal Europe,* 3 October.

24. S. Budiansky, 1995, *Nature's Keepers: The New Science of Nature Management,* Free Press, New York, pp. 167–168.

25. Reverse extrapolation from species area curves.

26. T. Brooks and A. Balmford, 1995, Atlantic forest extinctions, manuscript prepared for submission.

27. S. Budiansky, 1995, p. 170.

28. Endangered Species Act, section 2(b).

29. National Research Council, Committee on Scientific Issues in the Endangered Species Act, 1995, p. 17.

30. D. Murphy, 1995, An overview of The National Academy of Sciences report: Science and the Endangered Species Act, *Endangered Species Update* 12(9):8–10.

31. This is a major theme of Mann and Plummer, 1995.

32. D. Murphy, California and the Endangered Species Act: Part of the solution, not part of the problem, op-ed submitted to *Los Angeles Times,* August 1995 (edited here by Dennis Murphy).

33. U.S. Fish and Wildlife Service, 1993 (press release, March), Gnatcatcher to be listed as "threatened;" Interior's Babbitt promotes regional conservation efforts; L. Dwyer, D. Murphy, S. Johnson, and M. O'Connell, 1995, Avoiding the trainwreck: observations from the frontlines of natural community conservation planning in southern California, *Endangered Species Update* 12(9):5–7.

34. D. Ray (with L. Guzzo), 1993, *Environmental Overkill: Whatever Happened to Common Sense?,* HarperCollins, New York, p. 85.

35. Even Dan Quayle went after the now-famous bird when he was vice president: "[he] attacked the Endangered Species Act, the garter snake, spotted owl and unnamed 'radicals' who he said would stop growth by cutting off water to ranch lands" (P. Trounstine, 1992, Quayle attacks species protections: Democrats value owls over people, he says, *San Jose Mercury News,* 11 August).

36. D. Wilcove, 1994, Turning conservation goals into tangible results: The case of the spotted owl and old-growth forests, in P. Edwards, R.

May, and N. Webb, *Large-scale Ecology and Conservation Biology,* Blackwell, Oxford, pp. 313–329.

37. Those interested in a summary by a first-rate scientist should see David Wilcove's overview (1994). Especially interesting is Wilcove's view (pp. 326–327) that a nebulous "ecosystem" approach would not be as effective as an improved species-by-species approach.

38. The precedent-setting Interagency Spotted Owl Scientific Committee, enjoined by Congress to develop a "scientifically credible" plan for the owl, was constrained to focus on that species alone (J. Thomas, E. Forsman, J. Lint, et al., 1990, *A Conservation Strategy of the Northern Spotted Owl,* U.S. Forest Service, Bureau of Land Management, U.S. Fish and Wildlife Service, and National Park Service, Portland, OR; see also D. Murphy and B. Noon, 1992, Integrating scientific methods with habitat conservation planning: Reserve design for northern spotted owls, *Ecological Applications* 2:3–17). The final plan was a compromise that left both sides—loggers and environmentalists—dissatisfied.

A conclusion of a panel of scientists who examined that 1990 plan proposed for the preservation of the spotted owl was that the plan would have a high probability of maintaining the owls over the next century (J. Thomas, M. Raphael, R. Anthony, et al., 1993, *Viability Assessments and Management Considerations for Species Associated with Late-Successional and Old-Growth Forests of the Pacific Northwest,* U.S. Forest Service, Washington, DC). In contrast, the plan would give only a "medium low" probability of preserving breeding populations of marbled murrelets, and a "very low" probability of maintaining sensitive fish stocks (primarily salmon). For sustaining a functional old-growth ecosystem, the point of the entire exercise, the panel concluded that the chances of succeeding for a century were "medium low." The report of that panel remains the cornerstone of public lands planning in the Pacific Northwest, but it has been buttressed with conservation actions designed to protect hundreds of other species, from invertebrates to furbearers.

39. T. Egan, 1994, Oregon, foiling forecasters, thrives as it protects owls, *New York Times,* 11 October.

40. World Wide Fund for Nature, 1994, *For Conserving Listed Species, Talk Is Cheaper than We Think: The Consultation Process Under the Endangered Species Act,* World Wildlife Fund, Washington, DC, November.

41. A. Chase, 1995, *In a Dark Wood: The Fight Over Forests and the Rising Tyranny of Ecology,* Houghton Mifflin, Boston, pp. 248–251; A. Chase, 1994, Flying blind over owl terrain, *Washington Times,* 21 April.

42. H. R. Pulliam, 1988, Sources, sinks, and population regulation, *American Naturalist* 132:652–661.

43. H. R. Pulliam, in press, Providing the scientific information that conservation practitioners need, *Cary Conference Proceedings*.

44. Pullman cites W. Ripple, D. Johnson, K. Hershey, and E. Meslow, 1991, Old-growth and mature forest near spotted owl nests in western Oregon, *Journal of Wildlife Management* 55:316–318; and J. Lehmkuhl and M. Raphael, 1993, Habitat pattern around northern spotted owl locations on the Olympic Peninsula, Washington, *Journal of Wildlife Management* 57:302–315.

45. Here Pulliam cites J. Blakesley, A. Franklin, and R. Gutierrez, 1992, Spotted owl roost and nest site selection in northwestern California, *Journal of Wildlife Management* 56:388–392.

46. Mann and Plummer, 1995.

47. Ibid., pp. 164–175.

48. Ibid., 1995, p. 174.

49. Ehrlich and Ehrlich, 1981, pp. 182–185.

50. S. Pimm, personal communication, 29 November 1995.

51. S. Pimm, 1995, testimony to the Senate Committee on Environment and Public Works' Subcommittee on Drinking Water, Fisheries, and Wildlife, 13 July, pp. 3, 28.

52. Mann and Plummer, 1995, p. 210.

53. *Lycaeides melissa samuelis.*

54. *Nicophorus americanus.*

55. D. Wilcove, 1996, review of *Noah's Choice: The Future of Endangered Species,"* by Charles Mann and Christopher Plummer, *Biodiversity and Conservation,* in press.

56. Mann and Plummer, 1995, p. 24.

57. E. Wilson, 1987, The little things that run the world (the importance and conservation of invertebrates), *Conservation Biology* 1 (4): 344–346.

58. Ibid., p. 345.

59. T. Reid and D. Murphy, 1995, Providing a regional context for local conservation action, *BioScience,* supplement, S84–S89.

60. Murphy, 1995.

61. See, e.g., *Wall Street Journal,* 1993, The emotional species act (2 November).

62. See, e.g., P. Ehrlich, 1994, Energy use and biodiversity loss, *Philosophical Transactions of the Royal Society* 344 (B): 99–104.

63. Mann and Plummer, 1995, p. 214.

64. See, e.g., Ehrlich and Ehrlich, 1981, pp. 48–52.

65. Given tens of millions of years, Earth's biota has shown extraordinary resilience in regenerating diversity after catastrophic extinction episodes.

66. Mann and Plummer, 1995, chapter 8.

67. This does not mean abandoning the protection of individual species—see note 21.

68. Dwyer et al., 1995.
69. David Wilcove, personal communication, 21 November 1995.
70. P. Ehrlich and H. Mooney, 1983, Extinction, substitution, and ecosystem services, *BioScience* 33:248–254.
71. A partial model could be the evolution of attitudes toward cruelty to animals and the passage of humane laws over the past several generations (Ehrlich and Ehrlich, 1981, pp. 50–52). At one time mine owners and haulage companies thought it was their right to overwork the animals they owned and that such actions were nobody else's business. They purchased their animals with the expectation that they could abuse them. Try beating your horse to death in public today, and you'll find that's changed! Now, only a few generations later, the notion that you can abuse your land and its biota because it was purchased with certain expectations is also changing.

Chapter 8: Fables about the Atmosphere and Climate

1. R. Bailey, 1995, Prologue: Environmentalism for the twenty-first century, in R. Bailey, (ed.), *The True State of the Planet,* Free Press, New York, p. 2; J. Bast, P. Hill, and R. Rue, 1994, *Eco-sanity: A Common-Sense Guide to Environmentalism,* Madison Books, Lanham, MD, p. 62; see also M. Fumento, 1993, *Science Under Siege: Balancing Technology and the Environment,* William Morrow, New York, pp. 360–361; A. Wildavsky, 1995, *But Is It True? A Citizen's Guide to Environmental Health and Safety Issues,* Harvard University Press, Cambridge, MA, p. 437; R. Balling, 1994, Global warming: The Gore vision versus climate reality, in J. Baden (ed.), *Environmental Gore: A Constructive Response to Earth in the Balance,* Pacific Research Institute for Public Policy, San Francisco, p. 109; R. Lindzen, 1994, Global warming: The origin and nature of alleged scientific consensus, in Baden, 1994, p. 124; J. Simon, 1994, *Scarcity or Abundance: A Debate on the Environment,* W. W. Norton, New York, p. 55.

2. We say "could" because it is difficult to balance ameliorating effects of less extreme winter temperatures on respiratory disease in some places against increased risk of heat stroke and other summer problems in warmed areas. See A. Haines, 1993, The possible effects of climate change on health, in E. Chivian, M. McCally, H. Hu, and A. Haines (eds.), *Critical Condition: Human Health and the Environment,* MIT Press, Cambridge, MA, pp. 151–170.

3. R. Shope, 1991, Global climate change and infectious diseases, *Environmental Health Perspectives,* 96:171–174; P. Martin and M. Lefebvre, 1995, Malaria and climate: Sensitivity of malaria potential transmission to climate, *Ambio* 24:200–207. For further references and an overview

of the epidemiological environment, see G. Daily and P. Ehrlich, in press, Development, global change, and the epidemiological environment, *Environmental Economics and Development.*

4. For more details and references, see P. Ehrlich and A. Ehrlich, 1991, *Healing the Planet,* Addison-Wesley, Reading, MA, chapter 3.

5. This is the basic message of the brownlash; many references to it in its various forms will be given in following sections.

6. For a fine discussion of some of these complexities in layman's terms, see S. Schneider and R. Londer, 1984, *The Coevolution of Climate and Life,* Sierra Club Books, San Francisco.

7. This is a good example of a theory so well established that scientists treat it as a fact.

8. Intergovernmental Panel on Climate Change (IPCC), 1996, Summary for Policymakers, *Climate Change 1995—The Science of Climate Change: Contribution of Working Group I to the Second Assessment Report of the Intergovernmental Panel on Climate Change,* Cambridge University Press, Cambridge, U.K.; Atmospheric CO_2 levels have been recorded continuously since 1958 by C. D. Keeling's group at an observatory on Mauna Loa in Hawaii in a classic study that won membership in the National Academy of Sciences for Keeling.

9. See, e.g., J. Holdren, 1990, Energy in transition, *Scientific American,* September, pp. 157–163; Intergovernmental Panel on Climate Change (IPCC), 1996.

10. Intergovernmental Panel on Climate Change (IPCC), 1996; see also Intergovernmental Panel on Climate Change (IPCC), 1990, *Climate Change: The IPCC Scientific Assessment,* Cambridge University Press, Cambridge, p. 25.

11. M. Morgan and D. Keith, 1995, Subjective judgments by climate experts, *Environmental Science and Technology* 29 (10): 468a–476a.

12. See Schneider and Londer, 1984.

13. D. Ray and L. Guzzo, 1993, *Environmental Overkill: Whatever Happened to Common Sense?,* HarperCollins, New York, p. 27.

14. R. Kerr, 1995, It's official: First glimmer of greenhouse warming seen, *Science* 270:1565–1567; Intergovernmental Panel on Climate Change (IPCC), 1996.

15. International Panel on Climate Change (IPCC), 1996, *Climate Change 1995,* Summary for Policymakers, Working Group I, pp. 10–11.

16. Kerr, 1995; Intergovernmental Panel on Climate Change (IPCC), 1996.

17. W. Stevens, 1996, '95 the hottest year on record as the global trend keeps up, *New York Times,* 4 January; J. Hansen, R. Ruedy, M. Sato, and R. Reynolds, 1996, Global surface air temperature in 1995: Return to pre-Pinatubo level, *Geophysical Research Letters,* in press.

18. P. Gloersen and W. Campbell, 1991, Recent variations in Arctic and Antarctic sea-ice covers, *Nature* 352:33–36.

19. O. Johannessen, M. Miles, and E. Bjorgo, 1995, The Arctic's shrinking sea ice, *Nature* 376:126–127. Computer models that consider increasing CO_2 levels alone suggest that warming should be most pronounced in the polar regions, although more recent models that include regional cooling by aerosols do not show this effect.

20. D. Normile, 1995, Polar regions give cold shoulder to theories, *Science* 270:1566.

21. W. Stevens, 1995, In Rain and temperature data, new signals of global warming, *New York Times,* 26 September; T. Karl, R. Knight, D. Easterling, and R. Quayle, 1995, Trends in U.S. climate during the twentieth century, *Consequences,* spring, pp. 3–12; T. Karl, R. Knight, and N. Plummer, 1995, Trends in high frequency climate variability in the twentieth century, *Nature* 377:217–220.

22. W. Stevens, 1995, Experts confirm human role in global warming, *New York Times,* 10 September.

23. Ibid.

24. Intergovernmental Panel on Climate Change (IPCC), 1996, chapter 8.

25. R. Bailey, 1995, p. 2. Bailey goes into more detail in his 1993 book, *Eco-Scam: The False Prophets of Ecological Apocalypse,* (St. Martin's Press, New York, p. 147): "To the dismay of the apocalypse boosters, their data, on which the headlines are based, appear to be simply wrong. Satellites orbiting the earth for the last thirteen years . . . confirm that there has been only a statistically insignificant upward trend . . . during the 1980s."

26. S. Singer, 1995, Global warming remains unproved, *New York Times,* 9 September.

27. Kerr, 1995; Intergovernmental Panel on Climate Change (IPCC), 1996.

28. B. Rensberger, 1993, Blowing hot and cold on global warming: Two methods of temperature-taking are getting opposite results, *Washington Post Weekly,* 2–8 August.

29. As shown in the quote in the text, this fallacy is one that S. Fred Singer resurrected in a letter in responding to the *New York Times* report of the IPCC's conclusion that global warming had been detected (letters, 1995, Global warming remains unproved, *New York Times,* 9 September). See also B. Bolch and H. Lyons, 1993, *Apocalypse Not: Science, Economics, and Environmentalism,* Cato Institute, Washington, DC, p. 78, note 18; R. C. Balling Jr., 1994, Global warming: Gore vision versus climate reality, in Baden, 1994, p. 116. (Balling's discussion is a cut above most brownlash treatments, but it fails to point out the actual significance of the satellite data.)

30. The reference for the satellite data is R. Spencer and J. Christy, 1990,

Precise monitoring of global temperature trends from satellites, *Science* 247:1558–1562. Note that the title doesn't say where the temperature trends are measured, but they are *not* surface temperatures.

31. Intergovernmental Panel on Climate Change (IPCC), 1996.

32. Note that because of such phenomena as ozone depletion cooling the troposphere more than it cools Earth's surface, there is no expectation that surface temperature measurements and those recorded at various levels in the atmosphere by satellites should be identical; see, e.g., J. Hansen, H. Wilson, M. Sato, R. Ruedy, K. Shah, and E. Hansen, 1995, Satellite and surface temperature at odds? *Climatic Change* 30:103–117.

33. Letter sent to the *Washington Post,* 9 September 1993, unpublished.

34. Stevens, 1996.

35. This was not the only error in Singer's letter. He also wrote that the 1995 IPCC report stated that "only 50 percent to 79 percent of [the] temperature increase will be realized by the year 2100." The 1995 IPCC report actually said that its projected warming range of 1.8° to 6°F (1° to 3.5°C) by the year 2100 represented only 50 to 90 percent of the warming that was eventually expected to occur (i.e., in equilibrium) from the gases emitted up to that time (Intergovernmental Panel on Climate Change [IPCC], 1996.) Slight differences in projected temperatures appearing in various sources trace to the media reporting on preliminary documents from the IPCC process. The lag is due to the heat absorption capacity of the oceans, which slows the warming of the atmosphere. As physicist Michael Oppenheimer put it, "Mr. Singer gets it backwards by arguing that only 50 percent to 70 [sic] percent of the 1.5 to 6 degrees will be realized by 2100" (M. Oppenheimer, 1995, Global warming, unfortunately, is all too real, *New York Times,* 26 September). The warming projected by then is 1.8° to 6°F, which, if it were 70 percent of the equilibrium value, would indicate the ultimate warming to be 2.6° to 8.6°F.

36. See, e.g., G. Easterbrook, 1995, *A Moment on the Earth: The Coming Age of Environmental Optimism,* Viking, New York, pp. 22–23, which states that "water vapor accounts for 99 percent of natural global warming." Easterbrook emphasizes that "the human impact on the greenhouse effect . . . [is only] roughly 0.04 percent of the total annual effect." This estimate of human impact is wrong twice: first, because the human impact is about 1 percent, and second, because it ignores the increased water vapor added to the atmosphere by the heating caused by anthropogenic greenhouse gases (the latter is not yet measurable directly). And, of course, it is irrelevant for the reasons given in this section (without water vapor, which is the largest contributor, the average surface temperature of Earth would be below the freezing point of water).

37. See, e.g., Intergovernmental Panel on Climate Change (IPCC), 1990, p. 48. This is actually a difficult parameter to give a single number on, since it depends on factors such as feedbacks. If there could be only CO_2 in the atmosphere, warming due to an increase in its concentration could not lead to higher water vapor concentration as it would now, removing that positive feedback.

38. Ray and Guzzo, 1993, p. 16; see also Easterbrook, 1995, p. 296.

39. Intergovernmental Panel on Climate Change (IPCC), 1996, p. 20.

40. Ray and Guzzo, 1993, p. 21.

41. Bolch and Lyons, 1993, p. 79.

42. Simon, 1994, p. 59.

43. G. Reisman, 1992, The toxicity of environmentalism, in J. Lehr (ed.), *Rational Readings on Environmental Concerns,* Van Nostrand Reinhold, New York, p. 831.

44. W. Beckerman, 1995, Why worry about the weather?, *Wall Street Journal Europe,* 25–26 August.

45. See, e.g., L. Haimson and B. Goodman (eds.), 1995, *A Moment of Truth: Correcting the Scientific Errors in Gregg Easterbrook's "A Moment on the Earth,"* Environmental Defense Fund, New York, p. 23.

46. See, e.g., Martin and Lefebvre, 1995; L. Kalkstein, 1991, Potential impact of global warming: Climate change and human mortality, in R. Wyman (ed.), *Global Climate Change and Life on Earth,* Routledge, Chapman, and Hall, New York, pp. 216–223.

47. S. Vogel, 1995, Has global warming begun?, *Earth,* December.

48. See, e.g., Wyman, 1991; R. Peters and T. Lovejoy, 1992, *Global Warming and Biological Diversity,* Yale University Press, New Haven, CT; T. Root and S. Schneider, 1993, Can large-scale climatic models be linked with multiscale ecological studies?, *Conservation Biology* 7 (2): 256–270.

49. W. Beckerman, 1995, *Small Is Stupid: Blowing the Whistle on the Greens,* Duckworth, London, p. 96.

50. W. Nordhaus, 1990, Greenhouse economics: Count before you leap, *The Economist,* 7 July, p. 21; G. Daily, P. Ehrlich, H. Mooney, and A. Ehrlich, 1991, Greenhouse economics: Learn before you leap, *Ecological Economics* 4:1–10.

51. Morgan and Keith, 1995.

52. See, e.g., G. Schuh, 1995, The world food problem and population growth, *Proceedings of the American Philosophical Society* 139 (3): 240–246; L. Brown, 1995, *Who Will Feed China? Wake Up Call for a Small Planet,* W. W. Norton, New York; U.S. Department of Agriculture, Economic Research Service, 1995, Food aid needs and availabilities: Projections for 2005 (GFA-6), U.S. Department of Agriculture,

Washington, DC, October; P. Ehrlich, A. Ehrlich, and G. Daily, 1993, Food security, population, and environment, *Population and Development Review* 19:1–32; P. Ehrlich, A. Ehrlich, and G. Daily, 1995, *The Stork and the Plow: The Equity Answer to the Human Dilemma,* Putnam, New York.

53. Easterbrook, 1995, p. 294.

54. Ibid., p. 282.

55. Intergovernmental Panel on Climate Change (IPCC), 1990, chapters 1 and 2; Intergovernmental Panel on Climate Change (IPCC), 1992, *Climate Change 1992,* Cambridge University Press, Cambridge.

56. Intergovernmental Panel on Climate Change (IPCC), 1996, chapter 8.

57. J. Mitchell, T. Johns, J. Gregory, and S. Tett, 1995, Climate response to increasing levels of greenhouse gases and sulphate aerosols, *Nature* 376:501–504.

58. Fumento, 1993, p. 361; R. Bailey, 1993, *Eco-Scam: The False Prophets of Ecological Apocalypse,* St. Martin's Press, New York, p. 80; Bast, Hill, and Rue, 1994, p. 231. See also attacks on Stephen Schneider and his work in Ray and Guzzo, 1993, p. 26; Easterbrook, 1995, chapter 17; Wildavsky, 1995, pp. 442–445; R. Lindzen, 1994, Global warming: The origin and nature of alleged scientific consensus, in Baden, 1994, p. 125; T. Bray, 1989, The media and the greenhouse hype, *Detroit News,* 3 December; and many others.

59. Fumento, 1993, p. 361.

60. G. Will, 1992, Al Gore on the environment: Bad ideas with big price tags, *Washington Post,* 3 September.

61. S. Rasool and S. Schneider, 1971, Atmospheric carbon dioxide and aerosols: Effects of large increases on global climate, *Science* 173: 138–141.

62. S. Schneider and L. Mesirow, 1976, *The Genesis Strategy: Climate and Global Survival,* Plenum, New York, p. 184.

63. Ibid., p. 90.

64. Ibid., p. 10.

65. Ibid., p. 11 (our emphasis).

66. Intergovernmental Panel on Climate Change (IPCC), 1996.

67. Rasool and Schneider, 1971.

68. Intergovernmental Panel on Climate Change (IPCC), 1990, 1992, and 1996.

69. Reisman, 1992, p. 831.

70. If the climate warmed sufficiently (and for long enough) to melt the Antarctic and Greenland ice caps and smaller glaciers, this combined with thermal expansion of the ocean's waters would raise sea level al-

most 250 feet (the current estimate is about 70 meters—230 feet) (Intergovernmental Panel on Climate Change [IPCC], 1990, pp. 257–281).

71. S. Leatherman, 1991, Impact of climate-induced sea level rise on coastal areas, in Wyman, 1991, pp. 170–179; S. Schneider, personal communication, September 1995.

72. Ehrlich and Ehrlich, 1991, pp. 92–94.

73. Intergovernmental Panel on Climate Change (IPCC), 1995.

74. R. Watson, 1995, *Climate Change, Meeting Population, Environment and Resource Challenges: The Costs of Inaction,* report prepared for scientific panels, Third Annual World Bank Conference on Effective Financing of Environmentally Sustainable Development, Washington, DC, 4 and 9 October 1995, p. 7.

75. The history of this surprise is well told in an accurate popular book, S. Roan, *Ozone Crisis: The 15 Year Evolution of a Sudden Environmental Emergency,* Wiley, New York.

76. See, e.g., R. Jones and T. Wigley (eds.), 1989, *Ozone Depletion: Health and Environmental Consequences,* Wiley, New York, pp. xi–xii.

77. Controls placed on the manufacture of CFCs by an international agreement called the Montreal Protocol recently led to a small decline in the chlorine content of the atmosphere, although the total ozone-destroying power of human-made chemicals has not declined yet. That is because the bromine released from the halons (which are scarcer than CFCs), perhaps forty times as potent an ozone destroyer, is taking up the slack (R. Kerr, 1996, Ozone-destroying chlorine tops out, *Science* 271:32). See also AP, 1996, Data point to ultimate closing of ozone hole, *New York Times,* 31 May.

78. The current scientific consensus on the problem of ozone depletion and the current state and future prospects of the ozone shield can be found in World Meteorological Organization, 1995, *Scientific Assessment of Ozone Depletion: 1994,* National Oceanic and Atmospheric Administration, National Aeronautics and Space Administration, United Nations Environment Programme, World Meteorological Organization.

79. T. Graedel and P. Crutzen, 1995, *Atmosphere, Climate, and Change,* Scientific American Library, New York, pp. 62–63. The precise history of the ozone shield is far from certain (see, e.g., A. Knoll and H. Holland, 1995, Oxygen and proterozoic evolution: An update, in National Research Council, *Studies in Geophysics: Effects of Past Global Change on Life,* National Academy Press, Washington, DC), and the estimate here seems grounded in part on the fossil record of terrestrial life, so there is some circularity in the argument.

80. Ray and Guzzo, 1993, p. 32.

81. M. Molina and F. Rowland, 1974, Stratospheric sink for chlorofluo-

romethanes: Chlorine atom catalyzed destruction of ozone. *Nature* 249:810–814.

82. Boston, 14 February 1993; published in *Science* 260:1571–1576, 11 June 1993.

83. J. Farman, B. Gardiner, and J. Shanklin, 1985, Large losses of total ozone in Antarctica reveal ClO_x/NO_x interaction. *Nature* 315:207–210.

84. There is a cautionary tale here. The *Nimbus 7* satellite carried the TOMS (total ozone-mapping spectrometer), which sent back several hundred thousand measurements every day, covering essentially all of the sunlit Earth (the TOMS operated by measuring solar ultraviolet radiation backscattered from the lower atmosphere through the stratospheric ozone layer). The first satellite measurements in October, the time of year when the "ozone hole" is formed, were made in 1979. They showed consistent ozone values of around 250 Dobson units (300 Dobson units is the approximate global average value at any time). Apparently, the TOMS was programmed in its early years to reject any reading below 180 Dobson units as erroneous because such low values had never been known to occur. On reexamination of the data, values below 175 Dobson units were found to have been appearing before 1983. However, the deep plunge during 1980–1982 was not detected because, although earlier readings above the 180 Dobson "throw-out" value showed a decline, the data were not examined closely enough to detect the downward trend immediately. American scientists eventually noted some decline, but by then the TOMS was beyond its expected useful life, a factor that added uncertainty to interpretation of the data. The way the TOMS was programmed, combined with NASA's failure to make any provisions for adequately handling the flood of data that came from it, conspired to let Farman and his team first publish the news of the ozone hole. When these situations were corrected, reexamination of raw TOMS data quickly confirmed and expanded the findings of the Farman team. (This reconstruction of the *Nimbus 7* story is based on e-mail correspondence with F. Sherwood Rowland, December 1995.)

85. Bailey, 1993, p. 135.

86. P. Rigaud and B. Leroy, 1990, Presumptive evidence for a low value of total ozone content above Antarctica in September 1958, *Annales Geophysicae* 8 (11): 791–794.

87. F. Rowland, e-mail message, 29 September 1995; edited by us.

88. The French also had, apparently for other reasons, another instrument at Dumont d'Urville Station that was the predecessor of the filter instrument and that used the 1920s style of recording light—by darkening photographic plates. This was the kind of instrument first used to measure ozone with observations of the sun. At Dumont d'Urville, however, there is no sunlight during the critical period in September.

The French tried to take the measurement with moonlight (reflected sunlight). They found they could not get useable results, apparently because of the irregularity of light intensities from the varying surface of the moon.

The French did, however, report values obtained with starlight. Almost everyone who knows anything about this kind of measurement knows that the problem of separating the signal (actual UV-B/UV-A ratio) from the noise (random variation due to instrument error or other problems) is virtually insurmountable. Dobson himself reported trying it in 1934, with the Pole Star as the source of light, and failing. His equipment then was essentially the same as that used by the French in 1958, when they got enormous differences in their readings throughout the winter (from 100 to 450 Dobson units; 300 is the world average). Then there were several low values in September, the start of the Antarctic spring. The latter were the basis of Rigaud and Leroy's claim, cited by Bailey. Rigaud and Leroy further postulated that the Antarctic polar vortex was unusual in 1958, so the low temperatures required for ozone loss appeared over their station but not over the British station at Halley Bay (which did not record an unusual drop in ozone that year). They ignored the existence of vertical temperature profiles taken with radiosonde balloons that showed that, in fact, Halley Bay had been within the vortex for the entire period, while Dumont d'Urville was mostly outside it.

Everyone else's measurements show very little variation during Antarctic winters. Ozone loss over Antarctica appears with the first sunlight of approaching spring. (Information is from Rowland e-mail message, 29 September 1995.)

89. R. Maduro, 1989, *Executive Intelligence Review* 27:19.

90. Ray and Guzzo, 1993, p. 35.

91. R. Bennett, 1993, *Wall Street Journal,* 24 March, p. A15.

92. National Oceanic and Atmospheric Administration, 1962, *U.S. Standard Atmosphere, 1962,* National Aeronautics and Space Administration, U.S. Air Force, Washington, DC; see also World Meteorological Organization, 1995; its Executive Summary specifically addresses the absurd notion that CFCs can't reach the stratosphere because they are heavier than air (p. 21).

93. F. Rowland, 1993, President's lecture: The need for scientific communication with the public, *Science* 260:1571–1576.

94. Ray and Guzzo, 1993, p. 34.

95. R. Limbaugh, 1992, *The Way Things Ought to Be,* Pocket Books, New York, pp. 156–157. Limbaugh's mistakes and misinterpretations of the ozone situation are recounted in L. Haimson, M. Oppenheimer, and D. Wilcove, 1995, *The Way Things Really Are: Debunking Rush Limbaugh on the Environment,* Environmental Defense Fund, New York.

96. D. Johnston, 1980, Volcanic contribution of chlorine to the stratosphere: More signficant to ozone than previously estimated?, *Science* 209:491–493. In that paper, Johnston did an analysis of the explosive 1976 eruption of Mount St. Augustine, Alaska, and drew the quoted conclusion. He also called for additional work on ". . . the role of groundwater in volcanic eruption columns; (iv) the distribution of gas and particulates in tropospheric and stratospheric eruptions . . . and (v) the efficiency of gas scavenging." That work was done, and it eliminated volcanoes as a central culprit in creating the ozone hole.

97. While eruptions that are powerful enough to inject material into the stratosphere do temporarily add to ozone depletion, that does not alter the conclusion that CFCs are the major cause of the Antarctic ozone hole (see, e.g., R. Watson, 1989, Present state of knowledge of the ozone layer, in Jones and Wigley, 1989, pp. 49–51.) Careful measurements have shown buildups of both hydrogen chloride and hydrogen fluoride, exactly as one would expect from the breakdown of CFCs but not from volcanic activity.

98. Rowland, 1993. This article also contains references to the original research, published between 1983 and 1992, which demonstrated that volcanoes did not play a signficant role.

99. S. Singer, 1989, My adventures in the ozone layer, *National Review* 41 (30 June), p. 37.

100. G. Taubes, 1993, The ozone backlash, *Science* 260:1583.

101. D. Ray and L. Guzzo, 1990, *Trashing the Planet,* HarperCollins, New York, p. 45.

102. [Footnote in Rowland, 1993], Ray and Guzzo, 1990, p. 13.

103. Rowland, 1993, p. 1574.

104. J. Russell III, M. Luo, R. Cicerone, and L. Deaver, 1996, Satellite confirmation of the dominance of chlorofluorocarbons in the global stratospheric chlorine budget, *Nature* 379:526–529.

105. Easterbrook, 1995, p. 536.

106. Ibid., p. 541.

107. See, e.g., ibid., pp. 542–543.

108. See Jones and Wigley, 1989, part 5, Ultraviolet-induced carcinogenesis, pp. 147–189; S. Madronich and F. de Gruljl, 1993, Skin cancer and UV radiation, *Nature* 366:23.

109. G. Reisman, 1992, The toxicity of environmentalism, in J. Lehr (ed.), *Rational Readings on Environmental Concerns,* Van Nostrand Reinhold, New York, p. 831. (The comma after "exposure" is in the original.)

110. For overviews of what is known of the direct health and ecosystem threats of ozone depletion, see Jones and Wigley, 1989.

111. See, e.g., Graedel and Crutzen, 1995, pp. 108–109.

112. A. Wildavsky and R. Rye, 1995, CFCs and ozone depletion: Are they as bad as people think?, in Wildavsky, 1995, pp. 304–339. Rye, "a fresh college graduate," was hired by Wildavsky to do a paper on ozone depletion, and he and Wildavsky "achieved a common view" (p. 3).

113. Ibid., p. 339.

114. G. Likens, 1992, *The Ecosystem Approach: Its Use and Abuse,* Ecology Institute, Oldendorf/Luhe, Germany, p. 114.

115. Comments by F. Sherwood Rowland on the Wildavsky-Rye analysis (personal communication from Rowland, 24 October 1995, edited slightly for clarity):

     "One of the most persistent sets of false statements made by the ozone skeptics has been concerned with the analysis of ozone trends from the ground-based Dobson network performed by the NASA/WMO Ozone Trends Panel in the period 1986–1988. The conclusions from this work were released at a press conference on March 15, 1988, published in condensed form in August 1988, and finally [printed] in the regular two-volume publication around Dec. 1989/Jan. 1990 (Volume 1, *Report of the International Ozone Trends Panel 1988,* World Meteorological Organization Global Ozone Research and Monitoring Project—Report No. 18, sponsored by NASA, NOAA, FAA, WMO, and UNEP). The key conclusions from this study are summarized in the following paragraph (p. 4):

     > Analysis of data from ground-based Dobson instruments, after allowing for the effects of natural geophysical variability (solar cycle and the quasi-biennial oscillation [QBO]), shows measurable decreases from 1969 to 1986 in the annual average of total column ozone ranging from 1.7 to 3.0 percent, at latitudes between 30 and 64 degrees in the Northern Hemisphere. The decreases are most pronounced, and ranged from 2.3 to 6.2 percent, during the winter months, averaged for December through March, inclusive. Dobson data are not currently adequate to determine total column ozone changes in the Tropics, sub-Tropics, or Southern Hemisphere outside Antarctica.

     "These conclusions reversed the previous interpretations of the ground-based data, which had been that no statistically significant trends in total ozone had yet been observed. (The basic analysis of the Ozone Trends Panel report was done by a group of five scientists, with me in charge. The other four were a graduate student of mine, Neil Harris; a statistical analysis specialist, Peter Bloomfield; an ozone measurement specialist, Rumen Bojkov; and DuPont scientist, Mack McFarland.) Prior to the formation of the Ozone Trends Panel, Harris and I had already concluded in an abstract and presentation to the American Geophysical Union in late 1986 that a wintertime loss of ozone was occurring in three northern hemisphere stations: Arosa (Switzerland), Bismarck (North Dakota), and Caribou (Maine). There were two significant conclusions drawn by the OTP report—(1) that the Antarctic ozone hole was caused by CFCs; and (2) that ozone loss was being observed in the North Temperate Zone, i.e., it was not restricted to Antarctica. Within two weeks after the March 15 release of the Executive Summary, the DuPont Company switched its position on CFCs and announced that it was going to phase out their manufacture. Within the knowledgeable industrial circles, opposition to the phaseout of CFCs disappeared within two or three months of the OTP report—it really had a very significant effect. The objections of the skeptics took two forms: (1) that we had 'corrected' the official measurements as reported to the international data center and published in *Ozone Data for the World* and then analyzed the corrected data, with the implication that we had adjusted them to produce the desired result; and (2) that we had chosen a time period from 1969–1986 for our analysis, corresponding to a transition from a period of solar maximum [of sunspot activity] to a period of solar minimum. Because UV intensity around 200 nanometers is more intense at solar maximum (however, difficult to measure accurately over the necessary 11-year solar cycle), producing correspondingly more ozone, the solar variability decline from maximum to minimum was then stated as being added to whatever trend there might be.

"The answers to the first objection are two-fold: (a) comparisons of ground and satellite ozone data for individual locations demonstrated that the basic data reported by many ozone stations had demonstrable glitches at times of re-calibration; and (b) on pages 241–245, Vol. 1, OTP report, we demonstrated that the important conclusion of loss in ozone was already present in the official numbers in *Ozone Data for the World,* that the revisions in the data had no consistent effect on the trends, with approximately ⅓ showing more ozone loss, ⅓ showing less ozone loss, and ⅓ showing little or no change.

"The second contention, that we used the time period from 1969 to 1986 for our analysis, has been very widely quoted and is simply false. The following is quoted from S. F. Singer, 'My Adventures in the Ozone Layer,' published in the *National Review,* June 30, 1989:

> The latest phase in the war against CFCs began in March 1988 when the NASA Ozone Trends Panel (OTP) announced its findings, after a massive reanalysis of data from ground stations and satellites. After subtracting all the natural variations they could think of—some of them as large as 50 per cent within a few months at a given station—they extracted a statistical decrease of 0.2 per cent per year over the last 17 years.

Making these corrections is very difficult and very technical and very uncertain—especially when the natural variations are a hundred times larger than the alleged steady
change. Furthermore, there is the matter of choosing the time
period of study. . . . Now, 17 years is only one and a half
solar cycles, and solar cycles have a very strong influence on
ozone content. Another letter to *Science*—not accepted.

"Wildavsky takes up this subject in paragraph 3, p. 316, and follows
it for several pages. In paragraph 5, he correctly notes that the OTP
analysis was based on 22 years of data (1965 to 1986), basically from
one minimum to another. However, he then says: '[B]ut the trends reported are from 1969 to 1986, going from a solar maximum to a solar
minimum. When the OTP's predictions are firmly negative, our re-
analysis (formulated in Table 10.4), which takes into account solar
variability, shows either no change or a very slight depletion in the
53–64° latitude band.'

"The statistical analysis we used did not 'subtract all the variations
we could think of' but took as a model a situation in which a basic
level trend lasted for one period of time to be followed by some
smooth trend in each month, provided parameters for other factors
such as the sunspot cycle and the QBO, and then did a least-squares
fit [a statistical test] to all of the data to evaluate the various parameters. In each case, we evaluated two models of the time-split: (a) flat
period from 1965 to 1975, followed by trends for 1976 to 1986; and
(b) flat period from 1965 to 1969, [followed by] trends from 1970 to
1986. In the first case, the trend is evaluated from solar minimum to
solar minimum; in the second, from maximum to minimum; but in
both cases, the time period for the trend is irrelevant because the data
being fitted cover the entire 22-year period from solar minimum to
solar minimum. With a coverage of two full solar cycles, the data were
not 'corrected' for solar cycle variability but were evaluated for its
magnitude.

"The corrections applied in the last two columns of Table 10.4, page
317, are statistical nonsense. All they have done is assume, with no
evidence, that the statistical variation from solar maximum to solar
minimum is 3% and subtract the difference between that number and
what they call 'solar correction used' from the trend. For example, in
the 40–52°N latitude belt, the Winter (%) from our data is given as
−4.7 ± 1.5%, and the 'solar correction' is −0.8 ± 0.7%. They have then
subtracted (3.0 minus 0.8), or 2.2%, from −4.7% to obtain −2.5%. If
they wanted to evaluate the trend for the hypothesis that the solar
variability was 3%, then they would need to correct each individual
data point for its position on the solar cycle and then re-run the
trends. Because the data set that was used included 22 years of data
and not just 17 years (1.5 cycles), the outcome of the forced fit to a
3% solar cycle would actually not change the trend very much.

"However, the errors concerning the work of the OTP are much worse than the previous paragraph might indicate. The same data set between 40 and 52°N used to give the −4.7 ± 1.5% for the winter months was also analyzed in OTP for the assumption of a constant value from 1965 to 1975 and a trend from 1976 to 1986. In this case, the trend is from solar minimum to solar minimum, so no Wildavsky-Rye kind of 'correction' would be applicable. I now quote from Vol. 1, p. 377, for the trends calculated for each of the 12 months (QS70 is flat from 1965 to 1969, then trend for 17 years through 1986; QS76 is flat from 1965 to 1975, then trend for 11 years through 1986). If the Wildavsky-Rye statistical 'calculation' had any significance, then the calculated trends should be uniformly much less.

Latitudes 40–52 Degrees North, Total Ozone Loss (Dobsons)

Time Period	QS70	QS76	QS70 × 17	QS76 × 11
January	−0.56 ± 0.45	−0.40 ± 0.67	−9.5 ± 7.7	−4.4 ± 7.4
February	−1.18 ± 0.51	−1.33 ± 0.77	−20.1 ± 8.7	−14.6 ± 8.5
March	−1.33 ± 0.55	−1.61 ± 0.83	−22.6 ± 9.4	−17.7 ± 9.1
April	−0.58 ± 0.41	−1.18 ± 0.62	−9.9 ± 7.0	−13.0 ± 6.8
May	−0.30 ± 0.24	−0.72 ± 0.37	−5.1 ± 4.1	−7.9 ± 4.1
June	−0.39 ± 0.21	−0.77 ± 0.32	−6.6 ± 3.6	−8.5 ± 3.5
July	−0.43 ± 0.20	−0.78 ± 0.30	−7.3 ± 3.4	−8.6 ± 3.3
August	−0.46 ± 0.18	−0.78 ± 0.28	−7.8 ± 3.1	−8.6 ± 3.1
September	−0.53 ± 0.19	−0.86 ± 0.29	−9.0 ± 3.2	−9.5 ± 3.2
October	−0.27 ± 0.26	−0.61 ± 0.40	−4.6 ± 4.4	−6.7 ± 4.4
November	−0.44 ± 0.25	−0.64 ± 0.37	−7.5 ± 4.3	−7.0 ± 4.1
December	−1.08 ± 0.33	−1.10 ± 0.51	−18.4 ± 5.6	−12.1 ± 5.6
Average			−10.7	−9.9

"In five of the months, the best fit ozone loss is larger if the ramp-trend is started at 1970; in seven, if started at 1976. Because the average ozone loss is slightly larger when the downward trend in the model is started at 1970, the implications are that most of the ozone loss occurred after 1976, but enough occurred between 1970 and 1975 to quote most of the results in terms of losses of ozone since 1969.

"Thus, on p. 318, Wildavsky says, following Singer, that 'the time period chosen by the OTP for its analysis, 1969–1986, maximized the potential effect that solar variability might have on the results.' This is simply a mistaken statement, for the reasons outlined above.

"Three other points:

"I. Wildavsky-Rye, p. 319, paragraph 3:

The Bojkov group is well aware that determining long-term trends from data with periodic swings of large amplitude is not an exact science. They remind their readers that 'over most of the stations considered ozone varies as much as 25–30% within a single year.'

"My reaction to this statement is that the authors have little understanding of what Bojkov has said. The amount of ozone in the North Temperate Zone has a maximum in March and April and a minimum around October. Here are the average values for March and October at Arosa (Switzerland) for the ten years from 1977 through 1986:

March: 347, 346, 373, 358, 357, 389, 331, 378, 353, 356   359 ± 17
October: 271, 287, 287, 278, 290, 282, 273, 284, 276, 279   281 ± 6

"The March data are on the average 28% higher than in October. All that is needed to avoid trouble in interpreting these data is a calendar.

"II. Wildavsky-Rye, p. 329:

Fortunately, the dip exists almost entirely over unpopulated areas. Also, the perturbed air generally does not bring low enough ozone levels over these areas to make for higher ultraviolet exposure, because the sun is lower in the sky. The dip therefore poses little or no health threat to humans or their livestock and crops.

"The ozone levels over Palmer station in the Antarctic Peninsula fell low enough that the measured UV-B intensity on the most exposed day of 1983 (late October) was 25% greater than on the most exposed day of 1983 in San Diego (late June); i.e., the Antarctic level was normal tropical UV-B. The sun was at a 52° angle on the maximum day in Palmer and at 10° in San Diego. The biology of the southern ocean, however, has presumably not evolved with such intense UV-B and did not heretofore need repair mechanisms against UV-B damage.

"III. Wildavsky-Rye, p. 329. paragraph 3:

[T]here are a number of other necessary conditions for the formation of the ozone hole. The temperature must be cold enough for the formation of [ice] crystals. The vortex must stay coherent long enough for the chlorine and chlorine oxide to do their damage. Ozone depletion is tied to the strength and the temperature of the inner and outer polar vortex. The lack of an observed dip from 1957 to 1979 seems to implicate CFCs, but by the same token, it indicates that the conditions for the formation of the hole are not always present.

"Regular vertical profile temperature measurements well into the stratosphere have been made throughout the winter at the Halley Bay station since 1957. These data show that the late winter temperatures during the late 1980s fell easily within the range established throughout the 1960s and 1970s. The difference was the much lower concentration of chlorine compounds."

116. R. Alvo, 1986, Lost loons of northern lakes, *Natural History,* September:60–64.

117. P. Drent and J. Woldendorp, 1989, Acid rain and eggshells, *Nature* 339:431; R. Schreiber and J. Newman, 1988, Acid precipitation effects on forest habitats: Implications for wildlife, *Conservation Biology* 2:249–259.

118. B. Cai, O. Loucks, and R. Kuperman, 1993, The Contribution of Soil Macroinvertebrates to Litter Decomposition Influenced by Acidic Deposition, poster presentation, meeting of the Ecological Society of America, Madison, Wisconsin, 14 August; O. Loucks, personal communication, 8 December 1995.

119. See, e.g., E. Gorham, 1989, Scientific understanding of ecosystem acidification: A historical review, *Ambio* 18:150–154; H. Rodhe, 1989, Acidification in a global perspective, *Ambio* 18:155–160.

120. G. Likens, 1989, Some aspects of air pollution effects on terrestrial ecosystems and prospects for the future, *Ambio* 18:172–178.

121. See, e.g., Bailey, 1993, pp. 160–161; Bast, Hill, and Rue, 1994, pp. 74–81; Bolch and Lyons, 1993, pp. 96–103; Ray and Guzzo, 1990, ch. 5; Ray and Guzzo, 1993, pp. 147–150, 179–180.

122. Wildavsky and Rye, 1995, p. 285.

123. T. Sullivan, D. Charles, J. Smol, B. Cumming, A. Selle, D. Thomas, J. Bernert, and S. Dixit, 1990, Quantification of changes in lakewater chemistry in response to acidic deposition, *Nature* 345:54–58.

124. Wildavsky and Rye, 1995, pp. 2–6.

125. W. Brown, 1986, Hysteria about acid rain, *Fortune* 113:125–126. The actual statement was "[A]cid rain is only a minor contributor to environmental damage. . . . So far as lakes are concerned, the principal sources of damage are likely to be natural sources of acid. . . . The amount of acid generated by nature is now known to be far greater than that contributed by industrial generated acid rain. Take bird droppings, which are a relatively minor contributor to the problem. A calculation . . . shows that the droppings hit the US at a rate of about one million per second, and that the 150 million tons of droppings per year outweigh sulfur dioxide emissions by something like six to one."

126. See, e.g., Ad Hoc Committee on Acid Rain, 1995, Is there a scientific consensus on acid rain? Excerpts from six governmental reports, Institute of Ecosystem Studies (Box AB, Millbrook, NY 12545), October.

127. O. Loucks, 1993, Science or politics? NAPAP and Reagan, *Forum for Applied Research and Public Policy,* summer, pp. 66–72. The study spent almost $600 million.

128. In what follows, we lean heavily on G. Likens, 1992, *The Ecosystem Approach: It's Use and Abuse,* Ecology Institute, Luhe, Germany. Gene Likens is a member of the National Academy of Sciences, a fellow of the American Academy of Arts and Sciences, and a Foreign Member of the Royal Swedish Academy of Sciences, and he has received many prizes for his scientific work. This book was written in response to his

receiving the Ecology Institute's Prize in 1988. The statement of the scientific prize jury was in part: "In 1962 [Likens] initiated and developed (with F. H. Bormann) the Hubbard Brook Ecosystem Study in New Hampshire. Comprehensive investigations in this study provided a model for ecological and biogeochemical studies worldwide. A major finding of the study was that rain and snow are highly acidic. "Acid rain" is now recognized as one of the major environmental hazards in North America, Europe, and elsewhere" (quoted in the Introduction).

129. For a more detailed discussion, see Loucks, 1993.

130. Likens, 1992, p. 132.

131. J. Nilsson and P. Grennfelt (eds.), 1988, Critical loads for sulphur and nitrogen, international workshop, UN-ECE and Nordin Council Ministers, Stockholm, Sweden, Miljorapport 1988:15.

132. Rohde, 1989; T. Abate, 1995, Swedish scientists take acid rain research to developing nations, *BioScience* 45:738–740.

133. Ray and Guzzo, 1990, p. 53.

134. G. Likens, F. Bormann, R. Pierce, J. Eaton, and N. Johnson, 1977, *Biogeochemistry of a Forested Ecosystem,* Springer-Verlag, New York, p. 18.

135. Ray and Guzzo, 1990, pp. 54–57; the quote is on p. 54.

136. G. Likens, W. Keene, J. Miller, and J. Galloway, 1987, Chemistry of precipitation from a remote, terrestrial site in Australia, *Journal of Geophysical Research* 92:13299–13314.

137. N. Myers, 1995, The world's forests: Need for a policy appraisal, *Science* 268:823–824.

138. O. Loucks, 1995, Air pollution as a threat to old-growth forests, *Proceedings of Eastern Old-growth Forest Conference,* Asheville, NC; O. Loucks, 1995, Analysis of U.S. Forest Service Long-term forest inventory data, Indiana, unpublished; O. Loucks, 1989, Large-scale alteration of biological productivity due to transported pollutants, in D. Botkin, M. Caswell, J. Estes, and A. Orio (eds.), *Changing the Global Environment,* Academic Press, New York; F. Bormann, 1985, Air pollution and forest: An ecosystem perspective, *BioScience* 35:434–441; F. Andersson, 1985, Air pollution and effects in Nordic Europe—the forests of Fennoscandia, abstracts, *Muskoka Conference, International Symposium on Acidic Precipitation.*

139. C. Federer, J. Hornbeck, L. Tritton, C. Martin, R. Pierce, and C. Smith, 1989, Long-term depletion of calcium and other nutrients in eastern US forests, *Environmental Management* 13:593–601.

140. D. Johnson, J. Kelley, W. Swank, D. Cole, H. Van Miegroet, J. Hornbeck, R. Pierce, and D. Van Lear, 1988. The effects of leaching and

whole-tree harvesting on cation budgets of several forests, *Journal of Environmental Quality* 17:418–424.

141. Federer et al., 1989.

142. Loucks, 1989, p. 114.

143. R. Monastersky, 1995, Ozone on trial: Congress gives skeptics a day in the sun, *Science News* 148:238 (7 October).

□ **Chapter 9: Fables about Toxic Substances**

1. For an excellent review of toxins to which you might be exposed, see J. Harte, C. Holdren, R. Schneider, and C. Shirley, 1991, *Toxics A to Z: A Guide to Everyday Pollution Hazards,* University of California Press, Berkeley.

2. S. Olshansky, B. Carnes, and C. Cassel, 1990, In search of Methuselah: Estimating the upper limits of human longevity, *Science* 250:634–640.

3. Harte et al., 1991.

4. For effects on human health, see Harte et al., 1991; L. Lave and A. Upton (eds.), 1987, *Toxic Chemicals, Health, and the Environment,* Johns Hopkins University Press, Baltimore; for effects on the environment, see J. Cairns Jr. (ed.), 1986, *Community Toxicity Testing,* ASTM Special Technical Publication 920, Philadelphia.

5. John Froines, University of California, Los Angeles, School of Public Health, Center for Occupational and Environmental Health, personal communication, 18 December 1995.

6. S. Simonich and R. Hites, 1995, Global distribution of persistent organochlorine compounds, *Science* 269:1851–1854.

7. Cairns, 1986; C. Edwards, 1993, The impact of pesticides on the environment, in D. Pimentel and H. Lehman (eds.), *The Pesticide Question: Environment, Economics, and Ethics,* Chapman & Hall, New York, pp. 13–46; T. Colborn and C. Clement (eds.), 1992, *Chemically-induced Alterations in Sexual and Functional Development: The Wildlife/Human Connection,* Princeton Scientific Publishing, Princeton, NJ, chapters 6–9; for more details and earlier references, see P. Ehrlich, A. Ehrlich, and J. Holdren, 1977, *Ecoscience: Population, Resources, Environment,* W. H. Freeman, San Francisco, chapters 10 and 11; and P. Ehrlich and A. Ehrlich, 1981, *Extinction: The Causes and Consequences of the Dissappearance of Species,* Random House, New York.

8. T. Colborn, D. Dumanoski, and J. Myers, 1996, *Our Stolen Future,* Dutton, New York; see also Colborn and Clement, 1992, especially chapters 14–21.

9. J. Graham, L. Green, and M. Roberts, 1988, *In Search of Safety; Chemicals and Cancer Risk,* Harvard University Press, Cambridge, MA; Lave and Upton, 1987; Harte et al., 1991.

10. For more details, see P. Ehrlich and A. Ehrlich, 1991, *Healing the Planet,* Addison-Wesley, New York, chapter 8, "Risks, Costs, and Benefits," pp. 216–238.

11. R. Bailey, 1993, *Eco-Scam: The False Prophets of Ecological Apocalypse,* St. Martin's Press, New York, p. 21.

12. M. Fumento, 1993, *Science Under Siege: Balancing Technology and the Environment,* William Morrow, New York, p. 20.

13. B. Bolch and H. Lyons, 1993, *Apocalypse Not: Science, Economics, and Environmentalism,* Cato Institute, Washington, DC, p. 39.

14. UDMH is chemical shorthand for unsymmetrical dimethyl hydrazine.

15. E. Marshall, 1991, A is for apple, Alar, and . . . alarmist? *Science* 254:20–22. See also letters from V. J. Kimm (1991, *Science* 254:1276–1278) and A. M. Finkel and L. Mott (1992, *Science* 255:664–65). A good description of the whole controversy can be seen in J. Hathaway, 1993, Alar: The EPA's mismanagement of an agricultural chemical, in Pimentel and Lehman, 1993.

16. National Research Council Committee on Pesticides in the Diets of Infants and Children, National Research Council, 1993, *Pesticides in the Diets of Infants and Children,* National Academy Press, Washington, DC.

17. *Consumer Reports,* 1986, Some bad news about apples and babies (September), pp. 598–603.

18. CBS News, What about apples?, *60 Minutes,* 14 May 1989.

19. E. Groth III, 1989, Alar in apples (letter), *Science* 244:755; Marshall, 1989.

20. Marshall, 1991, p. 21.

21. D. Koshland, 1989, Scare of the week (editorial), *Science* 244:9. See also the letters from E. Groth III and from B. Ames and L. Gold (*Science* 244:755–757). Koshland claimed that only 5 percent of the apples on the market contained Alar; several independent tests had found Alar in 20 to 55 percent of apples on the market. Even though Alar-preserved apples were supposedly not used in processing (for apple juice, applesauce, etc.), tests by *Consumer Reports* showed Alar in two-thirds of the juices on the market as well (Groth, 1989).

22. Marshall, 1991.

23. Ibid.

24. Ibid.; K. Anderson, 1991, After Alar: Growers learn a lesson, *Food Business,* 23 September, pp. 14–15; P. Roberts, 1994, Who killed the red delicious?, *Seattle Weekly,* 23 February.

25. See, e.g., J. Ackerman, 1985, EPA wants to ban use of chemical for ap-

ples, *Boston Globe,* 31 August; K. Schneider, 1986, Tiny traces of suspect chemical found in apple juice and sauce, *New York Times,* 14 January.

26. Ames and Gold, 1989.

27. Ibid., p. 757.

28. See, e.g., B. Ames and L. Gold, 1995, The causes and prevention of cancer: The role of environment, chapter 5 in R. Bailey (ed.), *The True State of the Planet,* Free Press, New York; C. Sjoberg, 1993, Pesticides don't cause cancer—they're good for you, *Tomorrow,* October–December, pp. 20–23.

29. E. Whelan, 1989, Apple dangers are just so much applesauce, *Wall Street Journal,* 14 March.

30. Even Gregg Easterbrook once said of Elizabeth Whelan, "She never met [a chemical] she doesn't like." (M. Hager, 1993, The anti-backlash, *Tomorrow,* November–December, p. 33.)

31. The ACSH's funding sources, which included numerous large corporations besides Uniroyal as well as the National Agricultural Chemicals Association, were for years listed in the council's publications, a practice that was dropped after 1990 (American Council on Science and Health, 1990, *Twelfth Annual Financial Report,* covering fiscal period 1 July 1989–30 June 1990, American council on Science and Health, New York.

32. American Council on Science and Health, 1992 (press release, 25 February), The great Alar scare three years later: Will it happen again?; Ketchum Public Relations, 1992 (media advisory, 25 February).

33. E. Whelan, 1992, memo to "selected ACSH friends," American Council on Science and Health, 20 February, with enclosures.

34. K. Smith, 1992, Alar three years later: Science unmasks a hypothetical health scare, special report, American Council on Science and Health, New York.

35. American Council on Science and Health, 1994 (press releases, 26 February). Five years after the Alar hoax, scientists call upon *60 Minutes* and the NRDC to set the record straight; Scientists give 1994 Pinocchio Awards to environmental advocacy group. Interestingly, the only scientists named were those on the staff of the ACSH.

36. D. Ray and L. Guzzo, 1990, *Trashing the Planet,* Regnery Gateway, Washington, DC, p. 74. It is ironic that Ray criticizes the scientists' cases (which are well substantiated) against Alar, asbestos, PCBs, and dioxin for using exactly the "technique" used by the brownlash: "unsubstantiated charges, endlessly repeated."

37. Ibid, p. 79.

38. Ibid., p. 78. This might be translated into the probability that one in 280,000 children consuming one pound of apples (or the equivalent

in juice or applesauce) every day for seven years would end up with cancer. But the actual incidence, according to a series of tests including several concluded after Alar was withdrawn, would be considerably higher—on the order of one cancer per 20,000 Alar-treated apples; see, e.g., *Consumer Reports,* 1986; Hathaway, 1993; National Research Council, 1993; Groth, 1989.

39. Graham, Green, and Roberts, 1988; Lave and Upton, 1987; National Research Council, 1993; Harte et al., 1991.

40. A. Arnold, 1990, *Fear of Food: Environmental Scams, Media Mendacity, and the Law of Disparagement,* Free Enterprise Press, Bellevue, WA. Arnold's father, Ron Arnold, is a leader of the Center for the Defense of Free Enterprise, a wise-use organization in Washington State. One chapter of her book, written by an apple grower and lawyer, J. Jarett Sandlin, discusses how to use product disparagement law to discourage environmentalists and media critics from speaking out on pesticide issues.

41. Ibid., p. vii.

42. See, e.g., D. Avery, 1995, Saving the planet with pesticides, in Bailey, 1995, pp. 49–82. D. Ray and L. Guzzo, 1993, *Environmental Overkill: Whatever Happened to Common Sense?,* HarperPerennial, New York; J. Bast, P. Hill, and R. Rue, 1994, *Eco-Sanity: A Common-Sense Guide to Environmentalism,* Madison Books, Lanham, MD, pp. 99–102.

43. R. Naylor and P. Ehrlich, in press, The value of natural pest control services in agriculture, in G. Daily (ed.), *Nature's Services,* Island Press, Washington, DC.

44. P. Ehrlich, A. Ehrlich, and G. Daily, 1995, *The Stork and the Plow: The Equity Answer to the Human Dilemma,* Putnam, New York, chapters 6 and 7.

45. D. Pimentel, H. Acquay, M. Biltonen, et al., 1993, Assessment of environmental and economic impacts of pesticide use, in Pimentel and Lehman, 1993, pp. 47–84; see also D. Pimentel, C. Kirby, and A. Schroff, 1993, The relationship between cosmetic standards for foods and pesticide use, in Pimentel and Lehman, 1993, pp. 85–105.

46. D. Pimentel, J. Krummel, D. Gallahan, et al., 1979, Benefits and costs of pesticide use in U.S. food production, *BioScience* 28:778–784; D. Pimentel, L. McLaughlin, A. Zepp, et al., 1991, Environmental and economic impacts of reducing U.S. agricultural pesticide use, in D. Pimental (ed.), 1991, *Handbook of Pest Management in Agriculture,* 2nd ed., CRC Press, Boca Raton, FL, pp. 679–718.

47. The pests evolve resistance (genetically) faster than scientists can evolve (culturally) suitable pesticides. P. Ehrlich and P. Raven, 1965, Butterflies and plants: A study in coevolution, *Evolution* 18:586–608; P. Ehrlich, 1970, Coevolution and the biology of communities, in K.

Chambers, *Biochemical Coevolution,* Oregon State University Press, Corvallis, pp. 1–11.

48. World Resources Institute, 1994, *World Resources: A Guide to the Global Environment,* Oxford University Press, Oxford.

49. G. Ware, W. Cahill, P. Gerhardt, and J. Witt, 1970, Pesticide drift IV: On target deposits from aerial application of insecticides, *Journal of Economic Entomology* 63:1982–1983; G. Ware, 1983, *Reducing Pesticide Application Drift Losses,* University of Arizona, Tucson, College of Agriculture, Cooperative Extension; F. Mazariegos, 1985, *The Use of Pesticides in the Cultivation of Cotton in Central America,* United Nations Environment Programme, Industry and Environment, Guatemala, July–September.

50. Simonich and Hites, 1995.

51. Technically, dichloro diphenyl trichloro-ethane.

52. Colborn and Clement, 1992; Harte et al., 1991.

53. See, e.g., C. Huffaker and P. Messenger (eds.), *The Theory of Biological Control,* Academic Press, New York; R. Frisbie and P. Adkisson (eds.), 1985, *Integrated Pest Management on Major Agricultural Systems,* Texas A&M University Press, College Station.

54. See, e.g., K. Holl, G. Daily, and P. Ehrlich, 1990, Integrated pest management in Latin America, *Environmental Conservation* 17:341–350.

55. P. Kenmore, 1991, Indonesia's integrated pest management—a model for Asia, *FAO Rice IPC Programme,* Food and Agriculture Organization of the United Nations, Manila; R. Denno and T. Perfect (eds.), 1994, *Planthoppers: Their Ecology and Management,* Chapman and Hall, New York.

56. Naylor and Ehrlich, 1996. This is also the source for the material that immediately follows.

57. J. Reganold, A. Palmer, J. Lockhart, and A. Macgregor, 1993, Soil quality and financial performance of biodynamic and conventional farms in New Zealand, *Science* 260:344–349.

58. D. Pimentel, C. Kirby, and A. Shroff, 1993, The relationship between "cosmetic standards" for foods and pesticide use, in Pimentel and Lehman, 1993, pp. 85–105.

59. M. Healy, 1989, Buyers prefer organic food, *USA Today,* 20 March.

60. Pimentel, McLaughlin, Zepp, et al., 1991. Costs of lowering pesticide use in industrial farming as practiced in the United States may well prove to be more expensive than similar reductions in poor nations, where agriculture is much more labor-intensive. Farmers' costs are only a very small fraction of food costs in the United States.

61. R. Repetto, 1992, Policy Implications of Possible Effects of Pesticides on the Immune System, paper presented at the World Resources In-

stitute's Conference on Pesticides and Health, Bellagio, Italy, 1–3 April; D. Newcombe, 1992, Immune surveillance, organophosphorus exposure, and lymphogenesis, *Lancet* 339, 29 February; P. Thomas et al., 1988, Immunologic effects of pesticides, in S. Baker and C. Wilkinson (eds.), *The Effects of Pesticides on Human Health,* Princeton Scientific Publishing, Princeton, NJ; see also National Research Council, 1993; T. Culliney, D. Pimentel, and M. Pimentel, 1993, Pesticide and natural toxicants in foods, in Pimentel and Lehman, 1993, pp. 138–139.

62. G. Daily and P. Ehrlich, in press, Development, global change, and the epidemiological environment, *Environment and Development Economics.*

63. F. Graham Jr., 1970, *Since Silent Spring,* Fawcett Crest, Greenwich, CT; R. Van den Bosch, 1978, *The Pesticide Conspiracy,* Doubleday, Garden City, New York.

64. See, e.g., Fumento, 1993, pp. 97–181; Bolch and Lyons, 1993, pp. 58–62; D. Ray and L. Guzzo, 1993, pp. 143–144; Bast, Hill, and Rue, 1994, pp. 163–176.

65. K. Schneider, 1991, U.S. officials say dangers of dioxins were exaggerated, *New York Times,* 15 August.

66. Harte et al., 1991, pp. 296–298; F. Tshirley, 1986, Dioxin, *Scientific American,* February, pp. 85–94.

67. Harte et al., 1991, p. 297; Lave and Upton, 1987; Culliney, Pimentel, and Pimentel, 1993.

68. J. Raloff, 1995, Beyond estrogens, *Science News* 148:44–46 (15 July); R. Sharpe, 1995, Another DDT connection, *Nature* 375:538–539; W. Kelce, C. Stone, S. Laws, L. Gray, J. Kemppainen, and E. Wilson, 1995, Persistent DDT metalolite p, p'—DDE is a potent androgen receptor antagonist, *Nature* 375:581–585.

69. M. DeVito, L. Birnbaum, W. Farland, et al., 1995, Comparisons of estimated human body burdens of dioxinlike chemicals and TCDD body burdens in experimentally exposed animals, *Environmental Health Perspectives* 103:827.

70. J. Bailar, 1991, How dangerous is dioxin? (editorial), *New England Journal of Medicine* 324:260–262.

71. M. Fingerhut, W. Halperin, D. Marlow, et al., 1991, Cancer mortality in workers exposed to 2,3,7,8-tetrachlorodibenzo-*p*-dioxin, *New England Journal of Medicine* 324 (4): 212–218.

72. Both quotes are from Bailar, 1991, p. 261.

73. Raloff, 1995.

74. Lave and Upton, 1987, p. 225.

75. Harte et al., 1991, pp. 296–297.

76. B. Baker, 1994, The dioxin dilemma remains unresolved, *BioScience* 44:738–739.

77. P. Abelson, 1994, Chlorine and organochlorine compounds (editorial), *Science* 265:1155; letters, Sources of dioxin, *Science* 266:349–352.

78. The statement is correct in implying that it would have been better to test separately those parts of the fish normally eaten. This could have shown that the concentration in the meat was higher than in the entrails, or vice versa, or that it was uniform throughout all body tissues.

79. Ray and Guzzo, 1990, pp. 4–5.

80. Harte et al., 1991.

81. See, e.g., E. Pryne, 1980, Lots of pipelines in Sound? Not so, Governor, *Seattle Times,* 17 May; M. Layton, 1980, Ray doesn't take a shine to sun power emphasis, *Seattle Post-Intelligencer,* 2 July; M. Layton, 1981, Dixy: A look back at what brought her down, *Seattle Post-Intelligencer,* 11 January.

82. This message, with variations, is a popular one with brownlash activists; it is frequently seen in books, articles, and even scientific literature.

83. Colborn, Dumanoski, and Myers, 1996.

84. Raloff, 1995.

85. Ibid.; Kelce et al., 1995.

86. Colborn, Dumanoski, and Myers, 1996.

87. M. Hines, 1992, Surrounded by estrogens? Considerations of neurobehavioral development in human beings, in Colborn and Clement, 1992, pp. 261–282.

88. See, e.g., D. Davis and H. Bradlow, 1995, Can environmental estrogens cause breast cancer?, *Scientific American,* October, pp. 166–172; R. Twombly, 1995, Assault on the male, *Environmental Health Perspectives* 103:802–805.

89. Colborn, Dumanoski, and Myers, 1996.

90. Raloff, 1995.

91. H. Bern, 1992, The fragile fetus, in Colborn and Clement, p. 14.

92. Colborn, Dumanoski, and Myers, 1996.

93. John Froines, personal communication, 18 December 1995.

94. B. Allenby and D. Richards (eds.), 1994, *The Greening of Industrial Systems,* National Academy Press, Washington, DC.

95. Harte et al., 1991.

96. Colborn, Dumanoski, and Myers, 1996; Colborn and Clement, 1992.

97. Cairns, 1986.

◻ Chapter 10: Fables about Economics and the Environment

1. See, e.g., R. Arnold and A. Gottlieb, 1993, *Trashing the Economy: How Runaway Environmentalism Is Wrecking the Environment,* Merril Press, Bellevue, WA.

2. See, e.g., J. Holdren, 1991, Population and the energy problem, *Population and Environment* 12:231–255.

3. A. Jansson, M. Hammer, C. Folke, and R. Costanza (eds.), 1994, *Investing in Natural Capital: The Ecological Economics of Sustainability,* Island Press, Washington, DC.

4. See, e.g., R. Repetto, 1989, Balance-sheet erosion: How to account for the loss of natural resources, *International Environmental Affairs* 1:103–137; C. Cobb, T. Halstead, and J. Rowe, 1995, If the GDP is up, why is America down? *Atlantic Monthly,* October, pp. 1–20.

5. There are also positive externalities, such as the unpaid-for increase in your property value when your neighbors plant a garden that beautifies the neighborhood.

6. See, e.g., K. Arrow, B. Bolin, R. Costanza, P. Dasgupta, et al., 1995, Economic growth, carrying capacity, and the environment, *Science* 268:520–521.

7. See, e.g., M. Hager, 1993, Enter the contrarians, *Tomorrow,* October–December, pp. 10–18. This view is implicit in much of the brownlash literature, which often equates those deeply concerned with environmental deterioration with Marxists or leftists (e.g., R. Bailey, 1993, *Eco-Scam: The False Prophets of Ecological Apocalypse,* St. Martin's Press, New York, pp. 5–15; G. Reisman, 1992, The toxicity of environmentalism, p. 839 in J. Lehr [ed.], *Rational Readings on Environmental Concerns,* Van Nostrand Reinhold, New York).

8. M. Feshbach and A. Friendly, 1992, *Ecocide in the USSR,* Basic Books, New York.

9. A. Smith, 1776, *An Inquiry into the Nature and Causes of the Wealth of Nations,* Clarendon Press, Oxford (1976 edition).

10. That is, they do not maximize net value—the value generated minus the costs.

11. Here we are not referring to the external costs, which, added to the private costs, you will recall, equal the full social costs.

12. In a sense, the government's levying of a carbon tax could be viewed as a way of doing this by asserting it had property rights in what was previously an atmospheric "commons."

13. K. Keller, 1992, Calculating the costs, *Tomorrow,* April–June, pp. 60–62. See also R. Gray, 1992, *The Greening of Accountancy,* Chartered Association of Certified Accountants, 29 Lincoln's Inn Fields, London, WC2A 3EE, Great Britain.

14. A. Smith, 1759, *The Theory of Moral Sentiments,* Clarendon Press, Oxford (1974 edition).

15. For a discussion of these and related issues see H. Daly and J. Cobb Jr., 1989, *For the Common Good: Redirecting the Economy Toward Community, the Environment, and a Sustainable Future,* Beacon Press, Boston.

16. W. Reilly, 1990, The green thumb of capitalism: The environmental benefits of sustainable growth, *Policy Review,* fall, p. 18.

17. D. Jorgenson and P. Wilcoxen, 1990, Environmental regulation and U.S. economic growth, *RAND Journal of Economics* 21:2 (summer), pp. 314–340.

18. These figures are expressed in real (inflation-adjusted) terms, as are the other examples in this chapter. See D. Myers and E. Diener, 1995, Who is happy?, *Psychological Science* 6 (1): 10–18; *Science,* 1995, Money isn't everything (267:1765).

19. D. Holing, 1994, Goodbye GNP, hello green domestic product, *Tomorrow,* April–June, pp. 23–25.

20. Ibid., p. 24.

21. There is a measure, net national (domestic) product (NNP), which is GDP minus depreciation of human-created capital. Most people are unfamiliar with it because depreciation of that capital is smaller than the new capital added to the stock each year. While we accumulate human-made capital, however, we are "dis-investing" in natural capital, using it at rates far above rates of replenishment. It is a simple matter, conceptually, also to include the depreciation of natural capital in accounting systems.

22. Cobb, Halstead, and Rowe, 1995, p. 20.

23. M. Porter, 1990, The competitive advantage of nations, *Harvard Business Review,* March–April.

24. Estimates vary, but the most comprehensive analysis is Management Information Services, Inc., 1993, *The Net Impact of Economic Protection on Jobs and the Economy,* Management Information Services, Washington, DC; it is summarized with other studies in R. Bezdek, 1993, Environment and economy: What's the bottom line?, *Environment* 35 (7): 7–11, 2–32.

25. Bezdek, 1993; E. Marshall, 1993, Is environmental technology a key to a healthy economy?, *Science* 260:1886–1888.

26. T. Rothermel and D. Shooter, 1994, Where to go and what to know, *Tomorrow,* October–December, pp. 52–55.

27. Much of what follows is based on Deanna Richards, personal communication (e-mail message), 4 January 1996; see also B. Allenby and D. Richards (eds.), *The Greening of Industrial Systems,* National Acad-

emy Press, Washington, DC; and C. Frankel, 1996, Green is as green does, *Tomorrow,* March–April, p. 11.

28. J. Holusha, 1993, Union camp turns a cleaner page, *New York Times,* 20 October.

29. This requirement is partly in response to German "take back" laws.

30. Electrolux, 1994, *Electrolux Environmental Report,* Electrolux, Stockholm.

31. M. Simons, 1992, Ecological plea from executives, *New York Times,* 8 May. See also S. Schmidheiny, 1992, *Changing Course,* MIT Press, Cambridge, MA.

32. Information on Monsanto is from P. H. Raven, personal communication (e-mail message), 7 January 1996.

33. Of course, Monsanto alone will not be able to affect significantly many of the global problems that hinder sustainability. Monsanto presumably is finding ways to internalize some environmental costs while maintaining profits; if firms in general begin to follow the same sort of course, significant gains in global sustainability will result.

34. These consultants include Peter Raven, David Pimentel, Amory Lovins, Herman Daly, Bill McDonough, Paul Portney, and Paul Hawken.

35. D. Richards and R. Frosch (eds.), 1994, *Corporate Environmental Practices: Climbing the Learning Curve,* National Academy Press, Washington, DC.

36. See, e.g., D. Korten, 1995, *When Corporations Rule the World,* Berrett-Koehler, San Francisco.

37. See, e.g., G. Durnil, 1995, *The Making of a Conservative Environmentalist,* Indiana University Press, Bloomington.

38. *New York Times,* 1996, Study says environmental laws aren't a big cause of job losses (18 March). See also S. Meyer, 1992, Environmentalism doesn't steal jobs, *New York Times,* 26 March.

39. R. Repetto, 1995, Jobs, competitiveness, and environmental regulation: What are the real issues?, *WRI Publications Brief,* March, pp. 7–8. See also the complete version of Repetto's report with the same name, published by the World Resources Institute, Washington, DC. The issue can also be framed in terms of *real wages* rather than jobs. Environmental regulations may lower real wages as conventionally defined (in terms of the ordinary goods and services an hourly wage will purchase). If, however, the "basket" of goods and services purchased includes environmental quality—that is, if the "real" is properly defined in terms of welfare—then real wages almost certainly go up as a result of environmental regulation.

40. This is the basic message of Bailey, 1993; see especially pp. 63–78.

41. G. Daily (ed.), in press, *Nature's Services,* Island Press, Washington, DC.

42. R. Naylor and P. Ehrlich, in press, The value of natural pest control services, in Daily.

43. See, e.g., W. Nordhaus, 1996, Elbow room, *New York Times,* 14 January.

44. See, e.g., P. Dasgupta and K. Mäler, 1995, Poverty, institutions, and the environmental resource base, in J. Behrman and T. Srinivasan (eds.), *Handbook of Development Economics,* vol. 3, Elsevier, Amsterdam, pp. 2371–2463. We are indebted to Lawrence H. Goulder of Stanford University Department of Economics for this formulation (personal communication, 10 January 1995).

45. P. Dasgupta and P. Ehrlich, in press. Recognition of this coming union has already been extended in W. Davis, 1995, Can we trust economists?, *British Airways,* August. In this article, Paul was formally inducted into the ranks of economists.

Chapter 11: Faulty Transmissions

1. Tom Meersman, *Minneapolis – St. Paul Star Tribune* reporter, personal communication, 10 April 1996.

2. Ted Turner's interest in the environment was clear to us when we met him in 1994; see also *SEJournal* 5 (4): 1.

3. R. Loftis and K. Carmody, 1995. Backing it up: Flawed anecdotes hurt journalistic credibility, *SEJ Journal* 5 (3): 1, 9–10. Both Loftis and Carmody are members of the SEJ's board of directors.

4. Ibid., p. 9.

5. K. Sagan, 1995, Easterbrook's environmental optimism: "A Moment on the Earth" spurs criticism. Contradictions and spin doctoring abound, *SEJournal* 5 (2): 22–23.

6. Quoted in Loftis and Carmody, 1995, p. 9.

7. P. Raven, personal communication, October 1993.

8. See, e.g., R. Limbaugh, 1993, *See, I Told You So,* Pocket Books, New York, p. 178.

9. G. Will, 1992, Al Gore's green guilt, *Washington Post,* 3 September.

10. C. Revelle, 1992, Global warming: What my father really said (letter), *Washington Post,* 13 September.

11. S. Schneider, 1992, Hot about global warming (letter), *Washington Post,* 26 September.

12. S. Schneider, 1993, Is the "Scientist-Advocate" An Oxymoron? paper

presented at the annual meeting of the American Association for the Advancement of Science, Boston, MA, 12 February.

13. Global Climate Coalition, 1995 (press release, 3 February).

14. R. Gelbspan, 1995, The heat is on, *Harper's Magazine,* December, p. 33. The *Global Climate Coalition* includes among its members the American Automobile Manufacturers Association, the American Petroleum Institute, the Atlantic Richfield Company, Chevron Corporation, Dow Chemical Chemical, Exxon Corporation, the National Association of Manufacturers, the National Coal Association, the Phillips Petroleum Company, Texaco, Inc., and the U.S. Chamber of Commerce. According to Gelbspan, the Global Climate Coalition planned to spend an additional $850,000 in 1996.

15. M. Morgan and D. Keith, 1995, Subjective judgements of climate experts, *Environmental Science and Technology* 29 (10): 468a–476a.

16. Received by forsythe.stanford.edu; Friday, 10 February 1995, 14:21:18 PST from David Keith.

17. This is the database referred to in D. Meadows, 1995, George Washington and I are subjects of groundless rumors, column e-mailed to Paul Ehrlich by Donella Meadows, 29 June 1995. *Valley News.*

18. The Keith Schneider story is based largely on V. Monks, 1993, See no evil, *American Journalism Review,* June, pp. 18–25. The detailed account given in this article is well worth reading and gives substantial insight into brownlash tactics.

19. Ibid. Schneider's article appeared in the *New York Times,* 15 August 1991.

20. K. Schneider, 1993, *New York Times,* five-part series on environmental policies, 21–23 March.

21. *SEJournal,* 1995–1996, SEJ at MIT: Sparks fly (5 [4]: 1).

22. Union of Concerned Scientists, 1996 (advertisement), *New York Times,* 26 February.

23. Easterbrook has not limited his journalistic coverage to environmental topics; he recently wrote a for-hire biography of C. Everett Koop, published in 1991 by Grand Rounds Press and distributed as an advertising vehicle for the Bristol-Myers Squibb Company.

24. G. Easterbrook, 1995, *A Moment on the Earth: The Coming Age of Environmental Optimism,* Viking, New York.

25. Ibid., p. 713.

26. P. Raven, 1995, review of "A Moment on the Earth" *The Amicus Journal* 17 (1): 45.

27. K. Sagan, 1995, Easterbrook's environmental optimism: "A Moment on the Earth" spurs criticism, *SEJournal* 5 (2): 22–23.

28. Easterbrook, 1995, p. 281. Easterbrook would doubtless claim that he meant "believers that human beings were enhancing the greenhouse

effect and causing global warming," but if *Moment* had had any knowledgeable reviewers they would have removed such transparent errors. Needless to say, none of the scientists mentioned is a "believer" in Easterbrook's sense, since all three adjust their conclusions to fit the latest data and models.

29. L. Garrett, 1994, *The Coming Plague: Newly Emerging Diseases in a World out of Balance,* Farrar, Straus, and Giroux, New York.

30. C. Pope, 1996. Television misses the future, *Sierra* March–April, pp. 12–13.

31. *SEJournal,* 1995, p. 16.

32. R. Limbaugh, 1992, *The Way Things Ought to Be,* Pocket Books, New York, p. 152.

33. Ibid., pp. 154, 156, and 166, respectively.

34. Ibid., p. 171.

35. There's a certain amount of truth in this view; scientists themselves have long noted that technical jargon often serves to separate subdisciplines and hinder participation in discussions and research by nonspecialists.

Chapter 12: How Can Good Science Become Good Policy?

1. For more details and references, see P. Ehrlich and A. Ehrlich, 1990, *The Population Explosion,* Simon and Schuster, New York, pp. 58–59; and P. Ehrlich and A. Ehrlich, 1991, *Healing the Planet,* Addison-Wesley, Reading, MA, introduction and chapter 2.

2. This is the principal area of environmental deterioration not readily handled under the *I = PAT* identity (see Ehrlich and Ehrlich, 1990, 1991).

3. Information on risk should include how people respond to voluntarily and involuntarily assumed risks, the importance of "no regrets" strategies, cost-benefit analyses, discounting in time and space, accounting for so-called environmental external costs in the prices of today's goods and services, etc.

4. Telephone 202-483-8491; fax 202-234-9194.

5. Early in our efforts at public education we used scenarios a great deal, but they have come back to haunt us dressed up as "predictions" by the brownlash. The scenarios in *The Population Bomb* were preceded by the following statement: "Scenarios are hypothetical sequences of events used as an aid in thinking about the future. . . . Remember, these are just possibilities, not predictions. We can be sure that none of them will come true as stated. . . ." (P. Ehrlich, 1968, *The Population Bomb,* Ballantine, New York, p. 72). Yet over the years, these sci-

ence fiction pieces from the *Bomb* have repeatedly been cited as failed predictions when the world did not follow the course described.

6. S. Budiansky, 1995, *Nature's Keepers: The New Science of Nature Management,* Free Press, New York, p. 153.

7. P. Ehrlich and E. Wilson, 1991, Biodiversity studies: Science and policy, *Science* 253:761.

8. *American Men and Women of Science, 1995–96,* (19th ed.), 8 vols., R. R. Bowker, New Providence, NJ.

9. Institute for Scientific Information, 1996, *Science Citation Index,* Institute for Scientific Information, Philadelphia.

10. To get some hints, you might want to consult J. Fremlin, 1964, How many people can the world support?, *New Scientist,* 29 October, and G. Hardin, 1959, Interstellar migration and the population problem, *Heredity* 50:68–70. Suppose we held Earth's population stationary by exporting people to other planets (ignoring the small logistical problems of doing so). At current rates, it would take less than a century to populate Venus, Mercury, Mars, the moon, and the moons of Jupiter to the same density as Earth, since the total surface areas of these planets and moons add up to less than three times that of Earth. Going to the stars would require strict population control on the interstellar ships, since it would take many, many generations to reach even the nearest star.

11. J. Harte, 1985, *Consider a Spherical Cow: A Course in Environmental Problem Solving,* William Kaufmann, Los Altos, CA.

12. R. Limbaugh, 1992, *The Way Things Ought to Be,* Pocket Books, New York, p. 154.

13. N. Borlaug, 1995, Food Production, report prepared for Scientific Panels, 1995 Third Annual World Bank Conference on Effectively Financing Environmentally Sustainable Development, Washington, DC, 4 and 9 October.

14. For an overview of the problem, see P. Weber, 1994, Net loss: Fish, jobs, and the marine environment. *Worldwatch Paper 120,* Worldwatch Institute, Washington, DC.

15. They should also be asked whether the trees really could grow back in the absence of the moist, shady conditions in which the seedlings of many tropical forest trees thrive.

▣ Chapter 13: One Planet, One Experiment

1. See, e.g., T. Homer-Dixon, J. Boutwell, and G. Rathjens, 1993, Environmental change and violent conflict, *Scientific American,* February,

pp. 38–45; P. Howard and T. Homer-Dixon, 1995, *Environmental Scarcity and Violent Conflict: The Case of Chiapas, Mexico,* American Association for the Advancement of Science and University of Toronto, Washington, DC (this and the two succeeding publications may be ordered by voice, at 202-326-6652; by fax, at 202-371-0970; and on the Internet, at bsmith@aas.org); V. Percival and T. Homer-Dixon, 1995, *Environmental Scarcity and Violent Conflict: The Case of South Africa,* American Association for the Advancement of Science and University of Toronto, Washington, DC; K. Kelly and T. Homer-Dixon, 1995, *Environmental Scarcity and Violent Conflict: The Case of Gaza,* American Association for the Advancement of Science and University of Toronto, Washington, DC; R. Kaplan, 1996, *The Ends of the Earth: A Journey at the Dawn of the Twenty-First Century,* Random House, New York; T. Rosenberg, 1996, Anarchy unbound, *World Policy Journal* 13 (1): 83–87.

2. See the in-depth examination of equity issues in P. Ehrlich, A. Ehrlich, and G. Daily, 1995, *The Stork and the Plow: The Equity Answer to the Human Dilemma,* Putnam, New York.

3. Union of Concerned Scientists, 26 Church Street, Cambridge, MA 02238.

Appendix A: Brownlash Literature

1. Gregg Easterbrook, 1995, *A Moment on the Earth: The Coming Age of Environmental Optimism,* Viking, New York. For other critiques, refer to World Resources Institute, 1995, *A Thoughtful Reader's Guide to "A Moment on the Earth,"* World Resources Institute, 1709 New York Avenue, NW, Washington, DC 20006; P. Raven, 1995, review of "A Moment on the Earth," *The Amicus Journal* 17 (1): 42–45; J. Harte, 1995, Optimism about the environment, *Chemical and Engineering News,* 3 July, pp. 26–27; R. Noss, 1995, The perils of Pollyannas, *Conservation Biology* 9 (4): 701–703; D. Meadows, 1995, Depressing case of environmental optimism, *Valley News,* 10 June; D. Davis, 1995, A "deadbody" approach to health, *Environmental Science and Technology,* August, pp. 370A–371A; J. Schulz, 1995, When nature writers get it wrong, *Natural History,* August, pp. 64–66; L. Haimson and B. Goodman (eds.), 1995, *A Moment of Truth: Correcting the Scientific Errors in Gregg Easterbrook's "A Moment on the Earth,"* Environmental Defense Fund, New York, NY 10010; T. Lovejoy, 1996, Rethinking green thoughts, *Scientific American,* February; and S. Pimm, 1995, testimony to the Senate Committee on Environment and Public Works' Subcommittee on Drinking Water, Fisheries and Wildlife, 13 July.

2. Much of what's wrong with the positions taken in the book is philosophical, which we do not have time or space to dissect. Those with

a professional interest in anti-science should read the books for themselves.

3. Easterbrook, 1995, p. 218.

4. Ibid., pp. xiii–xxi.

5. Ibid., p. xvi.

6. Ibid., p. 14.

7. Ibid., p. 150.

8. Ibid., p. 303.

9. Ibid., p. 307.

10. Ibid., p. 329 and several other places.

11. Ibid., p. 393.

12. Ibid., p. 443.

13. Ibid., p. 575.

14. Ibid., p. 585.

15. Ibid., p. 677.

16. See, e.g., ibid., pp. 218, 224, 296, 299, 303, 431, 440, 491, 492, 571, 572, 649, 660.

17. See, e.g., L. Goulder, 1991, Using carbon charges to combat global climate change, in T. Wirth and J. Heinz, *Project 88—Round II* (unpublished) Washington, DC; L. Goulder, 1992, Carbon tax design and U.S. industry performance, in J. Poterba (ed.), *Tax Policy and the Economy 6,* MIT Press, Cambridge, MA; J. Poterba, 1991, Tax policy to combat global warming: On designing a carbon tax, in R. Dornbusch and J. Poterba (eds.), *Global Warming: Economic Policy Responses,* MIT Press, Cambridge, MA; R. Dower and M. Zimmerman, 1992, *The Right Climate for Carbon Taxes: Creating Economic Incentives to Protect the Atmosphere,* World Resources Institute, Washington, DC; H. Faulkner, 1994, Some commments on the INC process, in I. Mintzer and J. Leonard (eds.), *Negotiating Climate Change: The Inside Story of the Rio Convention,* Cambridge University Press, Cambridge, p. 236; references in P. Ehrlich and A. Ehrlich, 1991, *Healing the Planet,* Addison-Wesley, Reading, MA, pp. 104–106.

18. Ehrlich and Ehrlich, 1991, pp. 213–214; C. Holl, G. Daily, and P. Ehrlich, 1990, Integrated pest management in Latin America, *Environmental Conservation* 17:341–350.

19. Easterbrook, 1995, pp. 443–444.

20. Ibid., p. 713.

21. Ibid., p. 223.

22. Ibid., p. 426.

23. Ibid., p. 656.

24. Ibid., p. 225.

25. Ibid., p. 558.
26. P. Ehrlich and J. Roughgarden, 1987, *The Science of Ecology,* Macmillan, New York, p. 519.
27. Easterbrook, 1995, p. 669.
28. Ibid., p. 254.
29. Ibid., p. 86.
30. J. Simon, 1980, Resources, population, environment: An oversupply of false bad news, *Science* 208:1431–1437.
31. Easterbrook, 1995, p. 9.
32. Ibid., p. 9.
33. See, e.g., P. Ehrlich and P. Raven, 1964, Butterflies and plants: A study in coevolution, *Evolution* 8:586–608.
34. Twenty-five of the worst errors are documented in L. Haimson and B. Goodman (eds.), 1995, *A Moment of Truth: Correcting the Scientific Errors in Gregg Easterbrook's "A Moment on the Earth,"* Environmental Defense Fund, New York (call or fax 212-505-2100/2375 for a copy).
35. Easterbrook, 1995, p. 283.
36. Ibid., p. 268.
37. Ibid., pp. 280, 286.
38. Ibid., pp. 277, 280, 281, 282, 294.
39. See Haimson and Goodman, 1995, pp. 18–26.
40. See Haimson and Goodman, 1995.
41. Easterbrook, 1995, p. 284.
42. Schneider, as we have seen, is frequently attacked for having been concerned about possible global *cooling* in the 1970s, and he made some colleagues very unhappy when during the "nuclear winter" studies of the 1980s, he concluded that a large-scale nuclear war might cause only a "nuclear autumn."
43. Easterbrook, 1995, p. 294.
44. See, e.g., ibid., pp. 218, 224, 296, 299, 303, 431, 440, 492, 571, etc.
45. See, e.g., ibid., pp. 54, 593.
46. See, e.g., ibid., pp. xiv, 153, 375, 465, etc.
47. Ibid., p. 713.
48. Ibid., p. xiv.
49. P. Ehrlich, 1968, *The Population Bomb,* Ballantine, New York, pp. 36–45.
50. Ibid., pp. 44–45.
51. D. Meadows, D. Meadows, J. Randers, and W. Behrens III, 1972, *The Limits to Growth,* Universe Books, Washington, DC.

52. Donella H. Meadows, 1995, George Washington and I are subjects of groundless rumors, *Valley News,* column e-mailed to Paul Ehrlich by Donella Meadows, 29 June 1995.

53. Easterbrook, 1995, pp. 658–660.

54. This general area is the subject of an enormous and rich literature; see, e.g., P. Ehrlich and L. Birch, 1967, The "balance of nature" and "population control," *American Naturalist* 101:97–107; R. May, 1973, *Stability and Complexity in Model Ecosystems,* Princeton University Press, Princeton, NJ; C. Holling, 1986, The resilience of terrestrial ecosystems: Local surprise and global change, in W. Clark and R. Munn (eds.), *Sustainable Development in the Biosphere,* Cambridge University Press, Cambridge, pp. 292–317; S. Pimm, 1991, *The Balance of Nature,* University of Chicago Press, Chicago; S. Levin, 1992, The problem of pattern and scale in ecology, *Ecology* 73:1943–1967.

55. See, e.g., M. Davis, 1981, Quaternary history and the stability of forest communities, in D. West, H. Shugart, and D. Botkin (eds.), *Forest Succession: Concepts and Application,* Springer-Verlag, New York, pp. 132–153.

56. We discuss issues of community stability in some detail in P. Ehrlich, A. Ehrlich, and J. Holdren, 1977, *Ecoscience: Population, Resources, Environment,* W. H. Freeman, San Francisco, pp. 135–142.

57. Easterbrook, 1995, p. 224.

58. Ibid., p. 571.

59. Peter H. Raven, personal communication (e-mail message), 18 July 1995.

60. Easterbrook, 1995, p. 440.

61. See, e.g., R. Chambers, A. Pacey, and L.-A. Thrupp, 1989, *Farmers First: Farmer Innovation and Agricultural Research,* Intermediate Technology Publications, London; I. Scoones and J. Thompson, 1994, *Beyond Farmers First,* Intermediate Technology Publications, London; P. Ehrlich, A. Ehrlich, and G. Daily, 1995, *The Stork and the Plow: The Equity Answer to the Human Predicament,* Putnam, New York, pp. 212–216.

62. Easterbrook, 1995, p. 492.

63. Ehrlich and Ehrlich, 1991, pp. 62–65.

64. Easterbrook, 1995, pp. 440–441.

65. G. Daily, 1995, Restoring value to the world's degraded lands, *Science* 269:250–254.

66. P. Ehrlich and A. Ehrlich, 1981, *Extinction: The Causes and Consequences of the Disappearance of Species,* Random House, New York, pp. xi–xiii.

67. S. Budiansky, 1995, *Nature's Keepers: The New Science of Nature Management,* Free Press, New York, back flap copy.

68. Ibid.

69. Ibid., p. 182.

70. Ibid., p. 183.

71. See, e.g., S. McNaughton, 1977, Diversity and stability of ecological communities: A comment on the role of empiricism in ecology, *American Naturalist* 111:515–525; S. McNaughton, 1993, Biodiversity and function of grazing systems, in E. Schulze and H. Mooney (eds.), *Biodiversity and Ecosystem Function,* Springer Verlag, Berlin, pp. 361–383; S. Naeem, L. Thompson, S. Lawler, J. Lawton, and R. Woodfin, 1994, Declining biodiversity can alter the performance of ecosystems, *Nature* 368:734–737; S. Naeem, L. Thompson, S. Lawler, J. Lawton, and R. Woodfin, 1995, Empirical evidence that declining species diversity may alter the performance of terrestrial ecosystems, *Philosophical Transactions of the Royal Society of London B* 347:249–262; D. Tilman and J. Downing, 1994, Biodiversity and stability in grasslands, *Nature* 367:363–365.

72. We are indebted to Thomas Brooks, Department of Ecology and Evolutionary Biology, University of Tennessee, for sending us his analysis of this chapter, which was very helpful in preparing our treatment (personal communication, 27 October 1995).

73. Budiansky, 1995, p. 159.

74. See, e.g., A. Lotka, 1925, *Elements of Physical Biology,* Williams and Wilkins, Baltimore; R. May (ed.), 1976, *Theoretical Ecology: Principles and Applications,* Blackwell, Oxford; J. Roughgarden, 1979, *Theory of Population Genetics and Evolutionary Ecology: An Introduction,* Macmillan, New York; R. Anderson and R. May (eds.), 1982, *Population Biology of Infectious Diseases: Theory and Applications,* Chapman and Hall, London; S. Pimm, 1982, *Food Webs,* Chapman and Hall, New York; D. Tilman, 1982, *Resource Competition and Community Structure,* Monographs in Population Biology 17, Princeton University Press, Princeton, NJ; J. Roughgarden, R. May, and S. Levin (eds.), 1989, *Perspectives in Ecological Theory,* Princeton University Press, Princeton, NJ; M. Rosensweig, 1995, *Species Diversity in Space and Time,* Cambridge University Press, Cambridge.

75. Budiansky, 1995, p. 164.

76. Ibid., p. 165.

77. Brooks, 1995.

78. For a recent discussion of this issue, see S. Pimm, G. Russell, J. Gittleman, and T. Brooks, 1995, The future of biodiversity, *Science* 269:347–350.

79. Budiansky, 1995, p. 165.

80. F. Preston, 1962, The canonical distribution of commonness and rarity: Part I, *Ecology* 43:185–215; Part II, *Ecology* 43:410–432.

81. R. MacArthur and E. Wilson, 1963, An equilibrium theory of insular zoogeography, *Evolution* 17:373–387; R. MacArthur and E. Wilson, 1967, *The Theory of Island Biogeography,* Princeton University Press, Princeton, NJ.

82. Budiansky, 1995, pp. 165–168; Brooks, 1995.

83. Brooks, 1995 (with minor editing of punctuation).

84. C. Mann and M. Plummer, 1995, *Noah's Choice,* Alfred A. Knopf, New York. The book's funniest errors come in the footnote to page 5, which will amuse knowledgeable taxonomists, if no one else. The generic (not "genus") name is *Nicrophorus,* and the specific name is *Nicrophorus americanus.* Linnaean nomenclature is called binomial because each species has a two-part name with generic and specific (or trivial) parts. Olivier refers to the person who first formally described the species. Although Olivier may have collected the holotype—the individual considered (among those available) by the describer as most representative of the species—in many cases the describer works with specimens collected by others. Indeed, species are often named after their collector-discoverers, as in the case of *Sandia mcfarlandi* Ehrlich and Clench, the only dramatically different butterfly found in the United States in this century, which Paul and a colleague named after Noel McFarland, who brought Paul the first specimen. Other howlers in *Noah's Choice* include the assertion that "Darwin spent much of the five-year mission [of the *Beagle*] in bed" (p. 33) and relocating the famous Oxford ecologist Charles Elton to Cambridge (p. 38). These errors are not important to the argument in the book, but, along with infelicities such as "the Colydiidae and Bothrideridae families" (p. 3), they are indicators of the lack of familiarity with science that characterizes the brownlash literature in general. The suffix "idae" automatically tells a knowledgeable reader that the taxon is a family, and the family name is not an adjective. If Mann and Plummer had wished to inform readers not familiar with systematics that the taxa were families, they should have said "the families Colydiidae and Bothrideridae."

85. See, e.g., ibid., pp. 24, 39.

86. Ibid., p. 39. Paul supports more effort being made to develop national biological inventories (such as should have been one duty of the ill-fated National Biological Survey—now the National Biological Service—in the United States), but he believes those inventories should be concentrated on greatly improving knowledge of an array of "indicator" groups such as birds, butterflies, vascular plants, and perhaps

others such as frogs or tiger beetles. Paul has dedicated much of his recent research effort to identifying and evaluating such groups, and that is in no way contradictory to his recommendations in the 1964 paper cited by Mann and Plummer (*Systematic Zoology* 13:109–123). The statement that Mann and Plummer attribute to Ehrlich and Wilson, "An essential step in dealing with the extinction crisis is to know how many species the Earth has to lose," is pure fiction; nothing like it appears in the cited paper (*Science* 253:758–762). Furthermore, neither Paul nor Ed believes it.

87. Ibid., p. 284.

88. Ibid., p. 226.

89. Ibid., p. 227.

90. R. Bailey, 1993, *Eco-Scam: The False Prophets of Ecological Apocalypse,* St. Martin's Press, New York.

91. A typical example of *Eco-Scam*'s approach is given in the first sentence of Bailey's chapter on global warming: "'The beginning of the end,' warns Paul Ehrlich [sic]." This is referenced to page 72 of Paul and Anne Ehrlich's *Healing the Planet*. The quote is "accurate" in that page 72 begins a chapter titled "Global Warming: The Beginning of the End?" The omitted question mark makes a difference; in that chapter we tried to give a balanced presentation of the possibilities as of the time of writing (1990). It includes the following statements: "But then, maybe none of the untoward effects mentioned above will happen. Maybe some as-yet-unknown negative feedback mechanism will stabilize the climate about where it is now, or perhaps the warming will be so small and slow that civilization can easily adapt. Such an outcome cannot be completely ruled out." (P. Ehrlich and A. Ehrlich, 1991, *Healing the Planet: Strategies for Resolving the Environmental Crisis,* Addison-Wesley, Reading, MA, p. 95.)

92. W. Beckerman, 1995, *Small Is Stupid: Blowing the Whistle on the Greens,* Duckworth, London.

93. Ibid., p. 37.

94. Ibid., p. 142.

95. A. Sen, 1994, Population: Delusion and reality, *New York Review of Books,* 22 September.

Appendix B: The Scientific Consensus

1. Reprinted with permission from *Population Summit of the World's Scientific Academies*. Copyright © 1993 by the National Academy of Sciences. Courtesy of the National Academy Press, Washington, DC.

2. Population Reference Bureau, *The U.N. Long-Range Population Projections: What They Tell Us,* Washington, DC, 1992.

3. Mahmoud F. Fathalla, "Family Planning and Reproductive Health: A Global Overview," invited paper presented at the 1993 Science Summit, Delhi, India, 26 October 1993.

4. Sponsored by the Union of Concerned Scientists, 26 Church Street, Cambridge, MA 02238.

Index

About Paul Ehrlich and Anne Ehrlich

PAUL R. EHRLICH is Bing Professor of Population Studies, Department of Biological Sciences, Stanford University. An expert in the fields of ecology and population biology, Ehrlich has devoted his career to studying such topics as the dynamics and genetics of insect populations, the interactions of plants and herbivores, and the effects of crowding on human beings. His field work has carried him to all continents, from the Arctic and the Antarctic to the tropics, and from high mountains to the ocean floor. Professor Ehrlich has written more than 700 scientific papers and popular articles as well as many books (some coauthored with Anne), including *The Population Bomb, The Process of Evolution, The Machinery of Nature, Extinction, Science of Ecology, The Birder's Handbook, New World/New Mind, The Population Explosion, Healing the Planet, Birds in Jeopardy,* and *The Stork and the Plow.*

Among his many scientific honors, Ehrlich is a Fellow of the American Association for the Advancement of Science and the American Academy of Arts and Sciences, an honorary member of the British Ecological Society, and a member of the United States National Academy of Sciences and the American Philosophical Society. He was awarded the first AAAS/Scientific American Prize for Science in the Service of Humanity, and the Crafoord Prize in Population Biology and the Conservation of Biological Diversity, an explicit substitute for a Nobel Prize in fields of science where the latter is not given. Ehrlich has also received a MacArthur Prize Fellowship; the Volvo Environment Prize; the International Center for Tropical Ecology's World Ecology Medal; and the International Ecology Institute Prize.

ANNE H. EHRLICH is Senior Research Associate in the Department of Biological Sciences, Stanford University, and Associate Director and Policy Coordinator of Stanford's Center for Conservation Biology. She has been involved with such issues of public concern as population policy, environmental protection, and environmental consequences of nuclear war. Anne Ehrlich was one of seven outside consultants to the White House Council on Environmental Quality's *Global 2000 Report,* issued in 1980. She currently serves on the boards of the Pacific Institute for Studies in Environment, Development, and Security, the Rocky Mountain Biological Laboratory, the Ploughshares Fund, Redefining Progress, and the Sierra Club.

A recipient of an Honorary Doctorate in 1990 from Bethany College, Dr. Ehrlich is a Fellow of the American Academy of Arts and Sciences and an Honorary Fellow of the California Academy of Sciences.

Paul and Anne Ehrlich have jointly received the United Nations Environment Programme (UNEP) Sasakawa Environment Prize, the United Nations' Global 500 Roll of Honour for Environmental Achievement, the Heinz Award for the Environment, American Humanists Association Distinguished Service Award, and the Nuclear Age Peace Foundation Distinguished Peace Leadership Award.

About the Center for Conservation Biology

In 1984, Paul Ehrlich founded Stanford University's Center for Conservation Biology specifically to develop the science of conservation biology and to help devise ways and means for protecting Earth's life support systems.

In pursuit of its mission, the Center for Conservation Biology designs experiments to address specific and general questions in conservation biology; conducts research on broad-scale policy issues, including human population growth, resource use, and environmental deterioration; communicates the results of this scientific and policy research to conservation biologists, reserve managers, planners, decision makers, and the public; and educates students and professionals as well as fostering collaboration with other scientists and conservation groups around the world.

The Center for Conservation Biology is part of the Stanford University Department of Biological Sciences and is supported by donations and grants from individuals, private foundations, and corporations.